The Letters of
DAVID GARRICK

Edited by
DAVID M. LITTLE and GEORGE M. KAHRL

Associate Editor
PHOEBE deK. WILSON

Volume III
Letters 816–1362

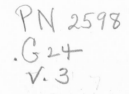

THE BELKNAP PRESS OF
HARVARD UNIVERSITY PRESS
Cambridge, Massachusetts
1963

DAVID GARRICK.

La premiere chose qu'on doit faire quand on a
emprunté un Livre, c'est de le lire afin de pou-
voir le rendre plûtôt.

Menagiana, Vol IV.

Volume III

Letters 816–1362

Contents

Volume III

Illustrations

Volume III

1*

Volume III

Letters 816–1362

Chronology of Garrick's Life

1717, February 9	Born at the Angel Inn, Hereford
1717–1737	Living and being schooled in Lichfield
1737, March 2	To London with Samuel Johnson
March 9	Enrolled at Lincoln's Inn
1738–1741	In the wine trade in London
1740	First theatrical entertainments produced: *Lethe* (Drury Lane, April 1); *The Lying Valet* (Goodman's Fields, November 30)
1741, June–July	Appearance at Ipswich Theatre under the assumed name of Mr. Lyddall
1741–42	Professional actor at Goodman's Fields Theatre; *Richard III* on October 19, thereafter eighteen more roles
1742, summer	Playing at Smock Alley Theatre, Dublin
1742–45	Playing at Drury Lane
1745–46	Co-manager and actor at Smock Alley
1746–47	Engagement at Covent Garden Theatre
1747, April 9	Contract as partner at Drury Lane
1749, June 22	Married Eva Maria Veigel
1749–72	Resident in Southampton Street, London
1751, summer	Visit to Paris
1754	Purchase of the Hampton villa
1763–65	The Grand Tour
1769, September	The Shakespeare Jubilee at Stratford
1772, March	Move to No. 5, The Adelphi
1775–76	Final season as an actor; sale of Drury Lane
1779, January 20	Death in London

816   To Joseph Cradock

Adelphi
Dear Sir.   Jany the 7th [1774]¹
I have been very ill wth a Cold & hoarseness, & am oblig'd to go
tomorrow into ye Country to try if the Air will be of Service to Me.
It will be impossible for Us, with the Engagements now upon our
hands to comply with Your request.—² I should have been very
happy to Obey Your Commands; but if You knew, what we have
to do, and ye little time we have to do it in, You would be assur'd
that the necessity of our affairs, & not a Mere Manager's Excuse,
compels Me to Act contrary to my Inclinations. We have not less
than 3 tragedies, a Comedy & two reviv'd tragedies to perform in
this & ye next Winter.

Sorry, & very Sorry I was, that I could not See Venice preserv'd— I have heard wonders of You & Co

This filthy cold I partly got, by Exhibiting my person in the
gallan⟨t⟩ Hastings, as the best Compliment I could Pay to the Noble
Host & Hostess where You are—³ but indeed my Pride was very
much mortify'd, when I found the Family did not come to their
box till in ye middle of the third Act— it will not be long in my
Power to pay many such Comp^ts.

I am Dear S^r Y^r most oblig'd humble Ser^t
D: Garrick

Source: FSL; Cradock, IV, 161.

1. The year is supplied in an unknown hand and is verified by the reference to
Cradock's invitation to Garrick to help with the Essex theatricals.
2. Under the auspices of William Ann Holles Capel (1732–1799), fourth Earl of Essex
(1743), and his wife Harriet (1734?–1821), a company of amateur players, including
Cradock, was at this time performing at Cashiobury, Hertfordshire, Essex's country seat.
Garrick had been invited to attend (Cradock, IV, 159f.).
3. Lord and Lady Essex had persuaded Garrick to play in *Jane Shore* (*ibid.*, 161f.).

817   To Herbert Lawrence

Monday Hampton
Dear Sir   Jany 10— 1774
I have been so untun'd with a Violent Cold & hoarseness, that in
Justice to you, & my self, I would not read the Comedy¹ you put

into my hands 'till Yesterday; I have consider'd it well, & sincerely wish'd that I might have an occasion to Shew the regard I have for you.— to be free & friendly with you, I think the Comedy not in the least calculated for representation, & if I did not know your hand, & that you had sent it to me, I should not have believ'd it, from the other performances I have seen of yours, to have come from the same Author— to speak my Mind without constraint & as Circumstances occur to me— The Character of your *Credulous Man* is surely unnatural & improbable, his Swallow is too large & too farcical— can it be possible that he could be so gull'd by flam, & his Brother cheat to take every thing for granted at so great a loss too? or granting that he could swallow all their Secrets is it credible, that he would agree to give his Daughter at once to a Stranger upon a days Acquaintance?— a Dupe so extravagantly absurd becomes an Idiot & unfit for the Stage— let us pass from him to the *Lover's* Scheme— & I fear that will prove as improbable. He is thought to be Dead, but returns, puts on a bob Wig, Visits his Mistress as her dead Lover's Uncle, & is not found out, till he discovers the plot himself.— I will grant you that some improble disguises have pass'd, & will pass upon the Stage— But tho' Love is painted Blind, Lover's are Suppos'd to have Lynx's Eyes, & it is Unnatural to think the Young Woman should converse with the object of her passion, still warm in her heart, and but lately left her, & not know him under so slight a Concealment?— to me it is impossible, & I fear would have a bad Effect upon the Stage,— but supposing (& it is supposing a great deal) that these Circumstances which are the main ones of the plot, could be made probable by Alteration, yet there still wants the Sine qua non, the Spirit of Dialogue, that vis Comica, that vein of pleasantry, without which, no Comedy can live upon the Stage— the *Credulous Man* is the only Character, & he I think too exaggarated to be pleasing; and we have so many *Cheaters & Cheatees* upon the Stage, Such as are in the Alchymist, Albumazar &c that I fear unless some very New Method & pleasant Method of galling the Credulous was found out,— an Audience would be very Squeamish— The Tychotho-licon of Feignwell would be thought an Imitation of the *Otacousticon* of Albumazar,[2] & the transmutation of Vegetables put 'em in mind of the transmutation of Metals in the Alchymist— Pandolpho & Sr Epicure Mammon are the old Gulls, & to be Sure had their Effect when the Transformation of persons, & transmutation of Metals were talk'd of, & believ'd by 19 in 20— even now by the force of writing they are Suffer'd— but indeed it is by a force upon the Understanding, & are but barely born, & I am certain would be condemn'd (with all their Merit) were they now for the first time to be Acted.

I hope my sincerity will not appear impertinent; I should think my self unworthy of your Confidence if I did not speak to you *as to my thinkings, as I do ruminate*,[3] and it is my honest opinion that you would have been unhappy had either Mr Colman or Mr Foote brought your Comedy upon the Stage I am

Dear Sir Your most Sincere wellwisher & humble Servant

D. Garrick

I write as you See with the Gout in my fingers— I can scarce hold my pen— I have written Slovenly & incorrectly, but you will excuse every thing. To convince you how over delicate the Publick may be at times— I will relate to you a passage in a Farce call'd *Neck or Nothing*—[4] Two Servants agree to impose upon an old Citizen Stockwell— one of 'em is to pass for his Master & to receive a portion with the Daughter, whom he is to marry— they agree to divide the Booty & run away— the business is comically enough manag'd & had great applause 'till upon the old Citizens asking the Sham Gentlemen to take a Mortgage upon Some Houses for part of the Fortune— the other Answers he is Sorry that he could not— but that he had bargain'd for an Estate that was *Contagious* to his own, & must be oblig'd to pay the Money in two days or forfeit— Is the Estate good, says the old Man? in fine Condition answers the cheat, & the Wood upon it will very near pay the Purchas⟨e⟩— indeed!— O Yes, says the Confederate, & then the fine ponds upon the Estate!— ponds (cries Stockwell) what signify Ponds— O Sir they make a great deal of the Ponds, many Pounds a year!— indeed! what are they good for?— Slip replies— to Catch Gudgeons Sir— great Proffit & pleasure.— I thought it dangerous and, so it prov'd, tho' but in a Farce, & which 'till the Gudgeons came had met with great applause. I mention this only to shew you that an audience will not Suffer the Dupe to be cheated too extravagantly even in a Farcical piece

Endorsement by Garrick: Letter to Mr Lawrence Apothecary about his play. *Source:* FC, copy; Boaden, I, 602f.

1. Apparently this play was never produced or published.
2. A "wondrous instrument," which amplified sound to such an extent

That you may know each whisper from *Prester John*
Against the wind, as fresh as 'twere delivered
Through a trunk, or *Gloster's* list'ning wall.

(*Albumazar*, I, iii).
  3. *Othello*, III, iii, 131f.
  4. By Garrick (DL, Nov. 18, 1766).

818   To The Reverend Doctor Thomas Francklin

Adelphi

Dear Sir   Jany 12. 1774

Your Letter which Surpriz'd me is half a letter of complaint &
without the smallest foundation, I never broke my word with any
body, nor do I expect a Murmur against me from a Liberal Mind
'till I do.— Dr Franklin might have known by the papers, that I
have been ill,[1] & very ill; so ill as to keep House for near a fortnight,
except Just the conveyance of me from the Adelphi to Hampton by
way of changing the Air— But you seem to think it hard that I will
not speak to Col. Dow, how such a request to the Col[1] could be
conveyd, is not in my power to determine, for he has been some
time in the East Indies, & left his play[2] in Guardianship; this I
thought I told You.— It has been your own fault, & yours only,
that you have not had your play, & other plays (if you had chosen
it) Acted at Drury Lane Theatre long before this.— As You seem to
be peevish I will speak the truth, because I will have none of your
faults added to a large bundle of my own— After your Warwick—
you were given to Coquettry, & after you had mention'd an intended
Tragedy to me often, you hung back, chang'd your mind &c &c &c
& never offer'd me one 'till that which I read last Summer.[3] I have
told you from the begining all my Engagements, & therefore it is
very hard to be distress'd about a Matter which I have wish'd to
be able to do, but had it not in my power— I have answer'd this
upon the Gallop, but could not rest till I had spoken my Mind as
freely as You have done. I am

Dr Sir Your most obed^t Servant
D Garrick.

What can You possibly mean by wishing to be now in my favour?
I would not break my word to gain the favour of Kings,— nor

should my Brother be preferr'd to a Stranger, had I given my word to the last— the Gout in my fingers makes my Letter scarce legible

Endorsement: To Dr Franklin, Queen Street, copy.   *Source:* FC, copy; Boaden, I, 603f.

1. "Mr Garrick, who has been much indisposed with a sore throat and hoarseness, is much better" (*Public Advertiser*, Dec. 30, 1773).
2. *Sethona.*
3. Presumably *Matilda.*

819   To George Steevens

Adelphi
Jany 13 1774

Never imagine, my dear Sir, that I can suspect Your friendship, or that I will suffer any body Else in my Company to defame You.[1] I have not seen Bell[2] but on Account of ye Letter he wrote to Me, for a long time— to do him justice he spoke, as he ought, about You; he complain'd of Baldwin's[3] partiality; & Exorbitance— I had Nothing to do but be an humble hearer: what ye D^r intends I know not, but this I know, if I were Mr Steevens, I would see Every thing that bears ye Name of Shakespear—[4] it must be a curious business, & you would shew too little Curiosity, not to attend his invitation— there are large Bills posted about the Town as tall as I am, & almost as broad—

Upon recollection, You mention'd in one of y^r Letters, as if I had said that Bell told me, he had acquainted You with his intended Edition of Shakesp^r[5]

Sure You must have mistaken Me, for I don't remember he said that to Me, I think Some time ago before the publication, that he mention'd Your bespeaking a Set of his books, & that is all. pray be present at ye Lectures

Most truly Yours
D Garrick.

Have You seen Bryant's book upon Ancient Mythology?[6] it makes a great noise—

Address: To George Steevens Esqr, Hampstead.   *Postmarked.*   *Source:* FSL.

1. Steevens had written Garrick on Dec. 27: "In the St. James's Chronicle of Thursday last, somebody has attacked Mr. Bell's new edition of Shakespeare . . . [I] take the earliest opportunity to assure you that the letter against his book (which includes some censure of you) was not mine *on my word and honour* . . . I have troubled you with this note, because you have people now and then about you, who are too apt to mistake their own groundless suppositions for established truth" (Boaden, I, 590; see also I, 591, 592).

2. Bell's edition of Shakespeare, which was dedicated to Garrick, contained "twenty-four of the author's most esteemed plays, each of which is ornamented with a beautiful frontispiece, and regulated by permission of the managers, agreeable to the present mode of performance at the Theatres Royal in London, by Mr. Hopkins, prompter, at Drury-lane, and Mr. Younger, prompter, at Covent Garden" (advertisement on publication, *LC*, vol. XXXV, Jan. 7, 1774, p. 27). Bell defied the copyright monopoly of the organized London printers and pioneered in bringing out cheap and often well-illustrated editions of standard authors.

3. Robert Baldwin (d. 1810), bookseller and publisher at 47 Paternoster Row from 1749 until his death; he was Steevens' publisher.

4. Kenrick had invited Steevens to a series of ten lectures on Shakespeare (Boaden, I, 606), the first of these to be given in the Apollo, the great room in the Devil Tavern, Temple Bar, on Jan. 19 (*LC*, vol. XXXV, Jan. 18–20, p. 72, and Jan. 20–22, p. 76). Not wishing "to hear any reflections thrown on Dr. Johnson," Steevens did not attend (Boaden, I, 607).

5. Boaden, I, 597.

6. *A New System, or an Analysis of Ancient Mythology*, 1774, by Jacob Bryant (1715–1804), the antiquary. Steevens replied, Jan. 26: "Mr. Bryant's book has deprived me of a great part of my rest for these two nights past" (*ibid.*, II, 129).

820   To Grey Cooper

Adelphi

my dr Sr   Febry 1st 1774

It is not possible for Me to believe what my Servt tells me, nay I shd scarce have believ'd my own Eyes had I seen it— He tells me that Mr Cooper in Compy with a Certain Lord,[1] whom I most honour & would Soonest Obey, call'd Yesterday at ye Adelphi!— impossible!— I beg & beseech You, my good friend, not to make me too vain, but if there are any commands to Either of ye Indies, if it is thought proper that I shd be Commander in Chief instead of Genl Clavering,[2] (whose nomination I & my friends intended to support next thursday)[3] or if I should be fix'd to make ye Bostonians drink their tea as they ought, or send them after ye tea into ye atlantic, pray let me know directly that I may seize the Kingdoms of England, & Scotland, (in ye Persons of Richd ye 3d & Macbeth)

& prepare to go any where or Every where, as that Noble Lord shall be pleas'd to command Me.

I am Dear Mr Cooper's most Oblig'd & Obed

D Garrick

Source: FC; Boaden, I, 611.

1. Lord North (see Cooper's reply of Feb. 3 in Boaden, I, 611).
2. John Clavering (1722–1777), K.B. 1776, Lieutenant-General, hero of the capture of Guadeloupe in 1759. At a meeting of the directors of the East India Company on Feb. 8 he was elected Commander-in-Chief of the Company's forces in India, having been nominated for the position at the meeting on Feb. 3 to which Garrick alludes (*London Gazette*, Feb. 1–5, 1774).
3. In 1768 Garrick and Nathan Carrington had each purchased five-thousand shares in the East India Company (manuscript note in Garrick's hand dated Nov. 29, 1768, FSL).

821   To   Richard   Cox

Adelphi

My dear Sir   Feb^{ry} 1st 1774

Since You read that letter to Me from your Friend at Vienna,[1] I have not dar'd to prance, & curvet as usual with my Pen—

My Genius is rebuk'd!

as Shakespear says:[2] therefore You must take what I have to say to you about Noverre, in plain, dull prose. that most fantastick toe, & great Genius & I have been in treaty for some time— I left the business to be settled by his Brother,[3] & I imagin'd that he, & his dancing crew, would have *caper'd* Tragedy at Drury Lane, as we are not at present in the highest repute to *Act* it. If he has preferr'd Milan[4] to London, We must be contented, the distance between us & the Brother's inexperience of Treaty-making may have Occasion'd some blunder.— This is as much of this Matter, as I know Myself.

I am my dear Sir most truly Yours

D Garrick.

You must excuse all my hurry & interlineations for I am wth three Lawyers & my Partner's Son—[5] I remember'd on a Sudden I was to write & so have sent this Scrawl.

Address: To Richd Cox Esqr, Albemarle Street.   *Source:* HTC.

1. Probably Sir Robert Murray Keith (1730–1795), K.B. 1772, Ambassador at Vienna (1772–1792). He and Cox were members of the little group which called itself "The Gang." On Feb. 16 Sir Robert wrote from Vienna to his sister "that about three weeks ago, *sixteen couple* of our chosen belles and beaux put themselves under the direction of the great Noverre, in order to learn from him one of the prettiest figure dances one can possibly conceive" (*The Memoirs and Correspondence of Sir Robert Murray Keith*, ed. Mrs. Gillespie Smyth, 1849, I, 454).

2. *Macbeth*, III, i, 56.

3. Augustin.

4. Following the end of his two-year contract at Vienna in 1774, Noverre moved to the Teatro Reggio Ducal in Milan (Deryck Lynham, *The Chevalier Noverre*, London, 1950, p. 74).

5. Willoughby Lacy (1749–1831), the only son of Garrick's partner, inherited his father's wealth but not his prudence. Following his father's death on Jan. 25, 1774, and his own marriage on March 22 to Maria Ann Orpen (d. 1788), he lived extravagantly at his father's old home in Islington and in a new town house on Great Queen Street. By the time Garrick retired, Lacy was already heavily in debt, eventually disposing of his inherited holdings in Drury Lane to Sheridan. First vanity, and later necessity, prompted his stage appearances, which seem to have been uniformly unsuccessful (*Registers of Marriages of St. Mary le Bone, Middlesex, 1754–1775*, ed. W. Bruce Bannerman and R. R. Bruce Bannerman, Harleian Society, 1918, pt. II, p. 149; Lysons, III, 335; Henry Angelo, *Reminiscences*, 1828, I, 52–54; *Thespian Dictionary*, 1805).

822   To Willoughby Lacy

Adelphi

S^r   Feby 26. 1774

After waiting till three o'Clock (according to y^r appointment) to receive your Answer on my several proposals for refering our differences,[1] I was surprised to find (by your Note, wch I rec'd late last Night) that you have consulted Counsell in a less amicable Way than I proposed—

You do me Justice in Supposing y^t I have no wish to deprive you of any R^t you are entitled to— I commend Your prudence, And before I give you a final answer I shall follow your Example and be properly advised

I am S^r Y^r hum^e Ser^t

D: Garrick

Endorsement by Garrick: Letter from Mr W. Lacy & my answer upon our affairs 26th of Feby 1774.   *Source:* FC, copy with corrections by Garrick; Boaden, I, 612.

1. Lacy had written Garrick on Feb. 25 that he had been advised by his lawyer that he had "an equal Right" with Garrick in the management of "every Branch of the Business, relative to the Theatre" (FC; Boaden, I, 612). Lacy replied to Garrick's letter on Feb. 28, and Garrick endorsed it: "From Lacy Junr to sell his part of the Patent" (FC).

823   To George Steevens

Hampton
My dear Sir   March 8th 1774
I came here this Morning almost dying with a headach attended wth a small fever, & some Symptoms of the Stone— I caught cold in ye house of Commons Yesterday,[1] & from my present feeling, I cannot, tho I am better this Evening, guess how my indisposition will end: the Gentlemen of the Club assemble before Nine,[2] if you are with Dr Johnson by 8, you will be in good time: I have receiv'd another letter from Mr Swan with his remarks upon that difficult passage in Othello—

> *a fellow almost damn'd in a fair Wife:*[3]

I will give you the letter, wth that curious one of Anti-mendax,[4] if I am able to attend You, & nothing but illness shall prevent me.

do You know a Gentleman whose name is *Gibbon*,[5] propos'd by Dr Goldsmith, & who was blackball'd ye Same Evening You was Elected? I have often taken Notice of ye bon ton you mention in many a Waistcoat![6] in hopes of being able to attend Your Entrance on Fryday, I am

Most Truly Your Sincere Friend & Ser^t
D: Garrick.

I write this upon ye bed for I can't hold my head up.

Address: To George Steevens Esqr at Hampstead. *Postmarked. Source:* Murdock Collection; *Proceedings of the Massachusetts Historical Society*, LII (1918–19), 148f.

1. On March 7, in the House of Commons, there were a number of reports and Lord North read the King's message on the "Information of the unwarrantable Practices which have been lately concerted and carried on in *North America* and particularly of the violent and outrageous Proceedings of the Town and Port of Boston in the Province of *Massachusetts Bay*" resulting from the tax on tea (*Journals of the House of Commons*, vol. XXXIV, 1771–1775, p. 541f.).

2. A recently elected member of the Literary Club, Steevens had written Garrick on March 6: "Many thanks both for your suffrage and your congratulations, for they are equally honourable to me. I shall not fail to join the club on Friday evening. Dr Johnson desires I will call on him, & he will introduce me.— Pray what is the usual time of meeting?" (Murdock Collection). For Johnson's invitation and letters to Steevens on this occasion, see Boswell, II, 273f.

3. *Othello*, I, i, 21.

4. Davies, the bookseller; in a letter to the *St. James's Chronicle*, Jan. 4–6, he criticized Garrick for allowing Hopkins, the prompter, "to deliver the Plays of Shakespeare in a State of Mutilation, as acted at his Theatre, to Mr. Bell." For identification of Davies as Anti-Mendax, see a letter to Garrick of Jan. 11, 1774, signed Detector, a letter which Garrick endorsed: "Whitchurch Pondport[?] Dorset Revd Mr Hawkins" (FC); see also Boaden, II, 130. In a copy of a letter from Davies to Garrick, dated only "Wed^y July 20," but probably written in 1774 since the day, month, and number agree with that year, the copyist has preserved what must doubtless have been Garrick's endorsement: "Mr Davies once an actor now a conceited bookseller nor is that all Anti-Mendax" (FC).

5. Edward Gibbon (1737–1794), the historian, the first volume of whose *Decline and Fall of the Roman Empire* did not appear until two years later.

6. An allusion to the following passage in Steevens' letter of March 6: "If the *bon ton* should prove a contagious disorder among us, it will be curious to trace its progress. I have already seen it breaking out in D^r G[oldsmith] under the form of many a waistcoat: but I believe D^r J[ohnson] will be the last man in whom the symptoms of it will be detected."

824   To Doctor John Campbell[1]

Hampton
March 22^d 1774

Mr Garrick presents his Comp^ts to Dr Campbell— He remembers well the taking some receipts from the D^r & in his removing from Southampton Street to ye Adelphi some of the receipts fell into his hands, but he cannot immediatly recollect where he put them: He will search for them, & what he cannot find he will certainly pay for— He imagines that[2] the D^r had M^r G's own Subscription,[3] but as it is too long to remember correctly, he will be determin'd by ye receipts themselves, when he is lucky enough to find them.

Source: FC, draft; Boaden, I, 615.

1. John Campbell (1708–1775), LL.D. 1754, miscellaneous writer, Scot of great industry and of wide knowledge, and a friend of Boswell and Johnson.

2. *Deletion:* "he paid for his own Subscription, as it is so long since, he believes now more than 20 Years' Mr Garrick will be determin'd by the receipts themselves, when he is lucky enough to find them."

3. A subscription to Campbell's *A Political Survey of Great Britain* (1774), on which the author had worked so many years that many of the original subscribers were dead. In his

reply, March 23, he wrote: "Dr Campbell is made exceeding happy by his good Friend Mr Garrick's obliging Favour of yesterday. He never had any account transmitted, neither can he find Mr Garrick's respectable Name as a Subscriber to the Political Survey in his general List" (HCL).

825 To L. M. N.[1]

Hampton
Sir   March 22^n 1774
I must take Shame to myself, & all ye blame which You attribute to Mr Anstey, I must with justice take to Myself: the Neglect of your Commands hurts me much, & yet when I relate ye Circumstances of that business, I flatter myself that I shall not plead for forgiveness in vain:

Tho I once met Mr Anstey at Mr Calvert's in Hertfordshire, & some little correspondence has since past by letter &c yet I really did not know, at ye time of receiving y^r favour, where to find him: I sent to his Brother in Law Mr Calvert who lives in Portman Square to transmit Your present to him— He unluckily being out of Town, and a greater hurry of business coming upon me, by my Partner's illness, & death, Your Commission with other Matters was lost in the confusion: it rather makes against Me, to say I am in general very punctua⟨l⟩ in my Care of & attention to my friends, but the Circumstances above may perhaps intitle me to indulgence— Shall I now write to my Friend Mr Calvert, & thro him convey the present, & my past Neglect to Mr Anstey? I am most willing to attone for my fault, I hate to be thought ungrateful, & to return favours with Neglect— I can say with Oedipus (altering one word)

My head was guilty, but my heart was free.

I am Sr Your most Oblig'd & Obed^t Ser^t
D: Garrick

a Line to ye Adelphi Terrace will oblige me much.
I write with ye Gout in my hand.

Address: To L. M. N. *Seal. Source:* FSL.

1. This is the reply to an undated letter signed L.M.N. and written from "Old Slaughter's Coffee house St Martin's Lane" (FC; Boaden, I, 29f.). The recipient was a

young man who had sent Garrick in January, before publication, two copies of "a little poetical Essay," entitled *A Bagatelle, a Dialogue* (1774). These were accompanied by an undated note, also signed L.M.N., asking the actor to keep one and deliver the other to Christopher Anstey, the writer not knowing his address (Boaden, I, 22). Believing that Anstey had received his poem, the author in his second letter to Garrick had accused Anstey of rudeness for failing to acknowledge the gift.

826   To The Earl of Sandwich

Adelphi

My Lord   March 30th [17]74
Your very favourable attention to my Solicitation in behalf of M[r]
M[iles][1] obliges me to trouble y[r] Lord[p] again— indeed he has
press'd me to it so warmly & for such reasons that I have not
philosophy enough to give him a denial— I flatter myself that he
will not discredit y[r] L[p's] kindness, or my recommendation, &
therefore I will venture to propose him as a proper Object for Both—
I was mistaken when I told y[r] Lord[p] that he was formerly in y[e]
Marines; he was bred to y[e] Sea, & was a Midshipman for some
time— His Utmost Ambition is to owe y[e] Salvation of himself &
family in this world to Lord S; how he will get clear in y[e] next by
being a Purser, if y[r] Goodness should make him one, will be his own
Concern: Whatever be his Lot, I shall always think of y[r] Lord[p]
wth gratitude & am My Lord Y[r] L[p's] most oblig'd

& faithfull hum: Ser[t]
D G.

Endorsement by Garrick: Lett[r] to Lord Sandwich for W. A. Miles Esq[r].   *Source:*
FC, draft.

1. William Augustus Miles (1753?–1817), political writer, had gained Garrick's
friendship in 1773 by publishing a *Letter to Sir John Fielding*, with a postscript to the actor,
protesting against Fielding's attempt to suppress the *Beggar's Opera* (William E. Schultz,
Gay's Beggar's Opera, New Haven, 1923, p. 245).

827   To Mary Latter[1]

Madam.   Easter Tuesday [April 5] 1774
I took y^r tragedy[2] into the Country with me, & have well consider'd it— I never make any Objections to ye Expence of decorating
a play, if I imagine that ye Performance will be of Service to the
Author, & the Theatre— Let me Assure You, Madam, that it is
my sincere opinion, notwithstand^g the Merit of some passages in y^e
Siege of Jerusalem, that it would fail of Success in the Representation—[3]

I am Mad^m Y^r most humble Ser^t
D G

Endorsement by Garrick: My Answer.   *Source:* FC, draft.

1. Mrs. Mary Latter (1725–1777), writer, lived much of her life at Reading; she describes herself as living "not very far from the market-place, immersed in business and in
debt; sometimes madly hoping to gain a competency; sometimes justly fearing dungeons
and distress" (*Miscellaneous Works, in Prose and Verse*, Reading, 1759, Appendix).
2. *The Siege of Jerusalem by Titus Vespasian* had been accepted by Rich, who had died
before it could be produced. It was published in 1763 and was performed at Reading in
1768, where it proved a failure. In Mrs. Latter's letter of March 26 (FC), to which this is
the reply, she submitted an altered version of the tragedy, stating that it had been "examin'd by *many* Theatrical Companies and favourably judg'd of. I presume not with standing, (at least I have been told,) that the Expenses attending its exhibition will frighten *all*
the Managers from bringing it on the Stage."
3. Mrs. Latter replied to Garrick in a long letter, dated June 12, 1774, which she
maintained had been wrung from her by "the withering blast of *Refusal*." Garrick endorsed her letter: "Mrs Latter from Reading about her Tragedy fine & conceited" (FC;
Boaden, I, 633f.).

828   To Peter Fountain

                                                      Adelphi
Dear Sir   [April] 15 [1774]
I will call upon You some Morning very soon & then We shall do
our business much better by Ourselves— I have ye pleasure of knowing Mr Tilson,[1] but have no particular Acquaintance with him.

I am truly y^{rs}
D Garrick

Address: To Mr Fountain, Lichfield Street.   *Endorsement by the recipient:* 15th Apr. 1774.   *Source:* FC.

1. Possibly Oliver Tilson (1717–1788), lawyer, of Hill St., Berkeley Square. He was admitted to Lincoln's Inn on Sept. 16, 1732, and was Commissioner of the Salt Duties in 1766 (*Alumni Cantab.*).

829   To The Bishop of Gloucester

Hampton
April 21— 1774

Will your Lordship permit me to recommend to your perusal the inclosed plan for a pronouncing Dictionary;[1] it is written by a most Worthy, ingenious Friend of mine who has studied his subject deeply, and I hope to the purpose— my regard for his Worth as a man, may make me partial to him as an author. I shall truly know what advice I should give him, if your Lordship would honour me with your sentiments— Let me assure you, that he is not one of the genus irritabile, and that he will be as grateful for your Lordships Objections as he will be proud of your approbation— the fear of interrupting your Studies, or being admitted when you have better Company, has often restrain'd my inclination of paying my respects to your Lordship, but I intend doing myself that honour in a few days. It is with great pleasure I have heard, that the Drs Hurd, Robertson, Beattie & other respectable names have written Letters in favour of literary property—[2] it will be of the greatest service to the Cause. Mrs Garrick presents her respects with Mine to your Lordship & Mrs Warburton,[3] I am

my Lord &c
D. G

Source: FSL, copy.

1. John Walker's *A General Idea of a Pronouncing Dictionary of the English Language on a Plan Entirely New*, dedicated to Garrick and published the previous month. Walker, under the patronage of Johnson, was at the time earning a livelihood by lecturing on elocution. The *Pronouncing Dictionary*, which was to appear in 1791, was long regarded as the standard work on English orthoëpy.
2. In March 1774 the booksellers had petitioned the House of Commons for a bill further to protect their privileges of copyright. James Mansfield declared in Parliament that he had by him "letters of Mr. Hume, Dr. Hurd, Dr. Robertson, Dr. Beattie, and

other Writers of established reputation ... lamenting the late decision of the House of Peers, as fatal to letters" (*LC*, vol. XXXV, May 14–17, 1774, p. 465).

3. Gertrude (Tucker) Warburton (d. 1796) who had been married in 1745.

830   To Mary Ann Yates

Adelphi

Madam.   April 27 1774

In all dealings the plain and Simple truth is the best policy: As Mrs Barry is in treaty with another Theatre,[1] it is natural for Me to Wish a treaty with another Lady; & it is as natural that my inclinations look towards You:[2] If *You* have no objections to Enter into a treaty with Me, be pleas'd to name Your time & place and I shall be as punctual as I ought to be to so fine a Woman, & so good an Actress.

[I am, Madam, your most humble servant,
D. Garrick.][3]

Endorsement by Garrick: Copy of a Letter Sent to Mrs Yates April ye 27th 1774. *Source:* FC, draft; Boaden, I, 623.

1. After the season of 1773–74 Mrs. Barry and her husband left Drury Lane for Covent Garden, where they both acted until Spranger Barry died in Jan. 1777.

2. Mrs. Yates had been engaged at Covent Garden by Colman in 1767, very much against the wishes of his partners Harris and Rutherford. With Colman's resignation in May of 1774 it was natural that she would seek a change, preferably to Drury Lane.

3. Matter in brackets is supplied from the printed source.

831   To Mary Ann Yates

Adelphi

Madam   May 4 1774

My Brother's dangerous situation[1] has made me unfit for business, nor did I see Mr Lacy till last night: this I hope will plead my excuse for not calling upon You Yesterday Morning:

We have consider'd your letter; in answer to which, we send you the following proposals. We agree to give You for *one*, *two*, or *three* Years 750 pounds including your cloaths—²

As We cannot do more, we hope for the good of the whole, (if Mrs. Yates will Accept of our terms) that She will come to an immediate Engagement.

I am Madam, Your most hum^le Servt

D: Garrick

as to the Benefit, Mrs Yates should well consider that Matter— We shall not stand upon *Triffles*, if Nothing Else can hinder our Engagement—³

Mr Garrick desires his Comp^ts to Mr Yates.

Source: FSL, draft in FC; Boaden, I, 623f.

1. See Letters 834, 835.
2. *Deletion in draft:* "should You chuse to wave Y^r Benefit, we will allow You (what we would not to any other Performer) 150 pounds in lieu of it— We cannot possibly, in any other manner, Shew the great desire, we have to Engage Mrs Yates."
3. Mrs. Yates had written on May 2: "I think I cannot in conscience take less than £700 a year for my salary; for my Clothes, as I love to be well dressed and the Characters I appear in require it I expect £200, as to benefit you shall settle that yourself, but as I have an infinity of *Scotch pride* had rather not take one tho' I am sure of losing by it" (FC; Boaden, I, 623).

832   To Mary Ann Yates

Madam.   Saturday May 7th 1774
As I flatter Myself by Your Note that you have accepted of our terms,¹ I shall wait upon you this Evening about 8 o'Clock & will bring Mr Wallis of Norfolk Street along with me to draw up a memorandum of our agreement,² as I would have it immediatly settled for Your Sake as well as Mine

I am Madam Y^r most hum^le Ser^t

D G.

If You chuse it You will have a Friend on Y^r Part   I beg My Comp^ts to Mr Yates.

N.B. no answer to this— I went wth Mr Wallis a little after 8 o'Clock, Mrs Yates had two Ladies wth her, & w^d not accept of ye terms.³ D G

Source: FC, draft; Boaden, I, 626f.

1. Actually all that Mrs. Yates had written was that "As Mrs. Y. thinks business cannot be so well settled by letter, she will be happy to see Mr. Garrick any day and hour he will please to appoint" (Boaden, I, 626).
2. See one dated May 28 in the Forster Collection (Boaden, I, 624).
3. Subsequently she accepted a contract, appearing at Drury Lane in Oct. 1774 and acting there for five seasons.

833   To Elizabeth Montagu

Adelphi
Fryday [May 13, 1774][1]

My Best And Most Amiable Friend—
When you called last Night my foot was flanell'd up wth y[e] Gout, and a Sight of you, and ten words from You, would have been a Charm for y[e] foul Fiend— but I was order'd to see Nobody, & did not know it was my cure till it was gone— I am much better, & so well, that I shall be able to appear in Old Lusignan tonight, & in a better Character tomorrow in Hill Street— in that of the faithful Friend, & admirer of Mrs. Montagu— I was reading, or rather dozing over the cold, Northern Critick[2] when you were at the door— notwithstanding his flattery to me, I can't bear the unfeelingness of his Soul. Shakespear no Tragic Poet!—[3] Shakespear not the *first* Tragick poet!— What insensibility!— but more of this when I have y[e] honour of seeing you tomorrow, which I most certainly will do, tho I am carried in a Litter & so lay'd at y[r] feet.

Dear Madam, most unalterably & faithfully y[rs],
D. Garrick.

I am always kissing Miss Gregory's hand & will make her cry if possible tonight.

Source: Blunt, *Mrs. Montagu*, I, 351f.

1. The date is determined by the references to Taylor and to Lusignan, which Garrick played on Friday, May 13, 1774.
2. Presumably Edward Taylor (1741?–1797), of Steeple-Acton, Oxfordshire. After studying at Cambridge and Göttingen and traveling abroad he retired to the country and spent the last twenty-six years of his life in the pursuit of literature (*GM*, vol. LXVII, Dec. 1797, p. 1076). Garrick's characterization of Taylor presumably stemmed from the critic's professedly English, detached, intellectual enjoyment of the art of tragedy rather

than an emotional involvement in the reality of illusion, a point of view antithetical to Garrick's concept of his role as dramatist and author.

3. Taylor, in his *Cursory Remarks on Tragedy, on Shakespear*, which had been published anonymously the previous month (see *LC*, vol. XXXV, April 19–21, 1774, p. 383), had commended Garrick's interpretation of Lear (p. 16f.), but had also asserted "with an impartiality that becomes every man, who dares to think for himself, let us allow [Shakespeare] great merit as a comic writer, greater still as a poet, but little, very little as a tragedian" (p. 37).

834 To The Reverend Doctor John Delap[1]

Adelphi

Dear Sir   May 14th 1774

The very dangerous Situation of my Brother's health for some weeks has made me incapable of any business; however within these last eight days I have well consider'd the Tragedy & read it twice— let me assure You by every thing that is dear to me, that the writing of this Letter is perhaps one of the most disagreeable tasks that I ever undertook, & the reason is, because I fear, that it will not be agreeable to You, whom I most sincerely wish to serve, & which is not to be done at the expence of my Reason & Judgment, & I fear of your Reputation.

I most willingly resign all my Claims to any knowledge of the Drama, if the Tragedy of the Royal Exiles is calculated for Success Upon the Stage—[2] The first Act with some small Alterations would have sufficient Merit for a first Act, but from the begining of the 2[d] to the End of the 5th it is very Languid, & undramatic that is, without a Spirited interest to keep up the Attention of an Audience. the false Oracle false Priest, & pitiful Character of Demophen sinks the whole, the death of Macaria by Accident the Unnatural Combat of the Brothers &c in the last Act are Shocking, but without Effect; however the Circumstances of the last Act (which to me is much the worst, & ought to be the best) might be alter'd— but indeed I find such a Languer thro' the whole that Representation can never Support— I would have desir'd some Gentlemen of Character in the Drama to have given me their Opinion, had I had your Consent— M[r] Whitehead seem'd to be averse to any farther trouble about plays, when we consulted him about a former Tragedy;—[3] I am really so much distress'd about it, that I could wish You would

let it be sent to the other House, the Managers since the parting
with Mr Colman,[4] have got M^r & Mrs Barry, & should they accept
of the Play, they would be more Capable of doing it Justice than I
possibly could with my present Company— I will take any trouble
You desire me, & be assur'd that your Name shall always be con-
ceald.

    I am Dear Sir Your Sincere wellwisher & humble Servt

                            D Garrick

I have had an Attack of the Gout, & am writing this Scrawl upon
my Bed— I write with double pain— but with the best wishes
towards You.

    Endorsement by Garrick: A Letter of mine to Dr Delap— & his very polite
answer May 1774.   *Source:* FC, copy; Boaden, I, 627.

    1. Delap replied to this letter on May 16 (FC).
    2. It was finally produced as *The Royal Suppliants* (DL, Feb. 17, 1781); the play was
taken from the *Heraclidae* of Euripides and *The Suppliants* of Aeschylus (BD).
    3. In a letter of Dec. 17 (no year), written in acknowledgment of Garrick's rejection
of his "Panthea," Delap states: "I will, in a post or two, desire y^r opinion of a plan, on a
story entirely new. M^r [William] Whitehead's opinion of it is, that, supposing the story
not to be *too romantic*, it is told in a very masterly manner— & he desires that I would send
it to You" (FC; Boaden, I, 126).
    4. With Colman's retirement to Bath, Thomas Harris took over the active manage-
ment of Covent Garden, for Powell had died in 1769 and Rutherford was retired (Eugene
R. Page, *George Colman the Elder*, New York, 1935, pp. 217–219).

835   To Peter Fountain

                                       Adelphi
My dear S^r   [May] 16th [1774]
My Brother George has been dying these 3 Weeks, he is in y^e
Country, & getting Strength Every day— I have had an attack
from ye Gout, And it was impossible to see You under ye apprehension for my Brother, & on my own Acc^t— You may depend
upon calling upon You after Wednesday— tomorrow I play,[1] &
ye next day I meet ye Company:[2] I sh^d be glad to Enter into any
treaty you approve of— Will you give me a hint of ye business that
I may be prepar'd for it—

The Picture has great Merit indeed— many thanks for ye perusal of it.

Ever & truly Y^rs
D: Garrick.

Endorsement by the recipient: Reced 16th May 1774 PF Directed to Mr Fountain at Mr Grignion's Litchf^d Street. *Source:* FC.

1. *King Lear*, for the Theatrical Fund.
2. In May 1766 Garrick had set up by donations and benefit performances the Theatrical Fund, later incorporated by Parliament as "The Society Established for the Relief of Indigent Persons belonging to His Majesty's Company of Comedians" of the Theatre Royal, Drury Lane. From its inception Garrick served as the nominal and later chief executive officer responsible to a committee of thirteen elected by the Company. According to the records of the Theatrical Fund of May 18, 1774: "Dav Gar Esq the father founder & Proct^r of this Inst this day convened the male members of the theater in the green R & then like a good and faithful Steward del into their hands the foll^g posessions & securities" amounting to £2918.11.9 (James Winston, "Theatrical Records," FSL; see also *The Fund, for the Relief of Indigent Persons, Belonging to His Majesty's Company of Comedians of the Theatre Royal, Drury Lane. Established, Endowed, and Incorporated by that Great Master of His Art, David Garrick, Esq., 1777,* 1819).

836   To Elizabeth Younge

Adelphi
Dear Madam.   May 17th 1774
It gives me much concern that we are not yet agreed, & indeed if You will not give up part of y^r demand, I fear, we shall still remain in a Situation disagreeable & very inconvenient to all parties— We will give You 12 pounds for 2 Years 13 for the 3^d and 14 for the 4th If fixing y^r Benefit play by Article to the Night, I gave you from Inclination, will be agreeable, it shall be done.

I have Something to propose about y^r Cloaths which may be likewise Agreeable & profitable— In short I will have You, if I can upon the fairest terms— but we must determine soon for all our sakes— when shall I see You?[1]

Most truly Y^rs
D. Garrick

Address: Miss Young.   *Seal.*   *Source:* FSL.

1. Miss Younge continued at Drury Lane.

837   To The Reverend John Home

Adelphi
My dear Home.   May 24 1774
You fled from London before I left Bath— I have seen the Person
mention'd in Yr Note, & have told him how he stands upon the list—
We are more regular in our Stage-promotions than they are in the
State— We Suffer None but those of extraordinary Merit, & Monsr
Arlequin to leap over Peoples heads— so much for that: I must
beg leave to recommend to Your good Word, for He well deserves
it, Mr Walker— You love honesty & ingenuity, he is well stor'd
with both, & intends reading lectures in Edinburgh upon ye English
language: tho *You* cannot be mended, there may be some of Your
Acquaintance who will profit by his knowledge in Every branch of
the English tongue— he has Studied it as a Gramarian Philosopher
Rhetorician, Orator Critick & What Not— his humility & Modesty
are Equal to his Ability, & if these Matters will not induce you to
like & Serve him, let me insure your favour for him at once & tell
You, that he is one for whom Your friend Garrick has the greatest
regard & the warmest wishes—

Ever & most Affecly Yours
D: Garrick

My Wife sends her best to You— pray remember me to the Chosen
Dr Carlisle, Mrs Home1 &c &c &c

Source: Maggs Brothers, Ltd.

1. In 1770 Home had married Mary, daughter of his friend and relation William
Home. Mrs. Home was unattractive in appearance, and when Hume asked how "he
could ever think of such a woman?" "Ah, David!" Home replied, "if I had not, who else
would have taken her?" (*Selections from the Family Papers Preserved at Caldwell*, ed. William
Mure, Glasgow, 1854, pt. 2, vol. II, p. 179, n. 3).

838   To Peter Fountain

Dear Sr   [ca. May 25, 1774]1
I never had a political illness in my life— I was at Covt Garden,
not with my Brother, but with Becket, & there I believe I caught,

2+L.D.G. III

what now I suffer— I came to Town from Hampton after four, & took it on a Sudden in my head to see *Rosamond*;[2] a finer Creature than M[rs] Hartly I never saw— her make is perfect— Yesterday Morn[g] I was Seiz'd with y[e] Gout in Southampton Street, & have kept house Ever Since— I love y[r] Suspicions they are friendly ones but ill-founded— You may depend upon my Secresy, but I cannot think as I am Situated that the Scheme can take place— I thank you for y[e] Loisirs,[3] I shall look into y[e] book this Afternoon— in the mean time

I am Dear S[r] very weak but Y[rs] truly

D Garrick

I am free from pain, & have my Cloth Shoe on— I am Subpœna'd by M[r] Foote in a Cause with him & M[r] Ross.[4]

Address: To M[r] Fountain, Lichfield Street. *Source:* FC; Boaden, II, 335.

1. On the assumption that the references in this and in the following letter are to the same subpoena and that both letters therefore were written at approximately the same time, the conjectural date is derived from the following letter. Other allusions in this letter support this dating.

2. Thomas Hull's *Henry the Second; or, The Fall of Rosamond* (CG, May 1, 1773). The play was repeated several times during the 1773–74 season, and the performance on Monday, May 23, is that which presumably Garrick and Becket attended.

3. *Les Loisirs du Chevalier D'Eon de Beaumont* (Amsterdam, 1774), reviewed in the *Public Advertiser* on March 21, 1774.

4. In 1770 Foote leased from David Ross for three years the Royal Theatre in Edinburgh; dissatisfied with the venture, he disposed of the lease in 1771 to West Digges, who shortly was arrested for debt. Ross thereupon sued Foote. From Garrick's references in this and the following letter it seems that the case was heard on May 26, 1774; the finding was against Foote (William Cooke, *Memoirs of Samuel Foote*, 1805, II, 214f.; James C. Dibdin, *Annals of the Edinburgh Stage*, Edinburgh, 1888, pp. 153–160).

839   To Hannah More[1]

Adelphi

[May?] 25 [1774?][2]

M[r] Garrick presents his best Comp[ts] to Miss More, & her Sisters[3] & as he is unluckily Subpœnad to attend Westminster Hall to morrow Morning, he must desire them to give M[rs] Garrick & him the Pleasure of their Company on Fryday— the Coach will be with them between Nine & ten— what can Mr Garrick say for the most flattering Compliment which he *Ever* receiv'd—? he must be Silent.

Address: To Miss More, Southampton Street.   *Seal.*   *Source:* FSL.

1. Hannah More (1745–1833) in May 1774, with two of her sisters, came up to London from Bristol for the first time and was introduced by Sir Joshua Reynolds and his sister to London society. To Dr. (later, 1792, Sir) James Stonhouse (1716–1795), a physician and clergyman in Bristol, who for many years had been a friend and counselor, she wrote a long account, notably of Garrick's acting. Perceiving how much meeting Garrick would mean to her, Stonhouse wrote the actor introducing her and enclosing a transcript of her letter (Appendix D; see also Roberts, *Hannah More*, I, 36).

2. It is assumed that this letter was inspired by Stonhouse's letter to Garrick of May 21, 1774, introducing the Mores. Garrick's letter is therefore conjecturally dated in the same month and year.

3. Sarah (1743–1817) and Martha (1747–1819).

840   To The Reverend Doctor Thomas Francklin[1]

Dear Sir   [May 29, 1774]
You did ask Me to lend you a 100 pounds, I told you fairly that I had calls upon Me which had almost drain'd Me: you then told Me If you had it by Michaelmas next it would be sufficient, I said I could by that time oblige you— whenever You please to speak *all* your Sentiments on *this* or any other Occasion to *Me*, I will most certainly *speak all mine to You*,— as to your *mentioning* them to *any body else*, it is in y^r own breast to do as you please— all I will say now is that what you said Yesterday Morning y^r letter, contradicts, & that to Me at least, You have always Acted & written unaccountably—

I am D^r S^r y^r most hum^le Ser^t
D Garrick

Endorsement by Garrick: Dr Franklin's Letter to me & My Answer about £100 May 29th 1774.   *Source:* William Salt Library, draft.

1. This is the reply to Francklin's letter of Saturday [May 28], in which he wrote: "I ask'd you this morning to lend me £100 for a short time which you refused. I will not speak *all* my Sentiments on this Occasion at present to you, nor will I mention them to any body *else*: all I shall now say is, that if you knew the distresses I have undergone, & the anxiety which you have caus'd in an unfortunate & numerous family by your refusal you wou'd sincerely pity [me]" (William Salt Library; see also Boaden, I, 632f.).

841   To Peter Fountain

Dᵣ Sʳ   May 30 [1774]
I have sent yʳ Book & print— both charming, Especially yᵉ Russian
Story—¹ yᵉ Print I had seen before— I am going to get some fresh
Air into yᵉ Country & shall not return immediatly When I do I
will certainly call upon You—

                                                             Yʳˢ truly
                                                             D G

Endorsement by the recipient: Mʳ G's Let May 30ᵗʰ Rec'd May 30ᵗʰ 1774 PF.
Source: FC.

1. Presumably the account of Eudoxia, Peter the Great's first wife, in the sixth
volume of d'Eon's *Loisirs*.

842   To The Reverend Doctor Thomas Francklin

                                                  June 5ᵗʰ [1774]¹
Mʳ Garrick has sent the Tragedy to Dʳ Franklin & desires him to
finish it as he intends it shall be Acted—² Mʳ Garrick thinks the
Catastrophe better for the alteration & differs wᵗʰ the Gentleman
who has made his remark upon that place. Mʳ Garrick thinks there
are weak parts, or rather languid scenes, & has not chang'd his
opinion wᶜʰ he Scribbled wᵗʰ a pencil the Tragedy appears to him
not so dramatic & calculate of Success as yᵉ Earl of Warwick—
He thinks Dʳ Franklin should read yᵉ Play to Mʳˢ Yates & know her
thoughts upon Matilda³

Source: FC, draft; Boaden, I, 632.

1. The year is from Francklin's reply of June 6, 1774 (Boaden, I, 632). Garrick
endorsed the wrapper to Francklin's letters about *Matilda:* "Letters from the righteous
Dʳ F—n about his Tragedy. wᵗʰ yᵉ account of Matilda's receipts" (FC).
2. *Matilda* (DL, Jan. 21, 1775), which netted the author £336. 7s. in nine performances (see Boaden, II, 44, and FC for the balance sheet). For Francklin's partiality for
Mrs. Yates, see Letter 531.
3. Miss Younge, however, took the title role.

843   To David Ross

Adelphi
Sir   June 5 [1774]¹
The present arrangement of our business for the next Season,
obliges Us not to enter into more Engagements, than those We have
already made: Be assur'd that it is not the least Objection to Yʳ
Abilities in Your profession that prevents our Acceptance of Your
Offer.²
                        I am Sir Yʳ most Obedᵗ Servᵗ
                                        D Garrick

Endorsement by Garrick in draft: To Mʳ Ross.   *Source:* Maggs Brothers, Catalogue, Christmas 1929, facsimile, draft in FSL; Boaden, I, 631.

   1. This is the reply to Ross's letter of June 4, 1774 (Boaden, I, 631).
   2. Ross had written: "I think my abilities, as things are circumstanced, may be of
some small use at Drury-lane, and of advantage to myself: as to my terms, give me what
you please when I may have deserved it . . . It is in your power to be of the greatest
service to me by rescuing me from my present situation, which that ungrateful fellow
Colman has put me in, by giving the preference to a man who, in my poor opinion,
never spoke one line naturally in his whole life."

844   To William Shirley

[*post* June 10, 1774]¹
Mʳ Garrick presents his Compᵗˢ to Mʳ Shirley— he shᵈ have answer'd
his last Note before had not he been almost prohibited reading &
writing:— He has consider'd his Plays² which have taken him up
some time, & he now Sends his Opinion of them with that sincerity
& frankness which Mʳ Shi[r]ley desires & practices: the Comedy
(he thinks) very unfit for representation— it is too low & uninteresting & grossnesses would never be suffer'd—³ Alcibiades after
the first Act falls off & fails in yᵉ requisites of Affection & Passion
as much as in moral tendency: Mʳ G. thinks that Mʳ Shirley seems
a little conscious of this himself by yᵉ Note he rec'd from him— the
Subject of the *Roman Victim*, has been upon yᵉ Stage Since Mʳ G's
Managemᵗ He Acted Virginius & Mʳˢ Cibber yᵉ Daughter—⁴ it

was well rec'd & the Author is Still living— M^r G: has been Accus'd of partiality for not reviving Mr Crisp's Virginia; to speak sincerely M^r G: thinks the Circumstance of Stabbing Virginia & ye Consequences better manag'd in the former play.— The Roman Sacrifice[5] bids fairest for Success— the Subject is not ye most pleasing for an English Audience— the unnatural rigour of Brutus is carried too far, but as it is a fact in history, it will Stand Criticism in that particular— M^r G: is going from home tomorrow betimes for 3 Weeks at his return he will let Mr Shirley know, & they will converse upon it— He has Return'd ye Plays as Mr S. may perhaps be willing to Offer Some of them to ye New Managem^t at Cov^t Garden— He may depend upon M^r G's Secresy.

Source: FC, draft.

1. This is the answer to Shirley's letter of June 10, 1774 (FC).
2. Shirley's four plays, according to a careful criticism sent Garrick by John Walker, were "All Mistaken," a comedy, and the tragedies "Alcibiades," "The Roman Victim," and *The Roman Sacrifice* (FC).
3. *Deletion*: "alterations of ye Comedy of Errors have been try'd & the original has been always better receiv'd."
4. In *Virginia* (DL, Feb. 25, 1754) by Samuel Crisp (d. 1783).
5. It was to be first performed at Drury Lane on Dec. 18, 1777, but was played only four nights and "very coldly received" (BD).

845   To The Reverend James Townley

London
Dear Townley   June 16 1774
I am told Your Curate of Hendon has left You— if so— let me recommend for Your Sake, not for mine,[1] or his, Mr Bate[2] to supply that place: He is a Man of Spirit, worth, & letters, if you would have a Stronger recommendation, I will give you one which I know will Weigh still more with You, he is a very warm friend of mine

Dear Townley Most affec^ly Y^rs

D Garrick

He lives upon a good Farm in y^r Neighbourhood.

Address: Revd Mr Townley, Suffolk Lane, Canon Street.   *Seal.*   *Source:* FSL.

1. Garrick owned the manor of Hendon, and Townley was rector of the church from 1772 to 1777.

2. Henry Bate (1745–1824), afterwards (1813) Sir Henry Bate Dudley, journalist, dramatic and miscellaneous writer. He succeeded his father as Rector of North Fambridge, Essex, but spent most of his time in London where he was known as a man of pleasure. As an early editor of the *Morning Post* (established 1772) his articles frequently involved him in personal disputes, earning for him the name "the Fighting Parson." In 1773 he had married a sister of Mrs. Hartley. Probably because of Garrick's solicitation, in 1774 he became curate to Townley (*Bath Chronicle*, Sept. 9, 1773; William T. Whitley, "An Eighteenth-Century Art Chronicler: Sir Henry Bate Dudley, Bart.," *The Thirteenth Volume of the Walpole Society, 1924–1925*, Oxford, 1925, pp. 25–66, with a portrait by Gainsborough).

846 To The Reverend Doctor
Thomas Francklin

Sir [June 16, 1774]¹
When I receivd y—r last favor I was so ill to be deny'd both reading & writing now I am better, I cannot pass yʳ last Extraordʸ Epistle without answᵍ it.

Whenever You put a play into my hands You desire my remarks, seem to express an Eagerness for them, but I always found that my Criticism was a very ill office— It gives me great pleasure to hear that you intend to shew yʳ Play² to Your *Friends*, & *approv'd Judges*, & let me request you, as yᵉ greatest favour You can confer upon Me, implicitly to follow their Advice; for I shᵈ indeed be very unhappy, if *you*, or *they*, should out of false delicacy, regard any Observations which I might have made— I may venture to say with you, *whatever you may think, I have no vanity about me*— I therefore repeat it again, that I hope yᵉ Catastrophe which I suggested will not stand.

Sorry I am to hear that mere Money is yʳ Muse and that You wᵈ never write again for yᵉ Stage but for yᵉ Sake of *Lucre*— pray wᵗ mortification has Dʳ Franklin met with by writing for yᵉ Stage? I will (without vanity) be bold to say that he had Every advantage with Us that an Author could have or his Merit's demand— if he did not succeed so well, when he turn'd from yᵉ Capulets, to the Mountagues,³ what can he blame, but his own inconstancy—

You are pleas'd to say that *I must* remember, when You first presented *Warwick* I told You it would not do at all— did not I add *without alterations*— & were not those Alterations made? or suppose it Otherwise— have not I a greater merit with You for performing y^r Play wch I thought *w^d not do at all*! why will you S^r call y^r past transactions, they will not make matters better between Us— If I thought about it as you say— why did I receive it— let me assure You, that I think now of *Warwick* as I always did: of *Men & plays*, (for I have known & try'd a great many) my guess is tolerably good— tho I will boast to have as little vanity as y^{r}self, yet I will venture to say, that *Warwick* was not ye worse for going thro' my hands—

Whether You think of retreating or not is *Your* affair, but *my* business is, to desire You to send me the Tragedy compleated to your own liking in two Months time, or I shall imagine that you have again chang'd y^r Mind— I shall take care to give You a good part of ye Season, & exhibit ye Play as well as I can for my own credit.

I am S^r Y^r humble Ser^t
D G:

Endorsement with address: To The Revd Dr Franklin; *and by Garrick:* Dr Francklin's letter & my answer yet unanswer'd. *Source:* FC, draft; Boaden, I, 456f.

1. This is the reply to Francklin's letter of June 6, 1774, a letter which Garrick endorsed: "Another Letter from Dr Franklin & my answer June 16, 1774" (FC; Boaden, I, 632f.).
2. *Matilda.*
3. Apparently a reference to the fact that Francklin's *Orestes* was produced at Covent Garden.

847   To Frances Abington

Hampton
June 18th [1774][1]

What still complaining, my dear Mad^m, of my Injustice?[2] Still seeking redress by producing a Catalogue of Grievances? for Heaven's sake let ye poor Manager have some respite from his many labours, & enjoy a few unmurmuring Weeks in the Summer; the Month of September will be soon here, & then it will be as Natural for you to find fault with him, as for Him to find fault with You: but my dear M^{rs} ⟨Abington⟩ Every thing has it's time &

season, & as the poor Devil has been ill lately, & very ill, let him rest from his torments till ye 17th of Sepr next,³ & then—

> Let him not look, stir, speak, or hold his tongue,
> But he means mischief, & is always wrong:

To be serious— why can't you ask a small favour without proving the infinite hardships you have suffer'd— bring me to my Tryal, and let the Jury be 12 of y^r dearest friends, & hang me out of y^r Bow-Window with a label on my breast to declare my Crimes, as a terrible Example for all future Managers. To be more serious— You shall be oblig'd upon certain conditions— first that ye Author or translator of ye petite piece,⁴ will assure Me under his hand, or face to face, that he will not think me impertinent for any little alterations I may make in adding, omitting transposing &c &c &c. *Secondly* that ye piece may be brought out as Early as I please, or I shall not be able to fulfill my Contracts— & 3dly When We have got it up with much Care, trouble, & Expense, that he will engage for M^rs ⟨Abington⟩ that she will not prevent the public from Seeing it, as often as they would wish— upon these Conditions I will set to Work directly, & if M^rs ⟨Abington⟩ could let me See her next thursday about two o'Clock at the Adelphi, We will Settle these mighty Matters.— I would wait upon her in half Moon Street, but I shall be oblig'd to stay at home upon very particular business.

I am, Dr Mad^m Y^r very humble Servt
D. Garrick

a Note Sent to ye Adelphi will be sent directly to ⟨Me⟩

Source: HTC.

1. This is the answer to Mrs. Abington's letter of June 14, 1774 (HTC).
2. Mrs. Abington had written: "Except for the very charming part which you Made for me in the Chances, I have not been permitted to speak one comic line in any new Piece these six years past— and Indeed Miss Pope is in possession of all the comic characters in Every class without Exception, while my Rolle has been confined to Melancholy walking gentlewomen only."
3. The opening of Drury Lane in 1774.
4. Identified in Mrs. Abington's letter as Bickerstaffe's *The Sultan; or, A Peep into the Seraglio* (DL, Dec. 12, 1775), in which Mrs. Abington was to play the part of Roxalana; of this part she wrote that "the author has been pleased Publickly to declare that it was My Stile of acting, which first suggested to him the Idea of Bringing Roxalana upon the English Stage; and my friends are, one and all, particularly anxious to see me in the character."

2*

848   To George Steevens

Hampton
My dear Sir   June 28 [1774?]¹
I shall be in Town Fryday and Saturday next & ready to receive
Your Commands— I have found the parcel of loose plays² &c with
a letter of Capel's³ which I will send by yᵉ Servant who brings the
books— I am really so much oblig'd to You for yᵉ trouble you have
taken, that I will send a Cart with pleasure for them if You will
appoint the Time— the Gout has again seiz'd upon my right hand,
& makes my Scrawl rather worse than usual— if Saturday should be
too soon, I Shall be in Town yᵉ Week after about Thursday— a Line
directed to yᵉ Adelphi will Convey Your Pleasure to, Dear Sir
                         Most Sincerely & faithfully Yours
                                              D: Garrick

Address: To George Steevens Esqʳ, Hampsted. *Postmarked.* *Source:* FSL.

   1. From the references in this and the next letter to the plays and Capell's letter, this
letter appears to precede the following.
   2. Listed by Steevens on the cover of Garrick's letter as follows: "Venus and Adonis
1592/ Titus Andronicus 1593/ Hen. 6. 2. p 1593/ Taming Shrew 1594/ Hen. V 1594/
King Leir 1594/ Winter Night's Pastime 1594/ K. Rich. III 1594/ Locrine 1594."
   3. It appears that Capell prepared for Garrick a catalogue of his Elizabethan plays
(Boaden, I, 586). Capell's letter which Garrick intended to send Steevens probably had
something to do with the catalogue, for Steevens complained, "The letter which accompanied [your] plays contains no other information but that you had lent Mʳ Capel
monies" (FC; Boaden, I, 450).

849   To George Steevens

Adelphi
July 2 [1774]¹
I am as Satisfy'd of Your Exactness, My dear Sir, as I am of the
trouble You have taken about my Collection of Old Plays:² they
will be taken out of yᵉ Boxes this Morning & plac'd in the Cases—
I have sent the unbound parcel with Capel's letter— & at the same
time let me Acknowledge that You have return'd my Collection of
Plays, & have greatly oblig'd me by yʳ careful inspection of them
                         I am my dear Sir most faithfully yʳˢ
                                              D. Garrick

I will Search for yᵉ tools You mention'd— I saw them some time ago— they are only mislaid.

PS. Dʳ Kenrick is going to Lecture at Mary'bone Gardens.[3]

Address: George Steevens Esqʳ, Hampsted. *Seal. Source:* FSL.

1. The year is determined by the reference to Kenrick's lecture.

2. Steevens replied: "I am sorry to let you know that very many tragedies and comedies are enter'd [at Stationers' Hall], the names of which are neither to be found in your catalogue nor any other . . . With the addition of a few more plays (which I believe I shall easily find for you) I can add two more quarto Volumes to your collection" (FC; Boaden, I, 449f.).

3. "On Saturday, Dr. Kenrick opened his School of Shakespeare, to a numerous auditory, in the Burletta Theatre at Marybone Gardens . . . In the Doctor's Lecture, which was materially different from that he read in the Apollo, at the Devil, he seemed to give great satisfaction to his audience, particularly in rehearsing the part of Falstaff, which he recites inimitably" (*LC*, vol. XXXIV, July 16–19, 1774, p. 64).

850 To Arabella and Catherine Garrick[1]

My dear, & very dear Girls— July 3ᵈ 1774

I take the opportunity by Mʳˢ Bulloigne yʳ aunt's Mantua-Maker to send my love to You both— I must do it in haste, for She can't stay— to You Madame Catharina I make my best Acknowledgments for Your very instructive, & curious letter— I read it with yᵉ greatest pleasure— shall I tell you of a very small, but constant fault, that you commit?— It is writing many insignificant words with a Great Letter— the best Writers never make Use of Capitals, but to proper Names of Men, Towns, & such like, or at yᵉ beginning of a Sentence— you see I have written *S*entence with a great S, which should be so, *s*entence, wᵗʰ a small one— if You were to write *D*ear Uncle, at yᵉ beginning of the letter, you shᵈ write it with a great D, but in yᵉ body of yᵉ letter, *d*ear: these are triffles but I would have you Accurate in every thing— Your Aunt Doxey is come to Town with her Daughter,[2] who looks very grave, that she is going to learn some thing at Mʳˢ Dennis's & has left Lichfield, Where she is Spoil'd— We are all togeather— yʳ Father who has been ill, but is now better, is going to Bath, & sends his Love & a thousand kisses— you see I have written *L*ove with a great L, which is wrong, it should be with a small one, *l*ove. I can no More, for I am call'd from you: God bless you both, to which y^r Aunt, with kisses more than would stiffle You, says Amen.

Dear Bell & Dear Kit Most affectionatly Yours

D: Garrick

I have ye Gout in my fingers & You can't read this Scrawl. Love to dear Miss Pratt, & my best Comp^ts to MonS^r & Mad^e Descombes.

Address: A Mademoiselles, Mademoisseles Garrick chez Mad^e DesCombes, rüe verte, F. B. St Honoré. *Seal. Source:* HTC.

1. This letter should be read with the one from Mrs. Garrick to Catherine, dated May 20, 1774 (Hedgcock, p. 383f.).

2. Merrial Docksey (b. 1761), the only daughter of Merrial and Thomas Docksey (Boswell, index, and III, 536).

851 To The Reverend Sanfoord Hardcastle[1]

Adelphi

Sir   August 4th 1774

I have obey'd y^r commands, & taken my time to answer your letter—[2] indeed I sh^d have postpon'd answering it, (as you did mine & for the same reason,) lest surprize might *have dictated sentiments, complaints &c,* such as a Manager very much surpriz'd might have utter'd— I had my reasons for not shewing the play[3] to any friend of mine, & y^r letter confirm'd them— it is a bad office to give an opinion of a play, & I think Mr Hardcastle's letter to me fully proves it. The two opinions which I gave of the same play, & which you think are sincere, were my honest judgement: I had not the least Idea *of raising Matter,* (as you are pleas'd to call it) *either for your vanity, or humiliation:*[4] Nor cou'd I have imagin'd that my considering the play a 2^d time (no very common thing & which I as readily agreed to as you civilly ask'd it) could have call'd your ⟨s⟩everity upon 3 plays[5] whose authors I am sure never offended Mr Hardcastle—

I thought in reading those plays, I saw enough in them to promise a certain Success, & I was not deceiv'd for they answer'd all my expectations— I ⟨li⟩kewise spoke my opinion, my honest opinion of *Manfred* & I had a right to do so, & if all the Scholars of both

Universities were to tye me to ⟨a⟩ stake for my judgement I cou'd not alter it— ⟨I⟩ have not the least curiosity to know the Scholar[6] ⟨y⟩ou mention'd in y^r last, nor have I the least ⟨o⟩bjection to his or the whole world knowing ⟨m⟩y sentiments of the Tragedy.

I shall have no objection to a principal ⟨p⟩erformer's having Manfred & Matilda for a Benefit— nor shall I obtrude my opinion of it upon any person you will please to favour with it.[7] Should I be ask'd whether I have seen it before (as it will be given to me in the course of business) & what is my opinion, I must desire Mr Hardcastle to tell me, what I must say, & I will obey his commands.

I am Sir Your humble Servt

D Garrick

PS. had you given me permission to wait upon you, I sh^d have offer'd all my objections, (as I told you) with freedom & Sincerity I really don't understand what particular triumph you have gain'd by y^r observation upon Shakespear's Cymbeline, Macbeth &c, &c.[8]

Endorsement by Garrick: Answer to Mr Hardcastles extraordinary Letter. Aug^st 5 1774. *Source:* FC, copy.

1. Sanfoord Hardcastle (1742–1788), Rector of Adel, Yorkshire (Walter W. Ball and John A. Venn, *Admissions to Trinity College*, Cambridge, vol. III, 1911, p. 194). As early as July 12, 1771, Hardcastle had submitted a tragedy, "The Jealous Father," to Garrick (FC).
2. Of July 13 (FC).
3. "Manfred and Matilda," which, according to Hardcastle's letter, Garrick had returned with a brief note stating that "The Author of this Tragedy, it is Mr Garrick's sincere opinion, would upon a better Fable write a good one." The play was never produced or printed.
4. Hardcastle had written: "Satisfied that you, Sir, gave y^r sincere opinion of the Play in Question— Let me as sincerely tell you— that I cannot upon cool reflection raise to myself matter either for vanity, or humiliation from those Remarks."
5. Having "seen the representation of Zingis— Alonzo— Sethona and many other modern Tragedies— Mr Hardcastle therefore cannot think representation the sole test of a Good Play— It were doubtless an office invidious as well as impertinent to try any one of these Tragedies by the exceptions M^r G has taken to that of Manfred and Matilda."
6. A great Cambridge scholar, according to Hardcastle.
7. An answer to Hardcastle's query: "Will you, Sir, in case I put a play into the Hands of one of y^r capital Actors or Actresses for a Benefit play will you *with hearty consent*, as a favor conferr'd from one Gentleman to another suffer that Play to pass without telling the Person I offer it to, that it has ever been refused, or seen by you." After receiving Garrick's answer, Hardcastle wrote on Aug. 15 to declare that "As Matters stand betwixt [us] at present, I can have no thoughts of obtruding my Play for representation upon a Benefit Night" (FC).
8. "Was the play of Hamlet— Macbeth— or Cymbeline put into y^r Hands by a modern author would not the Tale of the Ghost, the dancing of Witches, the chopping off of one Man's Head, and the thrusting of another Man, head and all, into a Cloaths Chest— appear as trifling, absurd, and unnatural" (letter of July 13).

852 To John Moody

Hampton

Dear Moody.   Augst 12 1774

I have been from home & but Yesterday rec'd Y^r letter— What a foolish double-fac'd Gentleman must Mr Swan be,[1] if You have been told a truth— I shall carry this letter wth Me to Town, & inclose if I can find one, a letter of Flattery— pray get to ye truth of this if possible, for if you will permit Me, I will return his papers & just mention, That as I find, *I have not been liberally educated enough to understand all the refinement of his remarks, I must beg leave to return them unread*— What say You? it will make him Stare— & he deserves to be made to Stare, if he is such a Hypocrite— Y^r Affair with Dodd[2] is extraordinary & very disagreeable. as to y^r desire, As I have no Articles, & George is at Bath, I cannot give You an Answer. I thought you were upon a rising Sallary for a term, & that the whole was y^r own making.

I have a great regard for You & should be glad to shew it upon a proper Occasion— We Shall see more of this Matter

Y^{rs} Ever

D: Garrick

PS. pray send me a Line about Swan— I have call'd again upon Y^r Wife[3] & sent her a Frank. always in a hurry— & I have miss'd writing upon this leaf—[4]

Source: FSL.

1. Moody reported that Swan believed no one understood Shakespeare but himself, and that Garrick had "neither learning nor understanding equal to the task" (Wilkinson, II, 152).
2. Apparently a quarrel with Dodd (see *ibid.*, I, 199).
3. Anne Moody (1717?–1805).
4. The postscript is written on the reverse of the first sheet.

853 To Francis Aickin[1]

Hampton

Sir   Augt 12th 1774

It is true, You had not a written Dismission from the Prompter,[2] because it was thought more civil to convey it by your Brother;[3]

as this was well understood by him, & confirm'd by Mr King, I am
a little surpriz'd at the mention of it.— So far am I from having *any
Violent Resentment*,[4] that I most sincerely wish You success,— wherever your Interest or Inclination may lead You.

Various circumstances (which I will not repeat) happen'd in the
course of last Winter,[5] by which I could not but imagine that you
intended we should part.— I hope I may say without Vanity that
Mr Aickin has met with some Indulgence in Drury Lane; and If I
expected in return some small Regard to me, as the *Older* Soldier,
& to my Rules & Orders as a Commanding Officer, I flatter Myself
that such an Expectation is not *inconsistent with honour & Manhood*,
& may be answer'd *without making any mean Sacrifices*. I am

Sir Your most Obedient humble Servant
D. Garrick

Source: FC, copy, with corrections by Garrick.

1. Francis Aickin (d. 1805), actor, left the trade of weaving to become a strolling
player in Ireland. After performing at Smock Alley, he made his debut at Drury Lane
in May 1765. He acted there until the close of the season of 1773–74, and then went to
Covent Garden.
2. Hopkins.
3. James.
4. Aickin had written in a letter of Aug. 10, to which this is the reply: "I have endeavour'd to flatter myself that the violence of your Resentment is by this time abated,
and I may yet hope for the pleasure of serving under your Command" (FC; Boaden, I,
651).
5. In reply to Garrick's letter, Aickin wrote: "When my mind was void of every
thing but the pleasure I received from your performance, [I was] reprimanded for
wearing my hat behind scenes before a number of hair-dressers, tailors, and many other
servants of the house; for doing even what *they* were doing; if taken so unexpectedly . . .
I did give any little hasty abrupt answer, I should imagine from a person of much less
candour than Mr. Garrick the offence . . . by no means merited so serious a resentment"
(Boaden, I, 653).

854   To Francis Aickin

Sir   August 24 1774
That no time may be lost, I take the first opportunity since the
receipt of Your letter to answer it: I must beg leave to repeat, that
I cannot enter into a discussion of the disagreeab⟨le⟩ Circumstances
which happen'd last Season. I am sorry to say that my Ideas of

them are very different from those of M[r] Aickin.[1] some late engagements Which the Managers of Drury Lane Theatre have Enter'd into, would make it inconvenient both to You & them, to alter their plan for the ensuing Winter.

I am Sir Your most Obed[t] Ser[t]

D: Garrick.

Endorsement with address: To M[r] Fran[s] Aickin, Bedford Coffeehouse. *Source:* FSL, draft; Boaden, I, 655.

1. The lines "It is not my fault, that you have not Engag'd Yourself Elsewhere— the Notice of our parting was deliver'd near 3 months ago" canceled in the draft, were in reply to the following statement in Aickin's letter: "If I wished to part with Mr. Garrick, I certainly should have taken some previous steps to provide myself a situation somewhere else, which I solemnly declare I have not done, nor shall, till I am ultimately convinced an accommodation of my unfortunate misunderstandi[n]g with him is impossible" (Boaden, I, 653).

855 To Catherine Clive

Hampton

My dear Pivy.[1]   Frid M[orning, ?August 26, 1774][2]
Had not the nasty bile which so often confines me & has heretofore tormented you, kept me at home, I should have been at your feet three days ago. If your heart (somewhat combustible like my own) has play'd off all the Squibs, & Rockets which lately occasion'd a little cracking & bouncing about me, & can receive again, the more gentle & pleasing firework of Love & friendship, I will be with you at Six this Evening, to revive by the help of those Spirits in your tea Kettle lamp that flame, which was almost blown out by the flouncing of your petticoat, when my name was mention'd.

Tea is a Sov'reign balm for wounded love.

Will you permit me to try the Poet's recipe this Evening?— Can my Pivy know so little of me, to think that I prefer the Clack of Lords & Ladies to the enjoyment of humour & Genius? I reverence most sincerely your friend & Neighbour,[3] not because he is the Son of one of the first, of first Ministers, but because he is himself one of the first Ministers of Literature:— in short your Misconception about that fatal Champetre[4] (the Devil take the Word) has made me so cross about every thing that belongs to it, that I curse all Squibs, Crackers, Rockets, Air-Balloons, Mines, serpents & Catherine Wheels, & can think of nothing & Wish for nothing, but laugh, Jig, humour, fun, pun, conundrum carriwitchet[5] & Catherine Clive!—

I am Ever my Pivy's Most constant & loving &c

D G

My Wife sends her love & will attend the Ceremony this Evening.

Endorsement by Garrick: My Letter to Clive about yᵉ renewal of our friendship.
Source: FC, copy; Boaden, II, 296.

1. Garrick's name for Mrs. Clive, given to her as early as 1768 (Boaden, I, 320, II, 295).
2. Conjecturally written on the first Friday following Garrick's *champêtre*.
3. Horace Walpole, who about 1755 had presented Mrs. Clive with a small house on his property at Twickenham.
4. "Last night," states the *London Chronicle* (Aug. 18–20, 1774, p. 175), "Mr. Garrick gave a splendid entertainment, or Fête Champêtre, at his gardens at Hampton. Signior Torre conducted a most brilliant fire-work; an elegant concert of music was performed; and the company, which consisted of a great number of Nobility and Gentry, expressed the utmost satisfaction on the occasion. The temple of Shakespeare, and gardens, were illuminated with 6000 lamps, and the forge of Vulcan made a splendid appearance."
5. Carry witchet: a sort of conundrum, puzzlewit, or riddle (Francis Grose, *A Classical Dictionary of the Vulgar Tongue*, 1785).

856 To Richard Cumberland

Hampton
My dear Sir   Augˢᵗ 29 1774
Had You directed yʳ letter (as I have always desir'd You) to the Adelphi, You wᵈ have had my answer to yʳ last 3 days sooner: I have been at Lord Camden's,[1] Yʳ letter went to Hampton, & was return'd to London, as I was going to the former place, so that I did not receive it till this Evening by yᵉ Coach— Therefore Mʳ Hanbury[2] & You must excuse this Seeming neglect of his, & Your friendly invitation:[3]

I have consulted with my Nephew,[4] who is as desirous as myself of his having the honour of making one in Your most liberal Amusements: He is oblig'd, as he will tell Mʳ Hanbury, to be at Cambridge ye 8th of Octr & term begins ye 10th when he will be fasten'd by ye leg till Xmas: could he have been then of the least Service, he should have Obey'd yr Commands wth pleasure: I really think (this I would not tell him) that his figure in any parts of tragedy would rather border on the ridiculous— he speaks well, & would not displease in a Character of Weight & Spirit— but surely he is too unweildy for any but Comic Characters— but as he does not feel it, I should not feel it for him, if his University business would permit him. as for Me, You may command an Epilogue if you should want one, or any thing in my Power, but alass, how can I be spar'd from my troops with so formidable an Alliance against Me? it will be impossible with the business I am preparing, & must produce with all convenient Speed, to quit the Field: You who know my Attendance at ye Theatre, & that Nothing can or will be done without me, must, as my friend, be my advocate to Mr Hanbury & his Sister—5 indeed, my dear friend, I will confess to You, that my time is so employ'd at this instant, that I could wish even to be excus'd from ye Epilogue— but rather than you should want that, or any thing in my power to do for You— *all Causes shall give way*!6 I could wish to have the *passionate Man*7 in my hands, & also that you would send me a Cast of ye Parts, according to yr Notion of ye Matter. the sooner ye better. I have seen ye *Lady-Author*8 we talk'd about— she is most worthy of Your friendship, & regard— She is very clever & very modest, & what will still make You, more her friend, she is distress'd. I have her play in my hands, she shd be much honour'd, if You would See it, & give yr opinion freely— She deserves all Encouragement— if I knew how to Send her play, I would— We wish much for yr Sentiments— You'll be Surpriz'd I assure you— pray write to Me soon again, & Speak yr Wishes, which I Shall always be happy to fulfil. I am Dear Sir

most affecly Yrs

D Garrick

Mrs G. joins wth Me in all respect & warm regard to Mrs C.9 Mr Hanbury & Mrs Th[ursb]y—

Among other misfortunes I have sprain'd my Leg & am afraid of a long confinement— a very disagreeable business. We have Engag'd Smith—10 & Madlle Hidoux from Paris to dance wth Slingsby.11

Address: Richd Cumberland Esqr at— Hanbury's Esqr, Kilmarsh, Northamptonshire. *Postmark:* AV 30. *Source:* FC; Boaden, I, 655f.

1. By a letter, dated Aug. 20, Camden had invited the Garricks to visit him at Camden Place on Aug. 24 (Boaden, I, 655).

2. William Hanbury (d. 1807), a friend of Cradock and of Cumberland, who lived at Kelmarsh, Northamptonshire.

3. Apparently they had invited Garrick to participate in private theatricals at Kelmarsh in the fall of 1774 (see Cumberland to Garrick, Oct. 23, FC; *LC*, vol. XXXVI, Oct. 27–29, 1774, p. 410).

4. Carrington Garrick, who had been admitted to St. John's at Cambridge in 1772; he was to receive his B.A. in 1776.

5. Anne (Hanbury) Thursby (d. 1778), wife of John Harvey Thursby. On her tomb in the church at Abington, Northamptonshire, is the odd inscription: "What sort of Woman she was the *last* Day will determine" (George Baker, *History of Northamptonshire*, 1822–1830, I, 15; Cradock, IV, 272–274; for her pleasant relationship with the Garricks, see her letter to Mrs. Garrick of Aug. 1776, Little Collection).

6. *Macbeth*, III, iv, 136.

7. *The Choleric Man* (DL, Dec. 19, 1774). There are in the Forster Collection several of Cumberland's letters written to Garrick during the rehearsals and production of the play.

8. An allusion, according to Boaden (I, 656n.) who knew her, to Mrs. Hannah (Parkhouse) Cowley (1743–1809), dramatist and poet. Her *The Runaway* was to be produced at Drury Lane in 1776.

9. In Feb. 1759 Cumberland had married Elizabeth, daughter of George Ridge of Kelmiston, Hampshire (*Memoirs*, 1807, I, 205f.).

10. Who was to appear at Drury Lane on Sept. 22.

11. Margaret Catherine Hidoux (spelled "Hidou" and "Hidon" in the playbills), a dancer, made her first appearance on the English stage with Slingsby at Drury Lane, in John Burgoyne's *The Maid of the Oaks*, on Nov. 5. Their performance was praised as "uncommonly fine" (*LC*, vol. XXXVI, Nov. 5–8, 1774, p. 445; see Boaden, II, 46; Adolphe Jullien, *L'Opéra secret au XVIIIᵉ siècle*, Paris, 1880, p. 174).

857   To Peter Garrick

Adelphi

Dear Peter   Augˢᵗ 31ˢᵗ [1774][1]

My Partner Mʳ Lacy Sets out for Birmingham next Saturday to perform the Part of Alexander—[2] I wish You would go there & see him— I think you will be pleas'd— He will be much pleas'd to see You— he Acts on *Wednesday* in yᵉ next Week wᶜʰ is the 7ᵗʰ: go if You can, & let me know your opinion, when you have seen him— pray go to him after yᵉ Play if you are there— Love to all.

I am Dʳ Broʳ yʳˢ most Affectʸ

D Garrick.

Address: To Peter Garrick Esqʳ, Lichfield.   *Postmarked.*   *Source:* FC.

1. The year is determined by the reference to Lacy's acting at Birmingham.

2. In Nathaniel Lee's *Alexander the Great; or, The Rival Queens*. Birmingham, Sept. 10: "Last night Mr. Lacy and Mrs. Yates played in Alexander the Great, at our new Theatre, to a very great audience. Mr. Lacy, like all young performers the first night, seemed a good deal confused; but after he had recovered himself a little, was received with general applause, and bids fair to make a good player. Mr. Garrick was present" (*LC*, vol. XXXVI, Sept. 13–15, 1774, p. 264).

858   To The Earl of Upper Ossory

Hampton
Sepr 3^d 1774

Mr Garrick from his Bed, (confin'd there by the Gout) presents his Respects to Lord Ossory, & thanks him for as fine a haunch of Venison, as Ever Quin roll'd an Amorous Eye at—

the Confinement occasion'd by the breaking of a blood Vessel brought on this Severe fit of ye Gout, he has not been able to walk since he had ye honour of Seeing his Lordship

Mrs Garrick joins with Mr Garrick in respects to Lady Ossory[1] & Your Lordship.

Address: To The Earl of Ossory at Ampthill, Bedfordshire.   *Postmarked.* *Source:* BM.

1. Anne (Liddell) Fitzpatrick (1738–1804), daughter of the first Baron Ravensworth, had married Lord Ossory in 1769 after her divorce from the Duke of Grafton.

859   To Sir Joshua Reynolds

Hampton
Sepr 5^h 1774

Dear Sir

I was too much in pain to write to you Yesterday— *Whoever will undoubtedly understand my answer to be an absolute refusal to take the play at any rate* will do me great injustice:[1] So far from refusing plays the Complaint is that I take too many: or supposing me capable of such a practice with Authors, at least don't think me so lost to my interest, to refuse a play, a Line of which I never saw, & which comes so recommended to me.

What I wrote to Sir Joshua Reynolds was upon my honour the real situation of my affairs at present— I have no less than Seven Plays, Each of 5 Acts, & two smaller pieces for representation; these with our reviv'd Plays will be as much as any Manager can thrust with all his might into two Seasons— When a disappointed author hears that I am so furnish'd, it is natural for him to imagine & to say that I don't care to receive his performance but that my Acquaintance Sir Joshua Reynolds, shou'd think for the Author, that I wou'd say the thing that is not, to clear myself from a performance recommended by him Dr Johnson & Mr Burke is not a little unpleasing to me—² To clear myself from so disagreeable suspicion, I will trust your honour with a sight of the Plays & in confidence you shall know the Names of the Authors

I am &c

Endorsement by Garrick: To Sir Jo^s Reynolds. *Source:* Waterston Collection, draft; Boaden, I, 658.

1. On Aug. 2 Reynolds had written Garrick: "The connexion which I have with the author [a nephew, Joseph Palmer (1749–1829)] of the tragedy ["Zaphira"] which accompanies this, makes it impossible for me to refuse him the favour of presenting it to you" (*Letters*, ed. Frederick W. Hilles, Cambridge, 1929, p. 40f.). Garrick replied, in a letter now lost, to the effect that he had so many new plays on his hands he could not produce for two years the tragedy in question even if he did approve of it. (His comments on the play are recorded in a note now in the Forster Collection; Boaden, I, 646.) On Sept. 4 Reynolds, taking Garrick's attitude as a refusal, asked for the return of the play (*Letters*, p. 41f.).
2. Subsequently Reynolds accepted Garrick's explanation (*ibid.*, p. 42f.).

860   To Richard Cumberland

From my bed
Hampton

My dear S^r   Monday [September] 5 [1774]¹

I am still in pain, but getting better; I have sent You the Lady's play, whose Conversation & manner would charm You: I am sure it would: She has desir'd you may see it; & begs that you will freely criticize it— We will all do our best for her— if you please to return it again to me with Your remarks, I will deliver 'Em to her Seal'd or unseal'd, as you please.

but my good friend, not a word of the *Comedy*?[2] I mean, of *when* I am to have it, the Season draws near, & we are making all kind of preparations— if you have any new thought about it pray communicate ⟨it⟩ for I am unhappy if I don't secure the proper Stores for yᵉ Campaign— My Elder Nephew[3] wrote to Mʳ Hanbury yᵉ same Evening I wrote to You— he is now from Hampton & returns tomorrow— by my honour he wrote his letter & sent it without my seeing a line of it— What he means by his Obligation to be at Cambridge, I cannot say, but I shall talk with him tomorrow. it grieves me that Mʳ Hanbury shᵈ think himself unprosperous with yᵉ house of Garrick— That House honours him Much, but indeed with regard to *Me*, the very tug of war with us, will be at yᵉ time of Yʳ Acting in Northamptonshire, & as this is a Season of some Consequence, I am sure my friends would not wish Me to leave my troops to be hack'd & hewn by yᵉ Enemy— in the Name of Every thing that is beautiful & Sublime where is my Rival the renowned Æolus? is not he to do such things?— pray in yʳ next let me know, if you intend the *Tragedy* you read to me, for Us, the Season after Next?[4] indeed plays come as thick as hail, & I must give an answer— let me once more beg an ansʳ about yʳ Plays, for a phrase in yʳ last puzzles me a little— *whenever it comes to be cast*: I desir'd you wᵈ send me what Cast you had thought of— don't think me too importunate. I am a great Lover of punctuality in business.

Dear Sir Most truly Yʳˢ
D: Garrick

pray present Our best Wishes to all about You. I rec'd yʳ letter but to day Monday, so I could not sent yᵉ parcel by yᵉ Northampton fly. I hope you have rec'd yᵉ Captⁿ'ˢ part, which I sent yᵉ Moment I found it— He is now better, but has been terribly ill with Us— he will much sooner be cured of his Asthma[5] than his Carelessness. I can scarce finish this scrawl.

Endorsement by Garrick: To Mʳ Cumberland. *Source:* Morgan Library, copy in FC.

1. The year is determined by the fact that this letter is obviously the sequel to Letter 856; the month is determined by the reference to the imminence of the start of the theatrical season. In 1774 Sept. 5 fell on a Monday.
2. *The Choleric Man.*
3. Carrington Garrick.
4. Perhaps *The Battle of Hastings* (DL, Jan. 24, 1778).
5. Presumably Garrick's nephew David had been assigned a part, perhaps that of

a captain, in one of the plays to be performed at Kelmarsh on Oct. 20 and 21 (see *LC*, vol. XXXVI, Oct. 27–29, 1774, p. 410). According to Cradock, David was "violently afflicted with asthma" (IV, 254). At Hanbury's the previous autumn he had acted in *Venice Preserv'd*, and when Cradock made him up for the part of Pruili, "in his uncle's grey locks," the resemblance to the great actor was "striking to every one" (*ibid.*).

861   To Thomas Evans[1]

Dear S[r]   Tuesday Sep[r] 6 [1774][2]
I beg that You will bring y[r] Company here,[3] whenever You please—my Nephew[4] (as I am not able) will attend You & shew you Every thing— I am sorry upon this Acc[t] that this nasty Gout still confines me still to my Couch—[5] dreadfull work, a Lame General & so strong an Alliance in y[e] field!

You have Shewn great partiality to Me in y[r] Letter to M[r] Woodfall:[6] Whatever he might have been pleas'd to publish against me I never thought they were so unmanly to go farther.

I am rather Sorry you wrote to him, M[r] W. about me: he may think that I apply'd to you upon that Matter— what I may have unwittingly done to that Gentleman I know not, but I must certainly have done him or his family some great injury— I seldom now read y[e] Paper (which by y[e] bye I think the most diverting) because I would not trust my sensibility with some of the violent paragraphs w[ch] are too often to be found there— I say this in Confidence & I am Dear Sir

Your most Obed[t] & Oblig'd Ser[t]
D: Garrick

Tho I can't see Y[r] Company, I shall desire You to come to my bed's side pray tell me when you will come

Endorsement with address: To M[r] Evans, Bookseller, Strand.   *Source:* FC, draft; Boaden, II, 269.

1. Thomas Evans (1742–1784), bookseller, who had started his shop in the Strand in 1774.
2. The year is determined by the reference to Evans's letter to Woodfall.
3. In a letter of Sept. 6 Evans had asked permission to bring his wife to see Hampton (Boaden, II, 268).
4. Carrington.

5. The *London Chronicle* for Sept. 17, 1774, announced that Garrick was still "at Hampton, much indisposed with the gout" (XXXVI, 271).

6. Evans had enclosed a copy of his letter to William Woodfall (FC; Boaden, II, 270); from that and from Evans's reply to Garrick on Sept. 8 it appears that Francis Aickin, who had been discharged by Garrick in August, had written some verses satirizing the *fête champêtre* held at Hampton on Aug. 19. These verses appeared anonymously in Woodfall's *Morning Chronicle* for Aug. 27. "If you suffer," Evans had written the editor, "The Morning Chronicle to be the vehicle for every insolent Actor to abuse a Manager . . . let us proclaim All Servants &c. who have behav'd ill & are discarded by their masters are welcome to abuse *gratis* in the Paper." According to Evans's letter of Sept. 8, Woodfall acknowledged "the justness" of the complaint and assured him that Aickin "shall no more *poison* the Paper" (FC; Boaden, II, 269).

862   To John Moody

Adelphi
[September?][1] 8th 1774

Inclosed you have a letter for Mr. Swan . . . Dodd has been much worse for his voyage [as I suppose he is not yᵉ better for his intrigue][2] he is money bound in Dublin and I shall release him . . . Mrs. Bakley is returned safe to her husband . . .[3] We are preparing Jubilee Fetes Champetres etc., etc. for opening our campaign

I am sure it will give you pleasure to hear that I am quite recovered.

Source: Chas. J. Sawyer, Ltd., Catalogue No. 8, 1955, extract.

1. The references here continued from those in Letter 852 make it probable that this letter was written in September before the opening of the theatrical season.

2. Matter in brackets is supplied from Sotheby's catalogue of July 24, 1935, which prints a shorter extract of the text.

3. Mrs. Bulkley, a niece of Mrs. Rich, had as Miss Wilford, before her marriage to a member of the Covent Garden band, made her debut as a dancer at Covent Garden in 1765. Her marriage early proving uncongenial, she embarked on what came to be a long affair with Dodd. During the summer season of 1774 she and Dodd went to Dublin to act, but "The connection between them was not of the most moral kind, and some recent transactions had excited strong prejudices against them" (Robert Hitchcock, *An Historical View of the Irish Stage*, Dublin, 1794, II, 259f.).

863 To Joseph Vernon

Hampton

Sir   Sunday, Sept^br 11th 1774
I did not expect to receive such a message & letter from Mr Vernon,
& a week only before the opening of the house. What would the
World have said, had we discharg'd Mr Vernon at this time without
any other notice, than that, which *you* have given *me*? Tho' I am
well accustom'd to strange things in a Theatre, yet I must own
that your behaviour in particular has surpriz'd me; it is as ungenteel, as it is unjustifiable. I have been all the Summer (three
weeks excepted) between Hampton & London, nay I met you at
Lord Stanlys[1] in the month of May,[2] & you never gave me the least
hint of your intentions till yesterday: According to the Rule &
Custom of the theatres you should have given me notice at the end
of the last Season that you expected an increase of Sallary for the
next, or by the same Rule & Custom, I had a right to expect your
attendance upon the same terms:[3] had you demanded double your
Sallary at the proper time, I should have no Complaint; I should
only not have agreed to your proposal & we had parted; but to
have no letter nor message from you till *yesterday* is very particular
indeed: I have depended upon you for the next Season, have plan'd
my business accordingly; your Sallary shall not be diminish'd &
y^r benefit shall come in course & at a very good time.
                              I am S^r y^r most humble Servant
                                                    D Garrick

Endorsement by Garrick: Answer to Vernon's Letter of the 9th of Sep^t 1774
answer'd ye 11th.   *Source:* American Autograph Shop; Boaden, II, 3f.

1. Edward Smith Stanley (1752–1834), later (1776) twelfth Earl of Derby and
establisher of the two great races at Epsom: the Derby and the Oaks. On June 9, 1774,
in honor of Lady Elizabeth Hamilton, whom he married on June 23, he gave an elaborate
fête champêtre at The Oaks, Epsom, Surrey, an estate belonging to his aunt, the wife of
John Burgoyne. For the *fête champêtre* Burgoyne wrote a two-act entertainment, or masque,
in which Vernon was one of the principal performers (*LC*, vol. XXXV, June 9–11,
p. 560, June 14–16, p. 569). Garrick later introduced the *fête champêtre* into Burgoyne's
Maid of the Oaks.
2. Presumably during the preparations for Burgoyne's masque.
3. In Vernon's letter, to which this is the reply, he had asked for an addition of two
pounds a week in salary and "my benefit in rank of salary" (Boaden, II, 3).

864 To The Reverend William Hawkins

Sir   Sepr the 20th 1774

Tho your threatening letter[1] found me in a fit of the Gout, which is a very peevish disorder, yet, I assure You it added Nothing to my ill humour, nay I could have laugh'd, tho in pain, had not the more humane Sensation of Pity, prevented it: Notwithstanding your former flattering letters to me, which I have luckily preserv'd, You now Accuse Me of Pride, rancour, Evil designs, & the Lord knows what, because I have refus'd your Plays,[2] which I most sincerely think unfit for representation, & which (some of 'Em, if not all) have had ye same fortune with other Managers. You are pleas'd to say, *that of all Animals, a Manager is ye Sorest*,[3] pray Mr Hawkins had you no feelings at the time you wrote this, which contradicted ye Assertion? can you really believe that this un-provok'd, intemperate behaviour can make me submit to y^r Inquisitorial Menaces? Perform my Plays, or I'll appeal to the Publick!— If You will publish Your Plays, with Y^r appeal, I will forgive You the rest—

Your insinuation that I formerly mortify'd You because you once *offended Me* in *the business of Henry & Rosamond* is unworthy of an Answer!— It is very well known that I bear no malice; and the offence which *you* so well remember, is as much forgotten by me, as Henry & Rosamond, the cause of it.

You Value Yourself much *upon laying a design to sound Me*, that is, to catch me tripping, in order to expose me, a very liberal design truly for a Scholar & a Divine, and I wish You joy of your success; but to convince you, if possible, how much Your intemperate Zeal contradicts Itself, You confess that Alfred, your tragedy-trap, was not well prepard, that the play was (as you are pleas'd to express it) *improperly digested, & you readily admit the Justness of my exceptions*: nay you go farther, & say *you give up Alfred & Acquiesce in my Judgment*: Can any thing I write, vindicate my conduct more than y^r own words? Have I seen Alfred *since* Your above confession? have I *refus'd* to see it?— I know my Duty too well— I am oblig'd by my Situation to read all You are pleas'd to send me, but I have ye same right to reject a Play, which I think a bad one, as You have to compose it.

May I without offence differ in opinion with a Gentleman who once was a Credit to the professorship of Poetry in Oxford?—[4] *It will be very hard Methinks,* (these are your words) *if that should not be a proper foundation of a Fable which happens to be Matter of Fact*— indeed Sir— the best dramatic Criticks I have read tell me that Matters of Fact are *not* always proper Foundations for dramatic fables— You say I wrote a Cavalier Note, if it were so, your very Cavalier letter produc'd it; I never begin first— Your last letter begot this, but I hope it is very unlike It's Father.

You conclude wth saying, *You don't desire to come to an open rupture with me, & that You wish not to Exasperate, but to convince; and you again tender me Y^r Friendship, & Your play*— so far, You seem to be returning to temper & Reason— but how was I deceiv'd!— for in order to promote the good Work, & bring about a reconciliation, You add— *that You have too much knowledge of human Nature in general, & the particular pride of my Situation to look for any good from this amicable overture*: ought You not as a Gentleman, and a Clergyman, & in justice, reason, & Good Manners, to have waited for my answer, before you had been guilty of such outrageous behavior? or is it the Revd Mr Hawkins's method of *Convincing,* & not *exasperating,* to call Names, while he is making a tender of his Friendship?

I am S^r Y^r humble Servt

D: Garrick

Give me leave to make another Observation upon Y^r peculiar behaviour to me & to y^r friends— tho You seem to think Me inexcusable for daring to differ wth them, yet when they don't agree wth you, it is to stand for Nothing— for Example— Mr Warton tells you, that your present Alfred, *is deficient in point of Bustle According to the Turn & taste of ye times*; and you tell me *so far as the Objection goes,* Mr W. *seems to think the Success of representation may be affected*— but this opinion (supposing it to have ground) cannot you presume affect a right of Representation— indeed!— I do not know, what most to admire, y^r Logick, or politeness to y^r friend.

Endorsement with address: To the Revd Mr Hawkins at Whitchurch near Bridport, Dorset. *Source:* FC, the better of two drafts; Boaden, II, 8f.

1. Hawkins' long letter of Sept. 14, written in anger at Garrick's final rejection of "Alfred" (FC; Boaden, II, 6–8).

2. Besides "Alfred," Garrick had rejected *Henry and Rosamond* (1749), *The Siege of Aleppo* (1758), "Troilus and Cressida," and "The Queen of Lombardy; or, the Ambitious Lover" (*ibid.,* and I, 656f.).

3. Hawkins had insinuated that Garrick had refused his plays because he had given "offence in the business of 'Henry and Rosamond'; and of all animals . . . a manager is allowed to be the *sorest.*" In the advertisement to *Henry and Rosamond* Hawkins had

stated: "This Tragedy having been offered to the Managers of *Drury-Lane* Theatre, who declined accepting it, for Reasons which appeared to the Author to be rather evasive, than satisfactory, he thinks proper to submit it to the Judgment of the Public."

4. From 1751 to 1756 Hawkins had been Professor of Poetry at Oxford.

865   To Frances Abington

Adelphi
Dear Madam   Sept 26 1774

As no Business can be done without being Explicit, I must desire to know, if you chuse to perform *M*^rs *Sullen*. The part is reserv'd for You, & the play must be Acted soon— whoever does it with *M*^r *Smith*, must do it with me— supposing that I am ever able to be the Rake again⟨.⟩[1] we talk'd a great deal last Night, & I am Sorry to Say it, without my having the least Idea what to do in Consequence of it. If the *Tender Husband*[2] can be done with Credit I shall immediately set to work, & with *the Hypocrite*—[3] I cannot Create better Actors than we have, & we must both do our best with them— Could I put you upon the highest Comic Pinacle, I certainly would do it;— but indeed (my dear Madam) we shall not mount Much, if your cold Counter Acting discourse is to pull us back at every Step— don't imagine that the Gout makes me peevish; I am talking to you in the greatest good humour, but if we don't do our best, with the best we have, it is all Fruitless murmuring & inactive repining— Something too much of this— I shall write to the Author of the Piece[4] to morrow Night, which I read to You— I have yet Obey'd but half his Commands, as he wrote the Character of *Lady Bab* for your Ladyship,[5] I must beg of you to Speak your Thoughts upon that— which after I had read it to you I promis'd to let him know your Sentiments— I could wish if You Say any thing to me of our Stage Business You would send it seperately from your opinion of The Maid of the Oaks & Lady Bab— with Your leave I would wish to inclose what you Say of the last to the Author

Yours most truly
D Garrick

Endorsement by Garrick: Letter to Mrs Abington in which her Manner of doing & saying is not describ'd omiss. *Source:* FC, copy; Boaden, II, 24.

1. Two days after Garrick's letter Mrs. Abington agreed to appear in *The Beaux' Stratagem* (Boaden, II, 24). The play was produced on Nov. 3, with Garrick playing Archer.

2. Sir Richard Steele's comedy was never played after the 1771–72 season during Garrick's management.

3. Bickerstaffe's play was given on Oct. 6.

4. John Burgoyne (1722–1792), soldier and dramatist, was at this time a Member of Parliament and a major-general. Encouraged by the public curiosity in the *fête champêtre* given by Lord Stanley, Burgoyne submitted his *Maid of the Oaks* to Garrick (Boaden, II, 10). "Mr. Garrick, after perusing the outlines of the two original acts, thought he discovered in the writer some talents for the higher species of comedy, and encouraged him to extend his plan" to five acts (*The Maid of the Oaks*, 1774, Preface). Shortly after the production of his play on Nov. 5 Burgoyne left for his disastrous military service in North America.

5. Hopkins wrote: "I cannot say too much of Mrs. Abington's Performance in this Piece" (Diary, *DLC*, p. 181).

866   To Henry William Bunbury[1]

Adelphi
Octr 5th 1774

To Henry Bunbury Esqr
upon receiving some game by the Bury Coach

Old Snarlers at the present times,
Whether they write in prose, or Rhimes,
Swear we have lost by innovation,
The social Spirit of the Nation;
That Christmas, ivy-crown'd of yore,
Is *merry* Christmas now no more,
And by the Muses, and Apollo,
Plumb-porridge gone, mince Pies will follow:
    Few Presents now to Friends are sent,
    Few Hours in Merry-making spent;
    Old fashion'd Folks there are indeed,
    Whose Hogs, & Pigs, at Christmas bleed,
    Whose honest hearts no Modes refine,
    They send their Puddings, & their Chine:
    No *Norfolk Turkies* load the Waggon,
    Which once the Horses scarce could drag on,
    And to increase the Weight, with these
    Came their *Attendant— Sausages*!

To Henry William Bunbury

Can you, dear Sir, a Man of Taste,
Revive old Whimsies gone, & past?
And (fie for Shame) without reproach,
Stuff, as You do, the Bury Coach?
With strange, old kindness, send me presents
Of Partridges and dainty Pheasants?
Nor is this all— not long ago,
(The World your vulgar deeds shall know)
You sent a Picture of your own,
(Laugh'd at indeed, as soon as shown)
Which by the Gout, as bound I lay,
Was brought before me Ev'ry day,
Of Groans the Tyrant to beguile,
And on the Rack to make me smile:
In short— of this same gen'rous turn
To clear your heart, your head must learn;
And if all Men of Taste, & fashion,
Explode this present-making passion,
What *Bunb'ry* will be said of You,
Who feast my *Eyes* and *Palate* too?

D: Garrick.

Address: Henry Bunbury Esqr, Barton near St Edmonds-Bury, Suffolk. *Postmark:* OC 5. *Source:* Morgan Library, copy in FSL with corrections by Garrick; *Correspondence of Sir Thomas Hanmer,* ed. Sir Henry E. Bunbury, 1838, p. 375f.

1. Henry William Bunbury (1750–1811), amateur artist and caricaturist, was a son of Sir William Bunbury. On July 5, 1776, Garrick wrote a poem in praise of Bunbury's talents which contains this description of him:

> Yet he's so whimsical, perverse, and idle,
> Tho' Phoebus self should bid him stay,
> He'll quit the magic pencil for the bridle
> And gallop fame and life away

(*Correspondence of Sir Thomas Hanmer,* ed. Sir Henry E. Bunbury, 1838, p. 377).

867   To Thomas Evans

Adelphi
D^r S^r   Oct 21 [17]74
I am much oblig'd to Mr Woodfall for his kindness, & let me add
Justice, to Me— I cannot conceive what ye Patriot Scribbers mean,
I voted for ye Lords P[ercy] & C[linton]^1 ('tis true), but I am no
party-man, & confine all my Services for my friends— this I Suppose
comes from my old friend the Doctor— as for that strange heap of
insincerity & contradiction Dr Franklin, I can say Nothing, but
that he look'd over ye Play for Mrs Yates's benefit At Cov^t Garden,
& it was play'd twice there— Mrs Yates entreated Me, that she
might appear first in it, much against my judgment,^2 this I told to
Dr Franklin, & he talk'd of preparing an Edition of ye Play— how
then Could he tell such a deliberate Falsehood to Mr Woodfall?
nay More— I have a play of his to Act,^3 I reliev'd his Wants
within this Fortnight wth a good round Sum, & procur'd him the
reversion of a very good living:^4 what now will You think of the
truth, justice & *gratitude* of ye Rev^d D^r?— I have long'd seen his
insincerity & double dealing— I avoid him as a Friend, but I do
him all justice as a Manager. I am much Oblig'd to You, dear Sir,
for Y^r Attachment to me & am

Most truly Y^rs
D. Garrick.

Tho I would not conceal any thing from Mr Woodfall as Dr Franklin
spoke to him, yet I could wish it went no farther, tho I am very
little solicitous about keeping Measures with such a Maskwell.^5
my finger is sore & I scarce can write as you may see.

Address: Mr Evans, Bookseller, Strand.   *Source:* HTC.

1. Hugh Percy (1742–1817), later (1786) second Duke of Northumberland, and
Thomas Pelham Clinton (1752–1795), later third (1794) Duke of Newcastle, had recently
been elected to represent Westminster in the House of Commons, having soundly
defeated two of Wilkes's "patriots," Lords Mahon and Mountmorres.
2. The play was *Orestes*, revived under the title of *Electra* for Mrs. Yates's reappear-
ance, after eight years at Covent Garden, at Drury Lane on Oct. 15, 17, and 22.
3. *Matilda.*
4. Unidentified.
5. See *The Double Dealer.*

868   To George Steevens

Adelphi

My dear S^r   Novr 7th [1774][1]
how do You do? in ye first place, after so long a cessation of our
Correspondence: I have receiv'd a letter from Mr Swan, this is a
part of it—

Accept my best thanks for y^r civility in sending my Mss: to M^r
Steevens: not knowing where to direct a letter to that Gentleman,
I must request that you will tender the same from Me to him, for
his favourable opinion of it: in which however I am somewhat
disappointed, as I own I did well hope, that he would have pointed
out such parts as appear'd to him to be exceptionable, & indeed I
could still wish that *You* (*having nothing to do*) or *he* would do this,
but dare not ask it: being desirous to satisfy Mr Steevens as far as I
am able, I beg that he may be told, that I do not at present mean
to publish:[2] the reason is I am diffident of my own judgment, &
cannot determine which of ye Notes to select for that purpose, if
therefore he is of opinion that they are, or may be made Worthy
of the publick Eye, & will himself take the trouble to revise & fit
them, they are much at his Service, only returning me, my own
books when he has done with them— & if he approves the Model,
& will pursue it thro' the rest of Shakespear's plays, I will most
gladly give him any assistance in my pow'r, but I have not yet
attempted any other of them Myself, nor shall I ever again undertake such a Work: so for Mr Swan: now, my dear Sir, a word or
two upon the above proposal will oblige both him & Your most
Sincere

& obligd
D. Garrick.

Address: To George Steevens Esqr at Hampsted.   *Postmarked.*   *Source:* FSL.

1. Steevens replied to this letter on Nov. 9, 1774 (Boaden, II, 16f.).
2. His notes upon *Othello* (Letter 814, n. 2).

869   To Frances Abington

Adelphi
Novr 9th [1774]^1

Mr Garrick's Comp^ts to Mrs Abington & has sent her on ye other side, a little alteration, (if she approves it, not Else) of the Epilogue,^2 where there seems to be a patch: it should, he believes, run thus—.

——such a persecution!
'Tis the great blemish of the Constitution!
No human Law should Nature's rights abridge,
Freedom of Speech, our *dearest* priviledge!
⟨our's is⟩ the Wiser Sex, tho' Deem'd the weaker,
I'll put the *Question*, if You'll chuse me *Speaker*:
Suppose me now bewig'd &c—

M^rs A: is at full liberty to adopt this alteration or not— had not our house overflow'd last Night in a quarter of an hour from the opening, Covent Garden had suffer'd much, as it was, there was great room in Pit & Gallery at ye End of ye 3^d Act: much joy I sincerely wish You at Y^r Success in Lady Bab, may it continue till we both are tir'd, you with playing ye part, & I with seeing it—

Endorsement with address in copy: Mrs Abington, 62 Pall Mall. *Source:* BM, draft, copy in FC; John T. Smith, *A Book for a Rainy Day*, 1905, p. 216.

1. The year is determined by the reference to Garrick's epilogue.
2. To *The Maid of the Oaks*; evidently Mrs. Abington adopted this alteration, for these lines appear in the published text of 1774.

870   To George Steevens

Adelphi
Novr 14 [1774]^1

don't imagine, my dear Sir, that I will ever lead you into a Scrape with Swan^2 or any of the other critical Geese, who cackle about Your Shakespear— if I said something in my letter to him which hinted a Sort of approbation from You, (if I don't forget) in a former letter to Me, You paid him some kind of Compliment, & calld him a *Swan among Crows*,[3] or some such thing, tho better express'd—

be that as it may— you shall not have a jot of trouble more wth him or his Notes: can You have any Objection to answer this letter, waving the *honour he has done You*,[4] & saying, in words which I may inclose to him, what you said in Your last to me?— however should this be disagreeable to You, I will plague You no more, but Send these illegitimate Brats to their respective Fathers, without laying them at Your door.

Most truly & affec^ly Y^rs
D. Garrick.

don't be angry at this Scrawl— I have the Gout in my right thumb & can scarce hold my pen.

Address: To George Steevens Esqr, Hampstead.   *Postmarked.*   *Source:* FSL.

1. This is the reply to Steevens' letter of Nov. 9, 1774 (FC; Boaden, II, 16f.).
2. "The history of the affair is briefly this," Steevens had written, "Mr G. tho' he wish'd to know somewhat about this Mr Swan, was too lazy, or too much better employed, to read his dissertations . . . He therefore gave them to Mr S. whose Leisure he might command, and whose opinion of them he thought he might adopt if favourable, or qualify, if unfavourable. Mr S., being somewhat aware of this, forbore to offer any judgment at all. Thus situated, Mr G. was reduced to the necessity of supplying such an answer as he supposed Mr S. ought to have delivered . . . I leave you now to clear yourself and me" (FC; Boaden, II, 17).
3. In reply to Garrick's letter, Steevens wrote: "Shakspeare (to whose words your memory is always faithful) has said that Juliet would appear *like a swan among crows* [I, ii]; and, if I remember right, when you mentioned Swan's communication, long before it arrived, I express'd my fears lest your *Swan should prove a Goose*" (FC; Boaden, I, 595).
4. Steevens had declined Swan's offer to allow him the use of his notes on *Othello* (*ibid.*, II, 16).

871   To Henry Sampson Woodfall

Adelphi
[November] 22 [1774][1]

Dr Woodfall.

Upon my return from Hampton I heard of y^r Accident—[2] can I be of the least Service to You, or Y^r Brother Culprit? tho full of business, if You have ye least desire to see Me, I will go to You directly—

I never see You while You are hopping between London & Islington,[3] but now they have Shorten'd your tether, & you are got into a Cage, one may take a peep at You.

Y^{rs} Ever
D Garrick

Becket will bring any message to me—

Address: To Mr H. S. Woodfall. *Seal. Source:* BM.

1. The month and year are established by the references to the imprisonment of the two Woodfalls.

2. On July 11, 1774, Woodfall was tried before Lord Mansfield and convicted of printing in the *Public Advertiser* for Feb. 16 a letter signed "A South Briton," containing "scandalous, traiterous, and seditious libel" on the Glorious Revolution of 1688. At the same time William Woodfall, "Y^r Brother Culprit," who had published the letter in the *Morning Chronicle* of the same date, was convicted for the same offense (*LC*, vol. XXVI, July 9–12, 1774, p. 39). On Nov. 21 both were committed to the King's Bench Prison, and on Nov. 26 they were sentenced to serve three months there and fined two-hundred marks (*ibid.*, Nov. 19–22, p. 496, Nov. 24–26, p. 512).

3. Woodfall lived at Canonbury in the parish of Saint Mary, Islington (Samuel Lewis, *The History of Saint Mary, Islington*, 1842, p. 96).

872   To Jean Baptiste Antoine Suard

My dear friend   Decr 2— 1774

Let me first Wish You & myself joy that the French Academy has honour'd themselves by the choice of You— that You were not chosen before, was to their discredit not Yours—[1] Votre discours[2] me plait infinem^t, & if You will keep Your own Secret I defy the keenest Critick of 'Em all, (not excepting Your *french Freron*,[3] for we have an English one) to *pick a hole* in the Composition— It is so closely *Weav'd* & *wrought*, & the *piece* (if you'll allow me to pun) altogeather is so well *work'd up*, that You may be assur'd that no Moths, bugs or any litterary Vermin can eat into it, or befoul it—

pray let all my dear Friends know, that I shall never forget their kindness or their affection to Me, they— (I hope no offence to make use of an Expression of that Barbarian Shakespeare to a french Academician)— They shall live

Within the book, & volume of my brain
Unmix'd with baser Matter—[4]

now I talk of my friends and Shakespear, (& I talk of Nothing so often) pray tell my dear Chattelleux that I am very unhappy upon his Account— he must think me a strange, cold, phlegmatic Englishman to forget his Commands— he sent me some Questions to answer about Shakespear for a Lady of his Acquaintance—[5] tho I was very ill when I rec'd his Commands, yet knowing how so Gallant & amiable a Knight Errant, would be impatient to satisfy the wishes of an imploring Lady, I sent them by a Gentleman who promis'd to deliver them safe into my Friends hands— behold he has been at Brussels & rambling about Flanders & return'd with yᵉ book, without seeing Paris— he has written to Me from yᵉ Country, & will return to London next Week, with my Notes upon the difficult passages— what shall I say for this Accident?— I feel too much Sensibility upon yᵉ occasion, not to desire You to Step between his Anger, & my distress— pray let me have a Line from him, or You to know, if I may give it to MonSʳ Garnier, or what I must do in this dilemma?— pray my Love to him, & all whom You know, I love— no offence I hope, to desire that Madame Suard, may be included in that Number— my Wife without any excuse at all, sends her Love & best Wishes to You & Yours.

Ever & most Sincerely Yours to the last Moment of my Life
                                                    D: Garrick.

I am this Moment going to yᵉ Theatre to perform Hamlet, with my Alterations— Could I write French half so well as You do when You are Sick, I would send a most grateful Academical discourse of thanks & Acknowledgments to Madame Helvetius for the honour & pleasure She has done Me, by the print of Mʳ Helvetius—[6] pray do You, or my friend Morellet speak for Me in this business

Source: FSL, contemporary transcripts in French and English in Stadt- und Universitäts-Bibliothek, Frankfurt-am-Main; Charles Nisard, *Mémoires et correspondances historiques et littéraires, 1726 à 1816,* ed. Jean-B.-A. Suard, Paris, 1858, p. 162, in French.

1. Suard's election to the Academy in May 1772 had been annulled because of his alleged contributions to the *Encyclopédie.* Cleared of the charge, he was reëlected and admitted in Aug. 1774.

2. Suard's *Discours de reception à l'Académie française* (Paris, 1774).

3. Elie Catherine Fréron (1719–1776), critic and controversialist, largely remembered today for his attacks on Voltaire and the Encyclopedists.

4. *Hamlet,* I, v, 103f.

5. Geneviève Savalette (1732–1795), marquise de Gléon, amateur actress and playwright, who was in love with Chastellux. On May 18 Suard had written that she had

filled a notebook with passages in Shakespeare's plays "inexpliqués, mais non pas inexplicables," and desired Garrick's interpretation of them (Boaden, II, 607).

6. Perhaps the print engraved by Macret after a painting by Louis Michel Van Loo.

873   To George Garrick

Drury Lane Theatre

My dear George.   Monday Decr 12 [1774][1]

I was much rejoic'd at your letter, & I hope your friend Dr Faulkener[2] will land You safe again amongst Us— I shall always hold him in great Esteem for his Care & attention, & am ready to give him more solid proofs of my Gratitude:

I have this moment finish'd ye long part of Hamlet, & my hand trembles while I am writing wth ye worst Pen in ye world— Johnston is in a damn'd humour, & I dare not ask for a better— We go on well, & shall play the Cholerick Man[3] for the first time on Monday Next— I was resolv'd to have it perfect & to do Every thing in my Power for it— I am surpriz'd that he did not write to me by this post, however I trust I shall have one tomorrow, & then I shall be Easy— Y^r Sons are Well & Mr Carrington says when he is better he will come to see Me— What can he have to communicate?

The 2^d Hospital has never sent for a Bill nor do I know where to go after them— so we shall have only one this Season—[4]

Foote is arriv'd & in great Spirits—[5] he ask'd much after You— they are now playing Dibdin's Nonsense[6] & as it met with some disapprobation ye first night We wish it well over—

There is a good ballad or two, ye rest Washy & Slop Dawdry— I really cannot write any more— they make a great Noise in ye house

Yours Ever & truly
D Garrick.

I believe it will be damn'd—

The Cobler has met wth much Obstruction—

Address: To George Garrick esq, three Tuns, Bath. *Postmarked. Source:* Wisbech Museum, two copies in FC.

1. The year is derived from the reference to the production of *The Choleric Man.*
2. Presumably William Falconer (1744–1824), M.D. 1766, who had moved to Bath in 1770, living there until his death.

3. Drury Lane, Dec. 19, 1774.

4. That is to say, there was to be only one charity performance that season. On Dec. 17, 1774, *Cymbeline* and *Miss in Her Teens* were performed "For the relief of persons imprisoned for Small debts" (*DLC*, p. 182).

5. On Sept. 15, 1774, he had written Garrick that he was leaving London for a vacation in France (Boaden, II, 5f.).

6. Dibdin's ballad opera, *The Cobler; or, A Wife of Ten Thousand*, first acted Dec. 9. Hopkins says of the first performance that it was "very much hissed, and with great Difficulty got thro'" (Diary, *DLC*, p. 182). Despite the opposition, it was performed nine more times that season.

874   To George Steevens

Adelphi
Decr the 16th [1774][1]

Pardon & Mercy, my dear Sir, for in my hurry of business I had forgot that I was to take care of y^r Friends for y^e *Chances* as well as *Hamlet*—[2] indeed my head in the mid'st of my Present hurry, wch is doubled upon Me by my Brother's absence, cannot hold all I endeavor to cram into it— the danger my Brother has been in, greatly increas'd my distress— Johnston, (who swears he always was partial to you,) was not in the least to blame— at first I thought y^r friends were jocky'd out of their places for Hamlet, & I was so Enrag'd at ye thoughts of it, that Lear was not half so mad as I was— so little was my remembrance of this matter, that I was oblig'd to have recourse to y^r letter to be assur'd of my Mistake— I wish after Hamlet you had refresh'd my memory— I beg Miss Collins's Pardon for disappointing them. We have a Tragedy of great Merit, from a Mr Jephson of Ireland;[3] there is a wonderful flow of Poetry, & something we have not seen in our time.

I am dear S^r yours most truly
D Garrick.

The Fable of ye Tragedy is the Revolutions of Portugal.

Address: To George Steevens Esqr, Hampstead-Heath. *Postmarked. Source:* Bodleian Library.

1. The year is established by the reference to Jephson's *Braganza*.
2. Presumably the performances of Dec. 15 and Dec. 12, 1774.
3. *Braganza* (DL, Feb. 17, 1775).

875 To George Colman

Adelphi

My dear Sir. Decr 28th 1774

a thousand thanks, merry Xmases & happy New Years to y^u for y^r delightful letter; Mrs Garrick sends the same with great warmth for ye Latin & English in which she is concern'd— it was impossible for you to satisfy Cumberland, had ye rack forc'd from you as much falsehood, as he has vanity— I am very glad you have prepar'd him for Me, had you been as Mischevous, as you were sincere with him, You might have sent him so high Season'd, & stuff'd so full wth conceit, that I should have had much ado to lower him; he has behav'd so disagreeably wth me,[1] that I must have a pluck at his feathers, whether they belong to Terence, Shadwell, or are of his own growth:[2] The *Two Misers* which are to be produc'd by y^r late Brethren, & written by O'Hara,[3] are from ye french of Sedaine, les deux avares, a very odd improbable piece, but ye french Musick[4] was thought good— Mr Tighe has endeavor'd to make me lose my hold of the Duke of Braganza—[5] the Barrys are Mad about it, & I am very stubborn not to say cross: if I can get a frank before I close this, you shall see how he has press'd me within these two days: *Harlequin's Jacket*[6] will make It's appearance *next Monday*; I announc'd it a few days ago in our paragraph, but it will appear in ye Bills— a *Medley Pantomime* call'd the *New Year's Gift* or *Harlequin's Jacket*. we shall take half price tho ye Scenes are all new— I shall do all I can to produce y^e *Silent Woman*[7] this season; but, it will work us much, if we keep Jephson's tragedy. I shall rely upon y^r Attachment to us to excuse our deferring it, if we find an absolute necessity for it— the Comedy will take thrice ye trouble & come off a modern one to Shew it, as it should be shown, & *ought* to be coming from *You* to *Me*: pray tell me truly w^t you think of *Henderson*? George is an Infidel— Entre nous has our friend [*tear*] had some words wth a certain Major?— pray tell George I have receiv'd his letter, & once for all I beg of him, not to think of leaving Bath, till he feels & finds himself wholly sound again— if he does, I'll never forgive him— a most disagreeable affair has happen'd— Mossop on his death-bed sends me his play, begging that I would Ease his Mind in his last moments, by taking his play, & doing all in my power with it for ye service of his Creditors—[8]

he is dead, & I have yᵉ Comedy— I have not yet read a speech—
a Friend has, & says it is like the *Patron*, wᵗʰ out yᵉ humour— What
a scrape— explanation more when I see you— when will it be?—
pray one letter more, if you follow it yᵉ next day.

Ever & most affectʸ Yours
D Garrick.

What a scrawl! Love to Foote

I was at Hampton or you should have had an answer by yᵉ
return of yᵉ post: pray tell George as I have written to you, I shall
not write to him this Week— Mʳˢ Gᵏ wishes that you wᵈ get her a
good Footman— tell my Brothʳ so

Address: To George Colman Esqʳ at Bath.   *Seal.   Postmarked.   Source:* Berg
Collection; Colman, pp. 302–304.

1. Presumably a reference to Cumberland's unsuccessful attempts to induce Garrick
to engage Henderson, after which, on behalf of the actor, he had approached Covent
Garden. In a letter to Mrs. Ireland, dated Dec. 22, 1774, Henderson says: "Mr. C—d
told me the other night, that he was ashamed of the part Mr. Garrick had acted in this
affair, and that he would undertake to get me whatever terms I pleased at Covent
Garden" (John Ireland, *Letters and Poems by John Henderson*, 1786, p. 147).

2. The *Universal Magazine* for December and the *St. James's Chronicle* for Dec. 22 had
asserted that Cumberland's *Choleric Man* was based on Thomas Shadwell's *Squire of
Alsatia* as well as Terence's *Heauton-timorumenos*, the dramatist's professed model (Richard
Cumberland, *Memoirs*, 1807, I, 378f.).

3. Kane O'Hara (1714?–1782), musician and writer of burlesques, whose musical
farce (CG, Jan. 21, 1775) was actually an alteration of Fenouillet de Falbaire's comedy,
Les Deux avares; Michel-Jean Sedaine (1719–1797) never wrote a play or comic opera
of that title.

4. By André Ernest Modeste Grétry (1741–1813).

5. Jephson's tragedy. Since Jephson was in Ireland, negotiations were carried on
through Tighe. Four of Tighe's letters to Garrick on the subject are printed in Boaden
(II, 19ff.). In one of these, dated Dec. 20, 1774 (*ibid.*, II, 22), Tighe declared that the
Barrys "were born" for the leading roles in *Braganza* and that he was "pressed by
multitudes" to give the play to Covent Garden.

6. "A Medley Pantomime was brought out last night at the Theatre Royal, Drury-
lane, called *Harlequin's Jacket*, or *A New Year's Gift*; which like most other medleys, is
a composition of the good, bad, and indifferent" (*LC*, vol. XXXVII, Jan. 3, 1775,
p. 11).

7. Colman's alteration of Jonson's *Epicoene; or, The Silent Woman*, was not produced
at Drury Lane until Jan. 13, 1776.

8. Mossop had died in Chelsea on Dec. 27 (*LC*, vol. XXVI, Dec. 27–29, 1774, p. 623).
Announcement that he had bequeathed to Garrick a comedy "in trust, the profits of
which are to be divided among his Creditors" appeared in the *London Chronicle* for Dec.
30, 1774 (p. 626) and the *Morning Post* for Jan. 2, 1775. Apparently this play was never
acted or printed.

876   To Peter Fountain

Sunday Night [?December 1774][1]
I am really so hurried with a double Share of Business on account
of George's dangerous Illness & absence from Me that I scarce
have time to write this— Why will You vex & fret Y^rSelf about y^e
Knight[2] & what he says— You praise him one day, & blame him
ye Next: You are an honest Man but too warm; you are likewise
a very *just* Man, & should recollect that *blindness* is a great Misfortune, & no Object of resentment— converse, & talk over y^r
Grievances calmly with y^r Wise Friend,[3] & avoid altercation with
ye Bow Street Magistrate— it really hurts you— as for y^r Friend
or Fiend you met upon Westminster Bridge, be assur'd that it is
somebody, who has been much oblig'd to Me— let him publish &
publish again, & do You laugh at him & despise him as I do— be
he as great or as little a being as he will— I fear none of the Scribbling Pest— if you can See in any Body's hands, any Promise of my
Brother's given for Me, be assur'd I will at any time fulfill it, but
for threats of Scs, I have had so many, & yet am belov'd by y^e
good & Creditable, that it is not worth mine, or any of my Friend's
while to listen to their Nonsense
                    I am in great haste Yours most truly
                                        D: Garrick.

Address: To Mr Fountain, Litchfield Street.   *Endorsed by the recipient.*   *Source:*
FC; Boaden, II, 57.

   1. The references to George Garrick and to Fountain's legal troubles place this
and the letter of Jan. 2, [17]75, in the same period, the second apparently repeating more
briefly the subjects common to both.
   2. Sir John Fielding, whose blindness is later mentioned.
   3. Presumably Thomas Lloyd.

877   To Thomas Rackett, Jr.[1]

                                                        1774
I must desire you to do a little commission for me, It is to see a
Mrs Hawkins, the Widow of a Revd Mr Hawkins,[2] who published
   3*

sometime ago some old plays (3 Vols)[3] He was of Magdalen College, I lent him great part of my old collection, which the Widow most justly returned me, she has lately found another very valuable book which I likewise lent him, and which she will send me whenever she can have a safe carriage— I sh[d] be glad that you w[d] take care of it, & bring it with you. pray present my Compt[s] to her, & let her know that I w[d] not trouble her with another Letter, as she might know I consented to her proposal by my silence.

Source: Little Collection, a transcript in a copy of an A.L.s. from the Rev. Thomas Rackett and F. Beltz Lane to the Rev. H. H. Baber, June 18, 1823.

1. So identified in the source. Thomas Rackett, Jr. (1757–1841) was at this time at University College, Oxford. He became Rector of Spottisbury, Dorsetshire, and devoted his leisure to antiquarian studies. He was to become one of the executors of Mrs. Garrick's estate (Boaden, I, lxiv).
2. Thomas Hawkins.
3. *Origins of the English Drama.*

878 To John Taylor

Dear Sir,   [*ante* January 2, 1775][1]
I received last night a letter from you, and another from Mr. Henderson, upon the same subject— I shall therefore beg, that this answer to you may serve for both. In my opinion, your proposal would be a very injurious one to Mr. Henderson— can he or you believe, that his playing only twice,[2] a different character too each time, would give the public a proper idea of his merit?— The diffidence and apprehension, natural to a performer of feeling, might make him incapable of shewing his talents and powers the first time upon a new stage, and upon which the great and established estimate must be put upon his merit; should his fears prevail too much, which are ever strongest with actors of keenest sensibility, he might be essentially hurt— could Mr. H have an opportunity of performing ten or twelve different characters, his genius would have fair play, otherwise, as his well-wisher, I protest against the other scheme . . .

If Mr. H chuses to be with me, why should he not chuse three parts, Hamlet, Shylock, Benedick, or what he pleases to appear in next season, and to have elbow room to display all his tragick and comick powers. I will either come into *certain* terms with him, or *conditional*, as he and his friends please. I can say no more, or offer any thing fairer, or more for his interest.— I protest against the other partial manner of trial, which can be of no service to the manager, and may be of great prejudice [to] Mr. Henderson.

> I am, Dear Sir, Yours, &c.
> D. Garrick.

Source: John Ireland, *Letters and Poems by John Henderson,* 1786, p. 160f., extract.

1. The approximate date is determined by the fact that Henderson enclosed this letter to Taylor in a letter to his friend and biographer, John Ireland, dated Jan. 2, 1775 (John Ireland, *Letters and Poems by John Henderson,* 1786, p. 160f.).
2. "Mr. G. Garrick himself told Mr. C[umberlan]d, that I should have *two trial parts,* but they afterwards must devolve to their present possessors" (*ibid.,* p. 154f.).

879   To Peter Fountain

Dear Sir   Jany 2^d [1775][1]
Thank You for Your Warm & kind Wishes, the same to You most Sincerely from Me & Mine—

I am kill'd wth business— my Brother's absence has doubled my labours— Y^r hint could not be Us'd in this Entertainment it is a *Medley* made up from Other pantomimes, & therefore call'd *Harlequin's Jacket*: It will I hope be lively & make a laugh—

I am sorry for ye Landlord's seeming ingratitude & unkindness:[2] I beg that you will always despise any Sort of pettishness you meet from Justices of all kinds— you are a warm honest man & deserve better treatment; but I am so Us'd to Ingratitude, that I always Expect it, but am not hinder'd from being kind to Others for ye faults of a few— I wish you Merry today & Every day— I am at dinner but Ever

> Y^rs truly
> D Garrick

Address: To Mr Fountain.   *Source:* FC.

1. The reference to *Harlequin's Jacket* (DL, Jan. 2, 1775) establishes the year; Garrick mistakenly wrote 74 as the date.

2. Fountain had been living in Lichfield St., Soho, at Mr. Grignion's, that is, Reynolds Grignion (d. 1787), the engraver. Apparently wishing to terminate Fountain's tenancy, Grignion had resorted to Justice Fielding of the Bow Street Court (Ulrich Thieme and Felix Becker, *Allgemeines Lexikon der Bildenden Kunstler*, Leipzig, 1907).

880   To Préville

Londres
Janvier 7ᵉ 1775

Ne m'avez vous pas oublié mon cher Compagnon en ivresse?[1] n'avez vous pas oublié nos expeditions romanesques sur les boulevars, quand les tailleurs de pierre devenoint plus pierre que leurs ouvrages En admiration de nos folies?— si je suis Encore assez heureux d'avoir une place dans votre memoire permettez moi de vous recommander le fils de mon Ami particulier,[2] pour avoir le plaisir de voir le grand favour de Thalie[3] dans son propre Caractere:

Ai je assez d'interest avec vous, de vous soliciter pour votre permission et amitié de vous voir tems en tems sur le teatre?— si en retour, vous voulez m'envoyer une demi douzaine de vos amis les portes de teatre royal de Drury Lane, et de ma maison seront aussi ouverts que mes bras de les recevoir— faites mille et mille complimens a Madame votre femme de la part de Madᵉ Garrick et de son Mari— je suis avec la plus grande consideration pour vos talens rares, et vrament dramatiques

votre tres humble Serviteur et ami
D: Garrick

excusez je vous prie que j'aye envoyè mes regards [et] services dans le plus mauvais françois—

Address: A Monsieur, Monsieur Preville En France. *Source:* HTC; Baker, p. 29f.

1. "Un jour, en revenant avec Préville, à cheval, du bois de Boulogne, [Garrick] lui dit: 'Je m'en vais faire l'homme ivre; faites-en autant.' Ils traversèrent ainsi le village de Passy, sans dire un mot, et, en un clin d'œil, tout le village fut assemblé pour les voir passer. Les jeunes gens se moquèrent d'eux, les femmes crièrent de peur de les voir tomber de cheval, les vieillards haussèrent les épaules et en eurent pitié, ou, suivant leur humeur, pouffèrent de rire. En sortant du village, Préville dit à Garrick: 'Ai-je bien fait, mon maître?— Bien, fort bien, en vérité, lui dit Garrick; mais vous n'étiez pas ivre des jambes" (*Correspondance par Grimm, Diderot, etc.*, ed. Maurice Tourneux, Paris, 1878, VI, 320).
2. Henry Angelo (see the following letter).
3. Thalia, the Muse of Comedy.

881   To Domenico Angelo

Dear Angelo   [*post* January 7, 1775][1]
I have sent you two packets one for the Conte Chattelleux & y^e
other for Preville— Your Son[2] will seal ye last, & give it as directed,[3]
if I have time, I will send a letter for Monnet but that is doubtful—
Ever Yours &c

                                                                D G.
Love to madam—

Source: Little Collection.

   1. An approximate date is determined by the reference to the packet for Préville
(see preceding letter).
   2. Henry Charles William Angelo (1756–1839), son of Domenico Angelo, had been
a classmate at Eton of Garrick's nephews, Carrington and Nathan (Henry Angelo,
Reminiscences, 1828, I, 7f.).
   3. Young Angelo, who was at this time in Paris learning fencing and French,
states: "I received a kind note from Mr. Garrick, in a packet enclosing another to his
friend, Mons. de Preville, the celebrated French comedian, which obtained for me the
friendship of that excellent actor" (*ibid.*, I, 75).

882   To The Reverend David Williams

                                                              Adelphi
Sir   January 8th 1775
I thank you for your most affecting letter— your Account of poor
Mossop's death distress'd me greatly—[1] I have been often told that
his friends never spoke kindly of me, and I am now at a loss to
guess what behaviour of mine from the first moment I knew him
till the time of his death could have given him that unkind and I
hope unmerited turn of mind against me— with regard to his
returning to us, it was his own peculiar resolution of not letting us
know his terms, that prevented his engagement at our Theatre,
had I known his distress I Shoud most certainly have reliev'd it—
he was too great a Credit to our Profession, not to have done all
in our Power to have made him *easy* at least, if not *happy*—
   The Money transaction is past,[2] he is gone and I had long ago

forgotten that I thought in that instance he behav'd not kindly to me— let me once again thank you for your very polite & agreeable manner in giving me this intelligence of our departed friend, for he was truly *mine* in those moments, when the heart of man has no disguise—[3]

> I am S[r] &c
> D Garrick.

excuse this scrawl as I have the gout in my hand

Source: FC, copy, signed by Garrick; Boaden, II, 38.

1. Williams' letter of Jan. 7 gives a pitiful account of the actor's last moments (Boaden, II, 37).
2. The actor went bankrupt in Jan. 1772, his chief creditor being Garrick, to whom he owed £200 (Robert Hitchcock, *An Historical View of the Irish Stage*, Dublin, 1788–1794, II, 212).
3. Garrick had offered to bury Mossop at his own expense, but "out of delicacy" he first wrote to an uncle of the deceased actor, a bencher at the Inner Temple, "who took the charge out of Mr. Garrick's hand, and buried him himself" (*LC*, vol. XXXVII, Jan. 5–7, 1775, p. 23).

883   To Elizabeth Younge

Madam,   Monday [January 9, 1775][1]
If my business would have permitted me I should have sat down to write you a long letter, for I have much to say and to be sorry for. If you are able to play Viola, I suppose you will, as his Majesty of England, not the copper one of Drury-lane, commands it.[2] If you should not find yourself fit, I will do the best in the power of,
> Madam, your most humble servant,
> D. Garrick.

Source: Boaden, II, 64.

1. Misdated in the source, Monday 10, 1774, for no performance of *Twelfth Night* was given by command in 1774; there was, however, a command performance of the play on Wednesday, Jan. 11, 1775.
2. Miss Younge did appear as Viola at the command performance. In her reply to this letter, however, she wrote that she could not think herself "humanely treated, when I complain and feel the bad effects of playing with a cough, that you should send me this haughty style of letter" (Boaden, II, 65).

884 To Elizabeth Younge

Adelphi

Madam. [January] 10th [1775][1]
I have really been much hurt at what Your Sister said to Johnston
the first Night of y[e] distresst Mother—[2] *that if you play'd Viola on y[e]*
Fryday you would not play Hermione on y[e] Saturday— this I knew Nothing
of till the Night of y[e] Provok'd Wife,—[3] when it was doubtful
whether you would play, or not, & I was oblig'd to get a Lady of
y[e] other house to Undertake y[e] Part, had you found Yourself
unable: As you said you were not taken ill till Fryday morning, I
was much hurt at Y[r] *Sister's Speech*: You likewise said in y[e] Green
Room that *I promis'd You should not play on y[e] Monday*: had I promis'd
You the most difficult thing in my Power I always keep my word—
but indeed it was impossible to promise *that*, as it was impossible
You should not have heard it given out on Saturday Night—
     I am very warm & sincere in my Attachments, but if I find any
Actor, or Actress distressing me or y[e] Business unjustly or fantasti-
cally I will with draw my Attachment y[e] Moment, that they shew
Me they have none. the Theatre is quite destroy'd by a New fashion
among Us— I was long y[e] Slave of the Stage, I play'd for Everybody's Benefit, & Even reviv'd parts for them, & sometimes Acted
new ones— this was at a time When by Myself I could fill a house—
that favour luckily for Me the Publick still continues, o⟨r⟩ We
might play to Empty benches—
     While Miss Young continues a Friend to me & herself, I shall do
Every thing in my power to support her; but I could wish that her
Sister would [not] prophesy to M[r] Johnston & that She herself
would [not] mention in the Green Room promises I never Made,
or her intentions of not playing to any body, but to

Her very humble Ser[t]
D: Garrick.

I will not mention some Circumstances which claim a double
portion of Your regard to the Interest of Your theatre— but I
shall be ready to mention them & much more Whenever I am call'd
upon.

Source: FC; Boaden, II, 65f.

1. The date is determined by the reference to Miss Younge playing Hermione, a role which she first took on Jan. 4, 1775.

2. Ambrose Philips' tragedy was first played during the 1774–75 season on Wednesday, Jan. 4.

3. Jan. 6, 1775.

885   To George Steevens

Adelphi

My dear Sir   [January?] 10th [1775?][1]

I have sent the volume you want— poor Warner[2] has been tottering a long time— he is a very worthy pains-taking Gentleman, & will be a loss to his friends & the public. pray can You tell Me, Where that Speech is to be found, which begins thus in Cibber's Richard the 3^d— Henry speaks it

> ——w^t noise & bustle do Kings make to find it:
> When Life's but a short Chase, ye Game Content &c[3]

There is a Wager about it, which I can't decide— have You Ever thought of any Play unreviv'd in Shakespeare, that would bring Credit to Us well decorated & carefully got up?— What think you of Rich^d 2^d—?[4] or of the rest?— An^y & Cleopatra I reviv'd Some Years ago,[5] When I & Mrs Yates were Younger— it gain'd ground Every time it was play'd, but I grew tir'd, & gave it up,— the part was laborious— I Should be glad to Employ our Painter upon some capital *Creditable* Performance.

Ever & truly yours
D Garrick.

Address: To G. Steevens Esqr.   *Source:* FSL.

1. This letter was answered by Steevens in one dated simply "Tuesday Night" but conjecturally written on Tuesday, Jan. 10, 1775, as in it Steevens remarked: "Don't you long to hear the roarings of the old Lyon over the bleak Mountains of the North?" (FC; Boaden, II, 122), evidently an allusion to Samuel Johnson's *Journey to the Western Islands of Scotland,* which was to be published about Jan. 12, 1775 (Boswell, II, 290).

2. Richard Warner was to die on April 11, 1775.

3. Act I, sc. i. Steevens replied: "The lines about which you enquire, are undoubtedly [Cibber's] own— at least I can assure you they are not to be found in the most obscure corner of any of Shakspeare's Plays" (FC; Boaden, II, 122).

4. "As to King Rich. II," wrote Steevens, "it is surely the most uninteresting and flattest of all the number. A few splendid passages will not maintain a Play on the stage" (*ibid.*).

5. Edward Capell and Garrick's alteration of *Antony and Cleopatra* (DL, Jan. 3, 1759).

886   To Frances Cadogan[1]

My dear Madam   Wed^y [January] 11^h 17[75][2]
M^r & Mrs Garrick are most particularly oblig'd to you, for Your
kind tho alarming letter— I will not Endeavour to make You laugh
till You send me Word that Mrs Wilmot is better: my Cold, Cough
hoarseness & what are Ever attendant upon such matters, low
Spirits are gone, & I am myself again— however, I shall not be
quite Myself, till You send good Tydings to me about Mrs Wilmot—
Mrs Garrick sends happy Years by ye Score to You & our dear
friends—

One Line of Comfort about Mrs Wilmot, & then You shall (if
possible) be higher in my Esteem— His Majesty demands my
presence,[3] & I am & Ever will be
Y^r most Sincere Admirer & Affect^e friend
D. Garrick.

I sh^d say their Majesties, for they are now in ye house, & I am
writing this upon ye Gallop in my dressing Room.

Address: To Miss Cadogan at Mr Wilmots, Farnborough place near Bagshot.
Postmarks: IA 12, IA 13.   *Source:* FSL.

   1. Frances Cadogan (d. 1812), later Mrs. William Nicholl, was the only daughter
of Dr. William Cadogan.
   2. Garrick seems to have forgotten the new year, for he wrote "74"; in that year
Jan. 11 was a Tuesday and there was no command performance on that day, but in '75,
Jan. 11 fell on a Wednesday and there was a command performance.
   3. *Twelfth Night* and *Harlequin's Jacket*; while Garrick did not appear in either play,
he was under obligation to be on hand to welcome members of the Royal Family.

887   To John Taylor

Adelphi

Dear Sir   Jany 13. 1775
My health obliging me to go into ye Count⟨ry,⟩ I did not receive
Your Letter[1] till this Afternoon. What is Mr Taylor's Friendship,
so warmly express'd heretofore, and not forfeited by any Negle⟨ct⟩
of mine, to be given up to the later Acquaintance⟨?⟩—[2] I will not

quote Shakespear upon You, lest I shou'd make bad Worse: I will
say a few Words upon this disagreeable Subject, & never trouble
You or your Friend again upon it: let the Adviser of the proposals
to Me, be who he may, he can have little knowledge of the Concerns of a Theatre, if he thinks any Manager in his Senses will
accep⟨t⟩ them: but, You say Sir, that *these* proposals are built upon
mine: What because I wou'd not let the Young Man run any risk
by playing twice this Season, but like a friend offer'd every Assistance for his Appearance in the next to the greatest Advantage, that
therefore I should have this Young Man to say *No* to my Opinion,
that he should have his Choice of parts for three Years afterwards,
without regard to publick Approbation, Justice to Other performers,
or the rights of a Manager? his Words are so very extraordinary,
that I will copy them for your reconsideration— after saying that
he will chuse 4 Characters the first Year, 4 the 2^d, & 4 the 3^d—
wch are to be chosen from our plays in Acting— (*he adds*) *reserving to Myself
the same priviledge of rejecting Any parts but what I shall* MYSELF AGREE
FOR *at the beginning of Each Season: My reasons, Sir, for stipulating so
particularly are not in the least from an Apprehension of Your allotting Me
improper Characters, or forcing Me to appear to my disadvantage,* (then
why is my right of judging to be taken from Me?— We shall hear—)
*but lest your good Nature & partiality to Me might lead You to think more
favourably of my Talents, than they deserve, and of which I must beg leave*
ALWAYS *to have a Power of judging myself upon my own feelings*: thus I
say again this Young Actor is to be absolute Manager of himself,
*tho' he has not the least Apprehension of my allotting him improper Char-
acters, or forcing* ⟨*him*⟩ *to appear to his disadvantage*— Surely this reason
for depriving me of my right of judging is very particular at least:
towards the End of your letter You are pleas'd to say, *that You will
justify in any Shape that the proposals were both civil and proper*— to which
I answer, that I totally differ with You in every Shape, & declare,
that M^r H[enderson]^s, proposals were not only both *uncivil*, &
improper, but *unpracticable*.

I am Dr Sr Your most hu^ble &c

D. Garrick

Source: FC, copy; Boaden, II, 40.

1. Dated Jan. 9 (FC; Boaden, II, 39).
2. Henderson.

888   To George Steevens

                                                        Adelphi
My dear Sir   [January] 13 [1775]¹
Since I wrote to you I have read Rich^d 2^d in y^r Edition most carefully— you are perfectly right— it is one of ye least interesting of
his Historical plays— it will not do— I could make a fine Scene of
the Barriers & particularly if they had made an attack before Rich^d
had stop'd them— the Choleric Man came in² just as I had receiv'd
y^r letter— the *Essay on ye Theatre*,³ was anonymous, & printed in
the Morning Chron^e against Sentimental Comedy & written (as
he has been told) by our Lincoln's I⟨nn⟩ friend—⁴ It was a Stroke
at ye fashionable Lover. The *Unhappy Gentleman* was that Wretch
Bickerstaff, who, C[umberland] says, was Ever *attacking* him, in
the Papers I mean— The Work, which he hints at, is a *Tragedy* he
has in hand—⁵ upon my word, I imagin'd it must be Something of
a kind not to alarm ye Critics— but how a *Tragedy* will be what he
says, (till we see it,) I cannot guess— He is very particular &
Easily hurt, which has occasion'd so many Squibs to be thrown at
him— I never heard of y^e *Sicilian Usurper*⁶ before— Sheridan's⁷
Comedy⁸ has rais'd great Expectation in ye Publick— Franklin's
Tragedy⁹ will be perform'd for the first time on Saturday Sen'night—
                                    Dear Sr Most Faithfully Y^rs
                                                    D. Garrick

Have you read Burke's Speech upon American taxation?¹⁰
    It is said that 15 leaves of ye roarings from ye North¹¹ are cancell'd,
I grieve at it, I love to see Character in writing, as well as in
Company—
    Where is y^e *Puss in boots*?
    Not in ye 5th Act of Rich^d 2.¹²

Source: Bodleian Library.

    1. This is the reply to Steevens' letters of [Jan. 10, 1775] (see Letter 885, n. 1; FC;
Boaden, II, 122) and [Jan.] 12, 1775 (Boaden, II, 112f.).
    2. Published Jan. 12, 1775 (*LC*, vol. XXXVII, Jan. 10–12, 1775, p. 39).
    3. Steevens, in his letter of [Jan.] 12, asked "To what Essay on the Theatre does
Mr. C. refer at the top of p. 9 of his dedication?— and what does he mean by 'except
in the case of one unhappy gentleman,' in the last paragraph?— and 'something more
worthy of their approbation, and less dependent upon yours?'" (Boaden, II, 112).
    4. Murphy.
    5. Perhaps *The Battle of Hastings*.

6. Steevens had written: "I suppose you are already painting the barriers for 'King Richard the Second.' Are you aware that Tate altered it under the title of 'The Sicilian Usurper?'" (Boaden, II, 113). Nahum Tate had actually called his play *The History of King Richard the Second . . . [or] the Sicilian Usurper* (1681).

7. Richard Brinsley Sheridan (1751–1816), dramatist, statesman, and wit. He was familiar with the theater through his father, Thomas Sheridan, an actor and teacher of elocution, through his mother, a playwright, and with music through his marriage on April 13, 1773, to Elizabeth Ann Linley the singer. In 1775 Sheridan was to win a great popular success with a comedy, a farce, and a comic opera. In another year he was to succeed Garrick as manager of Drury Lane. The relations of the two men were cordial: Garrick wrote the prologue for *The School for Scandal* (DL, May 8, 1777) and Sheridan wrote *Verses to the Memory of Garrick spoken as a Monody* (1779) and was chief mourner at his funeral.

8. *The Rivals* (CG, Jan. 17, 1775).

9. *Matilda.*

10. In the House of Commons on April 19, 1774; published as *On American Taxation,* it went through many editions, at least three of which were brought out in 1774.

11. Perhaps a somewhat exaggerated report of James Macpherson's demand that the passages in Johnson's *Journey to the Western Islands of Scotland* be canceled where Johnson "in expressing his incredulity, with regard to the authenticity of the poems of Ossian, [made] use of the words *malice, audacity,* and *guilt . . .* such expressions ought not to be used by one gentleman to another" (Boswell, II, 511).

12. Steevens had written "if you revive King Rich[d] I beg that proper regard may be paid to old *Puss in boots* who arrives so hastily in the fifth act" (FC; Boaden, II, 122, where, in a footnote, Boaden suggests the Duchess of York).

889   To Richard Cumberland[1]

Adelphi

My dear Sir   Jan[y] y[e] 20 [1775][2]

Much business at y[e] Theatre prevented my writing to you this morning— I cannot alter my opinion of M[r] H[enderson]'s proposals— I say no more of them— You seem to wish that he should make his appearance upon our Stage— As I have not seen him Act, & cannot guess at his Merit, which is so variously Spoken of, I will agree that M[r] Henderson shall perform any two parts at y[e] beginning of next Season which *he* shall please to fix upon, & afterwards upon others that we shall both agree upon. for after his choice of two, I cannot give up my right of *proposing* & *consenting* to any body— after he has perform'd ten or twelve times, & y[e] Publick voice will be known, let two Gentlemen, who know Something of theatrical matters one chosen by him, & one by Me, & let them fix upon his Sallary for that Season—[3] upon their disagreement a third may be call'd in;

& he must determine ye difference— I cannot do or say more, but that I am very truly

Your most ob^t hum^e Ser^t
D G.

To make something certain for M^r H, & ye Referees to go upon suppose We agree that his Sallary shall not be less than 5 pounds a Week nor more than ten for the Season, with a Benefit— [After his salary is fixed, he must become like the other performers, subject to my management *wholly.*][4]

Source: FC, the better of two drafts; John Ireland, *Letters and Poems by John Henderson*, 1786, p. 166f.

1. So identified by Henderson (John Ireland, *Letters and Poems by John Henderson*, 1786, p. 166f.).
2. The year is established by the fact that Henderson enclosed the letter in one to Ireland, dated Jan. 23, 1775 (*ibid.*, p. 165f.).
3. Cumberland advised Henderson to accept this offer, but the actor declined it, and after making fruitless overtures to Covent Garden, reëngaged with Palmer to act at Bath for the next three years.
4. Matter in brackets is supplied from the printed source.

890   To Frances Abington

Hampton

Madam. Jany 28th 1775

The famous french Writer Fontenelle takes notice that nothing is so difficult to a Man of Sensibility, as writing to a Lady even with just grounds of Complaint: however having promis'd, I must answer your last very Extraordinary note:[1] You accuse me of incivility for writing to you thro' Mr Hopkins— did not Mrs Abington first begin that Mode of Correspondence? and without saying a word to Me, did she not send back her part in the new Comedy, & say that she had settled that matter with Mr Cumberland?[2] could a greater affront be offer'd to any Manager? and was not your proposing to Mr Hopkins, that *you* would speak my Epilogue, written for the Character, while *another person* was to perform the part, not only mere mockery of me, but destroying the play at once? let your warmest & most partial friend decide between Us. Whenever You are really ill, I feel both for You & myself; but ye Servant said last Wed^y that you *were Well, & had a great deal of Company*:

You mention *your great fatigue*: What is the Stage come to, if I must continually hear of your *hard labour*, when from the beginning of the season to this time, you have not play'd more than *twice* a Week? Mrs Oldfield perform'd Lady Townly for 29 Night[s] successively:[3] let us now examine how just & genteel Your complaint is against me: I promis'd You, that I would procure a Character of consequence to be written on purpose for You,[4] and that it should be Your own fault, if you were not on the highest pinnacle of Yr profession— I have been at great pains, & you know it, to be as good as my word— I directed & assisted the Author to make a small Character, a very considerable one for You, I spar'd no Expence in dresses, Musick, scenes & decorations for the piece, & now the *fatigue of Acting* this Character, is very unjustly, as well ⟨as⟩ unkindly brought against me: had you play'd this part *40* times, instead of *20*, my gains would be less than by any other Successful play, I have produc'd in my Management— the greatest favour I can confer upon an Actress, is to give her the best Character in a favourite piece, & the longer it runs, the more Merit I have with her, & ought to receive her *thanks*, instead of *Complaints*: in short Madam, *if you play* you are uneasy, & if you *do not*, you are more so— after what you said to Mr Becket, & what I promis'd, I little thought to have Your *farce*[5] drawn in to make up the Bundle of Complaints— however to make an end of this disagreeabl⟨e⟩ business, as the piece is written out, I am now ready to do it, & that You may have *Palmer*, I will give up the reviv'd Comedy— but even this, I know, will not satisfy You, nor can You fix in Your Mind, *what will*.

Were I to look back, what *real* complaints have I to make for leading me into a fool's paradise last Summer about a certain Comedy? and an alarming Secret you told me lately of a disagreeable quarrel!— on my return home the same Morning, I met one of ye Parties, & instead of a quarrel between them, they were upon ye best terms, had never had the least difference, & Mr M[urph]y was writing, at Mr T[ighe]'s desire, a prologue for his Friend's new Tragedy—[6]

Mr Garrick most Solemnly assures Mrs Abington that Nobody has in the least influenc'd him in this affair, & he hopes the above recital will convince her of the truth of his Assertion.

I am Madam Yr most Obedt Servt

D Garrick

Endorsement by Garrick: This Letter to Mrs Abington was not sent.   *Source:* FC; Boaden, II, 42f.

    1. Of Wednesday morning [Jan. 25] (FC; Boaden, II, 27f.).
    2. Mrs. Abington had been playing Laetitia Fairfax in *The Choleric Man.* In a note to Hopkins, dated Jan. 20, she wrote: "Mr. Cumberland has obligingly given his consent to her resigning of the part; and Mrs. Abington flatters herself that Mr. Garrick will have the goodness and complaisance to relieve her from a character so little calculated to her very confined style of acting" (*ibid.*, I, 609). Cumberland later wrote Garrick: "I have written her a Letter to the Effect you wished. I have told her the very unpleasant situation I was thrown into by having exceeded my power from a wish to gratify her Inclination & I have represented the high displeasure you have conceived both against her & myself from this attempt upon what is justly inherent in you alone" (FC). Mrs. Abington did continue in the part.
    3. Anne Oldfield (1683–1730), playing *The Provok'd Husband* in 1728 (Colley Cibber, *Apology,* 1740, p. 430).
    4. Probably Lady Bab Lardoon in *The Maid of the Oaks.*
    5. This allusion is not clarified by Mrs. Abington's letter of [Jan. 25]; she had apparently brought up the farce and Palmer in a letter now lost.
    6. Murphy, at Tighe's request, wrote the prologue for Jephson's *Braganza* (Murphy, II, 115f.).

891   To Peter Fountain

Hampton

D^r S^r   Saturday [January 28, 1775]

I have this moment rec'd y^r Note, & I have inclos'd a passport for you & ye Ladies if you chuse to go to Night— I came here to recruit my body & Mind from my Fatigues— I have no curiosity to read any praise of Mr Dagge's book,[1] I take it for granted—

    I shall wait for y^e *Wonder* you are so full of— I am sorry you leave y^r old habitation, y^r Landlord is surely an Obstinate Mortal— I wish you happiness wherever you go.

Y^rs heartily.
DG.

Endorsement by the recipient: 28th Jany 1775.   *Source:* FC.

    1. Presumably Henry Dagge's *Considerations on Criminal Law* (1772; enlarged, 1774).

892   To Charles Théveneau de Morande¹

[*post* February 23, 1775]²
Mʳ Garrick presents his compliments to Mʳ de Morande & ten
thousand thanks for his most agreable news about the Barbier de
Seville³ may that much wrong'd gentleman the Author always
vanquish his enemies in the same manner.⁴ Mʳ Garrick has really
been much concern'd at yᵉ accounts [that] were given out in
London about the success of that Comedy, but Mʳ de Morande has
made him quite easy

Source: Sotheby, Catalogue, June 12–19, 1899, extract.

1. Charles Théveneau de Morande (1741–1805), French pamphleteer and miscellaneous writer. He dealt chiefly in slander, supporting himself by his pen and the bribes
of apprehensive persons of prominence.
2. Dated from the reference to the "agreable news" about the *Barbier de Séville*.
3. The production of the play at the Comédie-Française on Feb. 23, 1775.
4. Pierre Augustin Caron de Beaumarchais (1732–1799), dramatist and pamphleteer,
had written his play as a satiric commentary on the rivalries which grew out of one of
his lawsuits. He had made many enemies through lawsuits, speculations, court intrigues,
and his *Mémoires* (1774), and these enemies had resorted to various maneuvers to prevent
the production of the *Barbier* (Louis de Loménie, *Beaumarchais et son temps*, Paris, 1858,
I, 451ff.).

893   To Frances Abington

Adelphi
Madam   March 7ᵗʰ [1775]¹
Whether a consciousness of your unaccountable & unwarrantable
behaviour to me, or that you have really heard of *my description of
you* in all companies, I will not enquire whatever I have said, I will
justify, for I always speak the truth. Is it possible for me to describe
you as your note of yesterday describes yourself? you want a day's
notice to perform a character you play'd originally & which you
have appear'd in several times this season;² you knew our distress
yesterday almost as soon as I did, & did not plead the want of a
day's notice, cloaths, hair dresser &c, but you refus'd on account
of your health, tho' you were in spirits & rehearsing a new farce.³

You suffer'd us to be oblig'd to another lady,[4] of another use, to do your business, when neither our distresses the credit of the Theatre or your own duty, & justice could have the least influence upon you. how could I give you a day's notice when I knew not of Mr Reddish's illness but in the morning and you were the first person I sent to between *12 & one* & not at *three* o'clock?— It was happy for us that we found a lady tho' not of our company, who had a feeling for our distress, & reliev'd us from it, without requiring 2 days notice, or wanting any thing but an opportunity to shew her politeness— these are serious truths Madam, & are not to be described like the lesser peccadillos of a fine Lady— a little time will shew that Mr Garrick has done essential offices of kindness to Mrs Abington, when his humanity only, & not his duty oblig'd him— as to your wishes of delivering me from the inconvenience of your engagement, that, I hope, will soon be another's concern; my greatest comfort is, that I shall soon be deliver'd from the capriciousness, inconsistency, injustice, & unkindness of those, to whom I always intended the greatest good in my power. I am Madam your most obed^t Servant

D. Garrick.

your refusing to play this evening has obliged me, tho' but just recover'd from a dreadful disorder to risk a relapse.[5]

Source: FC, copy; Boaden, II, 25f.

1. The year is from Mrs. Abington's letter, to which this is the reply, which while dated only Monday night was obviously written on March 6, 1775, from the references to productions and problems. This dating is confirmed by the calendar and by Boaden (FC; Boaden, II, 25).
2. Charlotte Rusport in *The West Indian*. The playbill had announced that *Matilda* would be acted March 6, but "Mr. Reddish, being a little out of his Senses, he could not play— therefore The West Indian was performed, and large Bills put up about two o'clock.— Mrs. Abington not being in a Humour to play upon such an Emergency, we borrowed Miss Barsanti from Covent Garden to play Miss Rusport" (Hopkins, Diary, *DLC*, p. 185).
3. Probably *Bon Ton; or, High Life Above Stairs* (DL, March 18, 1775), "said to be the production of the Author of the Maid of the Oaks. Certain it is, that Mr. Garrick hath revised, corrected, and altered it" (*LC*, vol. XXXVII, March 11–14, 1775, p. 248; see Letter 898).
4. Jane (or Jenny) Barsanti (d. 1795), a former pupil of Dr. Burney and a great favorite of his family, joined the Covent Garden company in Sept. 1772; one of her early roles was that of Miss Rusport (see *The Early Diary of Frances Burney*, ed. Annie R. Ellis, 1907, I, 55, 191).
5. Garrick played Lusignan on March 7, 1775.

894   To Frances Abington

Adelphi

Madam   March 7th [1775]¹
I beg that you will indulge yourself in writing what you please, &
when you please— If you imagine that I in the least countenance,
or am accessary to any Scribling in the papers, You are deceiv'd—
I detest all such Methods of Shewing my Resentment.— I never
heard of the disorder was occasion'd in the Maid of The Oaks, I
was too ill to be troubled with it, & Mr King, whom you have
always unjustly suspected, never mention'd it to me— nor did I
know of the Paragraph you allude to, till it was shewn to me this
Morning— Could the Country Girl have been done with Credit
yesterday, I should not have distress'd myself to have apply'd to
You, or to have borrow'd a Lady from another Theatre—² As I
will always retract the most insignificant mistake I may have made,
I find by the Prompter that the West Indian has been perform'd
but once—³ May I venture if Braganza can't be perform'd on
Thursday⁴ to put your name in the Bills for Lady Bab in the Maid
of the Oaks, or for any other part? I most Seriously Assure You
that I don't ask this to distress you, but to carry on the Business
in the best manner I am able

I am Madm Your most humble Servt

D Garrick

Mrs Yates has not yet Sent word that She cannot play on Thursday
and I hope you may be excus'd—⁵ I ask the question to prevent
trouble to both.

The writing peevish Letters will do no business.

Source: FC, copy; Boaden, II, 26f.

1. This is the reply to Mrs. Abington's letter dated only Tuesday morning but
obviously written (see preceding letter, note 1) on March 7, 1775 (FC; Boaden, II, 26).

2. See preceding letter, note 2. Mrs. Abington had written in her letter of March 7:
"it was plain that the country girl could have been acted from the Instant that Mr
Reddish's Illness was known: the design, therefore, of changing it, to the west Indian,
could only be to hurt and hurry Me— and if I refus'd, it was a good pretence for borrowing
a performer to play My part, in order to give colour to the abuse that was Intended for
me in the papers this Morning" (FC).

3. The actress had asserted that *The West Indian* had been acted at Drury Lane but
once that season (Oct. 4, 1774).

4. At the last performance, on March 4, the audience was much exasperated by
Mrs. Yates's failure to speak the epilogue. An apology appeared in the papers, to the
effect that "Mrs. Yates was really extremely ill, and the fatigue of having performed

for ten nights almost without intermission, with the very great exertion necessary in the last scene, rendered her totally incapable " (*LC*, vol. XXXVII, March 4–7, 1775, p. 223).

5. Mrs. Yates, however, was well enough to act the Duchess in *Braganza* on March 9. The audience would not allow the performance to begin until she had come upon the stage and personally assured it that she had been incapable of speaking the epilogue on March 4 (*ibid.*, March 9–11, 1775, p. 238).

895   To James Boswell

Adelphi

March 8th 1775

Dear S^r

Too much business, a severe attack of the Stone, & my Brother's dangerous Situation have prevented me from acknowledging your very obliging & friendly letter Sooner.[1] our learned Friend's Account of *You*, & *Yours*,[2] has occasion'd much Speculation, & had very near been productive of Mischief— You have heard I am Sure of Letters & Messages (very rough ones indeed) that have pass'd between the D^r & Mr Macpherson—[3] but Nine days have done wth their business, as they do with all other Wonderful Matters, almost annihilated it— our friend has this day produc'd another political pamphlet call'd, *Taxation no Tyranny*, a very Strong attack upon the Americans & Patriots— it is said to be well & masterly done— I shall devour it the Moment I have finish'd this letter. how the dispute about Fingal will end, I cannot Yet Say; I hope not wth bloody Crowns, as seem'd likely at first— an Acquaintance of the Doctor's & formerly an Antagonist of Macpherson, (Mr *Whitaker*[4] by name) by Some Strange literary Fatality, is bringing forth, in a two Shilling pamphlet, proofs of the Authenticity of Fingal!—! it has likewise been Whisper'd to me, that he will be pert with our Friend— He, you know, is too great a Philosopher, in the best sense of ye word, to regard, *The Whips & Scorns of* time—[5] He Superior to the little frail Sensibilities of inferiour beings, like Antæus, rebounds, & encreases in vigour from these attacks! and when he has blown up the billows— *He*

Smiles on the tumult, & Enjoys ye Storm![6]

have his *Hebrides* lost him any Friends at Edinburgh?— Fame says— *Yes.*—

Becket is a fool— & We plague him much about his Erse-knowledge & Learning[7] [*hole*]

Your theatrical Matters are ver⟨y⟩ ill manag'd— the Stage would have been a very comfortable business in Scotland for any *Sensible, good* Actor, wth good Management, but Your Directors are too great Rakes, & too fine Gentlemen, to serve themselves, or please their audiences.

pray Let us See You Soon, & bring your Spirits, good humour & unaffected Mirth along with You. I am D^r S^r

> Most Sincerely, Yours
> D Garrick.

I write in great haste & not in Spirits, but in great pain— ye Gout has fix'd upon my right thumb, & the post-man can't stay another Moment! adieu.

Address: James Boswell Esqr, Edinburgh.   *Seal.*   *Postmarks:* MR 8, MR 9. *Source:* Boswell MSS. Yale.

1. From Edinburgh on Feb. 4 (Boswell MSS. Yale).
2. Johnson's *A Journey to the Western Islands of Scotland*, 1775; not until 1785 did Boswell publish his *Journal of a Tour to the Hebrides, with Samuel Johnson.*
3. Johnson expressed a wish to see the original manuscripts from which Macpherson had drawn his Ossianic poems, and when they were not forthcoming had emphatically doubted their authenticity and existence. Macpherson threatened violence if Johnson persisted in his outspoken skepticism. The result was Johnson's famous letter defying the intimidations of a ruffian and asserting his determination to defend himself with a cudgel (Boswell, II, 296f.).
4. John Whitaker (1735–1808), clergyman, antiquarian, and historian, chiefly remembered for his *History of Manchester* (1771–1775). He had published in 1772 *The Genuine History of the Britons Asserted in a Refutation of Mr. Macpherson's "Introduction to the History of Great Britain and Ireland."* The pamphlet mentioned by Garrick has not been identified.
5. See *Hamlet*, III, i, 70.
6. Not identified.
7. Boswell had written Garrick on Feb. 4: "How could you let Honest Tom Becket put an Advertisement into the Newspapers gravely asserting that the *originals* of Fingal & other Poems of Ossian lay in his shop for the inspection of the curious, when for any thing that he knows those papers may have been muster rolls of the highland regiment, or receipts for brewing heath beer, distilling whisky, or baking oatmeal cakes; for, not a word of erse does he understand."

896   To William Augustus Miles

Adelphi

Sir   March 15— 1775

Tho' I particularly urg'd to you, my Ill state of health, my great hurry of Business, my Brother's dangerous Situation, & my great disinclination to write upon Nothing, Yet you resolve to *do* nothing that I desire You, & to persecute me with Letters, nay you not only disoblige me that way, but you make me your Letter Carrier to other people.— I most seriously think myself very ill us'd & treated by You, & must beg leave to wave all this matter for the future— You ask my advice upon sending Trifles to the Children of ———[1] — in my opinion you would destroy any interest you may have there for ever— that Lord immediately abandons any person who thinks to make an Interest thro' that Channel—

You will have another affair of more Consequence to take care of when you come to England. M[r] Macklin has got a Verdict in his favour,[2] & if the Parties (some of which I hear intend to take the Business to the House of Lords) don't make it up with him, Fine & Imprisonment must be the Event—[3] this is the Consequence of the most Childish Wanton imprudence that a Man in your disagreeable Circumstances could have been guilty of— the Testimony of *Evans*[4] was very severe against You— in short the Madness & injustice of that Night's Riot, & your unjustifiable Letter in the Papers afterwards made more irrational by signing your Name, appear'd in it's full Folly & brought on your Condemnation from all sides.—

Indeed M[r] Miles, You are the most thoughtless Acquaintance I ever had, & by what you call Spirit, and an unfeeling perseverance with regard to me, You make me almost lament that I ever had the pleasure of seeing You— In my Opinion your writing to M[r] Bates[5] may be thought too Officious unless you were desir'd, & however it be, I must be excus'd from the Office of *Go-between*.— As to the Affair of The Maid's Tragedy, I shall not prevent your going on with it, tho' if You wish to know my thoughts of that too, it is my Sincere Opinion by what I have Seen, & heard you Say, that You have No turn for the Drama & are losing your time in that Alteration[6]

> I am Sir Your humble Servant
> D Garrick

Endorsement by Garrick: My Answer to some of M[r] Miles's Letters from Holland. March 22[d] 1775.   *Source:* FC, copy; Boaden, II, 50.

1. Presumably Lord Sandwich, who in 1774, through Garrick's solicitation, had obtained for Miles the position of a ship's purser, and whose good will Miles doubtless wished to cultivate in hopes of a promotion. Sandwich had at this time two or three illegitimate children by Martha Ray.
2. Macklin had sued Miles and five others for going to Covent Garden on Nov. 18, 1773, with the intent of driving him from the stage by instigating the riot which indeed

led to his discharge. The case had come up for trial on Feb. 24, 1775, and the jury had decided that all had been guilty of the riot, and that all but one had been guilty of confederacy against Macklin "to have him turned off the stage" (James T. Kirkman, *Memoirs of the Life of Charles Macklin*, 1799, II, 61ff.).

3. All the defendants paid the damages but Miles, who "absconded" (*ibid.*, II, 253, 256, 290).

4. A Thomas Evans had testified that he had sat next to Miles and had seen him write a note to the managers demanding Macklin's discharge. In a signed letter to the *Morning Chronicle* for Nov. 20, 1773, Miles had denied writing such a note and vehemently defended his conduct at the theater (*ibid.*, II, 168f., 210).

5. Joah Bates (1741–1799), musician and author. He was at this time private secretary to Lord Sandwich, whose second son had been one of his pupils at Cambridge.

6. Apparently Miles abandoned his intention of altering Beaumont and Fletcher's tragedy.

897 ## To William Smith

Adelphi
Sir. March 15 1775

You have forc'd me to write this my last letter to You, & with this I beg that our Correspondence may End— Your intention of leaving our theatre was talk'd of behind our Scenes, & laugh'd at by me as impossible, before You open'd y^r mind to me last Saturday— You then hinted at *other* reasons for leav^g me nay Even condescended to speak of ye dressing room; & in y^r letter of that day, You mention that y^r *terms*, & *Employment* were not agreeable— I will venture to say y^t You have profited by y^r *Employment* at drury Lane, & the *terms*, I believe, are more, than you Ever receiv'd, which I did not know till yesterday— another circumstance of surprize!— in y^r Conversation wth me on Saturday, You told me you were neither *Engag'd* nor in *treaty* with another theatre; Some of ye Managers of Cov^t Garden make no Secret of some offers *You* made to them before our meeting & Seperation on Saturday last—[1] be that as it may, I receiv'd you wth open Arms the Moment I heard You were discharg'd. I have in Every particular done You not only justice, but shewn you friendship, to the great uneasiness of other Performers— I had great Satisfaction in being connected with You, & now, I know y^r regard for me I am not Miserable by the seperation.

I am Sr Your humble Servant
D G.

You may depend upon my not mentioning a certain person[2] indiscreetly whom I regard & am Oblig'd to. but a Gentleman told me yesterday, Unconnected with any theatre, that Mr S[mith]'s reason for quitting me & offering himself Elsewhere, was that ye Person in question wanted a protector: Mr S: shd desire his *present* friends not to be indiscreet

Source: FC, draft; Boaden, II, 49.

1. In his reply, of March 16, Smith protested that although he had seen Harris, the manager of Covent Garden, "No Terms were mention'd or Engagements made, nor any yet spoken of" (FC; Boaden, II, 51). A separate note by Garrick, apparently relating to Smith's letter, runs: "Mr Smith offer'd himself to Mr Harris on Thursday 9th March. 1775 & told me Saturday ye 11th do that he was neither engag'd or in treaty" (Murdock Collection; Boaden, II, 51).

2. Mrs. Hartley, Smith's mistress, then acting at Covent Garden (Boaden, II, 47).

898   To George Colman

Drury Lane Play house—
[*post March 18, 1775*][1]

The Author of Bon Ton presents his best Compts & thanks to Mr Colman for his excellent Prologue, & would wish to add to ye obligation by desiring him to look over the Farce & draw his Pencil thro' the parts his judgment would omit in ye next representation—

Mr Garrick not being present at ye representation, he likewise should be very happy if Mr Colman, would shew his regard to him, & take ye trouble which is wanting to make Bon Ton palatable.

Mr G. will do more or any thing at any time to Shew his Attachment to his Old Friend—

Source: Berg Collection; Colman, p. 305.

1. The approximate date is determined by the fact that *Bon Ton* was first acted at Drury Lane on March 18, 1775, and was next produced, with alterations perhaps by Colman, on March 27.

899   To Arabella and Catherine Garrick[1]

My dear Girls.   [*ante* March 21, 1775][2]
This little note is partly for You and partly for Mad^e DesCombes—
Your Aunt has express'd our Love for you both, & therefor⟨e⟩ I
shall now say Nothing but about business— in the first place let
Monsr & Mad^e DesCombes know that you will return to Us after
your next quarter which ends in June— if they cannot appoint me
any person here to pay the *3470 Livres & 9 Sous* which I owe them
& should chuse to pay here, I will draw upon Mess^r Panchaud the
Bankers if you will send me her commands in three Lines by y^e
next post or soon after— My best respects to Miss Pratt, Comp^{ts} to
M^r & Mrs DesCombes & Love to you both
                                          Ever & most affect^y Yours
                                                      D. Garrick.

Address: A Mademoiselle, Mad^{lle} Garrick chez Monsr DesCombes, rüe verte,
Fauxb: St Honoré a Paris.   *Postmark:* MR 21.   *Source:* FC.

  1. This letter is written at the end of an undated letter from Mrs. Garrick to Catherine
Garrick.
  2. The year is established by Mrs. Garrick's letter, in which she writes that "Your
Uncle Peter is with us till we set out for Bath" (see the two following letters).

900   To Elizabeth Montagu

                                                            Adelphi
Dear Madam—   March 27 [1775][1]
A new Footman, who being deaf, is not mov'd with the concord
of sweet Sounds,—[2] & being unmercurial in his heels could not
overtake the Coach, prevented us from having the pleasure we
devoutly (being Sunday) wish'd for last night— I could have
brain'd the fellow— a Son of Dr. Robertson[3] was wth us, & we
talked of Nothing but Mrs. Montagu, & Miss Gregory— Mrs.
Garrick was indeed just return'd from Hampton & my Elder Brother
was screwing up his Features to a parting ditty, which he sighed
forth, & left us before 5 this morn^g. The fool was so deaf he could

not tell us where you order'd y^r Coachman to drive, so that we could do nothing but fret and scold. I had two great favours to ask: the one was to beseech you not to be impress'd by any Acc^t of a late Separation from the house of Cumberland,[4] till you have heard the calm truth from y^r humble Servant— Such ingratitude! but I won't say any more at present, but be assur'd I will never do anything to any one Creature, that shall make *You* (& that is my only concern) think less favourably of me.

Suspend your Justice till the Cause is heard:[5] Your understanding naturally does this, & I flatter myself that your heart will not easily be misled to condemn me—

Something too much of this,— the next favour I had to solicit was Your name, *which I more Glory in than if Possess^d*[6] & to be added to ye most noble list I have got for a very ingenious man who has undertaken 6 etchings from the principal Characters of Shakespeare.[7] I have sent you a Sample of the work, which I must beg you to return to day or tomorrow— without your permission I have plac'd you at the head of my List, & Everybody agrees to the propriety of having such a Leader— Should you meet with any choice Spirits, whose names may be easily got, they will not discredit themselves, & do great Service to a most ingenious Man.— I am Madam with every Sense of Esteem & affection most devotedly Yours,

D. Garrick.

Mrs. Garrick presents her respects— I would send more than these to Miss Gregory were I not afraid of Mrs. Garrick's Curiosity wishing to read over this letter. I have had a little pain & worse symptoms this morning.

Source: Blunt, *Mrs. Montagu*, I, 360f.

1. The year is determined by the references to Dr. Robertson's son and "Shakespeare's Characters."

2. *The Merchant of Venice*, V, i, 84.

3. William Robertson (1754–1835), later (1805) Lord Robertson, was the eldest son of Dr. Robertson of Edinburgh and was a lawyer and miscellaneous writer. Bearing a letter of introduction from his father to Garrick, dated March 14, 1775, he had come to London at this time "to see the sights" (FSL; Boaden, II, 48).

4. Garrick had quarreled with Cumberland in late December (Letter 875).

5. As Garrick later quotes from *The Orphan*, it is possible that he is here paraphrasing another line from the same play, act, and scene: "Hear all and then let Justice hold the scales" (II, i, 241).

6. *Ibid.*, l. 212.

7. "Shakespeare's Characters" (1775–1776), a series of twelve plates by John Hamilton Mortimer.

4+L.D.G. III

901 # To John Moody

Bath

Dear Moody   April 1ˢᵗ [17]75
Had I ravish'd Yʳ Wife, burnt Your house & murder'd yʳ Children,
you could not have written Me a more doleful Letter— pray did
Not Tom King speak to You from Me?[1] I desir'd him to tell You
that as I thought no Dancing would add to yᵉ Number of Yʳ house,[2]
& that I had given You the best day I could, I was of opinion that
You might have transferr'd yᵉ Dancing to the Next Benefit, (Dibdin's),[3] who is Starving, & would want Every assistance— my
words to King were these, *tell Moody that I hate Dibdin, & like him,*—
but as yᵉ first may want Slingsby, & the other will not, I leave it to
him to decide how it shall be— could I do better, or behave in a
more friendly manner? however as You desire me to *reverse the
decree*, I Shall, & do it with more Ease, & pleasure, than I can shut
my doors against You: my best Compᵗˢ to Your Wife.
                                        I am Dʳ Sʳ Yours most truly
                                                                D Garrick

My Brother George will see You on Wedʸ next & shall tell you
more.
    You are a vile fellow— farewell.

Source: FSL.

    1. For examples of how King was managing affairs for Garrick, see Appendix E.
    2. For Moody's benefit on April 17.
    3. On April 18.

902 # To George Colman

Bath

Dear Colman   April 10ᵗʰ 1775
When I see You, I will talk over in friendly conference the Subject
of yʳ last Letter— I am at present very oddly situated— but as I
shall always wish to second your desires whenever I can, without
injury to myself, wᶜʰ I am sure you always imply at the time you

let me know them, I must open my heart to you, & beg that it may be shut up to Every body else— Smith cannot, with the people the Managers have engag'd, be employ'd at Covent Garden—[1] He has offer'd himself to Me by my Brother in a fit of honour, or Compunction— I still keep aloof, & have written a very spirited & refusing letter to him— this my policy & my Spirit requir'd— but I will not hide a thought from You— I really think we can't do without him,[2] & if so (for Henderson is yet disengag'd) how can I make it worth B[arr]y's while to change his Situation? however let Matters rest a little, the theatrical face of things may be greatly alter'd, before we meet, for I give you up, & ye Pleasure of seeing you here— I must intreat Your Secresy in this affair, & you shall know all my Politicks & Engagements when I see you

Ever & affect^y Y^{rs}
D Garrick.

Addressed. Seal. Source: Berg Collection; Colman, p. 306f.

1. Among others, Smith's rival, Macklin.
2. Smith did continue at Drury Lane.

903   To George Colman

Bath

My dear Colman.   Saturday Night [April 15, 1775][1]
Your very friendly agreeable letter came to my hand in a very lucky moment: I had been numb'd, as a Maccaroni, I should have said bor'd, to death by old Dr Barry for an hour & half, so that had not You electrify'd me, I had perish'd— Your illness alarm'd me, & your scheme with Captⁿ Phipps[2] to the North Pole freezes about my heart—

    I despair of seeing you here, so that I must beat ye parade with the folks here, whose conversation lies as heavy upon my mind as the hot cakes & devilments at breakfast upon my Stomach— I have seen ye great Henderson, who has Something, & is Nothing— he might be made to figure among the puppets of these times— his Don John is a Comic Cato, & his Hamlet a mixture of Tragedy Comedy pastoral farce & nonsense— however, tho' my Wife is outrageous, I am in ye Secret, & see sparks of fire which might be blown to warm even a London Audience at Xmas— he is a dramatic Phoenomenon, & his Friends, but more particularly Cumberland has ruin'd him— he has a manner of [r]aving, when he w^d be Emphatical that is ridiculous, & must be chang'd, or he would not be suffer'd at ye Bedford Coffeehouse—

Palmer³ goes on well, & will be elected into ye Corporation, I am kissing old Women, & giving young ones ye Liberty of Drury Lane Theatre by way of Bribery & Corruption— It is the fashion, you know, for Punch to do this Business at Elections,⁴ & Palmer can't have a better— joking apart I am really become a Punch— I have gain'd two inches in the Waist, & the Girls at Night call me Fatty! I wish you had seen S^r J's play—⁵ y^r opinion would have confirm'd me— I hate this traffick wth friends.

I long to be at Gray's Memoirs—⁶ You have made me smack my lips— Mr Mason is certainly peevish, but I think there is poetry about him— when shall I devour the true Art of Poetry?⁷ I dreamt of it some Nights ago— it is a special business for your Genius & worthy of You. how like you Master Twiss?— Y^r Intelligence about the Dedication is erroneous—⁸

Mrs Garrick sends her Love to you, but says with me, that you are a false Loon, & will not see Bath this Spring.

Ever Yours most affect^y
D Garrick

all in a hurry going to ye Play—

Addressed. Seal. Source: Berg Collection; Colman, pp. 309–311.

1. The date is determined by the reference to Palmer.

2. Constantine John Phipps (1744–1792), naval captain, explorer, and politician; he was to become second Baron Mulgrave in Sept. 1775. In 1773 he had sailed north of Spitsbergen in search of a route to India.

3. John Palmer (1742–1818), son and namesake of the owner of the Theatre Royal, Bath. At this time he was managing the theater for his father, and in April 1776 he was to succeed to the proprietorship. He was up for election as a member of the Common Council at Bath on Friday, April 21, 1775 (see the following letter).

4. In March 1774 voters of Shaftesbury, Dorset, had been guilty of accepting bribes from a "Mr. Punch," who had danced for their attraction at the Lion Inn (*LC,* vol. XXXVII, March 30–April 1, 1775, p. 310).

5. Presumably Joseph Palmer's "Zaphira," submitted to Garrick by Sir Joshua Reynolds.

6. The *London Chronicle* had announced publication of "The Poems of Mr. Gray: to which are prefixed Memoirs of his Life and Writings by William Mason" in the issue of March 28–30, 1775 (XXXVII, 303).

7. Colman's translation of Horace's *Ars Poetica* was not to appear until 1783.

8. *Travels through Portugal and Spain in 1772 and 1773*, by Richard Twiss (1747–1821), F.R.S., miscellaneous writer, was published in early April of 1775 (*LC*, XXXVII, 340); the book contains no dedication.

904   To George Colman

Bath

My dear Colman   April the 20th [17]75

I have waited till this Moment to ascertain my time of leaving this place, but till my Brother George quits me the beginning of next week I shall not be able to fix ye day—

You may depend upon my staying at least ten days after ye Day you receive this, but if you cannot be here before ye End of next Week, unless y^r health requires y^r Coming, I would not wish to see you here for a few days, for that will be tantalizing me wth a vengeance, & the result will be, that I shall only have a taste of you here, & lose my meal of you in Town— I must be in London ye 18th of May, for ye fund,[1] & I am not certain whether I shall not shew myself the 9th,[2] for that is one of our days,[3] & I am afraid to take the chance of the Plays we can act without me— but of this I am not yet determin'd— Should you not have set out before George arrives in Town, which will be on thursday next, he will tell you all, If I see you here before then, I will by Jasus tell you all myself;— pray let Becket shew you the last card I received from Smith, which I shall not answer— I have some small suspicions about that business which Becket will explain— the *inflexible Captive*[4] has been play'd here wth success, & I touch'd up Mrs Didier wth an Epilogue[5] which had a good reception— Henderson play'd Regulus—[6] & you would have wish'd him bung'd up with his nails before ye End of ye 3^d act—[7]

Palmer's Election for common councilman comes on tomorrow— he has brought down L^d C[8] to insure him Success, & he will have it— what a stirring indefatigable fellow it is!

My Wife & George send their best to You, & I my best of all—

Ever & most affect^y Yours

D: Garrick

I will tell you a Secret Brother Martin[9] shall make your hair stand on End!— I believe I may engage the blood of the Lindleys!—[10] don't let one syllable of this transpire till ye deed is done!—

Addressed. Seal. Source: Berg Collection; Colman, pp. 307–309.

1. The benefit was postponed until May 25 (see Letter 908, n. 3).
2. He did not appear until the Theatrical Fund benefit.
3. That is to say, not a benefit day.
4. Hannah More's first play, acted at the Theatre Royal, Bath, April 18 (*Bath Chronicle*, April 18, 20); it had previously been given a one-night performance at Bath in Feb. 1774 (*BD*).
5. Mrs. (Du Bellamy) Didier (1741–1829), actress, was the wife of the actor J. Didier, later manager of the Theatre Royal, Richmond. In 1772 she had been engaged by Palmer, remaining at Bath until her retirement in 1806 (*Theatrical Biography*, 1772, II, 107f.; Genest, V, 312, 380, VIII, 60). For the epilogue see Knapp, No. 326.
6. The leading role.
7. Regulus had been killed by being placed in a nail-studded barrel which had then been rolled down a hill.
8. Probably Camden, for he knew Palmer (see Boaden, II, 67).
9. *The Beaux' Strategem*, III, iii.
10. Presumably Elizabeth Ann (Linley) Sheridan (1754–1792), singer, daughter of the composer Thomas Linley and wife (1773) of Richard Brinsley Sheridan. Since 1770 Garrick had unsuccessfully sought to engage her; he was to fail again in 1775, for Sheridan could not "be prevailed upon to let his wife sing" (Boaden, II, 100; see also *ibid.*, I, 488, Colman, p. 150f., Sotheby, Catalogue, June 19, 1928).

905   To Peter Fountain

Bath

Dear Sʳ   Wedʸ [April] 26 [1775][1]

I take this opportunity by my Brother to let you know that I am greatly recover'd, tho not yet without my ailings— I am sorry you have reason to complain of yʳ late Landlord, but bear yᵉ Evils, You may meet with patiently, & you'll Easily overcome them: The Case you sent me is almost unintelligible to Me, & I have No friend, Lord Camden being in Town, to Shew it to, that can be of Service at this place:

I shall be soon in London till when

         I am Dʳ Sʳ yʳ most Obed Serᵗ
         D Garrick.

Endorsements by the recipient: Ap— 1775; *and* 26th April 1771. *Source:* FC.

1. While the endorsements appear to be contradictory, the year is established by the reference to Fountain's trouble with his landlord (see Letter 879) and the month by the reference in the preceding letter to George's leaving Bath.

906   To Peter Fountain

Dear S^r   Monday May 1st [1775]
Before this You have rec'd my answer to y^r former letter— I am
sorry it is not in my Power in this place to serve the cause of y^r
friend— it is a good one, & must prevail.

My health mends daily, but all ye Symptoms of my disorder are
not vanish'd, however I live in hopes to be quite purify'd before I
reach Town— Should our Friend succeed, & I have no doubts
about it, pray rejoice with him & felicitate him in my Name upon
ye Occasion—

                              I am Dr Sr Most Sincerely Y^rs
                                        D Garrick

I am in a great hurry for Ladies are waiting for me to go to a Ball.

Address: To Mr Fountain, Maiden Lane.   *Endorsement by the recipient:* May 1,
1775.   *Source:* FC.

907   To Hannah More

                                              Bath
Dear Madam   Thursday Morn^g [May 4, 1775]^1
I take up my pen in a great hurry to let you know that the inflexible
Roman will exert his patriotism again next Saturday^2

We think with great pleasure, (in Spite of my disorder), of y^e
happy day We Spent at Bristol: Mrs Garrick adds her best Wishes
to mine, & sends them warm from her heart to You all— We begin
to think of leaving this land of Circé, where, I do this, & do that,
& do Nothing, & I go here & go there & go nowhere— Such is y^e
life of Bath & such the Effects of this place upon me— I forget my
Cares, & my large family in London, & Every thing, but that I am
Dr Mad^m

                              Your most Sincere humble Ser^t
                                        D. Garrick.

When shall I see ye Lecturer^3 again— I fear this hot weather which
ripens Cucumbers will do him no good.

Source: Society of Antiquaries, draft.

1. The date is from the deleted reference to Mrs. Keasberry's benefit.

2. *Deletion:* "for the benefit of Mrs Keasberry— I have Fix'd the Speech of Barce with ye Messenger & I believe for ye better, only by omission—." Mrs. Keasberry (1737?–1812) had been a Miss Carr, a favorite Bath actress, before her marriage to W. Keasberry, actor and later manager of the Theatre Royal (*GM*, vol. LXXXII, supplement, 1852, p. 605; Belville S. Penley, *The Bath Stage*, 1892, p. 65). *The Inflexible Captive* was played for her benefit at the Theatre Royal on May 6, 1775 (*Bath Chronicle*, May 4, 1775).

3. Possibly Thomas Sheridan, who was at this time lecturing on elocution at Bath, Bristol, and elsewhere.

908   To Frances Brooke

Adelphi

Madam.   May 15 [1775][1]

I have Obey'd Your commands; I love to oblige tho sometimes to my own inconvenience— You are pleas'd to say, You are sure that I have chang'd the Night inadvertently— indeed, Madam, I have neither made the one Change or the Other *inadvertently*, for I mean by both to be very civil, & Obliging with my Eyes open. Miss Macklin[2] has Every claim to my good Wishes and Services—[3] tho she belongs to another Theatre, She has very generously exerted herself to carry on our business, when the Ladies belonging to us would not—[4] I beg my best Compliments to Mrs Yates[5] an⟨d⟩ Your Brother[6] & I am

Dr Madam Y^r most humble Ser^t

D: Garrick.

Endorsement by Garrick: My letter to Mrs Brooke about ye Opera & agreeing to her desire. *Source:* FSL, draft; Boaden, II, 54.

1. The year is determined by the reference to the change of nights for Miss Macklin.

2. Maria Macklin (1733–1781), actress, the daughter of Charles Macklin who had carefully trained her. She had made her debut, at Drury Lane, at the age of ten, and she continued to act until 1777. Her talent was limited, but her character was above reproach (*Theatrical Biography*, 1772; James T. Kirkman, *Memoirs of the Life of Charles Macklin*, 1799, II, 309f.).

3. On May 14, 1775, Miss Macklin wrote Garrick requesting him to postpone the benefit for the Theatrical Fund from May 18 to a later date, since her benefit at Covent Garden was set for the 18th and she feared the rival attraction would reduce her proceeds (Boaden, II, 53). Garrick generously complied with this request, and the benefit for the Fund was given at Drury Lane on May 25.

4. *Deletion*: "They indeed have urg'd some kind of indisposition, but one of our best Writers has observ'd— *When the M⟨ind⟩ is truly attach'd to any thing or Per⟨son⟩ it is amazing what exertion it will g⟨ive⟩ Even to an infirm body.*"

5. Mrs. Brooke was the intimate friend of Mrs. Yates (see *GM*, vol. LVII, July 1787, p. 585f.).

6. Edward Moore (1741–1792), Receiver-General of the hackney-coach office (*GM*, vol. LXII, July 1792, p. 676).

909   To Peter Fountain

Dear Sir   Thursday. [May] 18th [1775]
I am very ⟨we⟩ak wth ye pain I suffer'd Yesterday— I am now out of Pain, which I reckon half a Cure!— I return you ye Notes you Sent— pray my best Compts to Mr Lloyd.
                                        Yours sincerely from my Couch
                                                    D Garrick

Address: To Mr Fountain, Maiden Lane, No 46.   *Endorsement by the recipient:* 18th May 1775.   *Source:* FC.

910   To Peter Fountain

                                           Fryday May 19th 1775
Much better, Dear Sir, but still Weak & ruffled— the Author of the inclos'd is yr very good Friend, & will not from Love, let You do wrong, if he can help it— such hot-pepper'd brains as Yours & Mine require a Lloyd to keep them from boiling over
                                                    Ever Yours
                                                    D. Garrick

I am sorry for Your Accident— we shall send you to Tom King at Sadler's Wells,[1] if you [*tear*] for tumbling—

Endorsement by Garrick: Mr Fountain.   *Source:* FC.

1. King had acquired Sadler's Wells in 1772 (see Edward W. Brayley, *Historical and Descriptive Accounts of the Theatres of London*, 1826, II, 53).

4*

911 To Charles Macklin

Sir   May 19th 1775

I shall be always ready to Shew my regard to Miss Macklin she has Ever behav'd in the best manner to Me— If You are engag'd to the Managers of Covent Garden, & they have fix'd You to play upon the 25 I cannot see how You can avoid performing on that Night.[1]

I am Sr Your humble Servt
D: Garrick.

Endorsement by Garrick: Mr Macklins Letter & My answer with his reply. May the 19th 1775. *Source:* FC, draft; Boaden, II, 55.

1. This is the reply to Macklin's letter, of the same date, in which he had written: "I am much obliged to you for your Civility to miss macklin in removing the Benefit for the Theatrical Fund from her night to the 25th Ins^t . . . But, unforeseen, it has so happened that you from your Kindness to miss macklin have removed the Benefit of the Fund to the 25th on which night, as by agreement, I am ordered to play . . . I request that you will give me your opinion, whether my acting on Thursday the 25th will be operative to the Prejudice of the Theatrical Fund on that night, or will make me liable to the Imputation of Ingratitude to you" (FC; Boaden, II, 54f.).

912 To Grey Cooper

Adelphi

Dear Sir   June 2^d [1775][1]

Not Rachel weeping for her Children could shew more sorrow than Mrs Garrick— not weeping for her Children for Children she has none, nor indeed for her husband for thanks to the humour of the times she can be as philosophical upon that Subject as any of her betters— What does she weep for then? Shall I dare to tell You?— it is for the loss of a Chintz bed, & curtains— the tale is short melancholly & is as follows— I have taken great pains to Oblige the Gentlemen at Calcutta by sending them plays Scenes & other little service—[2] in return they have sent me Madeira & poor Rachel this unfortunate Chintz— She has had it 4 years, & upon making some Alteration in our little place at Hampton, she intended shew^g away with her prohibited present—³ she had prepar'd paper, Chairs &c for this favourite token of East indian Gratitude— but alass, as all human felicity is frail No care having been taken on my wife's part, & some treachery being exerted against her, it was seiz'd the very bed—

> By The coarse hands of filthy Dungeon Villans,
> And thrown amongst ye smuggled lumber.⁴

If you have ye least pity for a distressed Female, any regard for her Husband, for he has a sad time of it, or any Wishes to see ye Environs of Bushy Park made tolerably neat & clean, You may put y^r thum⟨b⟩ & finger to ye business, & take ye thorn out of poor Rachel's side—

I am

I was at y^r door Yesterday, & intended waiting upon you this Morning but was prevented by my gravel complaint⁵

Source: HTC, draft, copy in Enthoven Collection; *European Magazine*, XII (Aug. 1787), 107.

1. The year is supplied by Cooper's reply of June 2, 1775, which Garrick endorsed: "my letter to Mr Cooper about Chintz & his Answer" (HTC).

2. Concerning the Calcutta theater, the *London Chronicle* for Dec. 10–13, 1774, contains this notice: "The Officers of the Companies troops, and the Gentlemen of the factory at *Calcutta*, in BENGAL, having erected a most elegant theatre for their amusement, applied to Mr. GARRICK, through their friends in England, for his assistance and advice, respecting the conduct of it: In consequence of which, he sent them over the best dramatic works in our language, together with complete setts of scenery, under the care of an ingenious young Mechanist from Drury-lane, whom he recommended to superintend that department. The theatre thus embellished, was opened to a most brilliant audience" (XXXVI, 564; see also Boaden, I, 465).

3. From a letter of April 17, 1775, written to Mrs. Garrick by a Charles Hart (apparently a servant entrusted to deal with the customhouse), it seems that Mrs. Garrick had sent the material to Thomas Chippendale, the furniture maker, where it was seized by the customs officers. Hart reported that the customs official with whom he talked could only say that if the material was from India it was "so very Strongly prohibited that if the King Was to Send his Signmanul down they could not Deliver it" (Little Collection).

4. *Venice Preserv'd,* I, i. "Common," the next to the last word in the quotation, has been crossed out and "smuggled" substituted.

5. The last two words are deleted and the phrase "plaguy disorder" written in by an unknown hand.

913   To Elizabeth Griffith

Adelphi

Dear Madam   June 3. 1775

The breaking up of the Company for the Summer,[1] & the hurry of settling our affairs prevented my answering your Letter[2] sooner— indeed, my dear Madam, it will not be in my power to follow my inclinations and oblige you: the business at the Theatre is grown too mighty for me, & I shall retreat from it with all good speed— Mrs Lenox[3] who was so unfortunate at Covent Garden Theatre, put into my hand last Year an alterd play,[4] which upon my honour, I have not yet had leisure to consider as I ought— another Lady of great merit has likewise intrusted me with a performance of 5 Acts,[5] which I must immediately look over, with all the care and delicacy due to her Sex & her talents— these matters with my other necessary business will, I protest to you most Solemnly, engage more time than I can possibly spare in the present precarious situation of my health— If, notwithstanding what I have said, any plays to be imitated from the french, or reviv'd from our Old Stock, should appear to me, worthy of your notice, I will give you immediate intelligence, & shall be very happy to convince you, that I am

Dr Madam Your most Obed^t Hum Servt

D Garrick

P. S. Upon my word I have reced no french play or old English one of late that I think will bear transplanting or reviving upon our Stage.

Endorsement with address: To Mrs Griffiths, Hyde Street, Bloomsbury.   *Source:* FC, copy; Boaden, II, 567.

1. The season had ended on May 27.
2. Of May 30, requesting "a hint of any subject . . . suited to the Theatre" (FC; Boaden, II, 56).
3. Mrs. Charlotte Lennox (1720–1804), miscellaneous writer. Her comedy *The Sister* (CG, Feb. 18, 1769) had unfairly been damned on its first night.
4. Probably her comedy *Old City Manners* (DL, Nov. 9), an alteration of Jonson, Chapman, and Marston's *Eastward Hoe* (but see also Boaden, I, 647).
5. Perhaps Mrs. Cowley's comedy *The Runaway* (DL, Feb. 15, 1776),

914   To Jane Pope

Adelphi
June 3ᵈ 1775

The proprietors of the Theatre royal in Drury Lane present their
Compliments to Miss Pope, & hope she has no Objection to continue her Engagement with them for three Years more, or as long
as she pleases.

D Garrick.

Address: To Miss Pope.   *Source:* FSL; Boaden, II, 57.

915   To Grey Cooper

My dear Sir   June the 5ᵗʰ 1775
Let me return You my best thanks, for your best Endeavors in my
Wife's business—[1] as You mention'd Your application to my
worthy friend Mʳ Stanley,[2] I have had the presumption to back it
with a few doggrl Verses— Montaigne Observes that some Men
are sooner tickled than reason'd into kindness— I have try'd to
draw my feather under the Secretary's Nose, in hopes that it will
soften the rigour of his Advice to the honourable Board: as I would
not do any thing in this matter without your knowledge, I have
inclos'd yᵉ Feather wᵗʰ wᶜʰ I have try'd yᵉ Experiment— if amidst
the Truths & Lies that are daily arizing about American affairs,
my Nonsense can steal You a few minutes from yʳ Cares I shall have
my desire— for there is no one wishes more warmly & Sincerely,
& can do so little, for yᵉ Cause as
My dear Sir Most faithfully & gratefully Yours
D Garrick

The Petition of D:G: to his Friend
E: Stanley Esqʳ in behalf of his Afflicted Wife

—Earthly Pow'r doth then shew likest God's
When Mercy seasons Justice. (Shakespear).[3]
O Stanley give ear to a Husband's Petition,   ⎫
Whose Wife well deserves her distresful condition, ⎬
Regardless of his, & the Law's prohibition.   ⎭
If You knew what I suffer, since she has been caught,

(On the Husband's poor head ever falls the Wife's fault)
You would lend a kind hand to the Contraband Jade,
And screen her for once in her illicit trade:
'Tis true, as 'tis sad, since the first Eve undid 'Em,
Frail women will long for the Fruit that's forbid 'Em;
And Husbands are taught now a days spite of struggles,
Politely to pardon a Wife, tho she *smuggles*:
If their Honors & You, when the Sex go astray,   ⎫
Have sometimes inclin'd to go wth 'Em that way, ⎬
We hope to *her* Wishes you will not say nay;   ⎭
'Tis said, that all Judges this Maxim should keep,
Not their Justice to tire, but at times let it sleep;
If more by the Scriptures, their Honors are mov'd,
The *Overmuch Righteous* are there disapprov'd;
Thus true to the Gospel, & kind as they're wise,
Let their *Mercy* restore, what their Justice denies.

D G.

Endorsement by Garrick: June 5th 1775 my letter to Mr Cooper wth my petition to Mr Stanley Secretary of the Customs.   *Source:* FSL, copy of verses in Garrick's hand, Yale University Library; *European Magazine*, XII (Aug. 1787), 107f.

1. In reply to Letter 912, Cooper wrote on June 2: "I have . . . sent a Supplication to my friend Stanley, the best humoured, (tho diligent & active) secretary that ever was at that board, to use his best offices to prevail with the Harpies to come into a reasonable Composition for the restitution of the Chintz & yet the Linnen drapers and Cotton Printers & all that Cursed Bourgeoisie, I fear will be as powerfull as they merciless. But let Mrs Garrick be assured that all that the Secular arm can do shall be done" (*European Magazine*, vol. XII, Aug. 1787, p. 107).

2. Edward Stanley (d. 1789), of Ponsonby Hall, Cumberland, Secretary to the Commissioners of the Customs.

3. *The Merchant of Venice*, IV, i, 196f.

916   To Peter Fountain

D^r S^r   Thursday [June] 8 [1775]
George is so ill, that my Mind can attend to Nothing till he is better— I shall do Myself ye Pleasure of attend^g You ye Moment he is out of Danger.

Y^{rs} most truly
D Garrick

Endorsement by the recipient: June 1775.   *Source:* FC.

917   To Jane Pope

Adelphi
June 9th 1775

Mr Garrick's Comp^{ts} to Miss Pope— his Brother's great danger for these four days has prevented his attending to any business— the Patentees sincerely wish that Miss Pope would have no Objection to continue her present Agreement wth them: they should be very sorry to lose her, & hope that they may depend upon her being at Drury Lane for many Years to come— Should Miss Pope be induc'd to quit her present Situation, they shall expect an answer in the Course of next Week, as her place will be with great difficulty supply'd— If they have no Answer to this, they shall depend upon her continuing with them— they not only Acknowledge her diligence, but her Merit.

Source: Bodleian Library, copy in FC; Boaden, II, 58.

918   To Jane Pope

June the 12th 1775

The Patentees, with their best wishes to Miss Pope, feel as much regret in losing her, as she can possibly do in quitting them. Tho They cannot agree to the addition, wch she insists upon to her present salary: they assure her that they part on the terms of friendship she desires; they wish her Every happiness that her change of place & Sentiments can give her; at the same time, they beg leave to Observe, that if Mr Garrick would have agreed to let Mrs Barry perform Beatrice & Clarinda,[1] & Mr Barry to have had for his Benefit, the day which he gave last year to Miss Pope[2] they should not have lost those capital performers— Mr Garrick takes no merit to himself in having done this, but that of shewing a little more than *Swiss attachment*[3] to Miss Pope—

Source: FC, draft; Boaden, II, 59.

1. Two of Miss Pope's parts.
2. March 21.
3. An allusion to Miss Pope's statement, in a letter of June 10, that she was "determin'd at length to shake all affection off, & like the Swiss to perform only with those that pay the best" (FC; Boaden, II, 58).

919　　　To Arabella Garrick

Mistley

Dear Bell.　　　　　　　　　　　　　Monday June the 26 [1775][1]

Your letter[2] is so properly written, with such a feeling of yr Situation, a true compunction for the cause of it, & a resolution to take Warning for ye future, that I will forgive You, never upbraid You again with the distress you have brought upon Us, & yrself, provided that You will Shew Your gratitude, by telling Every circumstance of this unhappy affair,[3] that I may be ye better able to deliver you from ye villain,[4] & that hereafter You will let Your good Sense & delicacy combat with Your passions, & not involve Yourself & family in ye greatest Affliction by another unwarrantable, indecent & ruinous Connection— indeed, my dear Girl, I cannot Account for Your rash & almost incredible behaviour— you seem'd to have lost ye Greatest ornaments, & safeguards of yr Sex— *delicacy* & *Apprehension*— When that great barrier that Nature has cautiously fix'd between passion & prudence is so easily overleap'd, Even by *our* Sex, we see the daily ill Consequences— but when *yr* Sex, is possess'd with such a Madness, the horror that attends it, is best describ'd, by ye Number of the most miserable Wretches that have fall'n a Sacrifice to their imprudence. but we will now look forward, I will treat you with fatherly kindness, & you must return it with an unbounded confidence on yr Side, write & talk to me with an open friendly freedom, be greatly asham'd of yr past Conduct, but let yr confession to Me be as sincere as Your Sorrow— Thus taking Warning & learning Experience from Misfortune You will be happier & wiser for ye future: but should You Ever again relapse, then let me tell You my dear, that the same generous Mind which has now so readily forgiven you, & will warmly exert itself for Your happiness, must then be for Ever irrecoverably lost to You.

I am my dear Girl most affecty yrs

Yr Aunt joins with me in Love to both— pray send me a full state of this Matter, that I may be better able to cope wth him & his

friends— He says You are violently in Love with him, that you will
be unhappy without him— is this true— is not he near fifty & very
plain? *good God!* have you not met him Somewhere unknown to
Mrs Descombes? & was not he the Person You told me in one of
y^r letters was a painter, who knew me, & was wth you upon some
Water Party?— pray let me know— You'll receive this tomorrow
Tuesday, answer it, & put y^r lett^r in ye post on *Wed^y* or *Thursday*
Night

Source: FC, draft; Hedgcock, p. 387f. (in part).

1. The year is indicated by Arabella's reply of June 28, 1775 (FC).
2. Of June 24 (FC). Mme Descombes had accompanied Arabella and her sister to
London and alone on June 24 called upon the Garricks at the Adelphi to report. It was
on that same afternoon that Arabella wrote: "I am sure did you but know, or even
concieve, half the pains, and troubles, that are lock'd up in my bosom, far from aban-
doning me as you threaten, you would give me all the Assistance in your power . . . After
so many proofs of your Affection and goodness, shall I find you inflexible in the most
important Moment. Do Sir put an end to this thing, you see it is in your power; Act
as Nature and your natural propensity to do good direct you, and not according to *my*
deserts In the mean time, I hope I need not assure you of my total Obedience and Sub-
mission to all your commands, Dear Sir, shut me up for ever, rather than abandon me,
and cease for heavens sake to load me with your curses, I have many more ills than I can
bear, ease me of one, which outweighs all the rest; that is, your hatred."
3. In her long letter of June 28 Arabella unreservedly complied with this request:
In Mme Descombes' house lodged one Molière, professedly as "an Officer who having
had an Affair of honor, and having wounded his antagonist was obliged to conceal
himself." He courted Arabella first in the halls and later by letters, always professing his
desire to abide by her wishes and communicate with her family. When Mme Descombes
intercepted a letter, they ceased all communication except for a final exchange when
he asked permission to follow her to England and she refused. "His behaviour ever since
has been inconsistent with reason, or honor; since I find he has not only put what really
did pass between us, in the most favorable disposition (that is) for himself; but has added
to it the grossest falsehoods . . . I am not surprized to find that he says I am violently in
love with him, and can't live without him; judge of the truth of it, when I tell you, that
after the untruths and shamefull reports he has rais'd about me; were he everything
that is aimiable, had a scepter to offer me, and to crown all had *your encouragement*, I
would not accept of him."
4. Molière (d. *ca.* 1793) seems to have been a subordinate officer of dragoons in the
Légion de Corse, and was, according to Arabella's letter of June 28, 1775, a man of
about thirty-five years. In a letter to Arabella of July 26, 1775, he was to attempt to
renew his suit (Hedgcock, p. 389f.).

920   To The Duke of Northumberland?[1]

Mistley

My Lord   June ye 26 [1775?][2]

However innocent I might be of It's impropriety, yet it gave me great uneasiness that I should ask a favour,[3] which was so generously granted, that Seems to carry with it a due attention on my part: let me assure Your Grace, that I am very incapable of making an ill use of y[r] flattering partiality to me— I shall represent the circumstance to M[r] Bate in the best manner I am able, & I trust in his good Sense to be well Satisfy'd with it— in this & upon Every other Occasion, I shall be proud & happy to Obey Your Grace's Commands

I am my Lord Y[r] Grace's most Obed[t] & Oblig'd

humble ser[t]

D:G.

Source: Garrick Club, draft, copy in FC, copy in HTC.

1. The recipient is conjecturally identified as Northumberland on the assumption that the favor mentioned here and in Letter 929 is the subject of Bate's letter to the Duke of Aug. 4, 1775 (FSL).

2. The conjectural year is indicated by Bate's letter.

3. Apparently Garrick had solicited Northumberland, Lord-Lieutenant of Middlesex, for some office in the county for Bate, and the Duke had promised a commissionership of the peace. Subsequently, however, for reasons unknown, Northumberland was unable to make the appointment and Bate, who had, according to his letter of Aug. 4, "made no secret of declaring the honor . . . intended," found himself in an "indelicate situation" (FSL).

921   To William Brereton[1]

Sir.   [*ante* June 29, 1775][2]

I return'd this Evening from M[r] Rigby's & found y[r] Letter upon my table—

Had you signify'd y[r] inclination to quit Drury Lane at the time of y[r] going for Ireland, I should have no right to complain, but I think it ungenteel not to let me know y[r] proposal before I went into Essex y[e] Debts of y[e] Company were produc'd at y[e] Office, & a proposal made to write to Each Person who was in debt to yᵉ Office— I stop'd 'Em from writing to You because I intended to raise Yʳ Salary even for yᵉ last Season & take it from yʳ debt— with regard to yʳ proposal for yʳ future Salary I will not agree to it— I will make up yʳ Salary four pounds for yᵉ last Season— five & five for yᵉ two next & Six for the third— as for Parts you must rely upon my Judgment & Justice— If you prefer yʳ Situation in Ireland to that I propose to you, I wish you Joy of it, & will supply yʳ place at least as long as I am Manager, in yᵉ best manner I am able

I am yʳˢ

Endorsement: Answer of Mʳ Garrick to an application from an Actor—.
Source: FC, draft.

1. William Brereton (1741–1787) was the son of a Master of Ceremonies at Bath. Under Garrick's tutelage he had made his debut at Drury Lane on Nov. 10, 1768.
2. This is the reply to Brereton's letter of June 24, written from Dublin; Brereton in turn replied on July 10, 1775 (Boaden, I, 638f., II, 67). In 1775 Garrick was at Mistley on June 26, and in London again by June 29.

922   To Richard? Lancake[1]

London
Sir.   June 29ᵗʰ 1775
Let me thank You most sincerely for your kind intentions to me & mine: as I have not the honor of knowing or corresponding with the Marquis de lace D'Arcambal,[2] I beg leave to send my answer to You.

Mʳ Moliere a french Gentleman who declares *his first attempt shall be to obtain the consent of her relations*, has endeavor'd to gain the affections of [a] young English Girl at school, without the least knowledge of her friends here, or her Gouvernance in France, and desires, without any lucrative view (& so it must indeed for she has not a Shilling) to marry her, to make them both miserable! The proposal is as romantic, as it is ruinous:

If she expects any proofs of affection from me, it must be when *my* inclinations agree with hers, & that it shall be *my* opinion that so serious a connection will be attended with a probability of happiness on both sides. On the other hand, let me freely confess to you, that I am surprised a Man of honor & Character, should expose the letters of a Young, Simple Creature,[3] whose Passions have been very unjustifiably worked upon, & whose imprudence has thrown her into dangers, which her innocense & inexperience could not have foreseen— This has the more astonished me, as I'm told that M[r] Moliere is old enough to be her Father.

Such conduct in this Country is looked upon in a very different light, & all the satisfaction that can arise to him from this strange affair, is that he has thrown her Father into a very dangerous illness, made her Relations very unhappy & perhaps distroy'd the Girls peace & happiness for ever: if my Niece sees M[r] Moliere's conduct to her, as She ought, & as I believe she does; I will Sincerely restore her to my love, & will, if she exerts a proper Spirit of mind upon y[e] occasion, endeavor to counteract all those Evils, that this very unfortunate affair might otherwise bring upon her.

I am Sir Your most oblig'd & most Obedient humble Serv[t]

D Garrick.

PS: to be more explicit, as my consent is in a manner asked, I never *will*, or *can* give it upon this Occasion.

Source: FC, copy; Little, p. 7of.

1. "R[d] Lancake," according to his letter to Garrick from Paris on June 18, 1775, to which this is the reply, had first reported on the relations between Arabella and Molière through Monnet. Later, at Molière's request, the "Marquis des Lacs d'Arcambal" called on Lancake to report that "Moliere is an Officer who has long serv'd in his [d'Arcambal's] Regiment, is particularly esteem'd by himself, and generally belov'd— that from his earliest attachment to Miss Garrick, he has inform'd him of his real affection— declaring his first attempt shou'd be to Obtain the Consent of her relations, from whom he had no lucrative wish— The Marquis after proper encomiums on disinterested love, wisely hinted the Necessity of fortune's aiding the advancement of a Soldier," Lancake in reply assuring him that Miss Garrick was entirely dependent on her uncle. When Lancake returned the call, the Marquis asked that Garrick write him either directly or through Lancake (FC).

2. Of the military members of the des Lacs d'Arcambal family recorded in the *Dictionnaire de la noblesse*, it is impossible to determine which one had interested himself in Molière (see *Dictionnaire*, Paris, 1863–1877, XI, 248, 249, XV, 578).

3. Apparently Garrick sought Monnet's assistance in recovering these letters, but was advised to forget the whole affair (see Monnet's letters of July 10 and Aug. 24, 1775, FC).

923　　　To Frances Abington

July 1st 1775

Mr. Garrick presents his best compliments to Mrs. Abington, and she may depend upon his doing his best to give her piece[1] success. Had the author vouchsafed to have communicated with Mr. G the matter would have been better managed.

Source: Boaden, II, 29.

1. Presumably *The Sultan* by Bickerstaffe, who was then living abroad in disgrace, for which Mrs. Abington had assumed the responsibility (Hopkins, Diary, *DLC*, p. 192). She had written Garrick in her letter of June 29 that "I am very certain that a few of your Nice Touches, with a Little of your fine Polish will give it that Stamp of Merit as Must Secure it a reception with the Publick Equal the warmest of my Expectations" (FC; Boaden, II, 29).

924　　　To Herbert? Lawrence

Adelphi

Sir　　　　　　　　　　　　　　　　　　July 14 [1775?][1]

Many thanks to You for Your civility & good Offices about the Young Adventurer of ye Buskin—[2]

I long to taste for Myself— tho I have great reliance upon yr Experience & my Brother's in these Matters, yet I wish to see & hear him with my own Eyes & Ears— if You are not too Sanguine (from yr knowledge of ye Young Man, or from ye fairness of his private Character) by Your Account I shall be Able to make the Men Stare, & the Ladies cry at him, but still Mr Lawrence I must repeat, that I chuse to be my own Caterer, for according to the old proverb — one Man's meat is another Man's poyson—

I really don't believe that it will be the Case here in this instance— but Still according to another proverb— Seeing's believing, but tasting is better— I hope You & my Brother will propose Some Means of my hearing this Young Man, if he has talents I will foster 'Em provided that his behaviour answers half of yr Encomium. Waiting for more intelligence from You & George

I am Sr very much Yr Well Wisher & huml Sert

D: Garrick.

Source: FSL; *The Era*, June 3, 1877.

1. The conjectural year is dependent on the identification and first appearance of the "Young Adventurer."

2. Identified in a penciled marginal note as Grist; presumably Thomas Grist (d. 1808) of Nottingham, who "made his first Appearance upon any Stage [DL, Oct. 17, 1775] in the Character of Othello" (Hopkins, Diary, *DLC*, p. 189). He did not come up to expectations, and after two seasons at Drury Lane spent the rest of his career in the provincial theaters (*GM*, vol. LXXVIII, Nov. 1808, p. 1045). On Jan. 25, 1776, Grist wrote to Garrick from Norwich asking for a recommendation to the new managers of Drury Lane, and on April 15, 1776, he wrote to acknowledge Garrick's assistance (FC).

925   To George Colman

Adelphi

My dear friend   [July] 25 [1775][1]

We wanted you much at the Election to day— Foote in great Spirits but bitter against the L^d Ch[amberlai]^n— he will bully 'Em into a License—[2] ye D[uche]ss[3] has had him in her Closet, & offer'd to bribe him— but Cato himself tho he had one Leg more than our friend, was not more stoically virtuous than he has been—[4] you shall know all when I see You— We will most certainly attend you on *Tuesday next*— it is scarce possible for me to refuse dining with you any where but wth Mr Baldwin— I will not Ever again attend those meetings, tho I have been very happy among my friends there—

I have been insulted greatly— first to have a Paper, in which I have a property,[5] abuse me for puffing myself, & then I am suppos'd the Author of a paragraph, or letter in ye Morn^g Chronicle,[6] which the Printer himself almost avows, & which by my honor, I never heard of till you mention'd it to me:

I have done my Share to ye paper, nay I have told that worthy Gentleman Mr Baldwin, that I would look out things whenever he was in want of Nonsense— but I give ye matter up now, & as he may be assur'd I will trouble myself no more about it, he may abuse me as fast as he pleases— I don't expect mercy from such Gentry for past Services. This you may say or read as you please—

I long for y^e *Saucy Gentleman*[7] Becket will let me have it, as soon as he can.

Yours in great haste— your Servt waiting at ye door.

Ever & most affect^y Yours

D: Garrick.

damn ye pen.

Source: Berg Collection; Colman, pp. 316–318.

1. In the Harvard College Library copy of the *Posthumous Letters* the month and year have been added in longhand, presumably by the younger Colman. These additions are verified by the references to "The Gentleman" and *A Trip to Calais*.

2. His comedy *A Trip to Calais* (published in 1778), satirizing the exploits of the notorious Duchess of Kingston, had, at her complaint, been refused a license by the Earl of Hertford, the Lord Chamberlain (see Foote's letter in *LC*, vol. XXXVIII, Aug. 1–3, 1775, p. 120). The play was later brought out as *The Capuchin* (HM, Aug. 19, 1776).

3. Elizabeth Chudleigh, Countess of Bristol and sometime Duchess of Kingston, in May 1775 had been indicted for bigamy, having become the wife of Kingston while still secretly married to Bristol (see Walpole, ed. Toynbee, IX, 227).

4. Walpole repeats this story in a letter of Aug. 7, 1775 (*ibid.*, IX, 228f.).

5. Presumably the *St. James's Chronicle*, published by Baldwin.

6. References to Garrick had appeared in that paper on June 23 and July 12.

7. Apparently the third in the series of six essays by Colman, called "The Gentleman," which was to be printed in the *London Packet* on July 26, 1775.

926   To The Reverend Henry Bate

Hampton

Dear Bate.   July 31 1775

If You pass by Cheltenham in Your Way to Worcester, I wish you would see an Actress there, a *Mrs Siddon's*,[1] She has a desire I hear to try her Fortune with Us; if she seems in Your Eyes worthy of being transplanted, pray desire to know upon what conditions She would make ye Tryal, & I will write to her the post after I receive Your Letter— pray our Compliments to Your Lady,[2] & accept of our warmest Wishes for an Agreeable Journey, & safe return to London

Yours my dear Sr Most Sincerely
D: Garrick.

Address: Revd Mr Bate.   Seal.   Source: FSL; *Morning Post*, Aug. 27, 1823.

1. Sarah (Kemble) Siddons (1755–1831) whose father Roger Kemble, a provincial actor and manager, reared her along with her famous brothers in the profession of acting. Upon her marriage in 1773 to William Siddons, a young actor, she began appearing in various provincial theaters, until in June 1775, according to Mrs. Siddons, "Mr King by order of Mr Garrick who had heard some account of me . . . came to Cheltenham to see me act the Fair Penitent" and returned a favorable report (*The Reminiscences of Sarah Kemble Siddons, 1773–1785*, ed. William Van Lennep, Cambridge, 1942, p. 4; Mrs. Clement Parsons, *The Incomparable Siddons*, 1909, pp. 18, 20). Garrick also sought Bate's advice, and on his recommendation engaged her at Drury Lane for the season of 1775–76.

Between illness and immaturity her performances did not come up to expectation, and she was not reëngaged until 1782 when she entered upon her long and almost phenomenally successful London career.

2. On Sept. 9, 1773, Bate had married Mary, daughter of James White of Barrow, Somersetshire (*Bath Chronicle*).

927   To The Duke of Newcastle

London
My Lord,   Aug't 2. 177[5][1]
I had the honor of receiving your Grace's note, and tho' Mrs Garrick had intended to give me a holiday and to withdraw herself next Wednesday, that I might be the merrier, yet the honor of attending Lady Lincoln[3] is too flattering not to occasion an immediate change of measures— Mrs Garrick will most certainly be ready to wait upon her Ladyship and I shall very willingly give up the advantages of my Wife's absence for the honor of paying my respects, to Lady Lincoln.

I am my Lord Your Grace's most obliged and
Obedient humble Serv't
D. Garrick

Endorsement: Letter to the Duke of Newcastle.   *Source:* FC, copy.

1. The year 1773 given on Newcastle's letter of Aug. 2 and on this letter, which is Garrick's reply, is corrected to 1775 by Newcastle's reference to Lord and Lady Lincoln.
2. Newcastle had written on Aug. 2: "Lord & Lady Lincoln are returned from Brightelmstone and if Mrs Garrick will be at Hampton [next Wednesday] they will be of the party, provided M^r & Mrs Garrick will promise to dine with them next day at Oatlands" (FC; see also Boaden, II, 69). Oatlands lay above Hampton Court, on the Surrey side of the river. Frances Seymour Conway (1751–1820), daughter of the Earl of Hertford, had married Newcastle's second son and eventual heir, Henry Fiennes Pelham Clinton (1750–1778), styled Lord Lincoln (1752), on May 21, 1775.

928   To George Colman

My dear Colman,—   Monday [?August 7, 1775][1]
D—n all tragedies, the modern ones I mean, they are such mill-made matters that I sick at ye sight of 'em, however I shall read

that you have sent me with great care, but if it were Shakespeare's,
I could not perform it next Season, nor can I give a judgement on
it till next Fryday . . .² Dʳ Butler³ is with me, and I write upon
[yᵉ] Gallop.

Source: Puttick & Simpson, Catalogue, July 15, 1853, extract.

1. This letter was conjecturally written on the Monday before the Garricks' visit to
Oatlands on Thursday, Aug. 10, 1775 (see n. 2 and the preceding letter).
2. According to the source, Garrick here "alludes to his going to meet Lord [George
Augustus, 1759–1827] Herbert and Lady Pembroke [Elizabeth Spencer, 1737–1831, wife of
the tenth Earl] and that they have a feast, and then is going to Oatlands."
3. Presumably John Butler (1717–1802), D.C.L. 1752, who at this time was Arch-
deacon of Surrey; he was later to be Bishop of Oxford and then of Hereford.

929 To The Reverend Doctor Thomas Percy

Hampton

Dear Sir   Tuesday Night [?August 8, 1775]¹
I have made the Person, as Easy as such a disappointment can
make him— His Grace's letter was so proper & sensible that it left
my Skill very little to do— had I seen the church militant before,
You should have heard from me sooner— I hope there will be no
more be said upon the subject to make Mʳ B—— uneasy
                    I am Dʳ Sʳ very truly yʳ humble Servᵗ
                                        D: Garrick

Address: The Revᵈ Dʳ Percy, Northumberland House.   *Source:* Garrick Club.

1. The assumption that this and Letters 920 and 932 all refer to the same affair and
that B—— is to be identified as Bate is supported by the fact that Percy was chaplain
to the Duke of Northumberland, at whose house he usually stayed when in London.
Accepting the above assumption, this letter was presumably written on the Tuesday
following Bate's letter of Aug. 4, 1775, to Northumberland (FSL; see Letter 920, n. 3)
protesting his disappointment and before his letter to Garrick of Aug. 12, 1775, accepting
the situation (see Letter 932).

930   To William Brereton

Hampton

Sir   Aug[t] 9th 1775

The Spirit of your last Letter[1] is so very different from your former one[2] that I am oblig'd to say a few words to you, which shall be the last you shall ever be troubled with from me— had I not seen your Name at the bottom of your Letter, and known your hand writing, I could never have imagin'd that such a Letter could have come from You;

You write me word that you are offer'd Seven pounds a Week to stay in Ireland, But if I will give You Six, You had rather return to me, for whom You have the greatest regard, & what not—[3] You desire me to send a speedy Answer, because You are press'd for an Engagement, & you will wait my Answer. I write directly, & make You an Offer of what falls a Trifle short of your demand, with a hint at your Quaker,[4] to oblige You as much as possible— To this You Reply— in y[e] warm Spirit of Gratitude, *that You are amply Content with my very generous Conduct to you &c &c &c* and that I may depend upon You— Upon this I rested assur'd of You.— But behold another Letter comes, which tells me— what?— that You had Sign'd Articles with M[r] Barry before your Offer to me, and that You can't be at Liberty to fulfill your Engagement to Me: and this You tell me in an Angry Manner, *that You conceiv'd You gave me a very substantial proof of your valuing my favour infinitely more than raising your Salary &c &c*

It must first be known what advantages You *will* gain, & what lose— I will venture to fore tell, that You have lost the very Critical time of your Theatrical Life, and that you will sorely repent Your unkind, I had very nearly said, Ungrateful Behaviour to me: What! does M[r] Brereton (To whom, & to whose Family I have Shewn the most immoveable Attachment) offer me his Services after having Engag'd them to another?— This Sir, I did not expect from *You* of all Men— & I will even continue my open Behaviour to You, and Assure You that it is impossible that You can ever be engag'd with *me* again— I wish you no harm, but hope when you meet with a better Friend of a Manager that you will treat him more kindly

I am Sir Your humble Servant

D Garrick.

I cannot give a hundred pounds for Your Farce—[5]

What do you mean by *Chicane*?[6] I accus'd You of None, I only told You that I heard (from a Friend of Yours) You had put your Engagement to Barry in the Papers— but what Chicane was there in that— Your own Letters Confirm that You *were* engag'd, & the papers said *True*.

Endorsement with address: Copy To Mr Brereton at The Theatre in Cork Ireland. *Source:* FC, copy; Boaden, II, 73.

1. Of July 30 (Boaden, II, 70).
2. Of July 10 (*ibid.*, II, 67).
3. In a letter of June 24 (*ibid.*, I, 638).
4. Brereton had purchased Dibdin's *The Quaker*. "The general price for a piece of that description, was a hundred pounds; but he offered me seventy, reserving a right to part with it to the theatre, if he could prevail on the managers to buy it at a better price" (Charles C. Dibdin, *The Professional Life of Mr. Dibdin*, 1803, I, 145). Brereton had offered the piece to Garrick to help reduce his debt to the manager (Boaden, II, 67). There is no "hint at" *The Quaker* in the draft of Garrick's earlier letter to Brereton (Letter 921).
5. Garrick, however, did buy *The Quaker* for £100 (Dibdin, *Professional Life*, I, 146).
6. In his letter of July 30 Brereton wrote: "I never cou'd be guilty of such low chicane as to send any thing relative to myself to the newspapers and am very much concern'd that you cou'd entertain such an opinion of me" (FC; Boaden, II, 70).

931   To John Moody

August 11th 1775

Thank You, Dear Moody, for Your Letter— I have been much Shock'd twice this Summer with the Deaths of poor Atkins,[1] a very good Man, & poor Keene—[2] You say Nothing of *Shuter*, so I suppose he is recover'd,[3] the Accounts of him here were dreadful— As *King* &c have very willingly given up a few parts to Yates,[4] that he may not Eat ye Bread of Idleness, I hope You will not pout a Moment at my desiring You to give up *Ben* in Love for Love & Strengthen ye Play by doing Sr *Sampson*:[5] Those Actors who I know are attach'd to me & Mine, I Either talk with or write to myself in this friendly Manner— Should Mr Yates (which is not impossible) quit us,[6] You may depend upon having y^r Choice of Either of those I have mention'd— this is ye only part which I can recollect, y^t he in ye least interferes wth You— have You Ever heard of Mrs *Siddons* who is Stroling about somewhere near You?

Drury Lane Theatre will delight y^r Eyes, when You cast them upon the Old Lady—[7] Miss Pope has left us, as she says, *like a*

Swiss for better pay— but we don't know where— Mr Brereton has play'd me a whimsical trick— he had agreed with me, thank'd me for my most generous behaviour to me, & yet wrote me word Yesterday, that he had sign'd Articles with Barry, before he offer'd himself to me, & he cannot get releas'd from them— What comical times these are Master Moody!—

Yours Ever & most Sincerely
D Garrick

George is much recover'd. all in a hurry & the post-man stands ringing, like Mrs Oakly,[8] to let me know he is impatient & that I must not read my letter over,— so take it with all its hurry scurry.

Address: Mr Moody at the Theatre, Liverpool. *Postmarked.* *Source:* FSL.

1. Atkins, a "principal dancer" at Drury Lane had died in London on July 29 (*LC*, vol. XXXVIII, Aug. 1–3, 1775, p. 115).

2. No record of his death has been found. A Keen's name appears in the Drury Lane playbills from 1765–1775.

3. Moody, in his reply to this letter, wrote that "Shuter is a deplorable object! but I think he gets better notwithstanding his calamity. He is very profligate and wicked; he has been but once on the stage these six weeks" (Boaden, II, 75). According to the *London Chronicle* for Aug. 24, Shuter had left Liverpool "to perform a few nights at York."

4. Although Yates had been acting for nearly forty years, he was reëngaged at Drury Lane more for his wife than himself, and he appeared less and less frequently.

5. In his reply to this letter on Aug. 16 Moody wrote that he was "very unhappy to find . . . that any character of mine should be given to Mr. Yates, who . . . is not a better actor, however fortunate he may be to have a better income. I have gone through every stage of your business with great cheerfulness, since that gentleman meanly left you; and I think it very hard to give him up my honest-earned laurels without a recompense" (Boaden, II, 75). Ben, in Congreve's *Love for Love*, had been one of Yates's roles when he had previously been at Drury Lane. The play, however, was not to be produced again under Garrick's management.

6. Yates, however, remained at Drury Lane until 1780.

7. "The house has been quite altered since last Season, and is now fitted up in the most elegant Manner possible by the Adams's &c.— and is the compleatest Theatre in Europe" (Hopkins, Diary, *DLC*, p. 188).

8. In the *Jealous Wife*, who is always impatient.

932 To The Reverend Henry Bate

Hampton

Dear Bate,   August 15, 1775
Ten thousand thanks for your very clear, agreeable, and friendly letter; it pleased me much, and whoever calls it *a jargon of un-*

intelligible stuff,[1] should be knocked down if I were near him. I must desire you to secure the lady[2] with my best compliments, and that she may depend upon every reasonable and friendly encouragement in my power; at the same time, you must intimate to the husband,[3] that he must be satisfy'd with *the state of life in which it has pleased Heaven to call her.* You see how much I think myself obliged to your kind offices, by the flattering quotations I make from your *own* book. Your account of the *big belly*[4] alarms me!— when shall we be in shapes again? how long does the lady count?[5] when will she be able to appear? Pray compleat your good offices, and let me know all we are to trust. Should not you get some memorandum signed by her and her husband, and of which I will send a fac-simile copy to them, under frank, if you will let me know their address.

I laughed at the military stratagems of the Covent Garden Generals,[6] whilst I had your genius to oppose them. If she has merit (and I am sure by your letter she must have)[7] and will be wholly governed by me, I will make her theatrical fortune; if any lady begins to play at tricks, I will immediately play off my masked battery of Siddons against her. I should be glad to know her cast of parts, or rather what parts she has done, and in what she likes herself best—[8] those I would have mark'd, and above all, my dear Farmer,[9] let me know at what time she may reckon to lye-in, that we may reckon accordingly upon her appearance in Drury-lane. I repeat this to you, because it is of the utmost consequence.

Pray let me hear from you again in answer to this. I make no compliments or excuses to you for the trouble I give you, because I feel by myself that you take pleasure in obliging me.

I am, dear Farmer, most sincerely yours,
D. Garrick.

Mrs. Garrick joins with me in every good wish for you and your Lady.

Address: Rev. Mr. Bate, Hop-Pole, Worcester.   *Source: Morning Post,* August 27, 1823.

1. See the end of Bate's letter from Worcester of Aug. 12, 1775 (BM).
2. Mrs. Siddons.
3. William Siddons (d. 1805), actor, first played with Sarah Kemble at Worcester in 1767. After their marriage in Dec. 1773 his fortunes declined as hers rose. Eventually, in ill health, he retired to Bath where he lived until his death.
4. Mrs. Siddons was pregnant.
5. Bate, in his reply of Aug. 19, reported that the child was expected in early

December, and suggested that until Mrs. Siddons was able to appear on the Drury Lane stage Garrick support her and her family somewhere in the country (BM).

6. An allusion to Bate's warning that "some of the Covent Garden Mohawks were intrench'd near the place, & intended carrying her by surprize" (letter of Aug. 12). Apparently Mrs. Siddons did negotiate with Covent Garden, for John de la Bere, who was acting for the managers, wrote Siddons on Dec. 13: "They consider her subsequent engagement to Mr Garrick as an infringement of the agreement subsisting between them and Drury Lane, and they have no doubt that Mr Garrick when he comes to be informed that she was in treaty with them will refuse to take her . . . that Mrs Siddons absolutely promised . . . to drop all thoughts of connecting herself with Drury Lane" (FC; Boaden, II, 113).

7. Although Bate had criticized the harshness of Mrs. Siddons' voice, he added: "I should not wonder, from her ease, figure & manner if she made the *proudest* she of either house tremble in genteel Comedy:— nay beware yourself, *Great Little* Man, for she plays Hamlet to the satisfaction of the Worcestershire Critics" (letter of Aug. 12).

8. In his second letter from Worcester, on Aug. 19, Bate sent Garrick a list of twenty-three characters which Mrs. Siddons had played. Of these, he underlined seven as her favorite roles.

9. Bate had a continuing interest in agricultural reform, and for his services was later to receive the gold medal from the Society of Arts, Manufacture, and Commerce (*BD*).

933 To Joseph Cradock

Dear Sir   Aug. 17, 1775

I am greatly oblig'd to you for your favour[1] & shall most certainly treat myself with reading it from the beginning to the end, tho' at this time we are very busy in preparing for the Campaign, which it is said will be a brisk one— I had some thoughts of troubling you with a Letter, concerning a very unjust impression, you may have taken about a transaction of mine, a pecuniary one, with the Author of Braganza— if Mr Johnson of whose probity I have the highest opinion, Spoke sarcastically upon that Subject with regard to me, he was mistaken, for he never wrongs any body knowingly— The circumstances of that affair you may have from other people, as it might be thought Vanity to tell them myself— all I shall say upon the Subject is, that I hope my friends will know the facts, before they relate them from those, who either are ignorant of the truth, or wish to pervert it.

I am Sir
&c

Endorsement by Garrick: Copy of a Letter to Mr Craddock Aug^st 17. 1775.
Source: FC, copy.

1. Presumably a copy of Cradock's *Village Memoirs*, published anonymously in late
1774 and twice printed in 1775 (Cradock, IV, 143f.).

934   To Doctor Thomas Augustine Arne

Drury Lane Theatre

Dr Sir   Augt 24th 1775
I am very sorry that Mrs Greville (to whom I gave free leave to
assist you) should behave so Ill to you, and more so, that your loss
will be so great, by her ill behaviour—[1] The Managers of Drury
lane have no intention to employ a constant Composer, but to
engage with different gentlemen as business may arise in the
Theatre.

How can you imagine that I have an irrisistable *Apathy* to you?
I suppose you mean *Antipathy* my dear Doctor: by the Construction
and general turn of your letter— be Assur'd as my Nature is very
little inclin'd to Apathy, so it is as far from conceiving an Antipathy
to you or any Genius in this or any other Country—

You ask me why I won't make use of your Pupils— shall I tell
you fairly, because I have not the opinion of them which you have?—
I try'd Mrs Bradford, Miss Weller[2] and I have now Mr Faucet: the
two first (As I in a most friendly manner foretold) did no credit to
you or myself by appearing in a Piece which you obstinately insisted
upon bringing out, tho you knew it would be the means of making
a coolness between us— In Short dear Sir, your heart and your
genius seem more inclin'd to the Theatre of Covent Garden than
that of Drury-lane— and when I consider the additional music to
King Arthur,[3] and the Music to Elfrida,[4] I trust that I am justified
in my Opinion:[5]

whether I am mistaken or not, I have not the least Antipathy,
I give you my honor I have not, to Doctor Arne, but on the Contrary, if I had a work of consequence, I Shoud wish to employ him,
notwithstanding that our theatrical connections have not yet been
serviceable to either of us.

I am Dr Sir, your very sincere Wellwisher and
humble Servt
D Garrick

Source: FC, copy; Boaden, II, 79.

1. In a letter of Aug. 21 Arne complained that he had been "cut out of, at least, a clear £100" by Mrs. Greville's sudden refusal to perform the principal comic character in "the intended New Comedy at the Opera House" (FC; Boaden, II, 78). Mrs. Greville's name appears in the Drury Lane playbills only in minor roles, usually comic.

2. Hopkins observed: "Miss Weller . . . is a Piece of still Life, sings out of Tune, and will never make an Actress" (Diary, *DLC*, p. 163; see also Boaden, II, 85).

3. John Dryden's masque, altered by Garrick, with music by Purcell and Arne (DL, Dec. 13, 1770).

4. William Mason's dramatic poem, with music by Arne (CG, Nov. 21, 1772).

5. In his reply of Sept. 3, Arne wrote: "I must beg your permission to assure you that you are greatly mistaken in two Points: First, when you imagine that I have the least partiality either in favour of the other Theatre, or its Patentees: next, in saying that the Music in Elfrida is much superior to the Music I compos'd for you in King Arthur"; having denied the charges, he goes on to insist that the chief songs of *King Arthur*, "which for Air & Mastership I have never excell'd," were assigned to persons "who cou'd neither sing in time or tune" (FC; Boaden, II, 85).

935   To Peter Fountain

Dear Sir   Sunday Augst 27th 1775[1]
Thank you a thousand times for yr Letters— Mr Loyd is too partial
to Me, but I glory in it as he is honest as well as clever— What you
mean by improving Hampton, is a Mystery to Me, & to all, who
may read yr letter— I shall be in Town in 5 or 6 days, & shall be
glad to hear wt you can say upon that head—

When the Sr Knight of Ranelagh[2] pleases to send his Summons,
I shall be glad as well as my rib to meet you there. I have been
junketting but am oblig'd to be temperate in ye midst of Luxury—
pray remember me most kindly to yr very worthy friend, when you
write to him

Ever Yours most kindly
D. Garrick.

Address: Mr Fountain, Maiden Lane.   Endorsement by the recipient: Sunday
27th Sept 1775 Sr Thomas R.   Source: FC.

1. The month given in the endorsement is obviously an error, for in 1775 Sept. 27 fell on a Wednesday, while Aug. 27, as Garrick has written it, was a Sunday.

2. Sir Thomas Robinson.

936   To George Colman

Hampton
My dear Colman   Aug^st 29 1775
I expect to see You as brown, & as hearty as a devonshire plough
boy, who faces ye Sun without shelter, & knows not ye Luxury of
small beer & porter—[1] will nothing satisfy your ambition but
Robinson Crusoe? I think *little Friday* would do very well for you
to begin with, particularly as you are in company with those mighty
adventurous Knights Banks,[2] & Phipps!— if You are still happy
in risking your Neck with them, I beg my best compliments to them—
what say you if I should once more emerge from Stone & Gravel
& many other human infirmities & Curses, & spring out again an
active being, & Exercise wth ye best of you!— Since you left me,
I have been upon ye rack, & almost despair'd of fighting a battle or
committing a Murder again— but a fortnight ago my good Genius
led me to ye Duke of Newcastle's where I met with an old Naples
friend, & he recommended a remedy which has work'd Wonders—
It has taken away half the Evil of my life, & at this moment I can
piss well, and have ambition enough to think of something more—
but Lord help Us, we little Men make nothing of swelling ourselves
to a *Hercules* or a *Robinson Crusoe!*— to be serious— You will be
pleas'd to see me, as I am— My spirits are return'd, and redeant
Saturnia regna—[3]
By the bye I had some thoughts to make a farce upon the follies
& fashions of ye times & y^r friend *Omiah*[4] was to be my Arlequin
Sauvage—[5] a fine Character to give our fine folks a genteel dressing—
I must lick my fingers with you at y^e *Otaheite Fowl & Potatoes*— but
don't you spoil ye Dish, & substitute a fowl, for a young puppy?—[6]
Pray my Love to George—[7] they who don't like him, are not fit
company for You or Me, so no thanks to 'Em for their good reception— notwithstanding *Foster*'s Oath,[8] Foote has thrown the Duchess
upon her back, & there has left her, as You & I would do— She is
Sick & has given up the Cause, & has made herself very ridiculous,
& hurt herself much in ye struggle— Foote's letter[9] is one of his
best things, in his best manner.
Miss Ford demands all kind attentions from Every one, by her
most agreeable & natural Manner. We sh^d have been at her tea-
table, this week, had not Lord Camden & family, honour'd us w^th
their Company, & is now wth us—

5+L.D.G. III

We shall desire to see her once more—

pray come away, & see my Sword drawn— yᵉ Theatre is noble!—
Entre nous: Pope has squeak'd & sent her penitentials, but I cannot
receive 'Em—

Ever & most affect^y Y^{rs}

D Garrick

My Wife sends her best Love to George. I have Scribbled away—
such Stuff! but we rise! WE! *We Apples!*— ha ha ha—

Source: Berg Collection; Colman, pp. 311–314.

1. At this time Colman was a member of an informal scientific expedition to Mulgrave, the seat of Captain Phipps, situated in the wild and desolate surroundings north of Whitby, Yorkshire (see Peake, *Colman*, I, 354f.).

2. Joseph Banks (1743–1820), later (1781) Bt., botanist and explorer.

3. Virgil, *Eclogues*, IV, vi: "the reign of Saturn returns."

4. Omai, the Otaheitan (Tahitian), the first South Sea Islander to visit England, was with Colman at Mulgrave.

5. A play (1722) by Louis François Delisle. Nothing came of Garrick's idea.

6. The younger Colman wrote in his account of the Mulgrave trip: "[Omai] cooked fowl instead of dogs, which last he would have preferred, in his own country, as the greater delicacy . . . for yams, he had potatoes, for the bread fruit, bread itself" (Peake *Colman*, I, 370).

7. Colman the Younger.

8. The Rev. John Foster (1694–1780?), the Duchess of Kingston's chaplain, on Aug. 18 had sworn out an affadavit that Foote had threatened the Duchess with publication of his *Trip to Calais* if she did not pay him £2000 (*LC*, vol. XXXVIII, Aug. 17–19, p. 176).

9. Written in reply to one of Aug. 13 from the Duchess of Kingston; it appeared in the *London Chronicle* (Aug. 15–17, p. 168).

937   To William Brereton

Adelphi

Sepr 9th 1775—

Sir

Tho I had resolvd never to write to you again yet lest you shou'd
add Error to Error, and plunge yourself deeper into mistakes which
may become a very serious consideration; I shall once more say a
word, Or two, in answer to yours— by your own account your
Circumstances are none of the best and your taking such an expensive journey & Voyage to England to convince me, that you have
not behav'd *unkindly* and *unjustly* to me, will be as ineffectual as

expensive, unless you cou'd give me a new head to conceive differ-
ently, and a new heart *not* to feel— Your proposition of breaking your
Article to come to me at all events, is adding worse to bad, and what
I would never consent to, had you all the talents of all the great
Actors put together— that you may not be misled again by a false
light or Deceive yourself with an Expectation of what cannot
happen; I once more assure you that it will not be in my Power
to give you the Situation you might have had, while I continue
Manager of the Theatre—[1] You may depend upon it that this is
the resolution of your once very Sincere
friend and not your Ill wisher even now
D G

Endorsement: Mr Brierton Sepr 9th 1775. *Source:* FC, copy; Boaden, II, 93.

1. Brereton, however, did break his article with Barry, and acted as usual at Drury
Lane during the season of 1775–76.

938   To Jane Pope

Adelphi

Madam   Sunday Sepr 10th 1775—
I was from home upon a Visit or you shoud have heard from me
directly— your two last letters[1] have given me much uneasiness,
I need not say why the first occasion'd it; as I had always been
not only just and friendly, but fatherly to Miss Pope, the expressions
of *want of Affection, turning Swiss* &c were as harsh, as unexpected—
however I would not precipitately prevent you from recollecting
yourself and therefore I waited more than two months in hopes of
your seeing your error and returning chearfully to your business, &
let me add, (in spite of your frequent incivilities to me) to your
best friend:
My hopes were deceiv'd, and as I cou'd not but imagine you were
engag'd, I thought it time to prepare for your loss—
Many of your parts were dispos'd of, and sent at the time I
mention'd (which was in August) to the different performers in
order to be ready for the opening of the Season—
Why I am still more unhappy at the receipt of your last letter is,

that from the particulars already mention'd, added to some new engagements I have made, it is not in my Power to give you a Situation in our Theatre for the next Season, that can Possibly be agreeable to you.[2]

I am Madam Your most hum^le Servt, & well wisher

D. Garrick

Endorsement: Miss Pope's letter & my; *by Garrick:* Answer to it Sepr 10th 1775. *Source:* FC, copy; Boaden, II, 92f.

1. Those of June 10 and Sept. 7; in the latter she enclosed a letter from Harris, manager of Covent Garden, declining to engage her on the terms she desired (Boaden, II, 58, 92).

2. As a result of Garrick's refusal Miss Pope was obliged to spend a "year of Banishment" on the Dublin stage (Boaden, II, 131).

939   To Joseph Cradock

Adelphi

My dear Sir   Sepr 12th 1775

I am sure by what I have heard from many of your former Auditors, that Your brilliant Company was the least part of Your Entertainment— Your very polite offer of Your petite piece I most gratefully Accept, & will do it immediatly all the justice in my Power.

Poor *Miller*[1] I knew a little, & I believe he never troubled his head wth Terence for he never had any part of him in it— He took all he had from ye French, & if I remember right his Man of Taste[2] is Nearly copy'd from the *Precieuses ridicules* of Moliere— let me again thank You for y^r kindness to D^r S^r

Your most Obligd & Obed^t

D Garrick

My respects pray to y^r Lady.

Address: J: Cradock Esqr, Gumbley hall near Market-Harborough, Leicestershire. *Postmarked. Source:* FSL; Cradock, IV, 255.

1. James Miller (1706–1744), a clergyman who took up playwriting to increase his income. An unfortunate gift for satire impeded his advancement in theater and pulpit alike.

2. Miller's *Man of Taste* was originally produced at Drury Lane in 1735; it was later "cut into a farce" and played on March 10, 1752 (*BD*).

940   To The Reverend Henry Bate

Lichfield
Dear Bate.   Sepr 15^h 1775
I have indeed been rambling, & taking my pleasures— Her Grace
of Devonshire[1] is a most inchanting Exquisite, beautiful Young
Creature— were I five & twenty I could go mad about her, as I am
past five & fifty, I would only suffer Martyrdom for her— She is no
Gamester my friend, nor was there Ever any Gaming at Chatsworth—[2] I am going directly for London, & I shall then do what I
can, & more, than I would do for myself, for You— I wish You
much happiness where You are, which is one of the Sweetest places
in the three Kingdoms— I beg that You will present my respects
to the Noble owner of it,[3] & believe me, most truly Yours
                                                         D: Garrick

I am call'd to an Account Every where for the Sins You commit.
   I am scribbling to You surrounded by my chattering family—
three males & as many females—

Address: Revd Mr Bate, Hagley. *Seal. Source:* Shakespeare's Birthplace
Trust.

   1. Georgiana (Spencer) Cavendish (1757–1806), daughter of the first Earl Spencer,
had married the fifth Duke of Devonshire in 1774.
   2. In this Garrick was only too sadly mistaken.
   3. The second, "wicked," Baron Lyttelton.

941   To Charles Dibdin[1]

[ante September 23, 1775][2]
As you are pleased to add falsehood to ingratitude (for the very
reverse of the first paragraph of your letter[3] is the truth) I cannot
have any agreement with you

Source: Sotheby, Catalogue, Feb. 4, 1876, extract.

   1. So identified in the source.
   2. The approximate date is from Dibdin's reply of Sept. 23, 1775 (Sotheby, Catalogue, June 12–19, 1899).

3. Perhaps a reference to Dibdin's undated letter in the Forster Collection, the first paragraph of which runs: "The only reason as I Understand that you assign for not engaging me is my having neglected rehearsals and that therefore you think there is no placing any dependence on me I did neglect some Last Winter tis true owing to my fear of being arrested but had I been suffer'd to receive at the Office the money you yourself promised me I should have been able to have advertized my benefit properly which I did not do once to have had large bills which the printer of the House refused me because I could not send the Money beforehand and so far to have appeas'd my Creditors there would have been no fear of this for the future."

942   To The Earl of Upper Ossory

Adelphi

My Lord.   Sept 23ᵈ [1775]¹

As you have ever been most favorable to me, I must entreat You to plead my cause with Lady Ossory— I had written the inclos'd letter to her Ladyship thinking that I could find the verses she desires in Town, but to my great Mortification, upon my searching here for them, I have recollected that they are at Hampton, where I go tomorrow I will inclose them to your Lordᵖ Monday or Tuesday night— we are to be disappointed, when our minds are most eager to do anything— I was so very happy to obey Lady Ossory's commands, that I took it for granted I could either find yᵉ Lines, recollect them, or get them from yᵉ Person to whom they are address'd— but my Search has been in vain, my memory is very bad, and Mr Secretary Stanley is gone upon a sailing party— next week Lady Ossory will be sure to have them. Mrs Garrick presents her respects.

I am My Lord Your Lordship's most obedient
D. Garrick

Source: Rupert Robert Vernon, transcript.

1. The year is supplied by Lady Ossory's letter, dated only Sept. 19, in which she requested a copy of the verses which Garrick had sent Edward Stanley of the Customs on June 5, 1775 (FC; Boaden, II, 368).

943   To Samuel Cautherly

Octr the [2, 1775]
When Mr Cautherly's letter,[1] which will be ever memorable, in
the annals of a Theatre, came to Mr Garrick he was confin'd with
a fit of ye Stone, & could not write:— had not Mr Cautherly's
impatient vanity been too strong for his discretion & gratitude, he
would have waited at least till the Saturday Morning, when the
fullest, & best answer would have been given to his letter by the
treasurer— has this Young Man a proper sense of right & wrong?
for taking Mr Garrick out of ye Question, should not he, have given
Notice *before* the beginning of the Season to any *indifferent* Manager
of his intentions of quitting the Theatre?—[2] to begin the Season was
misleading the Manager, & not to go on, is not only contrary to y^e
Establish'd rules of a Theatre, but unjust, illegal, & dishonourable—
what would the publick & Mr Cautherly's friends have said, had
M^r G: discharg'd M^r C: during the Acting Season?— We shall
soon hear what they say upon ye present occasion: perhaps M^r
Cautherly thought that his going away at a time when the Manager
rely'd upon him, would be more distressing: in this, as in many
other things, he is very much mistaken— Mr Garrick said in a
former letter, that Mr Cautherly could confer no favour upon him,
which he now retracts; for he confesses, Mr Cautherly has found a
Way to confer a very great one.

Endorsement by Garrick: My letter to Cautherly Octr the 2^d 1775.   *Source:* FC,
draft.

1. Of Sept. 27, in which he wrote: "I have flatter'd myself till the last Minute with
hopes of receiving a favorable Answer to a Letter I did myself the Honor to send you
before I left Town and am sorry to find your silence proceeds from a determined resolution not to do anything in my favor. My Situation in the Theatre for these four Years
past has been worse and worse & the impossibility I find of living on my Salary without
involving myself in difficulties obliges me (tho' with the greatest reluctance) to take my
leave of Drury Lane beging you will accept my most grateful Thanks for all the favors
your bounty formerly bestow'd" (FC).
2. Cautherly's name does not appear in the playbills after the season of 1774–75.
He was "the hero of the Dublin theatre about 1778" (*Thespian Dictionary*, 1805).

944   To William Siddons

Hampton
Sir   Oct[r] 7th 1775
This is one of the first letters I have written, since my recovery
from a very Severe fit of the Gravel, which render'd me incapable
of any business— As I am now much better, I flatter Myself that
a letter from me will no⟨t⟩ be disagreeable— I wish much to know
how M[rs] Siddons is,[1] & about what time I may have the Pleasure
of Seeing You in London— I beg that she will not make herself
uneasy about coming, till she will run no risk by the journey— all I
desire is that I may have the earliest information that can be had
with any certainty, for I shall settle some business by that direction,
which may be of immediate Service to M[rs] Siddons & the Manager—
if in the mean time You find it convenient to have any pecuniary
Assistance from Me, I shall give it You with great pleasure— let
me once more intreat that M[rs] Siddons may have No Cares about
me to disturb her, & that she may not be hurried to y[e] least prejudice
of her health. I beg my Comp[ts] & best Wishes to her in her present
Situation, &

I am Sir Your most hu[le] Serv[t]
D. Garrick

PS. my hand shakes with weakness but I hope You will understand
this Scrawl.

Source: HTC; Little, p. 72f.

1. She was seven months pregnant at this date.

945   To George Colman

My dear Colman.   Wed[y] Night [October 11? 1775][1]
I fear that I cannot go to Hampton tomorrow— I have been
rehearsing Othello, as Bensley will tell you, & my head shakes—
I have read over & over the tragedy[2] You have so warmly
recommended, & am sorry to say, that I most sincerely think it

w^d fail of success upon the Stage— the Fable is very improbable horrid & I fear would create disgust instead of pleasure— the Author I think a Man of Merit, & there are many Speeches taken Separately which denote Genius, but he should have a better fable to build upon— I write this in great haste & to my friend, for I always speak to him, as I to my thinkings as I do ruminate— pray let the Author know my Sentiments in better language for I write upon ye Gallop—

Your Ever most truly
D: Garrick.

Your being upon Your travels[3] has prevented my Sending Yo ye Play Sooner— let ye Author know, that ye delay must not be imputed to me.

Source: William Le Fanu.

1. Bensley played in *Othello* only in 1775; the tone of the letter implies that Garrick was referring to a rehearsal before the initial performance on Tuesday, Oct. 17—hence the conjectural date of the preceding Wednesday, Oct. 11.
2. Unidentified.
3. See Letter 936, note 1.

946   To Hugh Kelly[1]

Octr 16th 1775

Indeed, my Dear Sir, You have put into my hands a performance of very great hurry, & which cannot possibly be Represented with Success—[2] I never read More dangerous Scenes in all my Life— [an Audience in my opinion, would immediatly take Offence at M^r & Mrs Buzzard & particularly at the last— her culinary jokes when alter'd & made less strong, would be dangerous Even in a farce— but his peculiarity, & desire of lying with ye Widow Keenly, in ye Spartan manner would never be borne— *Wellwould* has Marks of a Character but surely his being kick'd & sent to Bridewell[3] is carrying ye joke much too far— and the Widow, which seems ye favourite female Character has a most abandon'd Mind, & tho she does not forge bonds, Yet she forges falsehoods to carry on her Schemes, & falls but little short of what is suppos'd of Mrs Rudd: *Comodore Sulky* is rather a trite Character, & little use made of him

5*

hitherto— the idea of a Fribble officer & a Foxhunting Girl (tho the last is in another play) is a good one, but there are no Circumstances, no Comic incidents to shew them off.— that of yᵉ Widow Keenly's against Wellwould wᵗʰ Dʳ Dismal is in my opinion is very dangerous tho an imitation of Moliere— But what is still more disheartening than all yᵉ rest, is the want of a Spirited Interest, in the plan; the Wheels of the fable are clog'd with a dialogue which, notwithstanding some good Speeches taken Seperately, go heavily on & become languid & without Effect—] in short for both our Sakes I cannot receive this Comedy, nor can I propose any alteration, that will take away my very strong objections to it— these are my Sincere Sentimen⟨ts⟩ which I communicate to You with all the freedom of friendship— for

I am most truly my Dear Sʳ Your most Obedᵗ

Endorsement by Garrick: Letter to Mʳ Kelly.   *Source:* FC, draft; Boaden, II, 103.

1. Because it is uncertain which passages Garrick wished to delete and which to retain, the entire letter is given with brackets surrounding what appears to be the intended deletion.

2. Writing to Garrick in a letter which is endorsed "Mʳ Kelly about his Play Sepᵗ 7 1775," Kelly described this untitled work: "The piece I hinted at my dear Sir, is not a pitite piece; it is a full five act piece, and I flatter myself most egregiously if you will not find the *Cub* . . . extremely *lickable*" (FC; Boaden, II, 102).

3. Principally a prison for "vagrants, harlots, and idle and disobedient apprentices, sentenced to short terms of imprisonment. Their chief employment seems to have been in beating hemp and picking oakum" (*London*, I, 242).

947   To William Siddons

Sir   Octʳ 19— 1775
Whenever You please to draw upon Me for the fifteen pounds I shall pay it immediatly— I am glad to hear that Mʳˢ Siddons is so Well, & Expect You will give me Notice when she is worse, & better—

if You find any difficulty in getting the Money on a draught upon Me, I will inquire, & get the money paid in Gloucester.

I am Sir (With very best Wishes & Compliments to
Mʳˢ Siddons) Yʳ Most Obedᵗ Serᵗ
D: Garrick

Source: FSL.

948   To George Colman

Hampton
My dear Colman.   Sunday [*ante* October 28, 1775][1]
I take yᵉ opportunity by Young Wallis[2] to say three words to You—
I forgot to give Becket yᵉ King & no King—[3] I Shall be there
toMorrow & will leave it out for You— What a precious Genius is
Master Steevens?— has our friend Woodfall frighten'd him that
he bitches so soon— I had prepar'd a Whisker for such treachery,
but 'tis better as it is— his letter to day (for I am sure it is his) is
most unaccountable— I hope when I see You next you'll make
me merry by giving me a little Spleen:[4] I am somewhat puzzled
about introducing my little jew Girl—[5] she is surprizing!— I want
to introduce her as the little Gipsey with 3 or 4 exquisite Songs—
More when I see You

Ever & most truly Yʳˢ
D: Garrick.

Address: G. Colman Esqʳ.   *Seal.*   *Source:* FSL.

1. Dated from the reference to Miss Abrams' introduction.
2. Albany Charles Wallis (1763?–1776), only son of Albany Wallis, was a student at
Westminster (G. F. Russell Barker and Alan H. Stenning, *Records of Old Westminsters*,
1928, II, 959).
3. By Beaumont and Fletcher; Colman was preparing an edition of their plays
(published 1778).
4. Presumably a reference to Colman's farce, *The Spleen* (DL, March 7, 1776).
5. Harriet Abrams (1760–?), singer, a pupil of Dr. Arne, made her debut on Oct. 28,
a Saturday, in a new production: Garrick's *May Day; or, The Little Gipsy* (Elizabeth P.
Stein, *David Garrick, Dramatist*, New York, 1938, pp. 153, 155). "She is very young and
small,— has a very sweet Voice and a fine Shake, but not Power enough yet.— Both the
Piece and the Young Lady were received with great Applause" (Hopkins, Diary, DLC
p. 190). The music was by Arne (Boaden, II, 86f.).

949   To Richard Yates

Sir   Sunday October 29ᵗʰ 1775
I shall beg leave to discuss our Theatrical Matters with You, in
order to prevent their being discuss'd any where else, which they
must be, if our Business for the future is to be unsettled & destroy'd

by our present uncertainty— You left word with Mr Hopkins *that we are to think no more of Mrs Yates, 'till She will let us know her pleasure,* or words to that Effect. Do You, & Mrs Yates imagine that the Proprietors will submit to this manner of going on, or that they will pay such a large Sum of Money for having their Busines⟨s⟩ so destroy'd as it was in great part of the last Season and has been wholly this, by waiting for Mrs Yates's pleasure to perform?— She play'd but Thirty times last Season, and as She goes on, in the proportion of four times in Six weeks she will play Twenty times in this Season.— Indeed Mr Yates this will not do, and I give you fair Notice. We lost greatly by her not playing the first Night she was advertis'd, & to this day no reason could be given for the disappointment, nor did you offer any to my Brother, but *that you could not help it, and you did all in your power to oblige her to Act.* It was observ'd by many of the Audience last Night that she never perform'd better,[1] and therefore She gives Notice that She must not be advertis'd 'till *She* pleases. As I was at the Theatre, & heard with my own Ears that her Voice was never clearer, I shall not Submit to this very unaccountable & unreasonable Behaviour— I pass'd over your own ill defended Argument about *Sterling,*[2] and think my self very ill us'd in that matter.— But now to something very unaccountable indeed!— Mrs Yates desir'd to have some Comedy parts— You mention'd Araminta, in the School for Lovers, and Hippolita in She wou'd & She wou'd not,[3] they were immediately given to her, and then indeed She wou'd not, because She would not be so indelicate to take em from a performer, who only play'd them because our great Ladies would not.[4] Yet she would take Belinda in All in the Wrong, tho' it has long been in the Possession of a Capital Actress.[5] what a Contradiction? but to go on still farther She that wants to save herself by Acting Comedy has refus'd to perform the Widow Knightly in the *Discovery* with me, tho' she did it originally, and it is now reviv'd for the Entertainment of her Majesty.[6] to finish this Business at once, & that we may be more explicit— It is my greatest pleasure to live in the greatest Harmony with my Capital performers, and more particularly so with M^r & Mrs Yates.— But if they persist to distress us; & Mrs Yates is resolv'd to withdraw herself so often, and sometimes without a Cause, I shall be oblig'd to do, what I would most wish to avoid. I am Sir

Your most humble Servant

D: Garrick

a little Gout in my right hand obliges me to make use of anothers to write the Letter.[7]

Source: FC, copy, corrected and signed by Garrick; Boaden, II, 106f.

1. As Calista in *The Fair Penitent.*
2. In *The Clandestine Marriage.*
3. These plays, by Whitehead and by Cibber, were acted on Oct. 24 and Nov. 23 with Mrs. Henry King taking the roles mentioned.
4. Mary King, the wife of Henry King the actor, after appearing at Edinburgh, Hull, and Dublin was with Wilkinson at York when Garrick engaged her as a foil to Mrs. Abington and Miss Younge. She made her debut at Drury Lane on Oct. 13, 1775, and continued to play only through that season. In Oct. 1778 she returned to York, but she never regained her former popularity and was forced to retire with a final benefit on Feb. 27, 1779 (Tate Wilkinson, *The Wandering Patentee,* York, 1795, I, 69ff., II, 14; Boaden, II, 74ff., FC).
5. Mrs. Abington; Mrs. Yates had created the role when Murphy's comedy was first performed on June 15, 1761.
6. On Jan. 20, 1776. "This Comedy is revived for (the) Queen to see Mr. Garrick in the Character of Sir Anty. Bramble [Branville]" (Hopkins, Diary, *DLC,* p. 193).
7. The letter is in Hopkins' hand.

950 To Joseph Cradock

Adelphi

Dear Sir, October 31, 1775

Though I shall be Sir John Brute in three quarters of an hour,[1] yet I would answer your letter directly. It is not in my power to make room for any new piece this winter. My list is so full, that I have been obliged to desire one of the Gentlemen to defer the exhibition of his play till the winter after this; which he has kindly agreed to. What shall I say to you, my dear Sir, about the Farce you were so obliging to put into my hands? I fear that there is such a similitude between part of it, and some scenes in the "Country Girl," not to say any thing of your friend Cumberland's "Choleric Man," that I fear it will want the force of novelty to give it the success I would always wish to attend your handy-works of every kind. I was in hopes that the Farce had been upon the subject of Miller's "Man of Taste," which is taken from the "Precieuses Ridicules" of Moliere. If these reasons weigh with you, as they do with me, I will return the Farce to your order; if not, I shall be ready in this, as in other matters, to obey your commands. Dear Sir,

your most obedient, humble servant,

D. Garrick.

Source: Cradock, IV, 255f.

1. Garrick "never played better, and had a remarkable Head drest with Feathers, Fruit &c. as extravagant as possible to burlesque the present Mode of the Ladies.— it had a monstrous fine Effect" (Hopkins, Diary, *DLC*, p. 190).

951   To William Smith

Adelphi

Sir   Wednesday Morning Nov: 1. 1775
In the middle of the play last night[1] I rec^d your very extraordinary Note—[2] I gave you leave to quit the Theatre for a few days upon your own private business but I little thought that my Management was to be arraignd during that absence by Mr Smith— I believe he is the first Actor that has been pleasd to find fault with the Acting any plays during the absence of that Actor from the business of the Theatre— I would have Mr Smith know, that I am as incapable of doing an unjust thing, as I think myself very ill used to be calld to an Account for what the Accuser had not the least shadow of right to interfere in— I shall not describe my distresses & troubles for many days last past in fixing upon plays— I have waited 3 & 4 hours at the playhouse before I could ascertain a Single play for the next day— but is an absentee who may partly be the occasion of those distresses, when he returns to town, instead of seeming oblig'd for the favour has been done him, announc'd his return with a Complaint of the Manager? Indeed these frequent Billets of Complaint betray an unsatisfyd Mind, & I am as little able to Account for this dissatisfaction as I find that no Act of mine is able to remove it.

I am Sir Your very H^{le} Ser^t
D G.

Endorsement: Copy, To Mr Smith Beauford Buildings. *Source:* FC, copy; Boaden, II, 108.

1. When Garrick had acted Sir John Brute.
2. It seems apparent that Smith had resented the production of Sir Richard Steele's *Conscious Lovers* on Oct. 30 without him, for having played the role of Young Bevil once, on Oct. 21, he considered that part his own.

952   To The Proprietors of Covent Garden Theatre[1]

                                                        Adelphi
Gentlemen   Novr 2^d 1775
I believe no precedent can be produc'd of the Managers returning
to five days a Week after they had play'd Six: and indeed, tho I
should be very happy to Oblige You, such a measure at this time,
would not only Subject Us to very injurious Suspicions, but it would
likewise, *as it is a time of dearth & Sickness,* bring on great distresses
upon the lower part of our Companies—
                                            I am Gentlemen

My Company has but this Minute left me

   Source: FC, draft; Boaden, II, 109.

   1. In their note of Nov. 2 the proprietors wrote: "If it would be agreeable to Mr.
Garrick that Drury-lane only should be open tomorrow, and to give Covent-Garden
Tuesday next, or make any arrangement of the kind, now in the time of dearth and
sickness, it would be complied with" by them (Boaden, II, 108).

953   To Peter Fountain

Dear Sir   Sunday [November] 5th [1775]
After all I am told by a Letter rec'd from France that the Chevalier
proves an Amazon— is it true— & more, which I am glad to hear—
that 15000 Liv: p an: are Settled upon him or her?—[1] pray resolve
me this question: I have been very ill— am not Well, & don't
know when I shall be—
                                            Yours Ever &c
                                            D: Garrick.

Address: Mr Fountain, Maiden Lane. *Endorsement by the recipient:* Nov. 1775. *Source:* FC; Boaden, II, 109.

1. On Nov. 4, 1775, d'Eon had agreed with the French government to surrender all the diplomatic papers in his possession in return for a life annuity of twelve-thousand livres; he had also agreed to the condition, which the government imposed in an effort to curb his political activities, that he wear for life the female attire in which he had occasionally appeared earlier. D'Eon's transvestism aroused wide interest and heavy wagering on his actual sex (John B. Telfer, *Chevalier D'Eon de Beaumont*, 1885, pp. 243-251).

954   To George Garrick

Almacks[1]

Dear George.   Novr 7th [1775][2]
We rejoice at your visible alteration of health & Spirits— Palmer says, that you begin to pick up, I don't mean at ye Whist Table, but in Your looks— pray keep y^rself quiet in Mind & y^r Body will get better of course— I beg you will let me know the progress of your health & I likewise must insist that you never think of leaving that fountain of *Your* health, till you can shew us a pair of rosy Cheeks, Spirited eyes, and a Belly out of the perpendicular— the Little Gypsy goes on Hummingly, & rises nightly in repute— there was a little odd talk of some party against us, but to this Minute there has not been one Single disapprobation— Weston is dying, & with him goes a good Actor, & a very bad Man— Mrs King is useful, but not excellent— she stops gaps but will not allure— Y^r Son David is not yet arriv'd, he is they say, at Lichfield with his Uncle— all the rest of y^r Olive Branches are well, Mr Carrington is better & worse & will continue so, till he dyes— I shall write to you by Palmer— just let us know that you are better—

Ever & affect^y Y^{rs}
D Garrick

Address: G. Garrick Esqr, Bath. *Frank:* Free Geo: Selwyn. *Postmarked.* *Source:* Hyde Collection, copy in FC; *The R. B. Adam Library*, Buffalo, 1929, I, 9f.

1. The fashionable club in Pall Mall, later known as Brooks's. In a letter to Garrick of Feb. 18, 1773, Pembroke had written: "The Almackists, my Dear Sir, have, in one respect, done a foolish thing in choosing you of their club, as it will often bring me there, who have no other employment amongst them, but that of watching the cheats of the nobility, gentry, & others, who compose it" (HTC).
2. The year is supplied by the reference to *May Day; or, The Little Gipsy*, which was produced only in the season of 1775-76.

955   To Peter Fountain

Dear Fountain.   Sunday 3 o'Clock [?November 12, 1775]¹
This is the Clerk of the Morning Post— I hope You will let him
[have] the Chevalier's paper,² if you print it to Morrow

>   Yours Ever
>   D: Garrick.

Address: Mʳ Fountain, Maiden Lane.   *Source:* FC.

1. The conjectural date is determined by the reference to the Chevalier's paper.
2. The rumors about d'Eon's sex again became current in the fall of 1775. Betting
odds ran high. In the *Morning Post* (Nov. 13–14, 1775) d'Eon published a protest,
earnestly desiring "the people of England, who hitherto have testified their benevolence
towards him ... not to renew any policies on his sex ... [He] has recently refused
great sums of money which have been offered to him to be concerned in such policies;
offers that he could never hear of but with the most sovereign contempt" (see also John B.
Telfer, *Chevalier D'Eon de Beaumont*, 1885, pp. 256–258).

956   To William Siddons

>   Adelphi
Sir   Novʳ 15ᵗʰ 1775
I wish You joy of Mʳˢ Siddons' safe delivery,¹ & I hope she continues Well—
    I am oblig'd to Mʳ Dinwoody² for his politeness, & shall return
him the Money upon the first Notice of his return to Town: and
now about Your coming to London— the Sooner I see You here,
wᵗʰ convenience to Mʳˢ Siddons, will be of more consequence to
her & to me— she may have something to do, if I see her soon,
which may not be in my power to give her if she comes later— nay
indeed, if she cannot safely set out before the time you mention'd
in a Former letter, it would [be better] for her not to appear this
Season, but put off her joining Us till the next opening of our
Theatre—³ but this I leave to Your own determination— & now,
let me desire You to give me the earliest Notice when you & Mʳˢ
Siddons can be here, & what part or parts she Would rather chuse
for her Onset, that I may prepare Accordingly— I should have no

Objection to Rosalind, as Mᵣ Bate thought it yᵣ favourite part,[4] but that a *Mʳˢ King* has made her first appearance in that Character—[5] if You will set down 3 or 4 that You & She think her most capital parts, I will make the choice, in yᵉ mean time

I am Sᵣ Your most huˡᵉ Seᵗ

D: Garrick.

Address: Mᵣ Siddons belonging to the Theatre at Gloucester. *Postmarked.* *Source:* HTC.

1. In a letter to Garrick, from Gloucester on Nov. 9, Siddons had written that his wife had been "unexpectedly taken ill: when performing on the stage And early the next morning produced me a fine girl" (BM); this daughter was Sarah Martha Siddons (d. 1803).

2. William Dinwoody (1740–1805), of the Excise Office at Gloucester, had been commissioned by Garrick to supply Siddons with money, and Siddons had just received twenty pounds (*GM*, vol. LXXV, May 1805, p. 491, Sept. 1805, p. 872; Siddons' letter of Nov. 9).

3. Mrs. Siddons was able to come to London with her husband in December. On the 29th of that month she made her debut, which was more or less unsuccessful because of her weakened condition and an attack of stage fright.

4. See Bate's letters of Aug. 12 and 19, 1775 (BM).

5. Oct. 13. According to Tate Wilkinson, Mrs. King pleased so well in *As You Like It* that "in order to mortify Miss Young . . . Garrick had interest at Court sufficient for his Majesty to have that play ordered" for Oct. 18; he then put the new actress' name in the bills as acting Rosalind "by Command," a circumstance which Wilkinson says was without precedent (*The Wandering Patentee*, York, 1795, I, 205).

957 To Mary Ann Yates

Madam   November 16ᵗʰ 1775

Your Letter of Yesterday came to me while I was at Dinner;— The fatigue in the Morning for near four hours, made me incapable of every thing after Dinner but sleeping in my great chair— I take the first Moment of leisure to answer your favour— at the same time I cannot but Lament that our Theatrical Affairs require so much writing about them.— You wish to be quit of the part of *Almeria*,[1] because you say it is *unfit* for You, and that you had given it up by my consent Fourteen Years ago; I dare not Contradict you, and if I was to own the Charge, it has nothing to do with the present question; You are pleas'd to say, it is not *fit* for you, If so, why would You take it again unsolicited by *me*, but why is it *unfit*, if it is the Capital part of the Play, and always perform'd by the first Actresses?— But there is still a stronger Reason for urging the Necessity of your appearing in that Character.— At the time of the Benefits last year, hearing how much the Plays suffer by the Performers taking parts for *one Night only*, I put up an order in the Green Room, that the Manager would expect every Performer to do for the House what they should do for the Benefits, and for this good reason; why is not the Publick at large to be as well entertain'd, as the Friends of any Single Actor? and why are not the Proprietors to be profited by the performance of Mrs Yates in Almeria as well as Mr Cautherley?—[2] to Convince You how Injurious this business would be to You, as well as to the Proprietors,— Mr Reddish sent word Yesterday, that he only perform'd Claudio in Measure for Measure, to oblige Mr King,[3] and that it would be hard upon him to Act such a part again.— I sent word that the Injury would be to the Play; (consequently to Mrs Yates) to the Publick, and to the Proprietors, and that I insisted upon his performing the part; he has consented.—[4] I hope therefore that Mrs Yates will not be the only one to oppose so reasonable an order of the Manager, and make him Guilty of an Act of Injustice,— I must therefore intreat her to comply with my Request, and to appear in Almeria next Tuesday Night,[5] which I intend immediately to advertise as it was in the papers a few days ago

I am Madam. Your most humble Servant
D: Garrick

P.S. The Forfeit[6] in this Case, cannot be accepted,— the part is not a New one You Voluntarily accepted of it, & perform'd it for a Benefit.

Source: FC, copy; Boaden, II, 110.

1. In *The Mourning Bride.*
2. For the latter's benefit on May 1.
3. For his benefit on March 18.
4. *Measure for Measure* was given on Nov. 18.
5. In her reply of Nov. 17 Mrs. Yates consented to play Almeria on Nov. 21 (Boaden, II, 110f.).
6. A system of forfeits was used in the theater to penalize actors who declined to play a role assigned to them.

958   To Henry Sampson Woodfall

Dear Woodfall.   Novr 28 [1775?][1]
I will most certainly rouse at y^r Flap as I always promis'd You I
Would— but still your fingers on y^r Lips I pray[2]— will not your
great & lesser Devils open my Notes to You—

Ever Yours most Sincerely
D Garrick

My best Comp^{ts} to Your Lady   She has not apply'd to me for a long
time— I begin to grow jealous—

Address: To Mr Henry Sampson Woodfall, The Corner of Ivy Lane, Pater
Noster Row.   *Postmark:* NICHOLSON 5 O'CLOCK. TUESDAY.   *Source:* BM.

     1. The conjectural year is dependent on the postmark, stamped either the day or
the day after the letter was written, and on the receiver's mark, "Nicholson," which
has been found only from March 8, 1774. In the years before Garrick's death and
after the first Nicholson mark, Nov. 28 fell on a Tuesday in 1775, and on a Monday in
1774; however (see address) in the latter year Woodfall was confined in the King's
Bench Prison during November.
     2. *Hamlet,* I, v, 188.

959   To Richard Bailye

Novr 30— [1775?][1]

M^r & Mrs Garrick would be glad to know Who at the Adelphi has
affronted or Offended Mr Bailye, that he has not vouchsaf'd to let
ye Light of his Countenance Shine there for some days.

Source: FSL.

     1. This letter was, conjecturally, written in 1775 when Bailye was visiting London
(see Letter 968 and Garrick's signed pass to Drury Lane for Bailye dated Nov. 11, 1775,
in FSL).

960   To Thomas Rackett, Jr.[1]

Adelphi
Dec. 2, 1775

What between Wandsworth and Oxford,[2] I shall have no occasion to trouble my Butcher or Poulterer any more . . . I play'd Hamlet last Wednesday[3] & after the play yr. Father & Mother went home with us to take part of my Chicken. the moment I got into my great chair, I was as lifeless as the Brawn's head you have sent me, but very unlike that I was tasteless too, and no mustard could quicken me— dead— dead— dead— however I recover'd the next day & play'd Archer on ye Friday, in short, my dear Tom, the Devil of a Duenna[4] has laid hold upon the Town, & nothing but your old Friend can get her a little out of her clutches—[5]

Hamlet was ye most crowded house we ever had & Archer was a most splendid one, tho not quite so profitable

Source: Sotheby, Catalogue, June 19, 1928, extract.

1. So identified in the source.
2. Rackett was at this time a student in University College, Oxford, and his parents were living at Wandsworth, Surrey.
3. Nov. 29, when the King and Queen had attended *The Duenna* at Covent Garden.
4. Richard Brinsley Sheridan's play (CG, Nov. 21) was to be played no less than seventy-five times during the 1775–76 season.
5. In an effort to offset the success of *The Duenna* Garrick appeared between Nov. 25 and Dec. 23 nine times, in six of his major roles.

961   To Frances Abington

Madam   Dec[r] 7th [1775][1]

I beg that you will keep M[r] Andrew's[2] Note, it is his justification to you, & had he been guilty of the least Endeavor to prejudice the Sultan,[3] I would never have spoken to him again— be assur'd that I have done my utmost for y[e] Piece, & had it not come out on Tuesday or Wed[y] *We* should, as well as *You*, have been great Sufferers— I shall take care that You are kept from playing till You appear in the new piece— we will settle the business of the table &

guitars when we meet, I cannot attend You to Morrow because I have a long & laborious part:[4] on Saturday I shall attend, & settle the whole— I took care that M[rs] Wrighten[5] should not have a gay Song, nor do I understand that it will in the least interfere wth Yours— & don't be uneasy; a Natural gay Chansonette, sung with natural Ease & pleasantry will be heard wth pleasure after the finest Embroider'd air of a Faranelli—[6] I believe an Emperor of y[e] Turks was never Seen before M[r] Palmer will make his appearance in y[e] Sultan— if You would have M[r] Shaw[7] oblige you most compleatly, a few half Guineas w[d] be well bestow'd, to have him to Your house, & settle the Song and Accompagniements with You— don't Starve y[e] business for triffles, I have done my Utmost for the piece, & it will be most splendid in Scenes & dresses.

I am Madam y[rs] very *truly*, when You are not *unruly*

D. Garrick

Source: BM, copy in FC; Percy Fitzgerald, *The Life of Mrs. Abingdon*, 1888, p. 80.

1. The year is determined by the reference to *The Sultan* (DL, Dec. 12, 1775).
2. Miles Peter Andrews (d. 1814), dramatist, M.P. for Bewdley, Worcestershire, affected the society of authors and actors and occupied a mansion in Green Park, where he lavishly entertained. A member of the Beefsteak and other clubs, he enjoyed a reputation for wit and hospitality (see also Boaden, II, 61).
3. Mrs. Abington had written on Thursday [Dec. 7] that she had "been put out of humour . . . by being told that M[r] Andrews talks of the Farce at the Coffee Houses, as the Work of Mr Kelly . . . and the report can only be Meant to bring popular prejudice against it" (FC; Boaden, II, 105). Kelly had made himself unpopular by adverse criticism of actors and by his support of the government as a pensioned journalist, and had already had to conceal his authorship of plays.
4. Hamlet.
5. Mary Ann (Matthews) Wrighten (d. 1796), actress and singer, was the wife of James Wrighten (d. 1793), a Drury Lane prompter. She acted at Drury Lane before her marriage as well as after. Hopkins described her as having had "a very fine Voice" but an "aukward and clumsy Figure" (Diary, *DLC*, p. 146; *Thespian Dictionary*, 1805).
6. Carlo (Broschi) Farinelli (1705–1782), the famous male soprano.
7. Perhaps the Shaw who is later noticed in the playbills as a member of the Drury Lane orchestra (playbills, HCL; see also *European Magazine*, vol. XVIII, Dec. 1790, p. 480).

962 To Domenico Angelo

My dear Friend   Dec[r] 8 [1775][1]
just going to bed— as I play Hamlet to morrow I can't have y[e]
Pleasure of attending M[rs] Garrick. She will be there at the place &
time, if you & M[rs] Angelo go, she will carry you if you will call in
your way— if not, she will follow your directions— she is greatly
oblig'd to you, as well as Your most sincere Wellwisher & hum[e] Ser
                                                                D Garrick

Address: M[r] Angelo.   *Seal.*   *Source:* Frederick W. Hilles.

1. Since Garrick says that he is to play Hamlet "to morrow" it seems that he either
misdated this letter or wrote it after the midnight preceding the day he was to appear,
for while he never performed the role on a Dec. 9, he did play it on Dec. 8, in 1775 only.

963 To George Colman

My dear Colman   Dec[r] 12 [1775][1]
Pray read over y[e] inclos'd if you have an hour's leisure— you shall
know It's history—[2] I must write to night about it, which letter you
shall see, if I can see you in the Evening— Shall I call upon you at
any time? I cannot get rid of an Engagement I have till about
Nine— where may you be till about 8—? I want to talk with you
about y[e] Silent Woman. poor Weston, Moody tells me will, he
thinks, never play again—[3] he wants to go to Bath— therefore as
we cannot stay his recovery, to whom shall I give *La Fool*?—[4] We
must go to work upon it directly— don't read these 4 Acts (tho but
short) if it is in the least inconvenient.
                                                    Yours Ever & Ever
                                                            D: Garrick.

My love to Miss Ford, & comp[s] to Miss Mills,—[5] you were not at
Cov[t] Garden, I like the Duenna much with some few objections—
It will do their business—

Source: Berg Collection; Colman, p. 314f.

1. The year is derived from the reference to *The Duenna* (CG, Nov. 21, 1775).

2. Presumably the manuscript of Jephson's play "Vitellia" (see Letter 966).

3. Weston's last part was that of Dozey in *May Day; or, The Little Gipsy;* when this piece was acted for the third time, Nov. 6, Weston's name was omitted from the bill. He was to die in January (*LC*, vol. XXXIX, Jan. 13–16, 1776, p. 51).

4. The part in *Epicoene; or, The Silent Woman* was assigned to King, who "did more than possibly could have been expected" with it (*ibid.*, p. 52).

5. Presumably the actress (d. 1792) who after performing in the provinces secured an engagement at Edinburgh and acted there from about 1775 to 1780 (see Peake, *Colman*, I, 107; *Thespian Dictionary*, 1805; Tate Wilkinson, *The Wandering Patentee*, York, 1795–96, II, 87, 96f.).

964   To Robert Smith[1]

Adelphi

Sir   Decr 12 [1775?][2]

The Theatre Royal in Drury Lane gives two Charity Benefits a year to the Hospitals, & they take their Turn in Succession— there are two fix'd for this, & two for the next, & how they go on afterwards I cannot say, not having the Book with Me— if the Committee would be pleas'd to know the future Arrangement of the Benefits, if they will send the Secretary, he shall see what we have done, what we shall, & what we can do— I came from Hampton Yesterday, or you should have had an answer before.

I am Sr Your most Obed^t Ser^t

D: Garrick.

Address: Mr Robert Smith, Fen Court, Fenchurch Street. *Postmark:* TU. *Endorsement:* 12th Decr David Garrick— (Concerning a Benefit-night at Drury-Lane, for the Misericorde Hospital). *Source:* FSL.

1. Robert Smith was an attorney who lived at a Fenchurch Street address, "1 Fan Court, Fenchurch Street," from 1775 to 1780 (London Directories, 1775–1780).

2. The conjectural year is determined by the fact that the letter was written before Garrick's retirement and during Smith's residence at Fen Court; in 1775 Dec. 12 fell on a Tuesday (see postmark).

965 To Peter Fountain

Dear Sir   Decr 15 [1775?]^1
I am unluckily engag'd to breakfast tomorrow with the famous
MonS^r Tessier—^{2} have not you heard of him?— Sorry I am I
cannot have ye Pleasure of Seeing you wth y^r Club: I hope y^e
inclos'd is right— if not— I'll alter it—

Your Ever & truly
D Garrick—

Address: Mr Fountain, Maiden Lane.   *Source:* FC.

1. The conjectural year depends on the reference to Le Texier, and the implication
that he has recently arrived in London.
2. A.-A. Le Texier (1737–1814) had been highly successful as a reader of plays until
he was accused of misappropriation of funds; he came to London in Sept. 1775 (Hedgcock, pp. 267–274).

966 To Robert Jephson

Adelphi

My Dear Sir   Decb. 18. 1775
I took Vitellia^1 with me to Hampton, & I not only read it myself,
to myself, but to some Ladies & a Gentleman of great taste in
theatrical matters— they were ignorant of the Author but agreed
that it was not at all calculated for success upon the Stage— that it
was romantick & what was worse, unaffecting— indeed you will,
in my opinion rue the hour that it is brought upon the Stage—
Your reputation is at present high on our dramatick list, & why you
would venture to throw away your well earn'd fame upon an uncertainty at the best, I cannot conceive— in short, I am so certain
of my Judgment in the present business that I cannot consent to
your undoing your well doing on the Same Theatre—
    I beseech you to consult your sincere & knowing friends— call
a grand Jury of 'em & let our friend Tighe be the foreman, and
after they have sworn upon our dramatick Gospel Shakespeare, let
'em bring Vitellia in a *true bill* if they dare— You have made me

unhappy, but nevertheless my best & warmest wishes attend you & yours— I am Dear Sir

Most Affectionatly Yours
D G.

P.S. It is impossible that any thing worthy of you should be resolv'd or done in this hurry scurry, patch work way— you adventure too much

Endorsement by Garrick: 1775— Answer to Jephson Dec[r] 19th. *Source:* FC, copy; Boaden, II, 113f.

1. When this play, retitled *The Conspiracy,* was finally brought out at Drury Lane on Nov. 15, 1796, it was, as Garrick predicted, a failure (Martin S. Peterson, *Robert Jephson,* Lincoln, Nebraska, 1930, p. 41).

967   To Hannah More

Adelphi
Dec[r] 19th— [1775][1]

My dear Madam

What can I possibly say to You, that can in the best manner declare the feelings of my heart, for the great honour you have done Me, & the great pleasure you have given Me— I am most truly & Sincerely sensible of Your very affectionate & friendly attachment to me, & I will venture to say, in Spite of my unworthiness for such a Mark of Your regard, there is no human being, however more deserving Your favours, that can be more grateful, more Sensible of Your partiality, or that would feel a tithe of y[e] Pleasure and Satisfaction, which I do, at the kind destinction your generous friendship has given me by Your dedication—[2] what I think of the work dedicated, I shall not tell you: but, as You keep *Your* Secrets I will tell you *mine*; my Sentiments shall be publish'd towards the latter End of the next Week,[3] the holidays destroy all the good intentions of a literary Nature, the Minds of Men are totally absorb'd in Plumb porridge & Minc'd-pies— M[r] Twiss is now with Me & has Shewn Me some exquisite imitations of Yours, upon my Credit, I don't know any thing that pleases me more, nor would I believe, that they have a Spanish Source, but that he swears himself black in y[e] face, that there is a Spanish Poet, who has conceiv'd, I am sure not executed, so well. It gives me great joy that you will be w^(th) us after Xmas— but why not *soon* after? if you cannot come till March, I dread my being oblig'd to go to Bath— besides if Your flattery has any foundation, & that my Fool's Coat draws You this way, why not draw You *Sooner*?

I have two little performances for You⁴ which are not worth Your Acceptance— I am oblig'd to write for us because other people will not at ye Same time— the one is a great favourite, & the other has answer'd the End of writing it.

> I am My dear Miss More with my Love & my Wife's
> Love to You all Most truly & faithfully Your Friend
> D: Garrick

I am oblig'd to write upon the gallop for Mr Twiss is in a hurry— I find I have written Nonsense in two places, you must make sense of it, as you can of any thing.

Address: Miss Hannah More, Bristol.   *Source:* FSL.

1. The year is determined by the reference to the dedication.
2. To *Sir Eldred of the Bower, and The Bleeding Rock* (1776). The dedication itself is dated from Bristol, Dec. 14, 1775. Walpole's copy of the book bears in his hand the date of acquisition: "December 22^d 1775" (HCL). The poems were announced by the *Public Advertiser* as published "this day" on Saturday, Dec. 23, 1775.
3. Perhaps "Upon Reading Sir Eldred of the Bower," with an introductory note, which, however, was to appear anonymously in the *Public Advertiser* three months later: April 3, 1776 (see Knapp, No. 239).
4. Presumably the published book of *May Day; or, The Little Gipsy, A musical Farce To which is added The Theatrical Candidates, A Musical Prelude* (1775). The advertisement states that *May Day* "was produced at an early part of the season, when better writers are not willing to come forth." *The Theatrical Candidates*, performed on Sept. 23, opened the season of 1775–76.

968   To Richard Bailye¹

Adelphi

My dear Dick   [December] 19 [1775]

Next Week You'll have a Barrel of excellent Oysters, & till they come you must take part w^(th) Peter & the Doxies for they will have some this Week— You were a damn'd fool to leave us so soon— The Brawn & minc'd Pyes would make your Chops Water— but we shall see You after Xmas & then We'll make you as drunk as a Piper— Tell all my Lichfield friends that I long to be with them, & that I certainly intend to shake Every dirty fist from Bacon Street to Green hill some time in yᵉ Summer—

I thank you dear Dick for your friendly letter, but yʳ friendly Company is worth all yʳ writing; So if You'll come again, I will prepare a new Influenza for You—

the Postman rings & I must conclude

Ever & affectʸ Yours
D: Garrick

Love to yʳ Brother.²

Endorsement: D: Garrick Esqʳ 19ᵗʰ Decʳ 1775. *Source:* HTC.

1. The familiar references—to Dick, the Lichfield members of the family, the recent visit to London, and to the brother—all point to Richard Bailye, Garrick's cousin, as the recipient.
2. William Bailye (d. 1785), of Lichfield, apothecary; Bailiff of Lichfield in 1757 and 1776 (Thomas Harwood, *History of Lichfield*, 1806, p. 434f.).

969 To William Smith

Sir   Tuesday Decbʳ 26ᵗʰ 1775
You have prov'd to Me that you have no attachment to me or my affairs— Would your wearing a domino & Mask, to take turn about with *Me* in walking down yᵉ Stage, be an injury to your Importance?—¹ I hope not— it would have been of Consequence to yᵉ Jubilee, which is got up at a great expence to support your & other Performers importance, which without it has suffer'd, & may Suffer more— but I am now, I must say, fully convinced that our connection is not rooted in the heart or in a Mutual desire to Serve each other.

I am &c.

I am this moment come home, and found your Letter upon the table— I am likewise in a great hurry for *I* am obliged to make one at yᵉ Jubilee.²

Source: FC, copy; Boaden, II, 117.

1. In a letter dated only Sunday but apparently written on Dec. 24, Smith had expressed a strong unwillingness "to appear as Benedick in the Procession" of *The Jubilee* (Boaden, II, 123). *The Dictionary of National Biography* reports that this actor was wont to boast that "he had never played in an afterpiece and never worn a beard or gone down a trap."

2. *The Jubilee* was revived on Dec. 26.

970   To James Boswell

Drury Lane

Dear Sir   Decr 26. 1775

Tho I am in the midst of Preparations for Shakespeare's Jubilee, & have my Fool's Coat on to sing his praises, I will not omit answering Y^r Letter[1] one post, as there is a little business in it— our Company is So full, & the Parts, or rather part, which Mr Johnston[2] perform'd, Supplied, that I have not ye least room for any new Performer— indeed my good Friend, We are at present so overburden'd with Histrionic Minors, that few Managers could bear their Weight— I am Sorry, that I cannot obey Lord Kaime's Commands,[3] I honour him much & read him often— as for our Friend the D^r, I have seen him but once since his return, he is full of Sarcasm against the french—[4] at present I cannot say more upon this Subject, but You shall have it all in ye Spring— I scarce have time to tell You how much I am D^r S^r

Your most Obed^t hum^{le} Se^t
D. Garrick.

Address: James Boswell Esqr, Advocate, Edinburgh. *Seal. Postmark:* DE 26. *Source:* Boswell MSS. Yale.

1. From Edinburgh on Dec. 21 (Boswell MSS. Yale).
2. Presumably Alexander Johnstone, who died in this year. He was long housekeeper at Drury Lane, and also had made a name for himself as Gibby, the Scottish servant in *The Wonder* (Lysons, III, 437f.).
3. Boswell had enclosed a letter (of Dec. 19) from Lord Kames asking Boswell to recommend to Garrick "Charles Young, formerly my Clerk, a well disposed peaceable creature, but unfortunate I think, in taking a violent passion for being a Player ... He has been more than a year with Mr Digges [in the Edinburgh theater] ... The death of Johnstone his Countryman employed in acting the Scotsman, gives him a glimpse of hope that he may be taken on by Mr Garrick to supply that vacancy." Boswell seconded the recommendation with additional information. Henry Home (1696–1782), Lord Kames, was the Scottish advocate and judge; though he wrote much on law, he had wide general

literary interests, and as Boswell reminded Garrick, "must be allowed to have considerable weight in the *Critick Department*."

4. From Sept. 15 to Nov. 15 Johnson and the Thrales had toured France.

971   To George Colman

Adelphi

My Dear Sir.   Decr 29th 1775
As I promis'd to let You know before I parted with my theatrical Property that You might be the purchaser if You pleas'd— I must now seriously acquaint You that I shall most certainly part with it— I Saw a Gentleman Yesterday of great property,[1] & who has no Objection to the price Viz: 35000 pounds for my Part— I must desire You to speak out, whether You have any thoughts of Succeeding Me in Drury Lane for I must see the Party again on Saturday Evening to talk over the Matter, & determine on my Part— I beg You will write to me directly & be explicit,[2] for I must determine or perhaps lose My Market— My disorder increases & distresses me much; my Friend Pott is to search for ye cause next Week— I beg that Your letter may be determinate— once again Many happy Years to You— I am Dear Colman

Most Affec^{ly} Yours
D: Garrick.

I have sent our friend Becket on purpose as this Matter is of great Consequence and I would not trust any other person with it— the Party wants to purchase the Whole, I must desire you to keep this business a Secret for More reasons than One—

Source: FC, draft; Boaden, II, 118.

1. Richard Brinsley Sheridan wrote his father-in-law, Thomas Linley, on Dec. 31 that he had met Garrick on Dec. 28 to discuss the purchase of Drury Lane. Garrick appeared to be "*really serious*" in the business, still, however, reserving the right of giving the refusal to Colman, though at the same time believing that Colman would decline it (Thomas Moore, *Memoirs of Richard Brinsley Sheridan*, 1825, I, 181f.).

2. Colman replied on Dec. 30: "If . . . your Letter . . . means to offer me *the refusal of* ONLY *your share of the* Property, to that offer I can immediately and most determinately say NO. I would not for worlds again sit on the throne of Brentford with any assessor, except it were yourself . . . If You are enabled to treat *for the whole*, or to reserve *your own half*, we must talk farther" (FC; Boaden, II, 118).

972   To Richard Brinsley Sheridan

[December 31, 1775][1]

Mr. Garrick presents his compliments to Mr. Sheridan, and as he is obliged to go into the country for three days, he should be glad to see him upon his return to town, either on Wednesday about 6 or 7 o'clock, or whenever he pleases. The party has no objection to the whole, but chooses no partner but Mr. G.—[2] Not a word of this yet. Mr. G. sent a messenger on purpose.— He would call upon Mr. S., but he is confined at home. Your name is upon our list.

Source: Thomas Moore, *Memoirs of Richard Brinsley Sheridan*, 1825, I, 182.

1. The date is from Sheridan's letter to Thomas Linley of Dec. 31, 1775, wherein he states that he has received "within this hour" a note from Garrick, "which . . . I here transcribe for you"; Garrick's letter follows in the source.
2. "On this, Mr. Garrick appointed a meeting with his partner, young Leasy, and, in the presence of their solicitor, treasurer, &c., declared to him that he was absolutely on the point of settling, and, if *he* was willing, he might have the same price for his share; but if he (Leasy) would not sell, Mr. Garrick would, instantly, to another party. The result was, Leasy's declaring his intention of not parting with his share. Of this Garrick again informed Colman, who immediately gave up the whole matter" (Sheridan to Linley, Jan. 4, 1776, Thomas Moore, *Memoirs of Richard Brinsley Sheridan*, 1825, I, 185).

973   To Peter Fountain

[1775][1]

Thank you, my dear Sir, for your Intelligence, I fear by what I heard Yesterday, that all Interest is quite Shut out— some powerful Influence, & perhaps a hint or plot to guide his Majesty will govern in this Unhappy Circumstance— I cannot yet talk of Successors to Weston, & hope to bid adieu to Management Myself—

Y[rs] Ever &c

D. G.—

Still Weak.

Address: M[r] Fountain.   *Source:* FC.

1. Written in 1775, presumably late in the year, when Weston was dying and Garrick was preparing to retire.

974 To Elizabeth Montagu

My dear Madam. [1775?][1]
We are unfortunatly Engag'd on Sunday next— but if We are able
to quit our Company, may we be permitted to pay our respects to
you?— if You should be Engag'd We will wait upon you ye first
opportunity— I have made bold to answer for You as a Subscriber
to Mr Capel's school of Shakespear—[2]
I will tell you more of this when I have the honour & pleasure
of Seeing you.
I am most devotedly Yours
D: Garrick.

Address: Mrs Montagu, Hill Street. *Seal. Source:* FSL.

1. The conjectural year is supplied by the reference to the subscription for Capell, presumably started immediately after the recall of his *Notes*.
2. When Capell's *Notes and Various Readings to Shakespeare* (dedication dated Dec. 20, 1774) met with a poor reception, he recalled it almost immediately, deciding to reissue the work by subscription and with the addition of a third volume on the "School of Shakespeare." The subscribers' list was "respectable, though not numerous," primarily because of "the inattention of a Friend [Garrick?] ... who had given him the most flattering hopes, through his personal interest, of a long list of names, which eventually amounted to very few" (Nichols, *Illustrations*, I, 472f.). The volumes were not finally to be published until 1783.

975 To Joseph Cradock

Adelphi
Jany 1st [17]76
A happy New Year to You my dear Sir, & many of them— So
said our less refin'd Ancestors, & I hope their Sayings will not be
disagreeable to Mr Craddock, tho they offend the delicate Ears of
our very Modish fine Gentlemen—
When Ever You please to open Your Budget, I shall attend it
with great pleasure— I shall have a double pleasure in the Operation,
first to hear You read a tragedy,[1] & next that tragedy is Yours.
I am Dr Sr Most sincerely Yrs
D: Garrick

I sh^d have been proud of seeing Mr Farmer—² a charming writer

Address: —— Craddock Esqr at Hinchinbrook near Huntington. *Post-marked. Source:* FSL, also copy; Joseph Cradock, *The Czar*, 1824, p. vii.

1. Identified in the printed source as *The Czar* (printed 1824, but never produced).
2. Cradock always avoided introducing Richard Farmer to Garrick. "I knew," he writes, "that Garrick duly estimated his 'Essay on the Learning of Shakspeare,' and I feared that his coarse manners would sink him in the estimation of the great Actor" (I, 36).

976   To The Reverend Doctor John Hoadly

Adelphi

My dear Friend. Jany 3 1776
I shall take my leave of the Stage, & bid Farewell to the plumed troops & the big Wars, & welcome content & the tranquil Mind— in Short— I will not stay to be Sixty with my Cap & bells— Active as I am, & full of Spirit, with the drawback of a *gravel-complaint*:
Mrs Garrick & I are happy wth the thoughts of my *Strutting & fretting no more upon ye Stage*,¹ & leaving to Younger Spirits the present race of Theatrical Heroines with all their Airs, indispositions, tricks & importances which have reduc'd the Stage to be a dependant upon the Wills of our insolent, vain, & let me add insignificant female trumpery— there must be a revolution, or my Successors will Suffer much, I had a resource in my own Acting, that counteracted all the Evil designs of these Gentry— Linley² will be of great Service— Sing Song is much the Fashion, & his knowledge of Musick & preparing fit Subjects for the Stage, will be a Strength, that the Proprietors may depend upon, when the Heroines are prankish— Dr Ford,³ the great Man Midwife, & very worthy Man will be concern'd in the purchase, as a Monied Man, not as one of ye Managers. The Story of my reading the Verses upon Grace to Miss Dutton⁴ at a Breakfast at Spring Garden,⁵ is most true, & I turn'd extempore the Line upon ye Dss of Cumberland⁶ upon her, & at ye time, I told you ye very words, which occasion'd a great laugh— *Mr Hardhead* (the foolishest of all foolish Scriblers), has certainly lost his wager, & his Verses in the BathEaston Collection⁷ Shew that he has lost his wits too, if Ever he had any— What a

6+L.D.G. III

prig of a Parson!— He was as important, & as Zealous to get M[rs] Miller's[8] Frippery prize, as if he had been after spiritual prefer- ment— I could not bear his absurd vanity, & shun'd him— E⟨rgo⟩ I am no favourite with y[e] Hardheads

have you read Anstey's last Work⟨—⟩[9] I fear it is short of y[e] Bath Guide— the *honnete Criminal*[10] I have read, & refus'd it in English— it has Merit, but y[e] Speeches too long, too french, & not quite dramatic Enough for our Audiences. I can say no More, but that I & Mine love You, & Yours— so

Ever & most Affectionatly (Manager or no Manager)
Your Friend & Serv[t]
D. Garrick.

We have found the lost Sheep Harry Fielding's *Good Naturd Man* that was missing near twenty Years—[11]

Address: Rev[d] D[r] Hoadly, S[t] Maries, Southampton. *Postmark:* IA 4. *Source:* FSL.

1. *Macbeth*, V, v, 25.
2. Thomas Linley (1732–1795), composer, singing-master, father-in-law of Sheridan, had come to London from Bath in 1774 to become joint-manager with Stanley of the Drury Lane oratorios.
3. James Ford (1718–1795), M.D., was physician-extraordinary to Queen Charlotte and a wealthy obstetrician in the West End of London.
4. Jane Dutton (1753–1800), sister of James, later first Baron Sherborne. Garrick's verses to her, called "Simplex Munditis," were printed in the second volume of *Poetical Amusements at a Villa Near Bath* along with a number of other verses praising her (1776, pp. 2–5, 49, 139). Garrick's lines must have been written during his visit to Bath in May 1775, for on Oct. 5 of that year Miss Dutton married Thomas William Coke, later (1837) Earl of Leicester.
5. Social gatherings by invitation from Mrs. Miller held on alternate Thursday mornings in Spring Garden at her Batheaston Villa during the Bath season.
6. Anne (Luttrell) Horton (1743–1808) whose scandalous conduct and clandestine marriage to the Duke of Cumberland brought her notoriety. Walpole describes the Duchess as "extremely pretty, not handsome, very well made, with the most amorous eyes in the world, and eyelashes a yard long" (ed. Toynbee, VIII, 103f.). Garrick's "On Grace" written to the Duchess were printed in *Poetical Amusements* (II, 1f.), and earlier in the *London Chronicle* for May 9–11, 1775, and elsewhere (Knapp, No. 112).
7. Volume II of *Poetical Amusements at a Villa Near Bath* was shortly to be published; it is advertised in the *London Chronicle* for Jan. 24, 1776, as published that day. The volume contains two poems by Sanfoord Hardcastle (pp. 14f., 162f.). Despite Garrick's inclusion in the volume, he wrote some scornful verses called "Upon the Batheaston Prize" (Sotheby, Catalogue, Feb. 17, 1930, No. 199).
8. Anna (Riggs) Miller (1741–1781), later (1778) Lady Miller, verse-writer, of Batheaston Villa, Bath. In a manuscript note in a copy of Richard Bull's *Lines Sent to Lady Miller's Vase* (1781), now in the Harvard College Library, Walpole gives an account of the Batheaston diversions: "at Bath, where 'tis fashionable to be foolish, a man has no chance of being thought either, who does not send some nonsense to Lady Miller's Vase. She gives out a Subject returnable that day fortnight. Every thing that is sent, is

put into an antique Vase, and when the Company is met, Sir John Miller leads up some young Lady to the Vase, who takes out the first Poem, she happens to lay her hands upon, which is given to some Gentleman present to read aloud, and which, by the Bye, is generally done most wretchedly, and it is usual for the men to run into a little room next that, where the Vase stands, to avoid being call'd upon to read . . . This ceremony is repeated till all the Poems are taken out of the Vase and read; after which the Gentlemen retire and decide which Poem is deserving the Prize; The author is presented with a Crown of Myrtle by Lady Miller, and gives it to some favorite Lady who wears it at the next Ball" (see also Ruth A. Hesselgrave, *Lady Miller and the Batheaston Literary Circle*, New Haven, 1927).

9. *An Election Ball in Poetical Letters from Mr. Inkle of Bath to His Wife at Gloucester*, written in imitation of *The New Bath Guide* and suggested by subjects given out at Batheaston. The verses are dated Dec. 6, 1775, and their publication is announced in the *London Chronicle* for Jan. 20–23, 1776.

10. A French verse-drama by Fenouillet de Falbaire (published in 1767; first acted in Paris in Jan. 1790). An English translation by "G.L." appeared in 1778. Garrick had rejected the play in Nov. 1767 (see Hedgcock, p. 275f.; see also Pembroke to Garrick, Jan. 28, 1768, HTC).

11. It was to be produced at Drury Lane under the title of *The Fathers; or, The Good Natur'd Man* (Nov. 30, 1778). According to a memorandum by Garrick: "The beginning of my Correspondence with Sir John Fielding was thus— The Late Mr Fielding was my particular Friend: he had written a Comedy call'd the *Good-Natur'd Man*, which being lent to his different Friends, was lost for 20 Years— It luckily fell to my lot to discover it, had I found a Mine of Gold upon my own land, it could not have given me more pleasure— I immediately ran to his Brother Sr John, & told him the Story of my discovery & immediately with all the warmth imaginable— offer'd my Services to prepare it for the Stage— he thank'd me cordially & we parted with mutual expressions of kindness" (FC; John Forster, *The Life and Times of Oliver Goldsmith*, 1854, II, 56).

977   To Richard Rigby

Adelphi

My dear Sir   Jany 7 [1776][1]

As I have flatter'd myself into a belief that whatever concerns Me much is not indifferent to You, I cannot finish the last Act of my theatrical life without informing my best friend of it— I am in treaty for the Sale of my Patent & all my property at the Theatre: I cannot free Myself from this great Weight, at a more proper or profitable time and therefore My Wife & I upon the most Mature Consideration, have thought it expedient upon many Accounts to make my Exit if possible at the End of this Season— As I have been long honour'd wth Your friendp, I thought it my duty to communicate it first to You— the business is not yet quite finish'd, but in a very fair Way— it is thought likewise necessary to keep it a Secret till We have sign'd & seal'd— If I fairly get quit of this

Matter the Burrough-Monger who return'd last Night from Bath much better than he has been for some time[2] will be wholly at leisure to Employ his great Electioneering talents in Your Service— may I be permitted to be a little Serious, tho I have not ye least right to trouble You in his behalf? it would make both him & Me Extremely happy, if he could deserve Your Notice in any way— he is honest & faithful & would (as well as his Brother) be the most Grateful of Men, if he could at any time & in any manner be number'd among Your humble Servants—

I am my dear Sir Very much asham'd but
Most truly attachd hu^le Ser^t
D. G.

Source: FSL, draft.

1. The year is supplied by Rigby's reply of Jan. 17, 1776 (FC; Boaden, II, 125).
2. George Garrick, who had doubtless participated in the election of Palmer (see Letter 903). "For my friend, the Borough Monger," declared Rigby in his reply, "if it should fall in my way to be of service to Him, I shall have great pleasure in publickly marking the regard I privately profess to have for you." However, by Dec. 22, 1776, Rigby had not yet come to George's aid, for on that date, writing from Bath to ask his brother for £50, George remarked: "I was in hopes that before this time, our friend Mr. Rigby wou'd have procur'd me some Employment, which wou'd have prevented my giving you so much trouble" (letter in the possession of C. F. Bishop).

978   To James Clutterbuck

Adelphi
My dear Clut.   Jany 18th 1776
You shall be the first Person to whom I shall make known, that I have at last Slipt my theatrical Shell, & shall be as fine & free a Gentleman as You would wish to see upon the South or North parade at Bath— I have Sold my Moiety of Patent &c &c for 35000— to Messrs Dr Ford Ewart,[1] Sheridan, & Linley—[2] we have sign'd to forfeit 10000 pounds, if the Conditions of our present Articles are not fulfill'd the 24 of June next—[3] in Short I grow somewhat Older, tho I never play'd better in all my Life, & am resolv'd not to remain upon the Stage to be pitied instead of applauded— the Deed is done & the Bell is ringing, so I can Say

no more, but that I hope I shall receive a Letter of felicitation from You— Love to Your better half & to the Sharps & all friends.

Ever & most affect^y Y^{rs}

D Garrick

Address: James Clutterbuck Esqr, Bath.   *Postmark:* IA 19.   *Source:* E. Percival Merritt; John P. Collier, *An Old Man's Diary*, 1871, pt. 1, p. 12.

1. Simon Ewart, referred to as an old man in 1782, was a relative of the Sheridans and a family friend; a wealthy brandy merchant of London, he lived on Thames St. Ewart later withdrew from the transaction (Anonymous, *Sheridaniana*, 1826, p. 39; Walter Sichel, *Sheridan*, 1909, I, 363, 388; Thomas Moore, *Memoirs of Richard Brinsley Sheridan*, 1825, I, 181f.).

2. "What a strange jumble of people," wrote Mrs. Clive to Garrick, Jan. 23, 1776, concerning the buyers of his patent. "I thought I should have died with laughing when I saw a man-mid-wife amongst them: I suppose they have taken him in to prevent *miscarriages!*" (Boaden, II, 128).

3. The sale contract was signed on the day this letter was written. For further details see Linley's letter to Garrick in the Forster Collection and Moore's *Sheridan* (I, 86ff.).

979   To Sir Grey Cooper

Adelphi

My dear Sir.   Jany 29th 1776

Tho I have not troubled You with congratulations upon a late Occasion,[1] I have not less rejoic'd than those, who have express'd the most Zeal at Your Welfare by their personal Attendance— if Ever it should happen that my Company will prove no interruption to better, & more important business, I shall beg to wait upon You & throw in a half-joke now & then among the Wits & Beaux Esprits that surround You— I had procur'd a Stage box for Lady Cooper this Evening, but the Festino, I fear, will allure her Ladyship from the Formal & unfashionable company of Sr Ant^y Branville:[2] may I be permitted to throw in a Line or two of Business— as I am quitting the Sock & Buskin, I cannot help continuing my Care to the Old & helpless of the profession— We have got a fund towards their support of near 5000, & with care & good Management, we shall make it of Some Consequence to the Invalids of ye Stage:

If we could procure an Act of Parliament to incorporate Us, & many of the grave & Younger part of the house seem desirous of doing it, I should finish my theatrical Life, as I would Wish, by presenting the Actors with this necessary & honourable Security for their Money— I would not dare to ask an impertinent favour, & should drop it directly, if it was disagreeable to HIM, for whom my Wishes & Services shall be ever Active, but, I am told, Mr Eliott,³ Mr Bacon⁴ & many of the respectable Members, are very desirous to be friendly & kind to any petition we may present to Parliament upon the Occasion—⁵ May I without offence intreat you to speak your Sentiments, which be assur'd, shall never be known, or declar'd upon any Account whatsoever, if you Wish it should be so, by

Sir Your most Obligd & Most Obedient humble Servant

D: Garrick.

Mrs Garrick presents her respects with mine to Lady Cooper.

Source: FSL.

1. Perhaps a reference to Cooper's having become a baronet in Oct. 1775.
2. Cooper, in his reply of the same date, regretted that Garrick was right (Boaden, II, 132).
3. Edward Eliot (1727–1804), later (1784) Lord Eliot of St. Germans, politician, was at this time M.P. for Cornwall.
4. There were two Bacons in the House of Commons at this time: Edward Bacon (1713?–1786), M.P. for Norwich and Recorder of that city, and Anthony Bacon (d. *ca.* 1799) of Woodford Row, Essex, a London merchant and M.P. for Aylesbury, Buckinghamshire (*GM*, vol. XLV, Aug. 1775, pp. 377, 383; vol. LVI, March 1786, p. 269; vol. LXIX, Aug. 1799, p. 718).
5. A petition for a bill "for better securing" the Theatrical Fund against "any Misapplication or Embezzlement," was to be introduced in the House of Commons on Feb. 7, 1776. It was referred to a committee, headed by Cooper and Burke. On Feb. 13 Cooper reported on the petition, and by order of the House the bill was drawn up; it was passed, and received the Royal Assent on March 25 (*Journals of the House of Commons,* 1776, XXXV, 517, 554, 633, 651, 679).

980   To Lancelot Brown

My dear Sir.   [*ante* February 5, 1776]¹
You make Me & my Wife mad— You shall be prefer'd to the whole body of Nobility, if you will give us Notice but one day of y^r Coming— I have kept places till 12 o'Clock the two last times of my Playing, but you never sent— There is not a Single place in the Whole house

but what is Engag'd— Don't use me so again for I love & esteem You & am moreover oblig'd to You— I shall Play Monday & Fryday Sen'night. Shall I procure You places for those days?

Since I wafer'd yᵉ Enclos'd, My Wife is resolv'd to make room for You, as well as She can in her Box— Come to the Stage door & Enquire for her box— yᵉ Ladies not in hats.

Address: To L. Brown Esqʳ. *Endorsed. Source:* FSL.

1. The conjectural date is based on the assumption that Brown wished to see Garrick play during his final season. During that season, the week of Feb. 5–9 was the only one in which Garrick appeared twice, on a Monday and a Friday, in different roles.

981 To Edmund Burke

Adelphi

My dear Sir   Febʳʸ 6ʰ 1776
Don't be Surpriz'd if you See my Name at the head of a Petition to Parliament for *Some provision to be made for Securing the Money we have got towards a fund for the relief of decay'd Actors* &c—[1] I should have waited upon You to have told You this, & to have desir'd Your Concurrence: We have found great favour with the Members, & I flatter Myself, that You will not oppose it, if it seems proper & to the purpose

Dear Sir Ever Yours most cordially
D. Garrick

I have not stirr'd abroad on acctᵗ of some disturbances in yᵉ theatre.[2]

Address: Eᵈ Burke Esqʳ. *Seal. Source:* Sheffield City Libraries.

1. In the Forster Collection there is a letter enclosing a bill (paid by Garrick on April 11, 1776) for £116.9s.10d. covering the expenses of the Act of Parliament to incorporate "the performers at Drury Lane Theatre Session 1775/6."
2. Occasioned by the production of Henry Bate's *Blackamoor Wash'd White* on Feb. 1. Bate, who had many enemies, had planted a number of ruffians and friends in the audience in case of trouble. As he had anticipated, a party came to damn the play; rioting ensued, continuing for four nights until it was announced that "the Authour had taken the Copy from the Prompter, and that it should not be done again" (Hopkins, Diary, DLC, p. 194; BD; Henry Angelo, *Reminiscences*, 1828, I, 165ff.).

982 To Jane Pope

Adelphi
Dear Madam   Feb^ry 11th [1776]^1
I thank you for Your polite letter, as I will not have any more
altercation with You, I will not Enter into a debate of our unlucky
difference— it gave Me great uneasiness that we were not together
this Season; & I now protest to You, that never did I in Word or
deed vary in the whole Course of Management from being your
warm & constant friend—

It was this that made me feel what I thought your disregard for
Me, more severely— I must desire now that any retrospect of this
business may wholly dropt— I suppose before this, that Mrs Clive
has told You that my first desire after ye Sale of my Patent, & before
I mention'd any other Person to them, Was the Establishing Miss
Pope in Drury Lane Theatre—^2 they, I must do them the justice,
seem'd as willing as Myself, to settle this Matter, if you would have
me say any thing more to them I will do it with great pleasure—
I am

Dear Madam Y^r very Sincere Well wisher
D: Garrick.

Address: Miss Pope.   *Seal.*   *Source:* Bodleian Library.

1. This is the reply to Miss Pope's letter of Jan. 28, 1776 (Boaden, II, 130f.).
2. She was to return to Drury Lane the following season, acting there until her
retirement.

983 To William Woodfall

Dear Sir   Tuesday [February] 13 [1776]^1
I was going to bed when your letter came last Night to the Adelphi,
& I have so much business with our change of Plays, Petition to
Parliament &c that I have Scarce a moment to answer Your
favour— As Your premises are founded upon a Mistake, I might
make my Conclusion very short, but I will not shew a peevish
turning away from the main object of the difference between Us—
in ye first place I never mention'd *rancour* respecting the *Blackamoor*,
but a *personal dislike* to *Me*, unconnected with the piece— You

must have known my very disagreeable Situation, that it was impossible for Me to give up the Author's property while it was suffer'd to be given out— & that if I had how many would have been ready to have imputed such behaviour to the meanest Motive: on the Saturday at Zara,[2] I was assur'd by Every body, for I was at home during the Farce, that had not Mr Roper[3] & two or three more come into the Boxes drunk in ye 3^d Scene of ye 2^d Act, the piece would have gone off wth gre⟨at⟩ applause— this all ye Performers agreed in— on the Sunday those Gentlemen who had bred the disturbance call'd upon Me, & seem'd much concern'd for what had happen'd, & assur'd me that it was mere Frolick, & that they meant No harm to ye author or Manager— after this, could I be warranted in Stopping it the 4th Night?— certainly not, as our Friend Colman will tell you— on the Monday Morn^g came forth y^r Paper, not only with a most severe Account of the Blackamoor, but some Cards or letters, for there were many, which tended to exasperate the audience again⟨st⟩ Me—[4] by good luck I Did not see them till the tuesday, or I should certainly have been so alarm'd, that I should have thought it necessary to have said something before my appearance in Sr John Brute—[5] now, Sir, this was what I thought ill natur'd, & personally disliking me— so far from condemning Your Spirit, I have often applauded it; but at the same time, I own that I may differ wth you in what is call'd ye impartial publication of letters which are brought to You—[6] if any tend by falsehood to prejudice even a Stranger to You, I think you would not be justifyd in publishing them, You will say y^r Paper is open for vindication, indeed friend Woodfall, I cannot think that a sufficient answer from You, or fit compensation for Me: I may be wrong but these are my sincere Sentiments, & I would not have printed such mischievous Matter upon you for any consideration— as to my Ears being open to Flattery, my dear Sir, & never hearing ye Truth that has been so often told me, that I almost begin to think myself a great Man indeed— if it is true, I am so us'd to it, that I am insensible of it— whatever may be my Genius or Abilities, I will venture to say that my Love of right, & attachment to my friends much exceed them— I could say much more, & will when I have an opportunity, but I write in too great a hurry, & have too much Matter in my head to write at all, did not I write to You with great Confidence

I am Y^r most obed^t hu^{le} Ser^t

D: Garrick.

Source: BM.

6*

1. Woodfall's reply to this letter is dated Feb. 13, 1776 (FC; Boaden, II, 136f.).
2. Feb. 3, 1776.
3. Henry Roper (d. 1788), a captain in the 30th Regiment of Foot and only brother of Charles Trevor Roper (1745–1794) later Lord Dacre.
4. Woodfall wrote in his reply: "You are wrong in saying there were *many* Cards or Letters, in Monday's Paper [*Morning Chronicle*, Feb. 5, 1776], to exasperate the Audience against you. There was only *one* Letter (beside the *Theatrical Intelligence Extraordinary*,) which at all tended to criminate you, and although I solemnly declare I am the Author of neither . . . I confess that from the face of Matters in the Theatre, I . . . think that both were justifiable" (FC; Boaden, II, 137).
5. On Feb. 5, which proved to be the last night of *The Blackamoor Wash'd White*.
6. Woodfall replied: "I acted against you, not as M[r] Woodfall, who honours, and respects you but as the Printer of the Morning Chronicle who ought to know, to hear to see— not through his own organs but those of his correspondents" (FC; Boaden, II, 136).

984   To Sir John Fielding

Adelphi
Feb[y] 22[d] [1776][1]

Mr Garrick presents his comp't's to Sir John Fielding— he return'd from Hampton yesterday very ill with the Gravel, or he shou'd have answer'd his Note before— With a proper regard for Sir John, he shall not now mention in its proper Colours, the false accusation and unjustifiable behaviour of one of his friends[2] to his Brother, whose warmth was too natural, to merit the severe censure it met with—[3] Mr Garrick imagin'd that the great compliment he paid to the Police by giving up his interest to their Opinion deserv'd justice at least from every Magistrate in Westminster. Mr Garrick wou'd have had as great pleasure in serving any of Sir John Fieldings family, as it wou'd have been a great honor to have had his Name join'd with that of his most excellent Brother; but as his present state of health may oblige him to go abroad for some time, he must beg leave to decline that business, & at the same time to express his satisfaction at being the Means of discover⟨ing⟩ the lost & valuable treasure.

Source: FC, copy.

1. This is the reply to Fielding's letter of Feb. 21, 1776 (FC).
2. William Addington (1728–1811), formerly a major in Burgoyne's regiment, was

at this time an official at Bow Street under Sir John Fielding. He wished, however, to be a dramatist; *The School for Wives* by his friend Kelly first appeared under his name, and his adaptation of Dryden's *Aureng-Zebe*, called *The Prince of Agra*, had been produced at Covent Garden on April 7, 1774 (George Baker, *History of Northamptonshire*, 1822–1830, I, 412f.; *BD*; *The Works of Hugh Kelly*, 1778, p. vii; *LC*, vol. XXXIV, Dec. 11–14, 1773, p. 573, vol. XXXV, June 2–4, 1774, p. 535).

3. After Garrick's offer of assistance in preparing Henry Fielding's newly found play, *The Fathers; or, The Good Natur'd Man*, for production, a misunderstanding arose that involved William Addington and George Garrick. Apparently Addington persuaded Sir John Fielding to allow him to make revisions in the play; this led to a disagreement between Addington as an author and Garrick as a manager, and George Garrick as a warm advocate of and emissary for his brother became involved in a sharp altercation with Addington (see the Fielding letters in FC).

985   To Sir John Fielding

Drury Lane Theatre
Feby 22 [1776]¹

Mʳ Garrick presents his compliments to Sir John Fielding and assures him that his ears are always open to conviction— the Play was returned to Mʳ Wallis from whom he had it and he imagines that a hurry of business has prevented that Gentleman from calling upon Sir John with it as he intended—² whatever Mʳ Addington may Say to the contrary I do assure you upon the word of a man that my behaviour to him, tho I was that instant going upon the Stage in the Character of Hamlet was as civil as if he had been the first Nobleman and my greatest friend—³ it is very Strange that my ill treatment of him should have happened upon the 8ᵗʰ of December and that I should not have heard of his complaints till two months after— Sir John will excuse my writing part of my letter in the first person and part in the third,⁴ I have so many people about me that I forgot I was scribbling a Note and not a letter

Endorsement: Mʳ Garrick to Sir John Fielding.   *Source:* FC, copy.

1. This is the reply to Fielding's letter of Feb. 22, 1776 (FC).
2. When Garrick, in the preceding letter, declined to assist in the preparation of *The Fathers; or, The Good Natur'd Man*, Fielding asked for the copy of the manuscript which had been prepared by Albany Wallis (Wilbur L. Cross, *History of Henry Fielding*, New Haven, 1918, III, 100f.).
3. The incident is partly explained by Addington's letter of March 1: "Mʳ Addington desires to inform Mʳ David Garrick, in justice to Sʳ John Fielding (whom He has always

considered as Mr Garrick's real Friend) that He never interfered or took part in the Dispute arising from Mr Addington's Opinion of Mr Garrick's Treatment of Him, behind the Scenes at Drury Lane Theatre; and if Mr Garrick's being then engaged in an interesting part, made Him forget the Civility, that was *so justly due to Mr Addington*, and He had at any time apologized for it, He should most undoubtedly have taken no farther Notice of it— and until a proper Apology be made, He must as a Gentleman, continue to be of the same Opinion— He is sorry that the above occurrence should have ocassioned any uneasiness to Sr John Fielding" (FC).

　　4. As Fielding had in the latter part of his letter.

986　　　　To Sir John Fielding

Adelphi

Febry 23d [1776]¹

Tho it is my profession to deal in *passion*, and yours in *Peace*, yet we seem to have chang'd hands— Your Worship grows out of humour, and I have not, I hope, been either uncivil, or out of temper— I write this just releiv'd from a fit of the Stone— my Spirits are tam'd by it, but not sour'd— We will if You please *not be the trumpets of our own Virtues* (as Shakespear says)² but take care that the innocent do not suffer by our Mistakes— there shall be *no Anathema denounc'd against them by Me*—³ if my thoughts & alteration of the plan of the good Natur'd Man will be of the least service to their Welfare I will go on with my Scribbling⁴ wth pleasure— my health is at present so precarious, that I am really afraid to undertake the Whole, (for much is wanted) lest the business shd be retarded by my leaving London or the Kingdom— What could you possibly mean by saying *that the mischief to the poor innocent family would not be so great as my Anger teaches me* to believe—? Surely these, Sir John, are the dictates of *Your* Anger, & not *mine*: & I will venture to say that now it is pass'd, you are sorry that you said it, as barbarity is as great a Stranger to my Nature, as falsehood to Yours— If you have oblig'd & honour'd me, I Thank You— that you never were in the Way to be oblig'd by Me is certain, or I should certainly have done it—⁵

　　Some reciprocal Acts of kindness pass'd between Your Brother & Me too triffling to be mention'd— but his praise is Fame: You might have guess'd at my Warmth to You & Yours by the pleasure

I had in ye discovery of the lost treasure— What You have said kindly I will remember, What unkindly I will Forget— I will not say farewel.

D Garrick.

Address: Sir John Fielding. *Seal. Endorsement by Garrick:* This letter was sent to Sr John & carry'd by Becket's Son ye 24th of Feb^ry 1776 & refus'd being taken in—. *Source:* FSL, copy in FC; John Forster, *Life and Times of Oliver Goldsmith*, 1854, II, 56n., extract.

    1. This is the reply to Fielding's letter of Feb. 23, 1776 (FC).
    2. *Much Ado about Nothing*, V, ii, 87f.
    3. In his letter of Feb. 23, written in reply to the preceding, Fielding had stated that because of his anger Garrick had revenged himself by refusing to be involved further in *The Fathers*, thus causing "an Anathema to be denounced against the innocent family of [Henry Fielding] to whom if Fame be of any Value Mr Garrick has the highest Obligations."
    4. After Sir John and Garrick were reconciled on July 23, 1776 (Letter 1033), Garrick assisted in some revisions and wrote the prologue and epilogue for the production at Drury Lane on Nov. 30, 1778 (Wilbur L. Cross, *History of Henry Fielding*, New Haven, 1918, III, 102; see also William Fielding to Garrick [*ca.* Nov. 1778], FC; Knapp, Nos. 313, 314).
    5. "You will be pleased then to take Notice," Fielding had concluded his letter, "that in the Course of my Life I have twice stood forth & once with great Danger to shelter David Garrick from the Resentment of the Public, that I have twice interfered to prevent Disputes between his Brother & Mr Addington being carried to improper Lengths, that I have twice been insulted for these Kind Offices, that I never received a Favour from Mr Garrick in the Course of my Life, have always done him Justice both publickly & privately, & sometimes done him much Honour. Farewell."

987   To Edward Tighe

                                           Adelphi

My dear Sir   Feby 24. 1776
I thank You most sincerely for y^r very flattering friendly letter— to quote my own lines in my own praise is surely the greatest luxury to a vain Mind.

    If I could have imagin'd that so worthy a Successor could have been found as a certain good Friend of Mine on the other side the Water, He most certainly should have had the refusal— deter Dignior would have weigh'd down the ballance at once in his favour— & yet why should I have been the means of his plunging into a Sea of Troubles, While I was sitting in my great chair on

Shore— it would have rous'd me from my lethargy, & Should have taken hold of the rudder again (as an Old Pilot is call'd off the Shore) to have shewn my regard & Esteem to the Captain— my Successors, (who are Young & Spirited Adventurers have no Notion of Danger, laugh at the rocks & quicksands, & tho they lower their flag now & then to yᵉ Old Admiral, yet they intend to Shew him I believe, that his manner Sailing will do well enough for a dung barge, but *not* for a first rate the Royal George— bon voyage to the Young Gentlemen— I have got so much into figure that I don't know how to get out of it— let me present my Wife's & my best & respectful Compᵗˢ to Your Lady,¹ & hope, without a figure, to have the honour & pleasure of kissing her hands at Hampton— Your approbation of my Conduct with regard to the last Tragedy² flatters me much, I have been a great friend to yᵉ author in that business, than in [*tear*] Now when I have yᵉ Pleasure of s⟨eeing⟩ You— pray my Love to [*tear*] Can you Serve Pope at her be⟨nefit⟩ An Admirable Actress & forgive her

Ever & most sincerely Yours
D. Garrick

the Postman rings & I can't read yᵉ Scrawl over

Address: Eᵈ Tighe Esqʳ, Member of Parliamᵗ, Dublin. *Postmark:* [F]E 26. *Source:* Walter R. Benjamin.

1. The former Miss Jones of Westmeath (John Burke, *Landed Gentry of Ireland*, 1904).
2. Jephson's *Braganza*.

988 To George Colman

My dear Colman   Tuesday Evening [March 5, 1776]¹
This moment return'd from my friend Wilmot's— I was sorry that fool Becket did not let you know that I was from home— Mʳˢ Garrick says & I say too, & when a man & wife agree it must be right, that the party you propose is yᵉ most agreeable of all parties, & therefore We will be disengag'd for yᵉ pleasure of meeting yᵉ Blackguards² you mention, from Thursday sev'night yᵉ rest of yᵉ year, till you fix your day— this being settled we will have no rehearsal next Thursday to interrupt yᵉ Engagement— We must

often meet I hope, before the blackguard day— I will certainly be at home all morning to morrow & if after you have done y^r business you will tittup over hither & take y^r mutton wth us, so much ye better— I would be with *You*, but I must stay to buy a little matter that is contiguous to my Wash house.

What Old Friend can you possibly mean?—[3] a laughing Friend too— Heav'n forefend that I should lose such a Jewel— I cannot guess whom You mean— I hope you'll let me know to morrow.

Ever & most cordially yours
D: Garrick.

Packet-Woodfall[4] pleases me much by doing justice to one of ye best Essays, that any *Gentleman* Ever Wrote— I shall send the *Gentleman* some Nonsense sign'd a *Gentlewoman*.

Source: Historical Society of Pennsylvania; Harry W. Pedicord, "Mr. and Mrs. Garrick: Some Unpublished Correspondence," *Publications of the Modern Language Association,* LX (Sept. 1945), 777.

1. The year for this letter, and for Letter 992, is derived from a letter by Hannah More written in [1776] in which she speaks of dining at the Adelphi at "an annual meeting, where nothing but men are usually asked . . . Colman and Schomberg were of the party" (Roberts, *Hannah More,* p. 48). The year is confirmed by her reference in the same letter to Garrick reading aloud "Sir Eldred" from the *Monthly Review* (vol. LIV, Feb. 1776, pp. 89–97). The reference in Letter 992 to *The Spleen,* first played at Drury Lane on Thursday, March 7, 1776, indicates that Garrick wrote his letter the next day: Friday, March 8. Finally, from the references in the present letter to the proposed party as "Thursday sev'night" and in Letter 992 as "*thursday* next," or March 14, it follows that the present letter was written on Tuesday, [March 5, 1776].

2. Colman had used "Blackguard" as his pseudonym for essays II and IV in "The Gentleman" series when they appeared in the *London Packet* during the summer and fall of 1775.

3. Perhaps Schomberg, see Letter 992 and Hannah More's letter quoted above; this was presumably Isaac Schomberg, to whom Colman had dedicated his translation of one of Terence's plays (1765).

4. William.

989   To Jean Baptiste Antoine Suard

Adelphi

My Dear Sir,   March 7th 1776

Ten thousand thanks for your great and friendly civilities to Dr. King.[1] He speaks of you all with the warmest gratitude. Pray let my dear friend, the Chevalier de Chatelleux, know that I am, on his account, a very miserable mortal. He sent me a letter some time ago, which, upon my honour, I can no more read, than if it was written in the Chinese language. I would have spoken to some French decypherer to have explained it, but fearing there may be some business, I have not yet dared to put it into other hands. If he will give me leave to do so, I shall be happy; for indeed, tho' I love and honour him so much, I have no profit or pleasure from his correspondence. Pray present Mrs. Garrick's and my most affectionate respects to him: you must likewise let my most dear and worthy Baron d'Holback know that his kindnesses and attentions to us, when at Paris, are never out of our hearts and minds: pray remember that Madame La Baronne is always included in our grateful remembrances: I have taken care that you shall have *Burney's History of Musick*[2] directly. Pray present my best compliments to M. l'Abbé Arnaud— if you forget to say every thing that is sincere and affectionate on our part to Mrs. Suard, and all our dear female friends we were connected with in France, you will for the first time be unjust and unfriendly. As for the essay you left in my hands, by our friend M. Diderot, you may depend upon my considering it well, and writing my remarks upon it.[3] Now for the other business:— An author who writes a piece of any kind whatever of five acts, is entitled to the third, sixth, and ninth night, and has no other profit from the theatre, but his liberty of the house. We have never had a three-act piece without a petite piece to make up the night's entertainment, and then it is the same thing with a performance of 5 acts; however I should allot 2 benefits and the 3d and 6th night for a 3-act piece; and the author of a farce, or any kind of piece acted *after* the first piece, is entitled to the 6th night. Should a performance have an extraordinary success, as at present the *Duenna* has at Covent Garden, which has already been play'd 99 nights,[4] then the managers will give the author of such a piece a 4th night during the run— but such 4th night cannot be claim'd by the author, it is a free gift from the manager for extraordinary merit. The managers of both theatres have agreed not to perform any of the new pieces which shall be done at either house, till the theatre where any new performance is first acted have enjoy'd it *two* seasons, then it becomes common property. An author, who has his entrées for writing a piece at one house has no privileges at the other. There can be no inconvenience arising from the manner of settling the profits of an author—he has his nights or night for his benefit, and there it ends. The copy-right is his own. The profits, with his copy-money, have sometimes risen to 8 or 9 hundred, and sometimes a thousand pounds. I can say no more, but that I am ever and most affectionately your

D. Garrick.

Source: New Monthly Magazine, XII (Dec. 1819), 535.

1. Presumably John Glenn King (1732–1787), D.D. 1771, previously chaplain to the English factory at St. Petersburg and at this time resident in London; he was a frequent visitor to the Burney household, where he became acquainted with Garrick (Frances Burney, *Early Diary*, ed. Annie R. Ellis, 1907, I, 119, *et passim*).

2. *A General History of Music*, the first volume of which had appeared in late February. Suard, in his letter of Feb. 28 (to which this is the reply), had asked for a copy of the volume so that a translation might be made "avec des notes de mon ami l'Abbé Arnaud, un des hommes de l'Europe qui entend le mieux et l'art et l'histoire de la musique" (Boaden, II, 614).

3. See Letter 787, note 4.

4. Actually played for the fifty-fourth time on March 7.

990   To Frances Abington

Madam   March 7th [1776]

at my return from the Country I found Your letter upon my table— I read it with great surprise, & can yet scarce believe that you are in earnest.[1] it would perhaps be as vain as impertinent in me to caution You against being too rash in determining upon so serious a Matter: my reasons for quitting ye Stage are many, & too strong to be withstood; You can have none but what will be easily conquer'd by your inclinations— it will therefore be worth Your while to consider seriously and if you have the least reason to repent of Your late determination, the best Night for a benefit which is the last Night of acting, before the Holidays, & which the Proprietors have purchas'd, is at Your Service— if you are still absolutely resolv'd to quit the Stage for Ever, I will certainly in May, do for Mrs Abington, what I have done for others who have made the Same resolution[2]

I am Madam &c

Endorsement by Garrick in copy: Mrs Abington's Letter dated March 4 & my answer to it sent By Ralph ye 7th of do 1776. *Source:* FC, draft and copy; Boaden, II, 142.

1. In her letter of March 4, 1776, she had informed Garrick of her "fixed determination to quit the stage"; Garrick endorsed the letter: "The Above is a true Copy of the letter examin'd Word by Word of that worst of bad Women Mrs Abington to ask my Playing for her Benefit & Why—" (FC; Boaden, II, 141).

2. Garrick did play for her benefit on May 7; she was finally to continue to perform at Drury Lane until 1782, when she transferred to Covent Garden.

991   To Edward Gibbon

Adelphi

Dear Sir   March 8th 1776

WhenEver I am truly pleas'd I must communicate my Joy: Lord Camden call'd upon Me this Morning & before Cumberland declar'd that he never read a more admirable performance than *Mr Gibbon's* History[1] & *he was in transport, & so was I— the Author is ye Only Man to write History of the Age— such depth— such perspicuity— such language force variety & what not?* I am so delighted with him, continues He— that I must write to thank him— I should be happy to know him— my Lord I have that honour, & will contrive if possible to bring You togeather—[2] said I too much—! My Coach is at ye Door— my Wife bawling for Me— & Every thing impatient— so hey for Hampton till Monday & in ye mean time as I am always

Most Truly Your most Obed^t & Oblig'd

D: Garrick

I have not a moment to read over this Scrawl—

Address: Ed^d Gibbon, Esqr, Bentinck Street, Cavendish Square. *Source:* BM; Edward Gibbon, *Miscellaneous Works*, ed. Lord Sheffield, 1814, II, 153.

1. The first volume of *The Decline and Fall of the Roman Empire*.

2. In his reply, dated March 11, Gibbon wrote: "With regard to the wish which his Lordship so politely expresses of my being made known to him, you must give me leave to say, that if he were still a chancellor or a minister, I might perhaps be inclined to meet his advances with some degree of coldness and reserve; but as he is now reduced to be nothing more than a great man, I shall eagerly embrace the first proper occasion of paying my respects to him" (Boaden, II, 145).

992   To George Colman

             Hampton
Dear Colman   Fryday [March 8, 1776][1]
Mrs Garrick will wait upon You with great pleasure on *Thursday*
next— pray let Schomberg be of ye Party, We have not seen [him]
a long long while & we love him—
 The Gentleman[2] is excellent: more when I see you.
           Ever & affect^y y^rs
            D Garrick

I hope y^r Spleen[3] will continue— We are jaunting it for a few days

Addressed. Seal. Source: Berg Collection; Colman, p. 292.

 1. See Letter 988, note 1, for the dating.
 2. Number VI of the essays was published on Dec. 4, 1775.
 3. Colman's comedy, with a prologue by Garrick (DL, March 7, 1776).

993 To The Count de Lauraguais[1]

             Adelphi
Sir   March 11th 1776
At my return from the Country I have this moment receiv'd the
honour of your letter—[2] As I shall be only solicitous to declare the
truth & w^d chuse to be as clear, as plain in my answer I hope, You
will excuse my writing in my own language.
 I should have been greatly flattered with your favour, had I not
so high an opinion of your wit, that I cannot but imagine you are
exercising it, when you talk of *my protection of M^r Le Texier.* The
humblest have their Attatchments, and I must confess that I am
yet prejudiced in his favour: by a recital of facts I depend upon
your own warmth of temper, and love of justice, to acquit me of
the least impertinence to you in my present regard for him: He was
recommended to me,[3] as a Man of *probity, family,* and *talents* by a
worthy Friend of mine in France, and from whom I had received
many favours. If I may be allowed to judge of his talents, I most
sincerely think that they are very extraordinary, and therefore I am

bound to believe that my friend has not deceived me in other particulars till I have certain proofs to the contrary. I will venture to declare to an understanding like yours, which never loses the substance in pursuit of the shadow, that the Comte de Guines[4] saying he never introduced M^r Le Texier to any body, and yet making frequent entertainments at his house, on his account, is a distinction without a difference: M^r Le Texier, in consequence of this countenance, and *this introduction*, (for what else can it be call'd?) became a favourite, and most welcome guest every where— nor has he yet forfeited this general partiality to him, as I can learn, by any indiscreet, or impertinent behaviour.

To confirm in part this opinion of mine, I was told by a Man of Fashion, whom you well know, that the Comte de Guignes assured him at his taking leave, that M^r Le Texier had been indeed *malheureux*, but not *malhonnéte*. After this stating of facts, I should appear very ungrateful to my friend, & shew little of the spirit of my Country, were I inhospitably to withdraw, what you so pleasantly call, my *protection*, till some stronger proofs of his ill conduct are produced.

There is a certain unpolish'd obstinacy in English Natures that will give way to nothing but demonstration, and I trust in the good sense and justice of the Count de Lauraguais not to think the worse of me for continuing my good wishes to M^r Le Texier till that demonstration arrives.

I am Sir with the greatest respect Your most
oblig'd humble & most obedient Servant
D. Garrick

I shall do myself the honour of paying my respects soon in Welbeck Street; my indisposition has prevented me from doing it sooner.

Source: FC, copy; Boaden, II, 616f.

1. Louis-Félicité de Brancas (1733–1824), comte de Lauraguais, essayist and dramatist, zealous patron of the arts and sciences. Prone to use his wit and sarcasm at the expense of the French government, the count was at this time spending one of his many exiles in London.

2. According to Lauraguais' long letter, written from Welbeck Street on March 9, Le Texier was a rogue who had found it expedient to flee Lyons (Boaden, II, 614ff.).

3. In a letter from Laplace, dated Sept. 15, 1775 (Boaden, II, 612f.).

4. Adrien-Louis Bonnières de Souastre (1735–1806), comte de Guines, French Ambassador from 1770 to Feb. 1776. On Jan. 3, 1776, Mme du Deffand wrote Walpole: "Savez-vous que ce M. Texier, qui vous charme et qui m'a charmée aussi, n'est pas bien dans ce pays-ci, et qu'on a blâmé M. de Guines de l'avoir reçu chez lui?" (ed. Lewis, IV, 254).

994   To Captain Edward Thompson

Adelphi
Sir   March 11 [1776][1]
As I never Satiriz'd my friends So I can never forget any un-
provok'd Satire from one I once call'd my friend— it is impossible
that Captn Thompson & I can Ever look upon Each other but with
pain, tho for different reasons & therefore the less we see Each Other
will be the better— I can never forget the very adverse manner,
with which you came to the Adelphi; with a friend,[2] whose Gentleman like behaviour too, I can never forget—
    You have own'd Y[r]Self y[e] Author of a Paper, which was publish'd
Some days before the Mermaid, in that paper I am represented by
the Author, as consulting about & abetting a design to destroy[g] the
force of the Syrens at y[e] other house: I can not conceive a more
Severe Attack upon Me as a Man a Manager & a Gentleman—
    You are pleas'd to say that there was Something in a Letter of
Yours written to me Years ago from Scotland w[ch] was mention'd
in y[e] Mermaid?—[3] Can M[r] Thompson imagine that the Man
whom he has known & try'd so long could be guilty of so much
baseness as to give up private letters for public ridicule? be assur'd,
Sir, that I have as totally forgotten Whatever You may have
Written to Me from Every part of the World, as I will Endeavor
to forget that Such a person as the Writer & his unkindness ever
Existed & that he was once connected with
                                    S[r] Y[r] most humble se[t]
                                          D Garrick

Source: FC, draft; Boaden, II, 145f.

1. The year is taken from Garrick's endorsement to the Thompson letter which had
provoked him to this reply: "The last letter I shall ever (I hope) receive from my good
friend Capt. Thompson March 1776" (FC; Boaden, II, 144). In the *London Packet* for
Feb. 29, 1776, there had appeared an article, signed "The Elephant of Drury-Lane
Theatre," charging Garrick with conspiracy to damn *The Syrens*, a masque by Thompson
which had been "dismissed with . . . contempt" after its third performance at Covent
Garden, Feb. 28, 1776 (*BD*). This article was known to have been the work of Thompson,
and Bate was so incensed by it that he published a reply, signed "A Mermaid," in his
Morning Post for March 1. In this Bate had informed his readers that, among other
kindnesses, Garrick had helped Thompson to obtain promotion in the navy and had
often lent him money. The article revealed such an intimate knowledge of his life that
Thompson had accused Garrick with having written it. On March 8, 1776, Bate swore
out an affadavit to the effect that Garrick had had no hand in the "Mermaid" article,
and Thompson then retracted his accusation. Thompson's letter, to which this is the

answer, is dated only Saturday, but was presumably written on the Saturday following Bate's affadavit of Friday, March 8 (Boaden, I, 143f.).

  2. Identified in Thompson's letter as a Mr. Crawford.

  3. The statement that he preferred "the Muses to Neptune."

995   To Peter Garrick

Adelphi

Dear Peter   March 21st 1776
Your Ale is exquisite & I must reward the Brewer, & pay my debts honestly— I wish from my Soul that I could tell You when I shall be at Lichfield, but till I have given my Successors possession, & receiv'd my Money I can't stir from ye Property— the day of payment is the 24 of June, & till that happy day is past, I shall not think myself my own Master— but then, I shall shake off my Chains, & no Culprit at a Jail delivery will be happier— I really feel ye Joy, I us'd to do, when I was a boy at a breaking up: I receive Every honour that a Man can do from all Sorts of people, & I was yesterday enroll'd a member among the first & greatest people in this Kingdom— We have a New house built in the best Taste in ye middle of St James's Street, & it is furnish'd like a palace—1 Each Member pays 12 Guineas at Entrance— It is ye first Society for titles & property in the known world— ⟨I need not tell You that with all this &⟩ 14 Dukes at the head of us, ⟨that I never was duller in all my Life.⟩ I [*illegible*] made my best bows to my Brethren, ⟨graces and Royalty, drank a Glass of Lemonade to keep me awake, which grip'd Me, the Effects of which I found burden'd me & went home as fast as I could.⟩— Dr Johnson & Mr Boswell will be at Lichfield almost as soon as this—2 he is coming to take his leave of you all before his departure for Italy—3

You are Johnson's prime favourite— I was sorry not to see Mr Fletcher, I sent after him, the Moment I got up, to his Hotel, but he was flown, & I could never after catch him— I am angry that Mr Lamb would not call upon me again— pray our Loves to all— My Wife will soon answer her Neice's letter— the Bell rings—

Yours most affecty
D: Garrick

George is again ailing I fear he never will be well. I am better, but not quite well— could I get rid of the pain at ye Neck of my bladder, wch is lately much better, I should have no complaint—

Source: FC; Little, p. 79f.

1. The Savoir Vivre, founded by General Joseph Smith, who, being excluded from Almack's, built "a magnificent house in St. James's Street, furnished it gorgeously, and enrolled both the clubs at White's and that of Almack's." On its opening night the management informed the members that at the gaming tables they would be furnished credit up to £40,000. The Savoir Vivre was to be closed in May, when Smith was jailed for bribery (*The Last Journals of Horace Walpole*, ed. A. Francis Steuart, 1910, I, 545f.; Roberts, *Hannah More*, I, 52).

2. They arrived in Lichfield March 23. "We then visited Mr. Peter Garrick, who had that morning received a letter from his brother David, announcing our coming" (Boswell, II, 462).

3. With the Thrales; a journey shortly to be postponed, then given up as a result of the death of their son (*ibid.*, II, 428, III, 6, 8, 27, 457).

996   To Christopher Anstey

Adelphi

Dear Sir   March 30 [1776]

having been from home for Some time, I did not receive Your most Obliging & agreeable present till last Thursday— I was made very happy with the first Edition of y^r poem,[1] & nothing could have added to my pleasure, but the pride of having receiv'd it from the Author

 I am Dear Sir with ye highest regard Your most Oblig'd
& Obed^t Servant
D. Garrick

Endorsement by Garrick: Letter of Thanks to Mr Anstey for his Election Ball. 1776. *Source:* Garrick Club, draft? copy in FC.

1. *An Election Ball in Poetical Letters.*

997   To The Bishop of London[1]

Adelphi

My Lord   April 2— 1776

I have been wholly engaged for these 3 days in comforting an
allmost distracted friend, whose Son, a most hopeful Youth at
Westminster School, was drown'd last friday—[2] the distress of the
father so affected me that I forgot my duty in not returning your
LordSp. my most respectful acknowledgments for what you were
pleas'd to say to Mr Townly— Your great kindness to my nephew,[3]
and your Confidence in me demand our warmest Expressions of
gratitude— but I have more instances in my Mind of your Lordships partiality to me— and my heart feels that in particular which
was given this Winter so publicly & which did so much honor to.

My Lord Your Lordships Most oblig'd Most Humble

& ob: Ser^t

D G.

Endorsement by Garrick: Copy of a Letter to the L^d Bp. London. Ap: 2. 1776.
Source: FC, copy; Boaden, II, 146.

1. Richard Terrick (1710–1777), D.D. 1747, Bishop of London (1764–1777). He
appears to have been Vicar of Lichfield at one time (Thomas Harwood, *History of Lichfield*, 1806, p. 91).
2. Wallis' only son had been drowned in the Thames on March 29. Garrick had a
monument erected to his memory in Westminster Abbey; it was inscribed with the
words: "his loving father's only hope" (*Westminster Abbey Registers*, ed. Joseph L. Chester,
Harleian Society Publications, vol. X, 1876, p. 421 and n. 2; *Records of Old Westminsters*,
ed. G. F. Russell Barker and Alan H. Stenning, 1928).
3. Evidently Terrick, acquainted with Garrick's intention of giving Carrington
Garrick the living of Hendon, then occupied by Townley, had written the actor that he
approved of the plan and had spoken to Townley, for the latter wrote Garrick on Dec.
16, 1776: "I find your Nephew is in Priest's Orders, and I therefore call'd upon you to
tell you that I am ready to resign the Vicarage of Hendon whenever You please" (FC).
Carrington Garrick, having completed his Cambridge B.A. in 1776, was to be ordained
Deacon on June 2 and Priest on Nov. 30, 1776, by the Bishop of London. He was appointed
Domestic Chaplain to the Duke of Devonshire on Nov. 16 in that same year and on
Jan. 10, 1777, was instituted Vicar of Hendon on the presentation of his uncle, who
owned the advowson.

998   To William Augustus Miles

Hampton

Sir   April ye 3^d— 1776

What I have often thought and you have as often deny'd, viz. *that you have no regard for m⟨e⟩*, I am now well convinc'd of— whoever says that I lend my Ear to a *detestable Sycophant*, wrongs me too much to have the least regard for me— I deny the charge, tho' Mr Miles is pleas'd to make it.[1] I despise Sycophants as much as he does, and have liv'd long enough in the World to know a Sycophant from a real friend, as well as he does. Such Mere Newspaper giving out is below the Notice, or repeating of a Man of Sense, and I am Old enough to chuse what company I like withou⟨t⟩ being Answerable to any Man in ye Kingdom for that choice— If I were to regard what peevish Persons say, there are Men for whose interests I have been anxious that have not the good Word or good Wishes of My other Acquaintance. Mr Miles has us'd me ill, not to say *who* is the Sycophant, and *what acts* of Sycophantism (if I may be allowed the word) he has been a Witness to— for I can not think he Would abuse me so grossly upon hearsay— I think the Man who suffers a Sycophant, a greater wretch than even the Sycophant himself— I therefore thank you, Sir, for the Compliment. I am glad that you can indulge your inclination by Resigning your employment, and no longer be made unhappy by any illiberal Service— all I am Sorry for, is, that you did not know this before, that I might have been spar'd much trouble, & uneasiness, and not have bound myself by an obligation, for what you think so ill suited to a generous & liberal Mind

I am, &c.

D G.

Endorsement with address: Willm Aug^s Miles Esq, Wills Coffee House, Charin[g] Cross.   *Source:* FC, copy.

1. Miles had written: "I am persuaded Sir you do not know me, and as a detestable Sycophant has obtain'd to the astonishment of Mankind your confidence, it is probable you never will, at least while he possesses your ear . . . If I am not enabled to proceed in my Ship, I shall wait upon Ld Sandwich with my warrant & entreat him to accept my resignation. Indeed I have had this matter already in contemplation as the Navy is a Service by no means suited to a generous & liberal mind" (FC).

999   To Peter Fountain

Hampton
Dear Sir   April 3ᵈ [1776]¹
Becket will tell you how miserable I have been wᵗʰ my poor friend
Wallis of Norfolk Street whose Son was drown'd last Friday! Such
a Scene of distress & distraction I never went thro— my Nephew
David & Neices too are ill here— & I am not quite right Myself,
nor ever shall be: You may depend upon my calling upon You
the first Time I return to London.

I am Dʳ Sʳ Yours very Sincerely
D: Garrick

I rejoice to hear yᵉ News about MonSʳ Beaumarchais.²

Address: Mʳ Fountain, Hand Court next door to № 46, Maiden Lane.   *Seal.*
Source: FC.

1. The year is established by the reference to young Wallis' death (March 29, 1776).
2. Presumably about a favorable turn in his long-standing and complicated lawsuit
(see Louis de Loménie, *Beaumarchais et son temps*, Paris, 1858, II, 54ff.).

1000   To The Reverend Doctor
Thomas Percy

Hampton
Dear Sir   April 3ᵈ [1776]¹
I am told that You have *a Young Man*,² whom I am to take care of
when a certain Person plays yᵉ fool upon Drury Lane Stage— Any
body that belongs to You shall not be neglected by Me— if he
would like to see plays at any time I will give orders that he shall
be admitted into a little private box of my own, & Every Night if
he pleases— let me know Your Wishes & they shall be fulfill'd—
I will call upon You the first time I pass by Northumberland house
in my way to my own— Shall I ask a favour of You? I am hunting
after the rise, progress & Establishment of Prologues and Epilogues,
from their first appearance to this Moment, in all Ages, & at all

times— May I not hope for a little of Your friendly assistance? if you will favour me with a Line in answer to this, pray direct for Me thus— Mr Garrick near Kingston[,] Surry

I shall receive it two hours sooner than if Hampton was mentiond on the direction— pray excuse this Scribble, for ye Gout is in my hand

I am Dr Sr Your most Obed^t Ser^t

D: Garrick

Address: Revd Dr Percy, Northumberland House, Strand.   *Seal.*   *Source:* FSL.

1. The year is determined by Percy's manuscript note on this letter.
2. Identified by Dr. Percy, in a note he appended to Garrick's letter, as his son Henry Percy (1763–1783), then a student at Westminster, "who was desirous to see Garrick the last Season of performing on the Stage" (FSL; *The Correspondence of Thomas Percy & Richard Farmer*, ed. Cleanth Brooks, Baton Rouge, 1946, pp. xiv–xvii; *Records of Old Westminsters*, ed. G. F. Russell Barker and Alan H. Stenning, 1928).

1001   To The Earl of Sandwich

Hampton

April 7th [1776]^1

My Lord

The Bearer of this has been an excellent Cricketer, & is now a good Butcher— his name is Piper,^2 & he once had the honour of Serving your Lordship in both capacities, when You liv'd near this place: As it is said that we shall be soon made happy by ye same circumstance, he has desir'd me to Solicit your Lordship's favour in his Character of Butcher; By Age & good living he is become a Spectator only at Cricket, but is ambitious of being Lord Sandwich's very humble Servant in any Capacity— as I am thought to be a good natur'd man in my Neighbourhood, I hope your Lordship will excuse my keeping up my Consequence in the Parish by this impertinant Solicitation.

I am My Lord Your Lordship's Most oblig'd &

most Obedient Servant

D: Garrick.

Source: Earl of Sandwich, transcript, draft in FSL.

1. The year is supplied by the apparent reference to Sandwich's impending residence during the summer of 1776 at Hampton in "a retired mansion belonging to Lord Halifax,

on the edge of Hampton Green" (Cradock, I, 153; Henry Ripley, *The History and Topography of Hampton-on-Thames*, 1885, p. 11; Walpole, ed. Lewis, X, 186).
   2. See Letter 1003.

1002   To Ralph? Lodge[1]

                                                        Hampton
Sir   Easter Monday [April 8, 1776]
If I am not mistaken, I hav⟨e⟩ receiv'd a Letter written by You,
and sign'd by Mrs Abington,[2] tho' this a little carries an Air of Ill
will to correspond with me by her Soliciter, Yet as You ar⟨e⟩ the
Gentleman, I shall rather think She does me a favour than an
incivility   Upon my word, I cannot conceive what Fetters I have
put on my Generosity by any Advertisement I have sent her,[3] and
if you will be pleas'd to unchain th⟨e⟩ Lady (tho' she is apt to
behave a little unruly to Me) I shall be much oblig'd to You—
indeed Sir, without a figure, I mos⟨t⟩ sincerely am at a loss to guess
her meaning   If She does not chuse to advertise as Mrs Pritchard,
& Mrs Clive did, pray let us have no more trouble about the matter,
but let her please her self; If She has any more to Say, or to unsay
about this Business, I shall be in Town on Wednesday Morning,
& a Note from You shall settle it with *Me* at least.
    Varium et mutabile Semper—[4] Be assur'd that I am quite
Satisfied, with the Declaration She has given me of her quitting
the Stage, & I am ready to fulfill my part of the Agreement on the
7th of May— therefore I hope that it will be impossible for the most
refin'd and Active Imagination to raise more doubts, tho' if they
should give me an opportunity of Seeing You, I shall certainly be
a gainer, for I feel my self at this Moment better for your recommendation of Dr Mierbach[5]
                    I am Sir Your much obliged humble Servant
                                                      D. Garrick

I have the Gout in my hand & must Send You this Scrawl.

Endorsement with address: Lodge Esqr, Gray's Inn, Holborn. *Endorsement by Garrick:* Mrs Abington's & My Letters about Mrs Abington Easter Monday 1776. *Source:* FC, copy; Boaden, II, 143.

1. Presumably the Ralph Lodge, "only son of George L., of the parish of St. James, Westminster, gent.," who was admitted to Gray's Inn on May 10, 1753 (*Register of Admissions to Gray's Inn, 1521–1889*, ed. Joseph Foster, 1889, p. 379).

2. Dated April 7, 1776, Easter Sunday (FC; Boaden, II, 142).

3. Although on March 4 Mrs. Abington had written Garrick of her intention to retire, and Garrick had then made the customary offer to appear at her farewell benefit, when he sent for her approval the paragraph announcing the occasion she declined it on the ground that she did not wish to rival the "eclat which must necessarily attend *your* retreat." She added that having "thankfully accepted of your offer to play for me . . . I confidently concluded from the unfettered generosity of the above declaration, that this business would not be further embarassed by advertisements, or any other unnecessary conditions." Garrick endorsed her letter: "A Fal lal from Mʳˢ Abington" (letter of April 7, FC). As her subsequent reëngagement at Drury Lane revealed, she did not wish to compromise her future by any notice whatever.

4. Virgil, *Aeneid*, IV, 569: "A fickle and changeful thing is woman ever."

5. Probably Dr. Meyersbach (d. 1798), "the celebrated water [kidney] doctor" (*GM*, vol. LXVIII, Feb. 1798, p. 175).

1003   To The Earl of Sandwich

My Lord,   Wedʸ in Easter Week [April 10, 1776]¹
Tho I would be very careful not to trouble Your Lordship with unnecessary Billets, yet I cannot refrain from making my Acknowledgments for the last favour— I shall always Obey Lord Sandwich's Commands with the greatest pleasure, & I think myself much honour'd to be appointed one of the Jury at the Gree[n?]-house² upon the Trial of William Piper—
                I am my Lord Yʳ Lordship's most &c

Source: FSL, draft.

1. From the references to Piper here and in Letter 1001 this letter would seem to have been written on the Wednesday of Easter Week in 1776: April 10.

2. Presumably Halifax's house on Hampton Green.

1004   To George Colman

                                                    Hampton
Dear Colman   April 12 [1776]¹
On Tuesday Next in all probability will finish our six nights of yᵉ Spleen: & if you chuse it, we will (as I propos'd to you) let you

have a sixth of the whole subtracting yᵉ Expences— or if you had
rather run the Chance of a Night, I will tell you all yᵉ Nights we
have, & you shall take your choice of them & of what play you
please with Mʳˢ Yates & which may Either appear as your Night
or as a Manager's—² We have bought two Nights, *Parsons*³ &
Aikin's the one Yesternight, & yᵉ other on Tuesday next— We shall
meet on Sunday Evening & whatever you will like best, will be
best to

My Dear Colman Ever & truly yʳˢ
D Garrick.

Addressed.　Seal.　Source: Berg Collection; Colman, p. 315f.

    1. The year is supplied by Colman's reply of April 13, 1776 (Boaden, II, 147).
    2. Colman risked the benefit night; on May 13, though it appears as a manager's
night, *The Spleen* was played with *Lear.*
    3. William Parsons (1736–1795), actor at Drury Lane from 1762 until his death.

1005　　　　To George Garrick

Hampton
April 12ᵗʰ [1776]¹

Dear George.
As Mʳ Linley sets off for Bath on Sunday morning, I chose to
write by him rather than the Post: it gave Us great Pleasure that
Your Change of Places has made such a Change in Your health—
I think that Bath for You, is what the Roman Catholicks think of
their religion, there is no Salvation out of it— You should [be]
absolutely resolv'd to fix Your Standard there— Your Girls &
David are almost well, very little remains of their Cough— I shall
transplant them next Sunday to their new apartments² wᶜʰ their
Grandmother³ has prepar'd for them, a fine bed on the first floor,
but David's bed is taken down in Nat's⁴ room— what meanness!—
they have forc'd the Lad to sell out,⁵ which has backen'd him some
Years in Life, & now they turn him out to starve, if some Chapter
of Accidents is not turn'd over in his favour— last Night I play'd
Drugger for yᵉ last time—⁶ the Morning Post will tell You yᵉ whole
of that Night— I thought yᵉ Audience were Mad, & they almost
turn'd my brain:

I must desire that my good friend Mr Squire, to whom I beg my best Wishes, & You would consider what our friend Linley means to give Me as a Security, for part of his Share: he is to raise £10 000 & wishes me to take some houses &c he has in Bath, which you will see, besides his Share, as a Security for the Mortgage— he likewise wants [m]e to take 4 & ½ Pcent— I demur to that, for as I have 5 from Lacy, will it not appear wrong to take less from a new purchaser, & for a less Sum?—⁷ pray both think of that & talk ye whole matter over together, & with Linley, & let me know, what it is, that I may do. He is a very honest man, but I must be secure, or what have I been doing? Love to all friends—

Yours Ever & Affec^ly
D Garrick.

My Wife sends her Love.

Source: FSL, copy in FC.

1. The year is determined by the reference to Garrick's last performance as Abel Drugger.
2. At their grandparents', the Carringtons, in Somerset House in the Strand (*Court and City Kalendar* for 1767, p. 92).
3. Catherine Spatcher of Little Eastcheap, widow, whom Carrington married as his second wife in 1746 (Nathan Carrington's will, Probate Court of Canterbury, Collier 413).
4. Nathan (1755–1788), third son of George Garrick, was a lieutenant in the Yeoman of the Guard (*Eton College Register, 1753–1790*, ed. Richard A. Austen-Leigh, Eton, 1921, p. 214). He was the namesake and favorite grandson of Carrington, who educated him, bought for him the commission in the Guards for £6000, and left him the bulk of his fortune (*LC*, vol. XLII, Nov. 20–22, 1777, p. 499).
5. His grandfather must have wished David to "sell out" sometime before Nov. 1775, for in that month Garrick apparently wrote Lord Edgcumbe, Captain of the Gentleman-Pensioners from 1773 to 1782, unsuccessfully soliciting for his nephew the post of standard-bearer (Boaden, II, 109).
6. Before a crowded house, Garrick acted Abel Drugger for the last time on April 11, 1776.
7. Garrick finally accepted 4 per cent, which Linley guaranteed by means of a bond and a mortgage on part of his Bath properties (Walter Sichel, *Sheridan*, 1909, I, 524).

1006   To Frances Brooke

Madam.   Saturday— April 20th 1776
From the great hurry and Multiplicity of Business in which I am engag'd, the misplacing or Mistaking a book¹ belonging to no set,

and therefore not of the greatest Value, may be a fault, but surely not of that Magnitude to merit so harsh a Letter.—[2] M[r] Highmore[3] whom I have not the honour to know, has been so obliging to give me my own time to find the lost Sheep, and to assure You that he is perfectly satisfy'd. This great & kind Civility has reliev'd my Mind from a most disagreeable concern, as it at once excuses you from the unpleasing task of writing Angry Letters, & me from the mortification of receiving them. I am

      Mad[m] Your most Obedient humble Servant
             D Garrick

Source: HTC, copy.

 1. From Mrs. Brooke's letter of April 17 (HTC) it appears that the book was a volume of miscellaneous plays.
 2. "I am asham'd," Mrs. Brooke had written, "of having kept so long a book which, at your request, I borrow'd of Mr. Highmore for a few days." Her letter, however, can scarcely be termed "harsh."
 3. Perhaps Nathaniel Highmore (1725–1790), a London attorney.

1007   To Frances Brooke

           [*post* April 23, 1776][1]
That M[rs] Brooke may not again be piqu'd at M[r] Garrick's failure in politeness,[2] of which he finds that he is totally ignorant, he has sent the inclos'd, which in looking over his Papers, he finds belongs to her—

Source: HTC, draft.

 1. This is the reply to Mrs. Brooke's letter of "Tuesday. April 23[d]," (HTC) an answer to the preceding.
 2. Mrs. Brooke had written: "If Mr Highmore is satisfied, Mrs. Brooke has not the least reason to be otherwise: she had not the least intention to write an angry letter, though she was exceedingly in earnest about the book, & a little piqu'd at what appear'd to her more a failure in politeness than punctuality."

1008   To Suzanne Necker[1]

Adelphi
Madam.   Friday Night [April 26, 1776][2]
What can I possibly say to You for Your most flattering, yet most
agreeable Note this morning— as I always speak the best from
Shakespear, I will say with him— *the praises of one of Which, must in
Your Opinion outweigh a Whole Theatre of others!*[3] Tho I give a great
deal to the Benevolence of your heart, Yet my Vanity draws great
Comfort from Your Sincerity: It has been resolv'd that I shall
perform the Character of Hamlet to morrow— the Copy of the
play You have got from the Bookseller will mislead You without
some direction from Me— the *first Act* which is very long in the
original, is by me divided into *two Acts*— the 3^d Act, as I Act it,
is the *2^d* in the Original— the *3^d* in the original is the *4th* in Mine,
and ends with the famous scene between *Hamlet* and his *Mother*—
and the 5th Act in my Alteration, consists of the 4th & 5th of the
original, with some small alterations, and the omission of some
Scenes, particularly the Grave diggers— all I could wish is, that M^{rs}
Necker would look over & consider the Scenes of Hamlet only— She
will be confounded if she Endeavors to study ye Whole, as there is
so short a time before it is play'd— I have taken care to place M^{rs}
Necker in the most commodious box for the Situation of the Scenes,
& to be near the Theatre. with my most respectful compliments to
Mr Necker[4]
            I am Madam Your most Obed^t and Oblig'd Ser^t
                                                    D: Garrick.

Mrs Garrick presents her Warmest Wishes & best Services.
Mrs Necker's box tomorrow will hold Nine persons commodiously

Source: FSL; George W. Stone, Jr., "Garrick's Long Lost Alteration of Hamlet," *Publications of the Modern Language Association*, XLIX (Sept. 1934), 890f.

1. Suzanne (Curchod) Necker (1739–1794), wife of Louis XVI's great finance
minister, mother of Mme de Staël, had at this time one of the most celebrated salons in
Paris. She had come to London with her husband at the end of March 1776 to see
Garrick act before he retired (Walpole, ed. Lewis, VI, 292, 302).
2. The date is from Garrick's acting Hamlet, April 27, 1776, the only time after
moving to the Adelphi that he took that role on a Saturday.
3. See *Hamlet*, III, iii, 30–32.
4. Jacques Necker (1732–1804), financier and politician.

1009 To Samuel Martin[1]

Hampton
Sir   April ye 29 1776
I am very sorry that an Engagement I have made wth Sr Thos
Mills to have the honor of dining with Lord North & Lord Mansfield
Next Wednesday will prevent my having the Pleasure of dining
with You on that day— I have Sign'd a Petition to the Lady of
the Manor,[2] to have a very small piece of Waste Ground granted
to my friend and Neighbour Mr Wood which lies at the End of his
Garden, & can be of no Use or convenience to any person in the
Parish, except himself— It is contiguous to Me on one side, & has
the Waste on the Other— the very disagreeable And offensive
things which are done there under *his Eye* & *My Nose*, are other
strong reasons for wishing that Mr Wood may be Accomodated with
this Slip of Ground the whole Size of which is not more than 28 feet
to the Water & thirty two wide—
                        I am Sir Your most Obed^t hum^e Ser^t
                                                    D. Garrick

Endorsement by Garrick: a Letter I wrote to Mr Martin Steward of ye Manor
of Bushy in favor of my Neighbor Mr Wood. *Source:* FSL, draft.

1. Presumably the Samuel Martin (d. 1788), lawyer and politician, who had been
secretary to the Princess Dowager of Wales from 1767 to 1772. Apparently at this time
he was serving as Steward of Bushey Park, of which Lady North was the Ranger (*Correspondence of George III with Lord North*, ed. William B. Donne, 1867, I, 100, 169; Walpole,
ed. Lewis, X, 64; *Annual Register*, 1772, p. 102).
    2. Lady North.

1010 To Peter Fountain

Dear Sir   April 29. 1776
I was pull'd to pieces for places last Saturday— Your friend & Mine
Mr Lloyd & Co may depend upon having the three places when
Hamlet appears again.[1] Lord Mansfield & the other great People

have made me very vain. I will call very soon upon You— I am
indeed all bustle.

Yours Ever & Truly
D Garrick

Address: Mr Fountain, Hand-Court, Maiden Lane.   *Source:* FC.

1. May 30.

1011   To James Boswell

Hampton
Friday [May 3, 1776?]¹

Mr Garrick presents his Comp^{ts} to Mr Boswell, & begs to have the
Pleasure of Seeing his Friend² & him at the Adelphi to breakfast
on Friday instead of Wednesday—

Mrs Garrick reminded him after Mr Boswell had left him, that
he had an Engagement of great Consequence on Wednesday, which
would Engage him soon in the Morning & keep him late.

Address: —— Boswell Esqr.   *Seal.   Source:* Boswell MSS. Yale.

1. So dated by the Yale editors of the Boswell Papers, presumably on the basis of
the chronology of Boswell's life.
2. Conjecturally identified by the Yale editors as Sir William Forbes (1739–1806)
of Pitsligo, the Edinburgh banker with general literary interests, the biographer of
Beattie, and one of Boswell's executors.

1012 To The Reverend Joseph Smith

Adelphi
May [9, 1776]¹

Dear Sir
I shall be very happy to meet You at any time or place, & Shall
expect & have the Satisfaction which Ever attends the meeting of
old Friends— my present Situation of my affairs— nay the last
hours of my theatrical Life, & my preparing for Another, not to

mention the Shifting of so great a Property, as my Patent, Scenes &c into other hands will require my attendance in Town till the middle of next Month, when I shall be glad to fix the *where* & *when* as soon as you please— a Greek Play!—² raises indeed my Curiosity! but as I deal in raising Curiosity Myself, & have not yet left off trade, I cannot, till I make my transfer, be absent from the Shop one Night— I am Sorry that You have a fellow feeling with Me, & are troubled with the worst of all disorders— but Yours will be Easily cur'd with a proper attention & perseverance— such an old Friend, & School fellow as you are shall command by best advice & Experience— If you will take Adams's Solvent, which is now known to be Perry's, & be a little careful of yʳ Food, & drink, I will answer for your Cure—³

> I am Dear Sir most truly Yours
>
> D: Garrick

just going to perform Benedict for the last time—

Address: Revᵈ Mʳ Smith, Stanmore, Middlesex.   *Source:* FC; Boaden, II, 149.

1. The year is determined by the reference to Garrick's playing Benedick for the last time: May 9, 1776. The letter is misdated May 8.
2. The *Trachiniae* of Sophocles, performed in May 1776 by the pupils of Dr. Samuel Parr, Master of Stanmore School; Smith was Rector of Great Stanmore. Foote furnished the scenes and Garrick the costumes for this performance (see *Works of Samuel Parr,* ed. John Johnstone, 1828, I, 69f., where there is a letter from Bennet Langton to Parr, dated May 8, 1776, informing him that Garrick would be unable to attend the performance).
3. Cradock reports that in the spring of 1776, when Garrick was deciding on his final roles, "Garrick said to me: 'I can play Richard; but I dread the fight and the fall. I am afterwards in agonies.' Some time afterwards, Dr. Brocklesby said: 'I do not know who your friend is that recommends such a medicine; but he'll be the death of you'; to which he [Garrick] warmly replied: 'I have taken all your medicines, and from this solvent only I think I feel some relief, and I had rather die than suffer as I do'" (IV, 250f.). Advertised in a pamphlet called *A Disquisition of the Stone and Gravel* (1773) as the work of "William Adams, surgeon," the real maker was soon known to be Samson Perry (1747–1823), a London surgeon.

1013   To John? Plumptre¹

Satʸ [May?] 11 [1776?]²

Mʳ Garrick presents his Compᵗˢ to Mʳ Plumptre & assures him that he could not this Morning procure 3 places for some intimate

Friends of his— there have been no places for Monday & thursday[3]
these two days.

Source: FSL.

1. The recipient may possibly be John Plumptre (1711–1791) of Jermyn St., Westminster, a commissioner of stamps and an M.P. who had retired from public life in 1774
(Thomas Bailey, *Annals of Nottinghamshire*, [1855], IV, 43, 141).
    2. The conjectural date depends upon the reference to "no places for Monday &
thursday," and the fact that May 11, 1776, fell on a Saturday. The pressure for tickets
was never so insistent as in Garrick's final season, when friends and strangers alike
addressed him for the favor of tickets. Although Garrick had several times earlier played
on a Monday and Thursday following a Saturday which fell on the 11th of a month,
the fact that he himself is having trouble getting tickets indicates the conjectural dating.
    3. Garrick played Lear on Monday, May 13, 1776, and Don Felix on the Thursday
following.

1014   To Sir James Caldwell[1]

                                                            Adelphi
Sir   May 14. 1776
Having been in the Country for a few days, your Letter was sent
after me & upon my returning to town a day sooner than my
Servant expected, I did not receive the great honour you have done
me till the day before Yesterday— I really want words to thank you
for the kind & hospitable Invitation you have Made me, & most
sincerely wish that it may be in my Power, as it is in My heart, to
Shew My gratitude for your favours. It has been long my wish to
visit a Kingdom, where I was honoured with every Mark of regard
& kindness— as I have not left Mrs Garrick one day since we were
Married, Near 28 years, I cannot now leave her, and She is so Sick
& distress'd by the sea, that I have Not had the resolution to follow
my inclinations on account of her fears.[2]
    Our poor friend Wallis has been most Miserable indeed, & has
imparted his distress to all his friends—[3] I have felt more on his
account than I ever did in my life— He is rather better, but still in
a very Melancholly Way. I hope some few Jaunts into the Country
and taking him from the sight of the Thames, which Was the Cause
of his Misery, will reinstate him in health & spirits which at present
are Much impaired. whenever I can settle my affairs which at this

time are in some Confusion (as I am to quit the direction in June) and can prevail on a fearful Wife to cross so small a branch of the sea, I shall Most Certainly pay My respects at Castle-Caldwell,— in the Mean time if you have any commands which My Care & Gratitude can execute, I shall most willingly obey them— I long to talk over Count Firmian & my pleasures with him at Milan. Mrs Garrick begs that her respects may be join'd with Mine, & bids me say that your temptations are so strong that they have almost conquered her fears.

I am Sir With the most grateful sense of your politeness
Your most Oblig'd & most Obedient Servant
D: Garrick

Endorsement with address: To Sir James Caldwell Bar^t at Castle-Caldwell near Ennishillen, Ireland. *Source:* FC, copy; Boaden, II, 150.

1. Sir James Caldwell (*ca.* 1722–1784), Bt. 1743, F.R.S., of Castle Caldwell, Fermanagh, Ireland.
2. Caldwell repeated his invitation in letters of May 16 and June 8 (FC).
3. Over the drowning of his son.

1015   To Gilbert Ford[1]

Adelphi
Sir   Monday Night May 20 1776
Give me leave to say that I think your Letter[2] a very particular return for my Civility, & what I should not have Expected from the Son of Dr Ford— did I complain of any impropriety in your asking for a friend to attend you in the Orchestra? and sure, Sir, I might without offence desire you to give up a place for one night to a friend of mine who had *not* seen Lear— had you not been there the last time,[3] I should not have presum'd to have done it, as I did not, for any of the other plays, which you have seen there— I have many friends to oblige,[4] & the Same favour, if it is to be call'd one, which I askd of you, I desir'd likewise of Mr Linley— if there are too many in the Orchestra the Mussicians cannot do their duty— was it refusing *you* a place in the Orchestra, because I could not admit your friend, & desird another Gentleman might take your

place at a play, you had seen before? this is a new kind of Logic to me: what follows is Still more particular— You are pleasd to say I have had *an unprecedented favour granted me of my box*— You will give me leave to smile at your mistake— I have had no favour granted to me— the Keeping my box is part of my bargain,[5] and your Father will tell you that in point of favour I have not been behind hand with the Gentlemen purchasers. this matter should not have been mentiond either in justice or civility, and I little thought before our matters had been settled that I should have been upbraided with receiving favours from Gentlem[en] to whom I gave the refusal of my share of the Patent in preference to many— this Surely is very *unprecedented*

I am Sir You[r] Humble Serv[t]

D G.

P.S. What I asked (I hope civilly) of you, I have ask'd likewise of Lady Hertford[6] for 4 Nights running which she granted most graciously

Endorsement with address: To M[r] Ford, Lincoln's Inn. *Source:* FC, copy; Little, p. 78.

1. Gilbert Ford (b. 1750?), lawyer, the son of Dr. James Ford who had been one of the purchasers of Garrick's patent (*Records of the Honourable Society of Lincoln's Inn: Admissions 1430–1799*, 1896, I, 459; *Records of Old Westminsters*, ed. G. F. Russell Barker and Alan H. Stenning, 1928).
2. On May 20 Ford had written Garrick a note requesting a place in the orchestra the following night for a Mr. Aikenhead. Garrick, however, had already written Ford asking him to give up his own seat for that evening. Garrick endorsed Ford's letter: "Correspondence. a very curious letter from M[r] Ford son to D[r] Ford May 20 1776 My answer likewise." Thinking that this was Garrick's reply to his note, Ford wrote the actor an angry letter, dated "Monday Night May 20th" (all in FC).
3. May 13.
4. During the final months of Garrick's long career on the stage the demand for tickets was tremendous. "The eagerness of people to see him," wrote Hannah More, "is beyond any thing you can have an idea of. You will see half a dozen duchesses and countesses of a night, in the upper boxes: for the fear of not seeing him at all has humbled those who used to go, not for the purpose of seeing, but of being seen, and they now courtesy to the ground for the worst places in the house" (Roberts, *Hannah More*, I, 59f.).
5. In the announcement of the sale it was stated that the "new Proprietors, as an act of their own, have stipulated, that Mr. Garrick shall continue to keep that box which has of late years been set apart for the accomodation of his family" (*LC*, vol. XL, Jan. 18–20, 1776, p. 71).
6. Isabella (Fitzroy) Conway (d. 1782), Countess of Hertford and daughter of the second Duke of Grafton, was a Lady of the Bedchamber to Queen Charlotte. In 1741 she had married Francis Seymour Conway, who in 1750 became first Earl of Hertford; he called her "the best woman, the best friend, and best wife that ever existed" (Walpole, ed. Toynbee, XII, 367n.).

1016   To Gilbert Ford

Sir   [May 21, 1776]
Logick that is good at yᵉ Theatre will be good at Westminster Hall
& vice versa—

As You have been pleas'd to repeat that the ⟨subject⟩ of my
Box,[1] & to Say again *unprecedented* I must take yᵉ Liberty of informing
you that there was a Certain Box call'd *Barton's* [Burton's?] *Box*
which was a part of yᵉ Gallery inclos'd & which upon Some Account
or another was made over to a Person of that Name for his Life &
not to his Assigns for many Years— the Said ⟨box⟩ was distroyd
in our Management— had the Gentlemen Purchasers of their own
free will, without any bargain, made over my little Box to my Wife
& Me, I cannot think it would have been any injury or discredit,
to their cause, as it is, I am oblig'd: Only to their genteel Manner
of agreeing to that part of the Conditions— as to the bargain Itself,
when there was some flying reports of our agreement being off—
Mʳ Hoare[2] my Neighbo⟨r⟩ whom You know I believe, made me
an offer of a larger Sum for the property I had sold to yʳ Father,
& others— as the Doctor is so deeply engag'd, I cannot but think
that you will find both leisure & inclination now & then to pry into
yᵉ Arcana of a Playhouse— but I shall say no more as that does
not concern me.

                                        I am Sʳ Yʳ huᵉ Seᵗ
                                        D G.

Endorsement by Garrick: Tuesday. May 21. 1776. *Source:* FC, draft.

    1. Ford replied to this on the same day: "I ought to make an Apology for mentioning
Your Box again, but whether You keep it next year by permission of the New Patentees,
or as part of Your Bargain with them the term I made use of 'of its being *unprecedented* is
in propriety of Speech, applicable for I believe there is no instance to be met with in
any of the former Conveyances of the Theatre of so considerable a reservation exclusive
of the other privileges You are to have. As it is however part of Your Bargain the mention
of it in my last Letter was certainly impertinent" (FC).
    2. Henry Hoare (1744–1785), banker, of Beckenham, Kent, and the Adelphi, son of
Sir Richard Hoare (1709–1754) of Barn Elms, Surrey. The namesake and heir of his
uncle who was head of the great London banking house, he was admitted to the firm as
a junior partner in 1774 (Frederick G. H. Price, *A Handbook of London Bankers*, 1876,
p. 81; Edward Hoare, *The Families of Hore and Hoare*, 1883, p. 56).

1017   To The Countess Spencer

Adelphi, May 23, 1776

Address: The Countess Spencer, St James's Place.   *In the possession of the Earl Spencer: Not made available for publication.*

1018   To Sir Grey Cooper

Hampton
My dear Sir,   Sunday [May] 26 [1776]¹
Your Letter this morning has hurt me greatly.—² When have I been inattentive to your and Lady Cooper's commands[?] I appeal to her Ladyship if I ever was remiss in shewing my regard to both. Her health indeed for some time rendered her attendance at the Theatre uncertain, but my regard was as constant and as regular as the Sun. What you tell me of the Dean of Derry³ was quite a secret to me— by my honour he never yet got a single place thro me:— If Bribery and Corruption have crept behind the Scenes, I am sorry for it, and tho my hands are clean, the Boxkeepers may plead the example of their betters.— The last Box I procured for you has caused much mischief to your humble Servant, and my Life on't, you never till your last note mentioned a desire to see King Lear— My likings and attatchments to my friends, will, I hope be remembered, when my Fool's Cap and Bells will be forgotten.

What you say about the Conditions of your moving for the Fund Bill, had escaped me:— I declare to you, and I back my word with my honour that my readiness to oblige Sir Grey Cooper, was ever independent of my interest, and I have found that his kindness was always exerted without conditions, towards

His most obliged and most obedient Servt

P.S. I plead guilty to Madame Necker: I recd many favours from her in France: she came over on purpose to see me act, and I thought myself bound in duty and gratitude to be attentive to her.—⁴

7*

Source: FC, copy; Boaden, II, 152f.

1. The month and year are from Cooper's reply of May 28, 1776 (Boaden, II, 155).
2. From Cooper's letter, dated only May 1776, it appears that he had requested a box but had been given instead a row of seats. "If I remember right," Cooper wrote, "you promised me some particular attention for moving your Fund Bill at the beginning of the Session; I have heard that a certain Monsr Necker, & a certain Dean of Derry have boxes every night you Play" (FC; Boaden, II, 152).
3. Thomas Barnard (1728–1806), D.D. 1761, Dean of Derry 1769–1806, a member of the Literary Club and a close friend of Goldsmith.
4. See her letter, dated by Garrick May 18, 1776, in the Forster Collection.

1019   To George Colman

Adelphi

My dear Sir   May 27. 1776
Your letter, which has astonish'd Me,[1] came to my hands at the most unlucky time, as I have so Much already upon my Mind— Was I in a dream when I imagin'd that you *gave* Us the alteration of the Silent Woman?— Did you not *say* so, and *Write* so?— I think no trouble too much for a performance with a Friend's Name to it, nor do I ever spare any expence to set it off.

The Silent Woman with all our Care did not succeed, & was left off under charges at the 4th Night, tho' we added the Jubilee to it— the impossibility of giving it a fashion was felt by You, as well as myself. If you intended to be consider'd as the *Alterer*, & not as the *Donor*,[2] why would you delay to this time to let me know Your expectations?— You must be sensible, that I would not that *You*, of all persons, should have a bad bargain:

Pray let me know what I must do, for I cannot have such a burden upon my Mind at this very distressing time, when my Theatrical Life is so Near It's End— It is the trouble of an Evil Conscience upon my Death bed.

I am my dear Sir Yours most truly
D: Garrick.

If I am confus'd or unintelligible impute it to Richard[3] what an Operation!—

Endorsement by Garrick in copy: Colman's letter about his Silent Woman & my answer May 26th 1776. Est il possible! Source: Berg Collection, copy in FC; Colman, p. 319f.

Mr. and Mrs. Garrick in 1773

Mr. and Mrs. Garrick at Shakespeare's Temple, Hampton

1. In his letter of May 25 Colman had intimated that he expected some money from the January production of his alteration of *Epicoene; or, The Silent Woman*, and was surprised, if not annoyed, at not having heard from Garrick sooner concerning the matter (Colman, p. 318).

2. Colman replied to Garrick's letter on May 28: "I am very sorry my Letter came so *mal-a-propos* . . . God knows I had no thoughts of profit, or *a bargain*, about the Silent Woman— yet I really did not pretend to make a gift of it . . . As to the popularity of the Piece, you can witness for me that it was what I never expected from it . . . I must confess myself so zealous for the honour for the Old School, that I think Epicoene . . . ought to keep the *stage*" (FC; Colman, pp. 320ff.).

3. Garrick played Richard III for the first time in four years on May 27.

1020   To Sir George Hay

Adelphi
June 2ᵈ [1776][1]

Mᵣ Garrick presents his respects to Sᵣ George Hay— he could not withstand the Solicitations of his Old Friend Beard to send him the inclos'd letter: at the same time he feels himself very aukward, without the least right to give Sᵣ George this trouble— but if some of the happiest hours of his life pass'd With him heretofore may be some claim to his favour, he begs to plead it on the present Occasion.[2]

Source: FC, draft; Boaden, II, 157.

1. The year is supplied by Hay's answer of June 2, 1776 (FC; Boaden, II, 158).

2. Hay replied: "You are grown formal in your Old Age, My dear friend.— Johnny Beard had no occasion to interpose so great a power in so slight a business.— Kiss the blooming Wrinkles of my antient Love for my sake, and believe me Always Your's & Her's."

1021   To The Bishop of London

My Lord.   [June 3, 1776]
Tho Your Lordship's politeness has excus'd a very great inattention of Mine in not Subscribing the letter I did myself yᵉ honour to

write to you Yesterday, yet from that very circumstance I am the less inclin'd to forgive Myself— upon considering the Matter, which astonish'd & vex'd me, when My Nephew told me of it, I remember being call'd away, when I wrote down the first page, & returning in a great hurry, I must have folded up yᵉ Letter without finishing it— I have nothing to plead in Excuse for this neglect but the multiplicity of business which has attended the preparation of parting wᵗʰ my property & my last theatrical Exit, which is to be this Week. I am with a true Sense of yʳ Lordship's favours[1]

Your most

Endorsement by Garrick: 1776 Letter from me to yᵉ Bishop of London June 3ᵈ.
Source: FC, copy.

1. Terrick had ordained Carrington Garrick as a deacon on June 2.

1022   To Hannah More

⟨Adelphi
⟨My dear Madam,⟩   Tuesday almost⟩ 11— [June 4, 1776][1]
I must gallop over this small piece of paper, it was yᵉ first I snatch'd up to tell you that my wife has yʳ letter & thinks it a fine one & a Sweet one— ⟨I am not to read it, till I have got over yᵉ fright of having the King's Command to morrow for Richard, tho' I play'd it last Night better than Ever—[2] it will absolutely kill me— What a Trial of breast, lungs, ribs & What not— Madam will answer yʳ letter soon, I shᵈ not have written but for yᵉ inclos'd— don't trouble yʳ head about franks I can have Thousands— the Bell is now ringing under my Window & I *must* finish—⟩

I was at Court to day[3] & Such work they made with Me, from yᵉ Archbishop of Canterbury[4] to the Page of yᵉ Back Stairs,[5] that I have been suffocated wᵗʰ Compᵗˢ— We have wanted You at some of our private hours— Where's yᵉ Nine? We want yᵉ Nine!—[6] Silent was Every Muse— I can ⟨Say no more, but in plain English we love & esteem You—

Yours my dear Miss More most affectʸ
D Garrick

Love to Y^r Sisters— I litterally cannot read it over.

My Partner Lacy would play Richm^d with me last Night & was hiss'd—⁷ Mum.⟩

Source: FSL, draft; Roberts, *Hannah More*, I, 75, extract.

  1. The date is determined by Garrick's references to acting *Richard III* "last Night," and to its command performance "to morrow."
  2. Garrick played Richard on June 3, 1776, and for the last time on June 5 at a command performance, when the house was so crowded that those standing interfered with the vision of those seated, thereby delaying the start of the play for about two hours (*LC*, vol. XXXIX, June 4–6, 1776, p. 544).
  3. In celebration of the King's birthday. "This day [June 4] the court at St. James's was very numerous and brilliant; when their Majesties received the compliments of the Nobility, Foreign Ministers, &c." (*ibid.*, June 1–4, 1776, p. 536).
  4. Frederick Cornwallis (1713–1783), D.D. 1748, formerly Bishop of Lichfield and Coventry and Dean of St. Paul's. He had become Archbishop of Canterbury in 1768.
  5. Nicholas Ramus.
  6. Garrick's nickname for Hannah More, because she was the epitome of the nine Muses.
  7. Palmer was to take the part on June 5.

1023   To A.-A. Le Texier¹

[*ante* June 10, 1776]²

En verité, mon cher fils, votre lettre m'a donné beaucoup de chagrin et d'etonnement— J'ecris cet Billet entourré de la Compagnie, et je l'envoye expres pour vous dire mes Sentimens, sans perdre le tems— J'ai un Si courte et foible Connoissance avec Monsr et Mad^e Necker qu'il ne seroit pas delicat pour moi d'ecrire votre Situation a Monsr Necker—³ Je vous conseille de le faire instamment vous meme, comme vous aviez une ancienne amitié avec lui, il est si sage, et si genereux q'un lettre ecrit, dans votre maniére, peut avoir un bon Effet— il faut au moins fair l'experiment— si cela ne succedera pas, Je suis pret toujours d'avoir une consultation avec vos amis sur votre compte le Moment que ma vie dramatique Est fini— Je suis votre ami

                                        D: Garric

Source: C. F. Bishop, draft, copy in FC; Hedgcock, p. 272.

  1. Le Texier is identified as the recipient by Garrick's use of the salutation "mon cher fils," for Le Texier was accustomed to write him as "mon cher maître" and "mon

cher père" (FC). Further, that it was Le Texier who was seeking a favor from Necker is confirmed by the following passage in a letter from Mme du Deffand of [Dec. 11, 1776]: "Je soupai hier chez M. Necker; je lui dis un mot de M. Texier, il ne fut pas reçu favorablement. Il a volé la caisse de la recette et de plus M. Boutin, qui s'était rendu sa caution; en un mot c'est un fripon; j'en suis fâchée, car il a un talent agréable" (Walpole, ed. Lewis, VI, 378).

2. Written sometime after Le Texier came to England in Sept. 1775 and shortly before Garrick's retirement on June 10, 1776.

3. Le Texier, who had fled France after a financial scandal, evidently wished Necker, who was influential with the government, to intercede for him.

1024   To Hannah More

[June 12, 1776][1]

Ten thousand thanks Madam Nine for Y^r last, which I rec'd this Night getting out of my Coach: I never pass'd two days with more real pleasure than I did Yesterday & today at Hampton, reliev'd from the Slavery of Government: such a Night as Monday last was never Seen!— Such clapping, Sighing, crying, roaring, &c &c &c— it is not to be describ'd!— in short— it was as we could Wish, et finis coronat Opus—[2] ye Bell rings— Exit Nonsense— Y^{rs} Ever & truly

D G.

Love to all[3]

Source: Bristol Public Libraries.

1. The date is determined by the fact that this letter was evidently written on the second night after Garrick's farewell performance on Monday, June 10, 1776; it is written in reply to Miss More's letter of the same date (Boaden, II, 159f.).

2. A current proverb—"The end crowns the work"—perhaps reminiscent to Garrick of the lines in *All's Well that Ends Well*: "All's well that ends well. Still the fine's the crown./Whate'er the course, the end is the renown" (IV, iv, 35f.).

3. There follows, in Garrick's hand, this letter from his wife: "We have not been at Hampton since you left us till yesterday, and from thence I thought to have wrote to you; but getting from one corner of the Ground to an other I was as usual all the day upon my legs, and so again this day, till we returned to this spot called Adelphi; and where I was just told by My fat lazy nephew, that he has not sent you the bill of the last day's Play, nor any thing you desired. I have then rousd *My* Lazyship just to tell you that all your naughty doings of running away from us are a little atoned by your two charming letters: the first to Me My Hus^d took from me, & answerd it but have not seen the answer nor the letter since. Your last, I shall serve him so, being wrote to him; but what is all this to what you want to know what has past in that awful moment? all that I can tell you is, that I never shall forget his Pale but charming looks when he took

his leave; how the whole house felt them you will better describe in your imagination than I can, had I even more time then I have at present, being within a Minute of Eleven, and have only time to tell you that I have sav'd his Buckles for you, which he wore in that last moment, and which was the only thing that They could not take from him— God bless you all, and say to all that I am their faithful M. Garrick in great hurry."

1025   To Nathan Carrington

Dear Sir [June 13, 1776]
I should have waited upon You had I not thought that this manner of addressing You, would be less troublesome & more agreeable to You— My Nephew & y^r Grandson David has surpriz'd me by Soliciting me to give him the means of return^g to the Army— I have refus'd him, & I hope wth propriety— When he first was fit to be sent into ye World, I procur'd an appointment for him in ye East Indies—[1] You were pleas'd to desire that he might not go— as Nobody had so good a right to command in Every thing which belong'd to y^r Grand Child, You was immediatly Obey'd, & he was taken out of my hands— He was then destin'd for the Army, & you generously bought him a Commission, upon his being lately ill, You propoz'd his Selling out,[2] & tho much against Lord Pembroke's & my opinion he obey'd, as he ought, y^r Commands & quitted the Army— Now finding himself better in health, & unhappy in his present idle disagreeable manner of living, he naturally thinks of the Army again, where he was bred & in which he can only make any figure— upon his being unsuccessful in his application to You He applies to Me, Who have never interfer'd in his destination & thought him wholly taken from my Care[3] nor have I been in ye least concern'd about him, except in ye Paym^t of some of his Bills—

I have I hope Sir in Your opinion I have done my duty, by taking 3 of the 5 wholly upon Me— if You likewise think that I Should take the fourth too, who has never yet been directed by Me I Could wish, if not disagreeable to You, to talk the matter over. he should not be thrown away as a near relation to both of Us, & I will Submit it to Yourself if I have not more than my Share of ye Burden by having four of ye Family upon Me out of Six. I am D^r S^r very truly

Y^r most Obed^t hum^{le} Ser^t
D G

Endorsement by Garrick: 1776 June 13th my Letter to Mr Carrington about David. *Source:* FC, draft.

1. *Deletion:* "by the help of my good Friend Governor Johnstone, that was said to be worth 2000, which sum I would have given ye Same appointment could it have been procur'd." George Johnstone (1730–1787), naval officer, was at this time Governor of West Florida, an M.P., and a self-appointed authority on American affairs (see Johnstone's letter of May 30 in FC).

2. He sold out presumably in the first half of 1776, when all cadets were replaced in his regiment and his fellow cadets promoted to lieutenant, the new lieutenant in his place being commissioned on July 24.

3. Carrington replied on June 16: "When I bought him his Commission, it was meant for a Provision for him in future, and was done entirely (as I understood) both with *your's* and his Father's consent, but I never meant, nor is there the least reason to conclude, because I had, (at a very great Expence) set him out in Life, that I had taken him out of your's and his Father's hands, so far from it, that for what I know to the contrary, he has always conducted himself agreeable to your Directions, nor did I ever take upon myself at all, the Care and Management of him, as I've already observed Sr I have, as his Relation, done all in my power, to set him off in the World, & I think I may venture to say, few Grandfathers wou'd have done so much towards it, It has Cost me for Nathan & him together, above £7000, exclusive of the assistance & helps I have given to the rest of the Family." Garrick endorsed this letter: "1776 Mr Carrington's Evasive anr to my Letter about David June" (FC).

1026   To Suzanne Necker

Hampton

Madam,   June 18th, 1776

I cannot say whether I am most happy or distressed by your very elegant and affectionate letter: such a sincerity of praise from such a lady has added a cubit to my stature; but the self-conviction I have, that I cannot answer it as such a letter ought to be answered, makes me miserable. I defy the whole French Academy, with my most critical and worthy friend Sicard [Suard?] at their head, to give such power to words as you have done; nor is it in their power to lower the joy of my mind, or the pride of my heart, from the present exalted state you have raised them to. Though every poet was a Voltaire, and every proseman a Rousseau, I now defy the devil of criticism and all his works. I can say with our Waller,

> "She smiled, and from her smiles were sped
> Such darts as struck the monster dead."

I flatter myself that you will not be displeased to know, that I departed my theatrical life on Monday the 10ᵗʰ of June— it was indeed a sight very well worth seeing! Though I performed my part with as much, if not more spirit than I ever did, yet when I came to take the last farewell, I not only lost almost the use of my voice, but of my limbs too: it was indeed, as I said, *a most awful moment.*[1] You would not have thought an English audience void of feeling if you had then seen and heard them. After I had left the stage, and was dead to them, they would not suffer the *petite piece* to go on; nor would the actors perform, they were so affected:[2] in short, the public was very generous, and I am most grateful.

Mrs. Garrick, who has taken your letter from me by force and keeps it locked up, begs to join her most affectionate respects with mine to you and Mr. Necker. If my multiplicity of business would permit, I should be at your feet almost as soon as this reaches your hands: but we have made a vow to be happy as soon as our worldly cares will permit us; till when, we beg that our warmest and best wishes may be presented to your fellow-traveller, the Chevalier Chatteleux, and all our friends: we never can forget them or your most flattering kindness.

I am, with the greatest truth, Madam, your most obedient and devoted,

D. Garrick.

Source: Boaden, II, 161f.

1. In his farewell address he said, "This is to me a very awful moment: it is no less than parting for ever with those, from whom I have received the greatest kindness, and upon the spot, where that kindness and your favours were enjoyed" (Murphy, II, 135f.).
2. "Every face in the theatre was clouded with grief; tears gushed in various parts of the house, and all concurred in one general demonstration of sorrow. The word, farewell, resounded from every quarter, amidst the loudest bursts of applause" (*ibid.*, p. 139).

1027 To Woodford Rice[1]

Hampton

Sir Sunday at dinner [June 23, 1776][2]

I am most sincerely oblig'd to You for Your polite Manner of communicating the false & scandalous Suspicions of my being the

Author of the inclos'd Libel— I have always been treated by Mr Rice with ye greatest civility, & I have never done any thing that could forfeit that civility— I am as incapable of doing so base an Action by a Gentleman who never offended me as I think *him* incapable of truth, who could in a Serious Manner hint to You, that I was ye Author. Let [me] assure [you] Upon my honour that I never in my Life wrote a Single Line upon You of any kind whatsoever & that I am wholly ignorant of ye author of ye inclos'd printed Lines.[3]

I am Sir Your most hum^le Ser^t

D: Garrick

Source: HTC, draft; Boaden, II, 360.

1. Woodford Rice (d. 1784), soldier, was long an officer in the 85th Regiment of Foot. His will, probated July 31, 1784, describes him as a bachelor, late of St. James's, Westminster (Probate Court of Canterbury, Admon. Act. Book, 1784).

2. Written on a Sunday after Bate founded the *Morning Post* in 1772 and presumably on the day following June 22, the date of Rice's letter (endorsed by Garrick: "Mr Rice's letter about verses against him in the M.P. wth my Ans^r"—FC, Boaden, II, 359). Within these limits Sunday fell on June 23 only in 1776.

3. *Deletions:* "I hope by this declamation that you will be Satisfy'd with regard to Me, & I hope You will not think Me unworthy of y^r Confidence but let me know to whom I am indebted for this very scandalous & false aspersion"; *and, as postscript:* "I shall wait for Your commands here, & be ready to attend You in Town if my Presence is necessary."

1028 To Thomas King

Adelphi
Dear King.   June 25 1776
Accept a Small token of our long & constant attachment to Each other— I flatter Myself that this Sword,[1] as it is a theatrical one, will not cut Love between us, and that it will not be less valuable to You for having dangled at my side some part of the last Winter—
May health, success, & reputation still continue to attend You

I am Dear Sir Yours very truly

D: Garrick.

Farewell remember Me![2]

Endorsement by Garrick: Letter to King wth a Sword June ye 25 1776. Source: FSL, draft; Boaden, II, 162.

1. In a note (endorsed by Garrick June 28, 1776) thanking Garrick for his gift, King wrote: "Your retiring from the Stage being justly consider'd as a severe stroke to every Performer on it, and regretted by every admirer of the Drama, how must I feel, who not only suffer in each of those capacities, but lament at the same time the absence of a worthy Patron and most affectionate Friend?" (FC; Boaden, II, 163).

2. *Hamlet*, I, v, 91.

1029   To Willoughby Lacy

Adelphi

My Dear Lacy.   June 27th 1776

I was in hopes, that I shou'd have seen you here for an half an Hour yesterday, or to Day (as was express'd in my Note) that we might talk over the Subject of your parting with the half of your Share, & to whom. I am much oblig'd to you for saying that you wou'd give the preference to any friend of mine; but the same regard, which makes me decline recommending any person not yet connected with you, obliges me from friendship to open my mind to you— I beg you will take this letter as the best legacy of a Man, who wou'd Scorn to give you any advice that means not your good & who most sincerely wishes to prevent any distress, which he fears & foresees may imbitter Your future life: as you have always flatter'd me that my advice & experience shou'd be ever welcome to you tho' I cannot say that you hitherto have much profited by it, as I cou'd prove to you in many instances, yet I cannot see you run into what I think a destructive measure, without holding out my hand to prevent you if possible— Your Idea is to sell part of your property to one, who shall be your friend & keep up a ballance of power in the Theatre.

In the first place, I am sorry that you shou'd think such a ballance necessary, because it infers that you have suspicions, a very bad foundation for good fellowship with your present partners, & in the next how will you be assur'd that by selling part of your property to this or that person, that you will at the same time purchase a friend?— on the other hand, why are you to distrust your present partners? I have had indeed no knowledge of them, but by our late transaction & in that I find them Men of their Words, & punctual in their dealings— they have ventur'd their all in this undertaking, & may be undone shou'd it fail of Success. What better security my good friend can you have for their zeal & attachment to your interest, which is the well doing of the theatre, than that your mutual all of fortune & happiness is embark'd on the same bottom, & that you will prosper by pulling together, or be sunk by a contrary behaviour— Dr Ford is a man of great reputation in his profession & of great probity in his private character— Mr Sheridan is certainly a man of genius, & appears remarkably fair & open in his Conduct & Mr Linley is an Example of great Merit & Industry without any view but that of labouring in the Cause & doing his duty like an honest man— What person can you introduce among them more likely to be your friends, than such Characters as the above?— however if you think otherwise, or what I am more afraid of, are taught to think otherwise, I shall dread the Consequences— I cou'd not have slept quietly, had I not said so much to you, because I most sincerely wish you well & the theatre which I have quitted— You are very Young & inexperienc'd in the ways of Men, you have done some things & I am afraid are doing more, which I very warmly caution'd you against— I wish you first to be easy in your Circumstances before you run into expence— If you would know more, I will tell you more, whenever you chuse it, for I never shall keep any thing from you that I think will be of the least service to your interest & happiness.[1]

I am Dear Sir Most truly your's

D: Garrick

If you cou'd call at Hampton next Saturday Evening about Six or Seven o'clock Mr Wallis & I shall be together, & glad to see you—[2] let me know if you will come— I shall be there this Evening.

Source: FC, copy, signed by Garrick; Little, p. 79f.

1. Contrary to Garrick's advice, Lacy later, when he received offers, sought to sell part of his share to Edward Thompson and to Abraham Langford, Jr., the auctioneer (see Lacy to Garrick, Aug. 18, 1776, FC). Eventually he was forced by Sheridan to agree to sell to him if he sold at all (*LC*, vol. XL, Oct. 15–17, 1776, pp. 374, 376; Boaden, II, 180ff.).

2. Lacy wrote from Isleworth on June 27 accepting the invitation (FC).

1030   To Hannah More

                                                        Adelphi
My dear Madam.   July 3ᵈ 1776
I have this Evening receiv'd Your 2 Acts,[1] & I set out for Suffolk
tomorrow— I cannot criticise as I ought, because I am in a hurry,
but they will do, & do well with a few Omissions, but more of that
Matter when I can do You, & my Self Justice at Hampton— there
I shall weigh Every Speech, & do the Needful, as yᵉ trading phrase
is: go on & prosper— I have Nothing yet to Object, but length—
keep up yᵉ fire, & We shall do Wonders!— I can do no more for
I am all hurry & Bustle, but most truly, warmly & unalterably
Yours Ever & Ever

                                                      D Garrick.

pray keep yᵉ printed scraps I sent You for my Wife— she is collecting
all yᵉ Nonsense about Me— don't lose any I beseech You— She
sends her best Love with mine to You & all about You— I am
truly in Such a hurry that I don't know what I write—

Source: Bristol Public Libraries.

1. Identified in Miss More's letter, which Garrick endorsed July 1, 1776, as the
first two acts of her tragedy *Percy* (FC; Boaden, II, 163f.). The play was to be produced
at Covent Garden on Dec. 10, 1777, with a prologue and an epilogue by Garrick.

1031   To John Rayner, Jr.[1]

                                                  Mistley in Essex
Sir   July 11. 1776
I received your letter at this place— The fatigues of the last Winter
were so great that I was obliged to take a jaunt into different parts
of the Kingdom, to recruit my health, and to rest after my great
labours. I shall move about for some time to Come, having Many
friends to see. I am very sorry and indeed surprizd at your letter—
Your Father,[2] I understood hath taken care of your Family; and
not to be able to avoid penury & other calamities you Mention,[3]

with your talents & knowledge of the law, rather, I fear upbraids your own Industry, than your Father's Obstinacy— I should not have taken this liberty had not you partly given it to me by your own letter— I have led a life of incredible fatigue, & it is one of my Maxims, that a Sensible Man in any business, Must thrive, if he does not oppose his own interest. Your Father's letter to me[4] was too Severe to Communicate, As I told Mr Fountain— our intimacy has been Much Weakened by my Zeal in your Cause— We have not (I believe) visited since that time.

As I have lost all interest with *him*, and Cannot possibly be of Any Service to *you* in your profession, it would only give me much uneasiness to hear, as it would you to relate, the disagreeable Situation which your letter so Strongly describes. Mr Rayner at the close of his life, and I cannot think it far off, may relent from his present rigor,[5] and still think of you, and act to you in the last Scene as your Father if you don't forfeit that chance, by some future Mistake in your Conduct.

I am, Sir, yr Well Wisher & obedt Servt

D G.

Endorsement by Garrick with address: Mr John Rayner Junr.   *Source:* FC, copy.

1. John Rayner, Jr. (d. 1784), barrister and legal author, was admitted to the Inner Temple on Jan. 14, 1752. According to a letter from his father to Garrick, written in July 1775, young Rayner had through dissipation gone from bad to worse, until about 1771 he deserted his wife and five children leaving them penniless and dependent on his father (FC). Sometime in early July 1775 Rayner, Jr., sought Garrick's aid in arranging a reconciliation with his father, but to no avail (see his letter to Garrick, July 24, 1775, FC; *European Magazine*, vol. V, 1784, p. 123).

2. John Rayner, of Skinner's Hall, London (will dated Nov. 19, 1776, proved April 3, 1777, Probate Court of Canterbury, Collier 178).

3. In a letter of July 3, 1776, to which Garrick's is the reply, Rayner complained of laboring under "extensive Penury . . . for near two years together, bereft of Roof, Rayment, and Food; and that too in the Life Time of a Parent bless'd with all in Abundance" (FC).

4. Of July 1775 (FC).

5. John Rayner, Sr., never did relent. In his will he referred to his son as following "a course of dissipation & ruin to himself & as far as lays in his power to me," and left him only some property which had formerly belonged to his dead mother. He did, however, provide for the younger Rayner's children.

1032   To Sir John Fielding

July 23ᵈ 1776

Mr Garrick presents his best Compts to Sr John Fielding & is very happy at receiving So flattering a Mark of ye Approbation,[1] of one, whom he always esteem'd, & respected— No Man is more Sensible of Sr John Fielding's Merit & probity than Mr Garrick, nor has more publickly declar'd it— if Mr G. appear'd hurt that his [*trim*] & jealous that an old family Connection of Love & regard was given up to a later Acquaintance,[2] he will bring old Montaigne, a most natural Writer, to justify him: he says, that Friendship in Minds of great sensibility almost equal the Warmth & Weaknesses of Love, & jealousy is as sure a Mark of one, as the other— Mr G: is much oblig'd to Sr John for his very friendly Wishes, & shall be much more cheerful in his retirement, if Sr John will now & then partake of his hospitality with those Select friends, he mentions in his Note.

Endorsement by Garrick: July 23ᵈ 1776 a Letter of reconciliation wᵗʰ Sr John Fielding. *Source:* FC, draft; Boaden, II, 170.

1. A letter from Fielding of July 23, in which, among other flattering comments, he wrote that "the Chastity of Mr Garrick, as a Manager of a Public Theatre, and his exemplary Life as a Man, have been of great service to the Morals of a dissipated Age" (FC; Boaden, II, 170f.).
2. William Addington.

1033 & 1034   To The Countess Spencer

Hampton

My very first of Ladies   Tuesday July the 23ᵈ [1776]

You will perceive the ill Consequences of Smiling upon an impudent fellow— as our intended jaunt into Wiltshire is put off for some days, May not Your humble Servants at Hampton hope that Saturday, Sunday or Monday next be appointed a day of Mortification?— We intreat You to make Yourself, & to persuade My Lord to be, miserable upon one of those days— Whatever Companions in affliction You would chuse, We will Endeavor to procure: We should rejoice that the Name of Howe[1] (Ever partial to my follies) should be of the chosen wretched— Your Ladyship & Lord Spencer have long promis'd & we could wish y^t Lady Harriet,[2] Miss Lloyd,[3] Lord Altrop[4] Gen[1] Koch,[5] & Mr Crawfurd[6] Would attend upon ye Melancholly Occasion with whomsoever else Your Ladyship pleases; Whatever the Company may Suffer, We shall be most happy, & most grateful for the honor conferr'd upon us.

I am, Ever was, & Ever shall be,

Your Ladyship's most Devoted

D. Garrick

Endorsement by Garrick: July 23. 1776 My Letter of Invitation to charming Lady Spencer— her Lad$^{p's}$ answer. *Source:* FC, draft; Boaden, II, 168f. *The final letter, of the same date, with minor alterations, is in the possession of the Earl Spencer but has not been made available for publication.*

1. The Hon. Caroline Howe (1722–1814), daughter of second Viscount Howe and widow of John Howe of Hanslop, Buckinghamshire. "Mrs Howe," wrote Lady Spencer in her reply (misdated July 22, 1776), "has put off her Journey on purpose to be one of the party" (FC; Boaden, II, 169).

2. Lady Henrietta Frances Spencer (1761–1821), commonly called Harriet, later (1793) Countess of Bessborough, was Lady Spencer's second daughter.

3. Rachel Lloyd (1720?–1803), in 1764 had become housekeeper of Kensington Palace (*Court and City Kalendar*, 1767, p. 83; see Walpole, ed. Toynbee, VI, 136). Walpole declared that Lady Spencer could not "keep up her drawing-room without Mrs. Howe and Miss Lloyd" (ed. Toynbee, VIII, 392f.).

4. George John Spencer (1758–1834), Viscount Althorp, Lady Spencer's only son, who was to succeed as second Earl Spencer in 1783.

5. Presumably Johann Baptist, Freiherr von Koch (1733–1780), Austrian soldier, at this time Governor of the Ostend fortress (Constant von Wurzbach, *Biographisches Lexikon des Kaiserthums Oesterreich*, Vienna, 1856–1891).

6. John Craufurd (d. 1814), a friend of Walpole and Boswell and like them tireless in his attendance upon polite society in England and France.

1035　　　　　To Henry Hoare, Jr?[1]

Hampton

Saturday [July 27, 1776][2] 7 o'Clock & a cloudy Morning

So So, My dear Fellow Traveller, here's a fine Kettle of fish! not unlike that You caught with our friend Bennet[3] wet up to Y^r A—s in Hertfordshire!— Here's a delicious Cordial to be presented to my Sight the Moment I get out of bed! and to such a tinder-like,

Combustible devil as I am! The World's at an End, & I shall prepare Myself for Execution— *Go without You*! go to Heaven without Virtue, or to a turtle feast without a Stomach— GO WITHOUT YOU!— I'll be d—d if I do!—

We shall wait, (not with patience), for the going off of Your cursed Gout— I am afraid that he likes his present Establishment too well not to Stay ye best part of the Summer— he is a Liquorish rogue & where can he revel so much in ye luxuries of the times as in his present tenement? all Your fasting & praying will not drive him from thence for some time— in short, (for Your Man is in Such a develish haste that he will not give me time to be Witty) the Jews shall not wait with More eager expectation for the coming of their Prophet, than I & Madam shall for Y^r coming to Hampton— We had got ourselves so Spruce for Your reception!— She has been cutting away leaves & branches with her Scissors to Make Vistas for You; We had prepar'd no less than a dozen fine Salmons to leap & frisk before You, while you were walking upon the terrace, & when we had set y^r Mouth a watering, You would have seen the Jowl of the largest upon the Table, with a new fish Sauce invented on purpose for You! what in the name of good fellowship would you have?— but to the purpose— as We are Married, & love our Wives— restet amica Manus—[4] & let us think of our *Feet*— may they be friendly to us & the sooner the better— would You think it?— if I don't sympathize with You I am a sous'd Garnet—[5] two Glasses of Champaign wch I drank Yesterday with Earl Spencer at Wimbledon, are now tickling the ball of my great toe— We were made for Each other in the Social Concert of Life, & tho You will always play the first Fiddle, yet I can be a good ripieno[6] to You, & may come to be a good Second, if I could keep You company, as much, as I intend to do— now for some answer to Your letter— the Devil saw we should be too happy, & so has put his damn'd foot into our broth— but our Virtues will be too hard for him— in Short— (this is ye 3^d in Short I have us'd in this letter) we shall be wholly at your Commands— write to our friends[7] & propose what will be most agreeable to You, & Your Gout, & You will please & Oblige her, & him who are most sincerely & Affectionatly Y^rs

D Garrick
for himself & Wife

Our Loves to Your Love[8]
  pray let us know at times how You are & what you fix for Us.

Source: FSL.

1. The conjectural identification of the recipient goes back to an anecdote, published in the *Morning Post*, Feb. 12, 1779, that "in August [1776] Mr Garrick, accompanied by his neighbour and friend, Mr Hen. Hoare, of the Adelphi, made a visit to Mr Hoare of Stourhead, in Wilts." The traveling companion and the occasion are substantiated by the fact that Hoare was with Garrick at Wilton on Aug. 9 (Letter 1039).

2. Presumably written on Saturday, July 27, 1776, from the reference in the letter of Aug. 19, 1776, to the effect that Garrick had been with the Spencers three weeks earlier, which agrees with his statement in this letter that he was with them the day before, or July 26.

3. Richard Henry Alexander Bennett (1744–1814), politician.

4. Statius, *Thebiad*, IV, 26: "Loving hand clings fast."

5. *Henry IV, Part 1*, IV, ii, 13.

6. A supplementary singer or instrument used to fill out the whole orchestra as against taking a solo or leading part.

7. The Henry Hoares of Stourhead.

8. Mary Hoare (d. 1820), daughter of William Hoare, a portrait painter in Bath, had married Henry Hoare, Jr. (no relation) on June 25, 1765 (Edward Hoare, *The Families of Hore and Hoare*, 1883, p. 56).

1036 To Hannah More

My Dear Nine, [*ante* July 28, 1776][1]
We have been upon the ramble for near three weeks, and your ode[2] did not reach me till Monday last. Good, and very good—partial, and very partial. Mrs. Garrick (who sends her best wishes) and her lord and master set out for Bath the beginning of next month. Though my doctors have extorted a vow from me that I shall neither dine out nor give dinners while I stay at Bath, yet I had a mental reservation with regard to Bristol. However, if I continue sick and peevish, I had better keep my ill-humours at home, and for my wife alone. She is bound to them, and so reconciled to them by long use that she can go to sleep in the midst of a good scolding, as a good sailor can while the guns are firing.

Mrs. Garrick is studying your two acts. We shall bring them with us, and she will criticise you to the bone. A German commentator (Montaigne says) will suck an author dry. She is resolved to dry you up to a slender shape, and has all her wits at work upon you.

I am really tired— my thumb is guilty, but my heart is free. I could write till midnight, but if I don't finish directly, I shall be obliged, from pain, to stop short at what I have most pleasure in declaring, that I am, please your Nineship,

> Most truly yours,
> D. Garrick.

Have you kindly excused me to Dr. Stonehouse? My friend Walker intends trying his lecturing acumen upon you very soon. Why should not I come one day, and kill two birds with one stone?

Source: Roberts, *Hannah More*, I, 72f.

1. Written before Miss More's reply of July 28, and in 1776 from the references to the three-week ramble, and to two acts of a tragedy which can be identified as *Percy* (FC; Boaden, II, 242f.; Letters 1031, 1030). Apparently Garrick changed his plan of going to Bath and visiting Bristol, for on Aug. 7 Miss More wrote him of her disappointment (FC; Boaden, II, 251f.).

2. Presumably her *Ode to Dragon, Mr. Garrick's House-dog at Hampton,* circulated in manuscript in 1776 before its publication in 1777 (Boaden, II, 282; *LC*, vol. XLI, April 8–10, 1777, p. 341).

1037　　To The Countess Spencer

July 30, 1776

Address: Lady Spencer. *In the possession of the Earl Spencer: Not made available for publication.*

1038　　To Peter Fountain[1]

Dear Sir　　　　July 31st 1776
You may depend upon my calling upon You the next time I take a broil in London— the winding up of my theatrical matters has taken up almost all my time; the little I had to spare was spent in a visit or two to some friends in Suffolk & Essex:

The little favours I conferr'd upon You were not worth the thanks you have given, besides I pleas'd myself more than I could you in bestowing them: so let that matter rest. I have heard of Sr Thomas's remarkable room— I have not yet seen it— it was mention'd to Me, as a most ridiculous affair— but I'll take y^r word— We don't quite set up our horses together, tho I have done a piece of service lately, he knows Nothing of, nor Ever shall— what you mean by the *black but fair defect*, Except that most Worthless Creature Ab[ington] I don't know— she is below the thought of an honest Man or Woman— she is as *Silly*, as she is *false* & treacherous—[2]

When I see You I shall be glad to see ye ring you speak of— I have very little faith in Such Matters— nor can I yet believe that the Gallant Chev^r is a female— c'est un peu trop fort pour moi mon Ami— as to Mr Rayner, I will meddle no more in that business— the moment I can lay my hand upon my Letter & his Father's Answer, You shall have them— his letter is a bitter one indeed—

I really think the Son to blame— if he is what you say, & all say, in his profession, the discredit falls upon him that he cannot take care of his own Subsistence & fame— I have my Objections to some part of his Conduct, tho I did my best Endeavors to serve him.

his Father & I are at present almost unknown to Each other— he is very ailing & I am told cannot last long— I beg I may hear no more of that business— ye letter you shall have, when I look over my papers: We must take care of ourselves & our own Credit, & let Mr Rayner Senr have his own feelings— nay he will have them— & he has so much sense & Resolution, that all we can Say would only prejudice ye Object of our Wishes— he is very clear & Strong in his Accusations, & some Fathers would think that he had been very ill us'd— I am going into Wiltshire for some time—

Yours Dear Sir most truly
D Garrick

I write upon ye Gallop & have not time to read it over so Yours—

Source: FC; Boaden, II, 171.

1. In the absence of evidence to the contrary, the identification of Fountain as the recipient is based on the inclusion of this letter among the group of ninety-three letters in the Forster Collection all classified as addressed to Fountain. The letter also agrees with the others in general tone and subject, particularly in the allusion to d'Eon.

2. Garrick had doubtless learned that instead of retiring she had signed a contract with the new managers of Drury Lane.

1039   To Richard Cox

                                                      Wilton
My dearest Richard   Aug^st the 9th [1776?]^1
Don't be angry with your Old dear Friend— We are so Water-
bound here that we cannot get from our Noble Landlord— We
vex at the Weather for we want to be wth You— but we cannot
leave this place till tomorrow at 7 or thereabout— we propose to
breakfast with You to Morrow Morning before ten & to dine with
You— We shall then set off for Overton, for our friend Hoare has
some business which will hinder us making an Inn of Your house—
pray return me a line of Comfort, for we are all in ye Dumps— if
our coming tomorrow will be inconvenien⟨t⟩ Say ye word, as freely
as I do, & we will see You another time— I write upon ye Gallop
because I will not keep ye Boy.
                              Y^rs Ever & Ever most affec^ly
                                             D. Garrick
My best respects to Mrs Cox—

Address: Richd Cox Esqr, Quarley. Seal. Source: FSL.

1. The year is conjectural, depending upon the fact that the letter is dated from
Wilton, the country seat of Lord Pembroke. In the postscript of a letter to Garrick of
July 13, 1776, Pembroke wrote from Pembroke House: "2^d of August we shall be, de
retour from Mount Edgcumbe, at Wilton, when we shall be daily looking out with
impatience for Casa Garrick, and their travelling companions" (HTC).

1040   To Frances Cadogan^1

                                                    Hampton
My Dearly Beloved   Aug^st 18 [1776]^2
We shall be most happy to see you & your Anti-Shakespeare
Father^3 on Sunday next— tho he has manifold Sins & much
Wickedness, they shall be all forgiven on Your Account— We are
going to Brighthelmstone^4 for 3 or 4 days next Wednesday & we
shall return on Saturday Night. but for fear we should not arrive
at Hampton till Sunday Morning— secure your breakfast at

Hurlingham,[5] & be with us about 12— stay with us all Night, & as long after, as it shall please *You*, for Nobody Else shall govern at Hampton, or Me—

Ever & most Affect[y] Yours

D Garrick.

No date & no place to your letter— there goes one fault— would I could find another!

Source: Baker, p. 68.

1. So identified in the source.
2. Answered by Miss Cadogan on Aug. 22, 1776 (FSL).
3. In a letter dated only May 19, Mrs. Montagu wrote Mrs. Vesey: "I have sent you enclosed a copy of verses made by Mr. Garrick the other day, Dr. Cadogan and he had at dinner a warm dispute about the merits of Shakespear, to which the Doctor is very insensible" (Blunt, *Mrs. Montagu,* I, 243; Knapp, No. 64). Some manuscript verses by Garrick in the Folger Shakespeare Library are superscribed: "G——k to Dr Cadogan on his abuse of Shakespeare," and endorsed: "My Verses to D[r] C——n & his Answer."
4. Brighton.
5. Hurlingham House, built by Dr. Cadogan in 1760 (Charles J. Fèret, *Fulham Old and New,* 1900, III, 242f.).

1041   To Peter Garrick

Dear Peter.   Aug[st] the 19th 1776

We have at last settled our peregrinations— they stand thus— the Duke of Devonshire meeting me 3 Weeks ago at Lord Spencer's at Wimbleton, desir'd me, in so affectionate Manner to go to Chatsworth that I could not resist him— Lady Spencer, the first of Women, hearing what was passing, insisted, as affect[y] that we should be there at y[e] Same time with them— which will be in y[e] first Week of y[e] next Month September— We have therefore resolv'd to go y[e] Second or Third to Chatsworth & after being there four or five days at Most, we will be with You at Lichfield for some days— George's Children are with their Grandfather, who is very ill, & does not care to part with them; so we shall come alone to You, & if You will let us keep house for a Week, with Some assistance to M[rs] Betty,[1] we will drink soft ale, & laugh like ten Christ'nings— we had rather live simply, Mutton & Pudding than upon all the dainties in the world— *Ben Victor* who is at Mr Piggot's^2 will meet Us at Lichfield, & I shall take him up to Town with Us— I wish among You, that you could get him a bed—

I will give both him & You notice when I shall beat up y^r Quarters— We intend this time, to be like Bobadil, *not too popular, or generally visited— private is ye word*—^3

If you like our Scheme say the Word, and we will be punctual— Our Loves to all of You.

Ever & Affec^ly Yours
D: Garrick

Send ye inclos'd as soon as You conveniently can—

Source: FSL.

1. Presumably the housekeeper for Peter, who was a bachelor. She was probably the Elizabeth Sadler to whom Peter, by will, left an annuity of ten pounds for life (Stafford Lent Assizes, *Docksey* vs. *Panting*, 1796).
2. William Pigott (1742–1811), lawyer, who left Oxford in 1770 and from 1779 until his death was Rector of Edgmond and Chetwynd, Shropshire. His name appears in the list of subscribers to Victor's *Original Letters, Dramatic Pieces, and Poems* which was to appear in the fall with a dedication to Garrick.
3. *Every Man in His Humour*, I, iv.

1042   To Frances Cadogan^1

My dear Madam—   Tuesday Aug^st 20 [1776]^2
Upon second thoughts, for fear our friends should press us to stay another day at Brighthelmstone, we wish that you would defer the Pleasure you are to give us at Hampton till Sunday sennight, when we shall hope for your Company as soon as you can give it us— We will take for granted that you will come, if we hear Nothing from you— write any thing you have to say to the *Adelphi* about Thursday next— if you could come Friday, or Saturday, the sooner the better. We live in hopes to ⟨see⟩ [you, and] am Yours^3 & my dear Doctor's most Affectionate,

Friends
The Garricks

Source: Baker, p. 69.

1. So identified in the source.

2. The reference to the Adelphi establishes that this letter was written after March 1772. From 1772 until Garrick's death Aug. 20 fell on a Tuesday only in 1776.

3. According to a note in the source, the manuscript read: "We live in hopes to see am Yours & my dear Doctor's most Affectionate," the word "see" being deleted.

1043   To Hannah More

Hampton
Aug^st 20 [1776][1]

We sincerely hope & believe, my dear Nine, that you were Woefully disappointed at our not peeping in at You at Bristol— You would be very hard-hearted Creatures if you were not— so say no more Madam Hannah upon that subject, We felt it, as well as Y^r Ladyship & Your pathetic Sisters— may I take the Liberty to say, that I don't think You were in y^r most Acute & best feeling when You wrote ye 3^d Act—[2] I am not satisfy'd with it, it is the Weakest of the four, & raises such Expectation from the Circumstances, that a great deal more must be done, to content ye Spectators & Readers— I am rather vex'd that Nothing More is produc'd by that Meeting, Which is the groundwork of the Tragedy, & from which so much will be requir'd, because such an Alarm is given to the heart & Mind— I have been in so much Company, & have had so little time to Study ye Matter, that I can say no more at present— I will at my return from Brighthelmstone— pore upon it, & give my thoughts more fully upon the business— till then rest you quiet & be assur'd, that I am Your sincere friend, tho at times more bold than wellcome.

My Wife sends her Love wth mine to You all— she has not yet seen ye 3^d & 4th, nor do I yet know whether she may be trusted wth it.

I am Dear Nine Ever & sincerely y^rs
D. Garrick.

You have not Sent us, what You reprinted about Me in ye Bristol paper.[3]

Source: Bristol Public Libraries.

1. The year is established by the reference to the impending visit to Brighton.
2. Of *Percy*.
3. Miss More had written on July 28: "the best thing that has appear'd, I think, on a certain subject [Garrick's retirement], was a long prose history in the *General Evening [Post]*, I know not who wrote it, but in general it was extremely well done. I had it reprinted here, and if Mrs G. wants a copy tis at her service" (FC; Boaden, II, 242). For the reprint, see the *Bristol Journal*, July 20, 1776.

1044   To George Colman

Brighthelmston
Dear Colman,   Friday [August 23, 1776][1]
Waldron[2] has purchas'd the Theatre at Richmond[3] & wants about 18 hundred pounds— had I not disposd of my Money, I should assist him— he is a very honest discreet Man, & will perform Every promise he makes—

I can say no more, if You have Money & don't dislike ye Security perhaps You may assist him—

I shall be ready for You about Wednesday, when I shall be quietly Seated at Hampton again.

I am Ever Yrs most affecly
D Garrick.

Address: George Colman Esqr.   *Seal.*   *Source:* FSL.

1. Waldron's negotiations for the purchase of the Richmond Theatre took place in 1776; in that year Garrick left for Brighton on Wednesday, Aug. 21, and was to return after three or four days (see Letter 1040).
2. Francis Godolphin Waldron (1744–1818), actor at Drury Lane (1769–1795), writer, editor, and bookseller.
3. In the summer of 1776 "the theatre was put up for sale, and sold to Mr. Waldron for 3600l., who forfeited the deposit, and the property reverted to the proprietors" (Thomas Gilliland, *The Dramatic Mirror*, 1808, I, 226).

1045   To Catherine Bunbury[1]

Chatsworth
Madam   Sepr 8 1776
The honour & favour You have bestow'd upon Me, are as properly felt, as it is out of my power to return them— what bare, but sincere gratitude can do, will certainly be done, but It's Circle is

8+L.D.G. III

but narrow, & confin'd within my own bosom: I had Notice by a Letter from my Brother of the arrival of the present,[2] upon which I shall set the greatest value— I thought Myself before so Oblig'd to yᵉ house of Bunbury, that I despair'd of shewing myself worthy of their very flattering regard a certain Gentleman has shewn Me; & now I am in the Situation of a person I knew, who being overwhelm'd with debts, told me, (upon my advising him to reflect a little upon his affairs) what signifies reflection Garrick, I never can get out of debt, so I must e'en be satisfy'd with letting things take their Course, & pray to Heaven to direct me for the best, as Nothing but prayers are left for Me, I beg that you will be assur'd that no blessing or Pleasure should be ever absent from my most amiable friends at Barton, if the prayers of a very unworthy Sinner could prevail.

I am Madam with great truth Your most Sincerely
Oblig'd humble Servant
D. Garrick

Mʳˢ Garrick presents her respects wᵗʰ mine to You & Mʳ Bunbury. as I find the little Nonsense I scribbled at Barton[3] has been approv'd of by some friends here, I take the liberty of troubling You to desire Mʳ B—— to alter yᵉ last Line, to yᵉ first reading— which was not— *Fortune plac'd*— but— *And Fate plac'd*

had I not been so far from Town I should not have been so long in Answering Your most obliging letter.

Seal. Source: FSL; *Correspondence of Sir Thomas Hanmer*, ed. Sir Henry E. Bunbury, 1838, p. 378.

1. Catherine (Horneck) Bunbury (1754–1799), had married Henry William Bunbury in 1771 (*Memoir and Literary Remains of Lieutenant-General Sir Edward Bunbury, Bart.*, ed. Charles J. F. Bunbury, 1868, p. 240).
2. Mrs. Bunbury had written on Sept. 3 that she had sent him a waistcoat she had made (Boaden, II, 369).
3. "The old Painter's Soliloquuy upon see[ing] Mʳ Bunbury's drawings

1

Shall *I* so long, old *Hayman* said, and swore,
Of Painting till the barren soil,
While this young *Bunbury* not twenty four,
Gets Fame, for which in vain I toil:

2

Yet he's so whimsical, perverse, & idle,
Tho Phoebus self should bid him stay,
He'll quit the magic Pencil, for the Bridle,
And gallop Fame, and Life away.

3

With *Reynolds'* matchless Grace, and *Hogarth's* pow'r,
   (Again He swore a dreadful Oath)
This Boy had rather trot ten Miles an hour,
   And risk his Neck, than paint like both.

4

Fix but his Mercury, He'd join the Two,
   And be my boast, Britannia cry'd:
Nature before him plac'd her Comic Crew,
   Fortune plac'd Beauty by his Side.

July 5ᵗʰ 1776/*Barton*" (Morgan Library; Knapp, No. 106).

1046   To The Earl of Upper Ossory

London   Adelphi
My good Lord   Sepʳ 24 [1776]
Mrs Garrick & I most devoutly wish to pay our respects to Lady
Ossory & your Lordship— Mr Crawford promis'd us to give us
information when our Company would be least troublesome at
Ampthill,[1] but as he is rather uncertain in his motions, I have
taken the liberty to trouble your Lordship— if the 8ᵗʰ or yᵉ 18ᵗʰ
of the next month will not be inconvenient to Lord & Lady Ossory
We shall with the greatest pleasure pay our Duty at either of those
times—[2] if your Lordship will be pleas'd to tell me the best &
nearest way to you, I will most certainly be with you at Dinner on
the Eight, or Eighteenth—
     I am most faithfully Your Lordships Obedⁿᵗ humˡᵉ Servᵗ
                                 D. Garrick

Mrs Garrick presents her respects with mine to Lady Ossory.

Endorsement: Mʳ Garrick 1776.   *Source:* Compton Mackenzie, transcript.

1. Ossory's country seat in Bedfordshire.
2. In Ossory's reply, Sept. 25, he wrote: "Your letter of yesterday made me extremely
happy, & I am only sorry to be obliged to fix upon the latter day you propose & even to
postpone that to the 20ᵗʰ on which day Lʸ Ossory & I most sincerely hope to have you
& Mʳˢ Garrick here at dinner" (HTC).

1047   # To Sir Thomas Mills

Hampton

My dear Sr Thomas.   Octr 2^d [1776?][1]

I have a Neighbour a very honest young man, & bred to Accounts: by no Sin of his own, but that of a foolish Father, he is become a Solicitor to Me for assistance— He thinks that I have interest to get him some Employment at the India house— Tho I have been, as You know, a very *steady* Proprietor, yet I have not troubled the Directors— many of my friends, are friends to Mr Roberts,[2] & I believe Your Worship among the rest— now if Your usual & constant good Nature to Me, was to be exerted in favour of my worthy Neighbour, with my Name tack'd to ye Petition, by way of a Make-Weight, who knows but Mr Roberts in a freak, (for he has as little reason to do any thing for Me, as I have to ask it) might give us his assistance, & make an honest man happy with about 50 pounds a Year?— if it should be *more*, the Man is so Obedient to my Commands, that I will answer he will not refuse it— to be serious, if Mr Roberts will be kind to us, we will be very grateful; and we are ready to give the best Security for his good behaviour. pray, dear Sr Thomas, exert your Winning Ways: & Even if he was heard-hearted, which I know he is not, Mr Roberts would melt before You— our best Wishes & respects Ever attend Lady Mills—

Ever Yours most devoutly

D: Garrick

I have ye Gout in my fingers— Ecce Signum! Scrawl!

I have no less than Six Garricks gabbling about me—

Source: FSL.

1. The conjectural year depends on the assumption that Garrick would have referred to Roberts as commanding great power in the East India Company during the time the latter was Chairman of the Court of Directors in 1776 (Joseph Haydn, *Book of Dignities*, 1890).

2. John Christopher Roberts (1739–1810), a Director of the East India Company for many years.

1048   To Thomas Harris

Hampton
Sir.   Oct^{br} 3^d 1776
I was at dinner with a great deal of company when your letter[1]
came to my hands— I am now risen from the Table to answer it—
Sr Thomas Mills ask'd me, if it were possible that you could have
struck off y^r Liberty list my Nephew, who, I find, had the freedom
of your House, when I was a Manager; I told him it was true, &
that I was surpriz'd at it, & so I really am— Mr Harris & Co had
the freedom of my Theatre, whenever they pleas'd, & I have had
6 & 8 of a Night sometimes, but without the least uneasiness on
my part— I suppose I have the Liberty of y^r House as an author,
for as such I have always taken it— Mrs Garrick always paid,
unless she was invited to a Manager's Box— If any Gentlemen,
who wrote for Covent Garden Theatre have not the Liberty of your
Theatre, I shall with pleasure pay for my place, nor can accept it
upon any other conditions, after the incivility, which was shew'd to
my Nephew in exposing him to y^r Boxkeepers & company in the
Lobby. I must confess that ye late behavior to him, & consequently
to me, *has not come up to my expectations*, & I hope, that my Vanity
does not make me singular on this occasion

I am &c.

If you had not said it, I could not believe that my Nephew, after
the disagreeable situation, he was put in, could have been satisfy'd,
with any favour that might have been shewn him— My present
situation must excuse the hurry & Scrawl of this letter—
     When we were first told that Mrs G. & I were upon the list— I
sent word that M^{rs} G: would always pay, & that I receiv'd my
freedom as an Author, & not from ye favour of ye Managers the
Message was Sent when Mr Colman Commenc'd Manager—

Endorsement: Mr Harris's Letter and a Copy of my answer.   *Source:* FC, copy.

   1. Of Oct. 2, in which he wrote: "I have been inform'd by Sr Thos Mills that You
have been very loud in your complaints in Public company's because your Nephews
were not continued on the Liberty list of Cov^t Gard^n Theatre— I suppose your eldest
Nephew must have inform'd You that he call'd on me the morn^g after our opening, he
was then told that it never was understood as a rule to give the freedom to the friends &
relations of the past as well as pres^t proprietors of this Theatre." When, however, Harris
had offered to continue Carrington Garrick on the free list as a friend, "Your Nephew

said he chose rather to have a liberty of sending for orders whenever he might have occasion. I requested that he wou'd" and he "express'd himself exceedingly satisfied" (FC).

1049   To The Countess Spencer

Adelphi, Oct. 4, 1776

Address: Countess Spencer, Althorp.   *In the possession of the Earl Spencer: Not made available for publication.*

1050   To Sir George Howard[1]

Adelphi

Sir   Oct[r] 5[th] 177[6][2]
a very honest poor Man of Chelsea College has foolishly apply['d] to Me to use my Interest w[t]h S[r] G. Howard to be rais'd from a pensioner at a penny a day to a Light Horse Man, or Serjeant—[3] I find (as he tells Me) that these favour[s] are granted as Vacancies happen— the only Vacancy that y[e] poor Man seems capable of filling is y[e] Grave, for he can scarcely stand, & what adds to the Whimsicalness of his request, is, that as he is so heavy & helpless, he would chuse to be a *Light* horse man— thus Sir without y[e] least pretension of troubling You, I feel a very great impropriety in addressing You— Nothing but y[e] honesty & age of the Object, & Your own Character, could have oblig'd me to be thus impertinent.[4]

I am S[r] Y[r] most Obed[t] & most hum[le] Ser[t]
D G.

Endorsement: Letter to S[r] G. Howard about Abbot. Oct[r] 5th 1776.   *Source:* HTC, copy.

1. Sir George Howard (1720?–1796), knighted 1763, soldier and politician, had been appointed Governor of Chelsea Hospital in 1768.

2. While the manuscript draft of this letter is dated 1778, the correction to 1776 is provided by the endorsement.

3. Pensioners in Chelsea College or Hospital were old or disabled soldiers; they were provided with food, lodging, other necessities, a special uniform, and a weekly allowance of 8*d.* A light-horse man or a serjeant received 2*s.* a week (Francis F. Grose, *Military Antiquities*, 1788, II, 185f.).

4. After looking into the records, Howard reported to Garrick on Oct. 22: "Abbott . . . *served only 8 Years,* and never was a Serjeant . . . if it was possible I would appoint him a Light Horseman, but that Station is particularly set apart for those who have served in the Cavalry. I would willingly appoint him a Serjeant in the College, but as he never served as such, it is too ridiculous to think, that in his State of Infirmity [gout] and at the age of 57, he should be able to learn any thing more than he knows at present" (HTC).

1051   To The Countess Spencer

October 9, 1776

Address: Countess Spencer, Althorp. *In the possession of the Earl Spencer: Not made available for publication.*

1052   To John Taylor

Althorp Northamptonshire
My dear Sir   [October] 18ᵗʰ [1776][1]
I receiv'd Your favour here in the Midst of Joy & the best Society; three of the most beautiful Young Women in Europe[2] are at this instant trying their Skill to prevent my writing this— My inclinations & Intentions have sent me, & will send Me to Bath but various Circumstances have happen'd & may happen to put a Spoke in my Bath Wheels. My theatrical Matters are not yet all Settled, & the late quarrel[3] among them hath been very disagreeable to Me & my friends— however that is well over, & peace & Success I hope will be the Consequence. I shall go from this place, (which I leave wᵗʰ yᵉ utmost regret,) to Ampthill, (Lord Ossory's) Where I think of staying till yᵉ End of Next Week— when I get to Town I must think a little of putting my affairs in a proper channel— when that

is done my thoughts will be Bath-ward— what may intervene to
Stop my progress, Heaven only knows, to that I resign Myself—
I never was in Such Spirits; no School boy is half so Wild & ridiculous, & I never was in a place Where all my follies are so much
indulg'd & forgiven— Lady Spencer is a divine Woman!

Yours Ever & most Sincerely
D Garrick

My best & Warmest Wishes from Me & Mine ⟨to⟩ You & Yours.
⟨I h⟩ope all y^r family Cares are Over.

Address: John Taylor Esqr, Circus, Bath. *Frank:* L Knightley. *Postmark:*
Northampton. *Source:* Morgan Library; Little, p. 81f.

1. The month and year are determined by Garrick's visits to Althorp and Ampthill
(Boaden, II, 179; Letter 1046).
2. Presumably Lady Spencer and her daughters.
3. Resulting from Lacy's attempts to meddle in the management. Sheridan stayed
away from the theater, and when remonstrances and threats had no effect he organized
a general strike of the actors until Lacy was forced to apologize and cease his interference
(Walter Sichel, *Sheridan*, I, 523ff.).

1053   To The Countess Spencer

Newport pagnell, October 20, 1776

Address: Lady Spencer. *In the possession of the Earl Spencer: Not made available
for publication.*

1054   To The Countess Spencer

Adelphi, October 26, 1776

Address: Lady Spencer. *In the possession of the Earl Spencer: Not made available
for publication.*

1055   To Elizabeth Montagu

Dear Madam.   Octr 26 [1776]¹
I congratulate all Your friends & Myself among that honourable,
happy Number for Your safe return to us—
    Mrs Garrick did herself the honour of calling upon You to return
her thanks in Person for the great care you have taken, & the
trouble you have had, with the friendly favour of Mrs Necker to
her—² I heard wth pleasure of y^r being at the french Academy
when Voltaire exhibited his malevolent Nonsense (for which too
among other Obligations I thank You) upon our belov'd & immortal
Shakespeare:³ could any thing possibly add to my Admiration of
Mrs Montagu, it was the Expression of contempt & astonishm^t
which, I hear You put on, at hearing the Weak and impotent
ravings of Age, Envy, hatred & Malice— it rejoices Me much to
hear, that this unchristian attack upon Genius had not a favourable
reception even from his own friends—
    I doubt not, but You have converted Numbers to the faith, not
wth Sword as Mahomet did, but by those emanations of Genius,
which You have caught from the divinity You have so powerfully,
& justly protected & admir'd— this Attack of Voltaire, I hope, is
not to pass unnotic'd— If the Champions will not mount with the
regulars, the Light horse, & hussars must begin a Skirmish— I most
devoutly wish for the honour of a little conversation, which I should
immediatly have Endeavor'd to enjoy in Hill Street, had not a
Small attack of ye Gout ob⟨lig'd me to⟩ Stay at home for a day or
tw⟨o. Yet⟩ may I not hope for that [tear] favour, as soon as the
more im⟨portant⟩ Matters have had their first dues, & ⟨we⟩ with
our little demands may present ourselves with all Love, & humility?
                    I am Dr Mad^m Y^r most devoted Servt
                                            D. Garrick

Mrs Garrick presents her respects— I w^d Send my best Wishes,
with my Wife's, to Miss Gregory, but alass, I fear the enchantments
of french Everything has destroy'd all my hopes—⁴
    I w^d not have sent this Scrawl could I have written better, but
ye illbred Gout has prevented me

Source: Huntington Library; Blunt, *Mrs. Montagu*, I, 562.

    1. This is the reply to Mrs. Montagu's letter of Oct. 20, 1776 (Boaden, II, 183).
    2. Mme Necker had sent Mrs. Garrick, by Mrs. Montagu, two "pots de pâte
d'amande" and a "petit sac de grains" (*ibid.*, 624).
    8*

3. Mrs. Montagu had sent him a copy of *Lettre de M. de Voltaire à l'Académie française* (Geneva, 1776) read before the Academy on Aug. 25, 1776. At the beginning of it some ridicule is cast on Garrick's Jubilee and temple to Shakespeare.

4. "I assure you," she replied on Nov. 3, "I am more alarmed for Mrs Garricks interests than ever, Mad^{lle} Gregory at Paris was more desperately in love with you than Miss Gregory at London" (FC; Boaden, II, 189).

1056   To Arthur Murphy

Dear Murphy,   October 27, 1776
I have a noble turtle to-morrow, the gift of the Right honourable Richard Rigby— if you have no objection to drinking his health, and meeting some of your friends, be to-morrow at my house at four, and you will oblige

Yours most truly,
D. Garrick.

Source: Foot, *Murphy*, p. 291.

1057   To George Colman

Dear Colman   Octr 3[1]^1 [17]76
I am setting this moment off for Hampton— I wish You most sincerely Success & Every pleasure from your new Engagement—^{2} I am truly partial to the *Old* Spot, from an Old habitual liking, but likewise from a principal of honesty that makes me Attach'd to people, who have bought my property, & behave so Well to me— were You Manager at the other house, I should have been much distress'd for then *honour would say, do this, & tender Love say nay*—^{3} I am sorry the Place is lett to a puppet-Show—^{4} & I rejoice you have not (as I hope) made a bad bargain— but more when I see You— I could wish that there were a proper Gentleman-like Agreement about Matters between You all—^{5} More when I see You— in y^e mean time God bless you my dear Friend

Y^{rs} Ever &c
D: Garrick

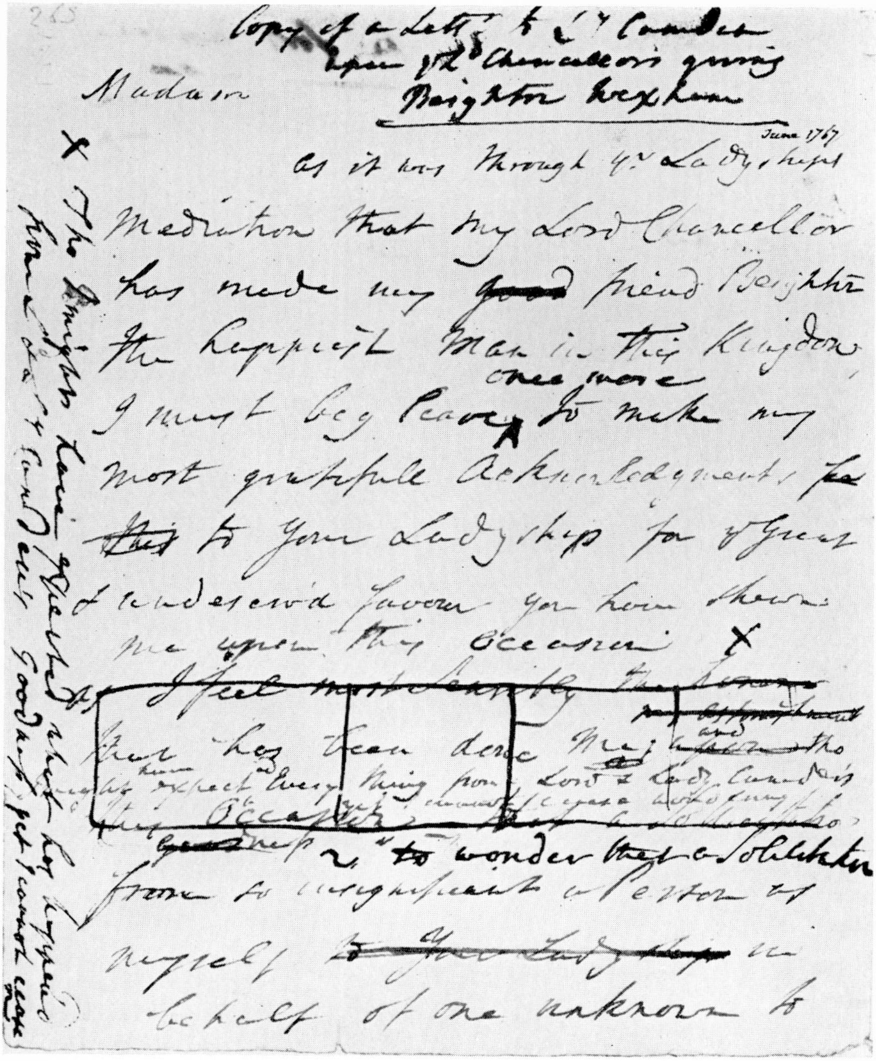

Copy of a Lett[r] to L[y] Camden upon y[e] L[d] Chancellor's giving Beighton his place

Madam

June 1767

As it was through Y[r] Ladyships Mediation that my Lord Chancellor has made my ~~good~~ friend Beighton the happiest Man in this Kingdom I must beg leave once more to make my most gratefull Acknowledgments ~~for this~~ to Your Ladyship for y[e] Great & undeserv'd favour you have shewn me upon this Occasion

to wonder that a Solicitation from so insignificant a Person as myself ~~to Your Ladyship~~ in behalf of one unknown to

An Example of a Draft: Letter 468, to Lady Camden [1767]

GARRICK
BY ZOFFANY

An Unfinished Portrait of Garrick

[I was very near losing 20p^ds as my vanity conceiv'd I Sh^d have heard of your Engagem^t before it had been in the papers—⁶ No friendly Miff I assure you]⁷

Endorsement by Garrick in copy: My answer to Colman's letter & his Letter upon his purchase of ye Haymarket. *Source:* Berg Collection, copy in FC; Colman, p. 322.

1. The date of Oct. 3 given in the manuscript copy and the printed source should be corrected, for the negotiations for Colman's taking the Little Theatre in the Haymarket ran from Oct. 8 to 18 and news of the agreement did not publicly appear until the end of the month (Peake, *Colman*, I, 412ff.; *LC*, vol. XL, Oct. 29–31, p. 424).

2. In return for an annuity, Colman obtained a transfer of Foote's lifetime patent to the Little Theatre in the Haymarket; Colman was to have the theater from May 15 to Sept. 15, Foote reserving the right to rent it during the winters.

3. *The Rehearsal*, III, v.

4. See the following letter, note 6.

5. An agreement among the managers about the closing of their winter season to allow the opening of the summer theater (Colman, p. 323).

6. Presumably Colman told Garrick the news before it appeared in the newspapers (see his undated letter in Boaden, II, 178). In an undated letter, which Garrick endorsed "Colman about his Haym^t purchase Novr 1776," he wrote that "the matter was scarce in embrio just as you were going to Ld Spencer's, & I went 3 or 4 times to the Adelphi & the house on purpose to consult you— but you were so lost in the dust made by the *New Brooms*, that I c^d not seize a favorable Moment— and indeed I did not then believe *him* in earnest" (FC; Boaden, II, 185).

7. Matter in brackets is supplied from the Forster Collection copy.

1058   To George Colman

My dear Colman   Monday N^r 4th 1776
I have this nasty Gout still nibbling at me & would fain damp my Spirits— You believe, I trust, that I am ye last man would advise You to bear Oppression, as I think You are the last man to take such advice— tho I am catechis'd on all sides about Your purchase, I will not own it, nor shall I, till I have *Your* leave— yet in ye name of good Management how can it be long a Secret?¹ for you must, like a wise General, prepare for ye Campaign—

Our facetious friend,² I hear, damns himself, that there is no such thing, & Jewel³ only owns to a treaty, but no bargain yet struck— I suppose HE w^d not proclaim his Abdication, till the tryal is Over—⁴ that will soon be & then you will come forth—

If you Wits & Managers (I don't include Messrs Leake & Fisher⁵ in this number) are not too much of the Game-Cock breed, You may settle y^r matters without sparring— they seem to be much hurt at ye 100 Nights for ye Fantocini—[6] all the three houses cry out Murder, & intend, as I hear, to petition against it— this I suppose cannot Effect *You*—

however busy & anxious I might be for the *New* brooms,[7] I am always constant to my *old* Friends, & shall be very sincere, however fallible in my advice to You

Y^rs Ever & most truly
D: Garrick

I saw you had secur'd *One* Author Yesterday— Much good may he do you— adieu & adieu!

Source: Berg Collection; Colman, p. 324f.

1. While the *London Chronicle* had announced that Colman had "absolutely engaged with Mr. Foote" at the end of October, the official announcement was not made in that paper until the middle of Jan. 1777 (vol. XL, Oct. 29–31, 1776, p. 424, vol. XLI, Jan. 16–18, 1777, p. 62).
2. Foote.
3. The treasurer of the Haymarket.
4. Under indictment since July, on Dec. 9 Foote was to be tried for and acquitted of homosexual assault on John Sangster, his former coachman (*LC*, vol. XL, Dec. 7–10, 1776, p. 558).
5. Of Covent Garden (Peake, *Colman*, I, 417).
6. Foote had rented the Haymarket for the winter season to a company which exhibited *fantoccini*: puppets.
7. See the preceding letter, note 6. The phrase "*New* brooms" alludes not only to the new managers of Drury Lane but also to Colman's prelude of that title with which the season of 1776–77 opened there on Sept. 21, Garrick providing the prologue (Knapp, No. 377).

1059   To The Countess Spencer

November 6, 1776

Address: Lady Spencer.   *In the possession of the Earl Spencer: Not made available for publication.*

1060   To The Countess Spencer

November 9, 1776

[Epitomized in the Historical Manuscripts Commission Report as follows: "Mentions a new fashion for ladies, of illuminated heads; head-dresses made of evergreens and lamps; a new invention, heard of by him, by a confectioner and toyman (Pinchbeck)"[1]— Report 2, Appendix (1874), p. 13.]

Address: Lady Spencer. *In the possession of the Earl Spencer: Not made available for publication.*

1. Christopher Pinchbeck (1710?–1783), inventor.

1061   To Suzanne Necker

Hampton

Madam   Novr 10th 1776

By the gracious permission of the Gout which has prevented my doing my duty 'till now I take up my pen, with fear & trembling, to thank you from my heart of hearts (as Shakespeare calls it)[1] for the most flattering, charming, bewitching letter that ever came to my hand—[2] I shall keep it as the most precious Monument of your unbounded partiality to me— & of my own Vanity— it Shall be left by my will to be kept in the famous Mulberry box with Shakespeare's own hand writing to be read by my Children's Children for Ever & Ever &

Exegi Monumentum &c![3]

Will you pardon me a fault for the Sincerity of Confessing it?— Mr Gibbon, our learned friend & excellent writer, happend to be with Me when I receiv'd the bewitching letter— in the Pride, & gratefull overflowings of my heart, I could not resist the temptation of shewing it to him— he read— Star'd at me— was silent— then gave it me, with these Emphatical words, Emphatically Spoken— *This is the very best letter that Ever was written*: Upon Which, a la mode d'Angleterre, The writer was remember'd with true devotion, & in full libations: An old English ballad Says—

> "Let your heart & your wine overflow,
> "To all that is matchless below!

And So they Shall as long as they can overflow wth me I am so bewitch'd to this Subject, that I had almost forgot my wife— Who is so full of her warm acknowledgments for the honour & pleasure she receiv'd with Your most elegant present,[4] that her great Sensibility upon the Occasion requires a more powerfull pen than mine to describe it; She begs me in particular to present her respects to M[rs] Necker, & that were She able to tell her feelings, that neither Shakespear or his Interpreter, her Husband, should outdo her in the true Sentiments of the heart:

It would be thought in general very Strange, that I should not before felicitate You Madam, and M[r] Necker upon his late, as it is call'd promotion—[5] I have a very particular way of thinking upon these Matters, & as I have the honour of knowing M[r] Necker, I sincerely think that no change of Situation can be any Promotion to Such a Mind & Such Abilities: I must beg leave to apply to You, & him, a Stanza in a little Ode which I wrote upon being ask'd, if I had been to wish Lord Camden joy of his appointment to the Great Seal—

> Wish him joy, & for what? I beseech you, declare:
> No Changes new honours can bring;
> To Necker the place will be labour, & Care;
> Wish Joy to his Country & King.

These are my real Sentiments in prose as well as Rhyme— And to be a little Selfish what Shall *I* get by the matter?— instead of seeing (should I go to Paris,) the warm, benevolent, Smiling, Social, Communicative, open hearted M[r] Necker, I Shall behold— the thoughtfull, absent, deep, wise, Grave Politician: Scheming every kind of good for France & perhaps in the moment that I am enjoying every hospitable pleasure under his Roof, he may be planning Mischief for poor Old England— I cannot bear it— No I'll Stay for his return to Social & private happiness, & then I will be the first to felicitate My best & much honour'd friends— If I can finish a little thought that I have, I will Send it— The only merit will be its Sincerity, I have left no room for Voltaire & Shake-

speare— There are rods preparing for the Old Gentleman by
Several English wits—[6] his Letter to the French Academy is no
Addition to his Genius or his Generosity— & his Errors are without
End— I pity his Ill plac'd Anger— I am
Your most faithfully Affectionate & devoted Servant
D Garrick

I have the Gout in my hand,

Endorsement by Garrick: A Charming Letter from Mrs Necker & my answer.
Source: FSL, draft; Boaden, II, 189f., repeated p. 625f.

1. *Hamlet*, III, ii, 78.
2. Of Oct. 5, in which she wrote: "Sçavez vous, Monsieur, que Voltaire et d'autres
beaux ésprits François ont profité de l'instant òu vous avez quitté le théâtre pour chercher
à détrôner Shakespear. Quand à moi c'est en vain qu'on veut me montrer dans cet
auteur quelques fautes de goût, et même de jugement; je réponds toujours, Vous n'avez
apperçu que son cadavre, mais je l'ai vû moi, quand son âme animoit son corps. Ils
repliquent, Vous vous trompez, ce n'étoit qu'un majestueux fantome que Monsieur
Garrick, ce puissant enchanteur, avoit évoqué du sein des tombeaux, le charme cesse,
il faut que Shakespear rentre dans la nuit" (Boaden, II, 624).
3. Horace, *Odes*, III, xxx, 1: "I have finished a monument more lasting than
bronze."
4. See Letter 1055, note 2.
5. He had been appointed Joint Controller-General of the Finance on Oct. 22.
6. Among them James Rutledge and Baretti, authors of *Observations à Messieurs de
l'Académie française* (Paris, 1776) and *Discours sur Shakespeare et sur M. de Voltaire* (1777).

1062   To The Countess Spencer

November 15, 1776

[Epitomized in the Historical Manuscripts Commission Report as
follows: "He mentions the Electrical Eels exhibited in the Haymarket, at 5*s.* a head; sends a bitter epitaph on Dr. Johnson, by
Soame Jenyns:[1]

'Here lies poor Johnson: reader, have a care;
Tread lightly, lest you rouse a sleeping bear.
Religious, moral, generous and humane
He was; but self-sufficient, rude and vain;
Ill-bred and overbearing in dispute;
A scholar and a Christian, and a brute.

Would you know all his wisdom and his folly,
His actions, sayings, mirth and melancholy,
Boswell and Thrale, retailers of his wit,
Will tell you how he wrote and talked, and coughed and spit!'"

Report 2, Appendix (1874), p. 13.]

Address: Countess Spencer. *In the possession of the Earl Spencer: Not made available for publication.*

1. Soame Jenyns (1704–1787), miscellaneous writer; though often criticized by Johnson, he waited until after the latter's death to publish the above lines (*GM*, vol. LVI, Aug. 1786, p. 696).

1063   To The Countess Spencer

Adelphi, November 30, 1776

Address: Lady Spencer. *In the possession of the Earl Spencer: Not made available for publication.*

1064   To William Woodfall

Adelphi

Dear Woodfall   Friday Morn^g [December 6, 1776][1]
As I intended to give You a very Satisfactory Criticism upon ye Play,[2] I waited till I could sit down at Hampton quietly & read it carefully— Mr Richards kept me in Town with his law Matter,[3] & I have been detaind since upon a business of great Consequence to those who are dearest to Me— I told Colman I had read it once over, & when I re'd y^r letter, I was in ye 4th Act for ye 2^d time— if You will call upon Me at y^r return from *Carractacus* about Nine this Ev^g I will be ready wth my remarks, & a Nibble from ye Mouse—[4] Send me word if You'll come—

Y^rs Truly
D: Garrick

I intended writing to day—

Address: Mr W. Woodfall, Dorset Street, Salisbury Court.   *Seal.*   *Source:* FSL.

1. The allusions to the "law Matter" (probably the deed of sale of the patent) and the criticism of *Sir Thomas Overbury* (CG, Feb. 1, 1777) in manuscript indicate that Woodfall was going to the first production of William Mason's *Caractacus* at Covent Garden on the evening of Friday, Dec. 6, 1776.
2. Presumably Richard Savage's *Sir Thomas Overbury*, which Woodfall was revising.
3. Probably relating to the preliminary arrangements for the signing of the deed of sale of Garrick's patent (see Letter 1072).
4. Presumably the contribution, mentioned in the following letter, to the *London Packet* of Dec. 11, 1776.

1065   To William Woodfall

Dear W.   [*post December 6, 1776*][1]
I have sent the Nibbler[2] to begin— it is a foul Copy, but correct— it may be made out— pray fill ye gaps with ye date wch I have forgot— don't let the Printer mistake the *pot pourri pomatum*—[3] 'tis all the ton— what says our friend to my Observations—[4] I wrote them with ye Stump of a pencil partly in bed & partly in ye Coach— all I contend for is the necessary alterations in the Episode— did you see the *New Morning Post*[5] of Saturday— there is an infamous paragraph about Foote[6] & the *Small Coal-Man*— It is Stupid as infamous; but this is ye paper set up against Bate's,[7] because it was so personal & slanderous— I don't remember so foul a paragraph as that any where— What Sc—ls!— I shall Send You Mouse ye first[8] soon—

                                      Yours Ever &c
                                      D G.

Address: ⟨Mr. W. W⟩oodfall, ⟨D⟩orset Street, Salisbury Court.   *Source:* BM.

1. Presumably written after the preceding letter and before the contribution signed "The Original Mouse in the Green Room" appeared in the *London Packet* for Dec. 11, 1776; that this letter refers to that article is made clear by the allusion to *pot pourri pomatum* which occurs in both.
2. Between Oct. 30, 1775, and April 26, 1776, eight contributions or letters addressed to Woodfall and signed "The Mouse in the Green Room" were published in the *London Packet*. In the last, of April 26, the "Mouse" gave his last will and testament and apparently terminated the series. However two additional contributions appeared signed "The Mouse": one on Sept. 30, the second on Oct. 30; both are almost certainly by Edward Thompson (see Letter 1078). That these two were not by Garrick is confirmed

by the signature to the Dec. 11 letter as "The Original Mouse in the Green Room," and by the fact that in the letter itself the contributor asserts that he (the Mouse) had written nothing since the "abdication of my royal master and manager, King David," that is, since Garrick's retirement in June 1776.

3. A cosmetic used by Mrs. Abington.

4. On *Sir Thomas Overbury* (see preceding letter and Letter 1078, n. 1).

5. The *New Morning Post; or, General Advertiser*, published by "G. Corral."

6. From his indictment for assault on his coachman (see Letter 1058, n. 4) until Dec. 9, 1776, with his trial and acquittal, Foote's character was consistently attacked in the papers by supporters of the Duchess of Kingston (Percy Fitzgerald, *Samuel Foote*, 1910, p. 364; see Letters 925, n. 2, 936, n. 9).

7. On Nov. 13, 1776, Walpole wrote: "Yesterday . . . I heard drums and trumpets in Piccadilly: I looked out of the window and saw a procession with streamers flying . . . this was a procession set forth by Mr. Bate, Lord Lyttelton's chaplain, and author of the old *Morning Post*, and meant as an appeal to the town against his antagonist, the new one . . . The new *Morning Post* I am told . . . exceeds all the outrageous Billingsgate that ever was heard of" (ed. Toynbee, IX, 439f.).

8. Presumably the letter in the *London Packet* of Dec. 18, or later, there being additional letters on Jan. 1, Jan. 12, Feb. 16, March 7, and May 9, 1777.

1066   To The Countess Spencer

Adelphi, December 12, 1776

Address: Countess Spencer. *In the possession of the Earl Spencer: Not made available for publication.*

1067 To The Earl of Buckinghamshire[1]

Adelphi

My Lord   Dec[r] 12th [1776][2]

Tho' I have for near Forty Years fac'd the most formidable Criticks, yet I could not till this moment have resolution enough to write and send this Letter to your Lordship: nothing indeed ought to distress a Man of Sensibility more than giving trouble without the least right, or pretence for it— thus, my Lord, having no excuse for my presumption, I must necessarily appeal to your goodness for my pardon: I have a Nephew, my Name Sake, whose dangerous State of Health obliged him sometime ago to sell out of Lord Pembroke's Dragoons, We never expected that he would have got the better of his disorder— He is now quite recover'd— is a young Man with a tolerable person, and his Character a good One— Lord Pembroke, and the Officers of the Regiment speak of him with great partiality— his Situation at present is very disagreeable to him, and if your Lordship would take pity on him, and honour him with your Commands to attend your Suite in any capacity you shou'd think proper, He would think himself most particularly happy, and I, my Lord should never forget the Obligation—[3] I might have procured a more powerful Interest for this Solicitation, but I was resolved to owe any favour I might recieve to Lord Buckingham alone, Or that He might have no difficulty in refusing

His Lordship's most humble and most Obedient Servant

D Garrick

Source: FC, copy; Boaden, II, 194.

1. John Hobart (1723–1793), second Earl of Buckinghamshire (1756), was to be appointed Lord-Lieutenant of Ireland on Dec. 18, 1776.
2. The year is determined by Buckinghamshire's reply of Dec. 13, 1776 (FC; Boaden, II, 194).
3. Buckinghamshire, in his polite refusal, wrote: "My taking the young gentleman with me without a prospect of making a permanent provision for him in Ireland would be only leading him and his friends into an unavailing expense."

1068   To Matthew Smith[1]

Adelphi

Sir   Decr 13th 1776
My Absence from Town for two days prevented my sending this Letter sooner: in Answer to Your favour relative to taking upon Me the Trust & Executorship of our late Friend's Will; tho I have ye greatest honour & Affection for his Memory, & Love for his Widow, which incline me to do Every thing in my power for her good & that of ye family, yet I fear the distance I live from the place where Every thing must be transacted, & the great confidence I have in my deceas'd Friend's judicious Choice of you (more capable & better qualify'd than Myself for Executing y^e

business) will oblige Me for the greater convenience & Ease of all parties to give up the interfering in the Trust, farther than yᵉ Nature of yᵉ Trust makes it absolutely necessary. I am told that as to the *real* Estate, it may be proper & necessary for Me to do some Acts which I shall be always ready to do whenever I am call'd upon: but the Personal & the Executorshp I would rather wish to relinquish— I must desire You to present Mʳˢ Garrick's & my Love to dear Mʳˢ Clutterbuck;² When I think a Letter from Me will not too much Affect her, I will certainly write & offer my most affectionate Services—

I am Sʳ yʳ most obed Serᵗ

D Garrick

Source: FC, draft.

1. Matthew Smith (d. 1777) had been appointed, with Garrick and others, an executor by James Clutterbuck who had died on Dec. 3 (Clutterbuck's will, probated Nov. 24 at the Probate Court of Canterbury). Smith had written Garrick on Dec. 6 asking whether the report was true that Garrick had declined to undertake the duties of executor (FC).

2. Just six months earlier, on May 13, Mrs. Clutterbuck had written Mrs. Garrick: "Mʳˢ Clutterbuck sends, by her Husband, who alas! is renderd almost incapable by Age & Infirmities, her most affectionate thanks to kind Mʳˢ Garrick for the well fill'd Box of excellent Cucumbers which was doubly wellcome because It brought the most pleasing Proof of her still living in the memory of the happy Couple who so highly merit every Felicity that They can either wish or enjoy; & a continuance of which She perpetualy prays for. Le pauvre Homme is equaly affected, but hath not words to express his Conceptions" (Little Collection).

1069 To George Colman

My dear Colman.   Decʳ 13 [1776?]¹
I like Your Neighbour so well & you not a little, that We shall put by our intentions of going into yᵉ Country to attend You— I had some Idea of calling upon You with my Gout to day— it is said our Friend² is sorry to part wᵗʰ Dominion, & that he has a Clause to take it again— so says Bannister³ (I hear) from him— the Bearer has heard so

Yʳˢ Ever &c &c—

D Garrick

Thank you kindly for thinking of Johnston.⁴

Source: FSL.

1. The conjectural year is indicated by Garrick's apparent reference to Foote's reluctance to relinquish the Haymarket summer seasons to Colman (see Letter 1057).
2. Foote?
3. Presumably Charles Bannister (1738?–1804), actor and singer.
4. Presumably John Johnston, of the Drury Lane management.

1070   To The Countess Spencer

Adelphi, December 16, 1776

Address: Lady Spencer. *In the possession of the Earl Spencer: Not made available for publication.*

1071   To The Earl of Sandwich

My good Lord.   Monday [December 16, 1776][1]
Ever Since Your Lordship's invitation to dine with you tomorrow I have been really unhappy that I coud not attend You— the person I was Engag'd to has given me leave to follow my inclinations & therefore they naturally point to ye Admiralty— will it not appear impertinent to desire to be ask'd again— it is not (I know) Selon les regles du bon ton, but when I consider that I am near Sixty; & that many such Holidays will not fall to my Share, may I be permitted to hope for a remission of my Sins & an admission to y^r table to Morrow.

                                                    I am

Source: FC, draft; Boaden, II, 162.

1. The date is supplied by Sandwich's reply of Tuesday, Dec. 17, 1776, where, however, he writes: "I am exceedingly happy to hear we are to have the pleasure of your company to dinner to morrow" (FC; Boaden, II, 195).

1072   To Hannah More

Adelphi
Decr 17 [17]76

Shame, Shame, Shame!

You may well say so, my dear Madam, but indeed I have been so disagreeably Entertain'd with the Gout running all about Me from head to heel, that I have been unfit for the Duties of friendship, & Every other, that a good Husband, & a good Friend should never fail performing. ⟨I have likewise been distress'd about my theatrical Matters. I never sign'd & seal'd ye last great parchment of all¹ till last Week— however I have— but before I tell You that—- I must tell y^o, the lost Sheep is found—² *the two Acts*— I have read & Studied ye four— the 3 will do & well do— but ye 4th will not stand Muster— that must be chang'd greatly but how, I cannot yet Say— it will require a few days in the Country uninterrupte[d] before I can pronounce, the *quomodo* (as Mr Bayes says) the *how*—³ have you thought of anything? for if I mistake not, I was very cold before about ye 4th Act— Mrs Garrick, who has been ill & attended by Dr Cadogan, has read you too with Care— she likes ye first 3, but can hardly believe you touch'd the 4th— and there is a report that Mr Twiss gave you that— he is return'd to us again,⁴ but I shall drop him, for he is so Absurd, not to say worse, that I am not Easy or feel pleasant in his Company— Your Ode to my house Dog⁵ is admir'd much— C⟩ambridge said Yesterday in a large Company at ye Bishop of Durham's⁶ where I din'd, that it was a ⟨Compleat Witty Composition⟩, & he thought there was Nothing to be alter'd or amended Except in ye last Stanza, wch he thought the only weak one: I am afraid that you ask'd me Something to do for You about ye Parliam^{ts} which in my Multitude of Matters was overlay'd— pray if it is of Consequence let me know it again, & you will be assur'd of ye intelligence you want. ⟨I write this in a hurry, in a little room at ye Playhouse with very bad paper & pen— but you are above all ceremony:⟩ the last new tragedy *Semiramis*,⁷ has tho a bare translation, met wth great Success— the prologue is a bad one as you may read in ye Papers, by ye Auth⟨or—⟩ the Epilogue is grave, but a Sweet pretty Elegant Morsel, by Mr Sheridan—⁸ it had deservedly great Success— Mr Mason's Carractaccus is not crowded, but the men of taste & Classical Men, admir⟨e⟩ it much— Mrs Garrick Sends a large parcel of Love to you all— I send Mine in ye Same bundle:— pray write Soon, & *forgive me all my Sins negligences & Ignorances.* I really have not time to read over this Scrawl— so pray decypher Me & excuse Me

Ever Yours most affect^y
D Garrick.

Source: FSL, draft; Roberts, *Hannah More,* I, 75f., extract.

1. Completing the sale of his share in Drury Lane.
2. The manuscript of *Percy.*
3. *The Rehearsal,* II, iv; the phrase, however, is spoken by the Gentleman-Usher.
4. In her reply of Dec. 21 she wrote: "so— that entertaining man is return'd, is he? I believe I have done with him too" (FC; Boaden, II, 282).
5. *Ode to Dragon.*
6. John Egerton (1721–1787) Bishop of Durham (1771–1787), formerly Bishop of Lichfield (1768–1771).
7. George Edward Ayscough (d. 1779) had adapted Voltaire's tragedy (DL, Dec. 13).
8. Miss More in her reply commented: "Of all the prologues I have seen, from the sober narratives of the Roman Terence, to the sprightly satires of the British Roscius, I think that to 'Semiramis' is the dullest. I long to see the epilogue."

1073   To The Countess Spencer

Adelphi, December 21, 1776

Address: Lady Spencer.   *In the possession of the Earl Spencer: Not made available for publication.*

1074   To George Colman

Dear Colman Decr 21 [1776?]¹
Many thanks from my heart of heart for your kind tokens to Me & Madam— she is better, but not quite as She should be— at my return from Hampton we must Settle a day for a laugh & a Minc'd pye wth ye Neighbors.

pray let me know when you have sign'd seal'd & deliver'd—

Yours Ever & affec^{ly}
D Garrick

What do you talk to me of Dress—?— Your fine Cloaths may please my Wife— but I always thought the dress was yᵉ least valuable part about You— there's for You Master Coley— Love to all about you—

Source: Bibliothèque publique et universitaire; Hedgcock, p. 424f.

1. The conjectural year is determined by the references to Mrs. Garrick's health (see Letter 1072) and to the apparent reference to Colman's leasing of the Little Theatre in the Haymarket (see Letter 1057, n. 2).

1075 **To George Garrick**

[*post* December 27, 1776][1]

If mine was an affectionate letter I am Sure Yours is the reverse— and since You have given Me a right (by yʳ unjustly charging Me *as yᵉ Cause of yʳ* EXPENSIVE *illnesses*)[2] of speaking my *Mind* & my *knowledge* I will open to you the Source of all yʳ Malady of Mind, body, & Estate— that I have Withdrawn my Affection at times from You is what I won't deny, but you had first withdrawn Yours in a Manner from us all, & which at this instant amazes Me!— I will not have your repeated *illnesses* laid at my door, and if You will not behave with justice decency & brotherly affection to Me, I cannot be a Hypecrite— You saw my distress & wᵈ not relieve it—[3] when had you any that I did *not* relieve?

Endorsement by Garrick: My Anˢ to George not sent. Source: FC.

1. This is the reply to George Garrick's letter of Dec. 27, 1776 (Boaden, II, 198f.).
2. George had written: "I can assure you that the pangs I have felt from your withdrawing your love and affection from me for a long time . . . has been the cause of my many and very long as well as very expensive illnesses."
3. Perhaps a reference to George's mismanagement of the Fermignac estate.

1076　　To The Countess Spencer

Adelphi, January 6, 1777

Address: Lady Spencer. *In the possession of the Earl Spencer: Not made available for publication.*

1077　　To Hester Thrale[1]

Hampton

Madam.　　　　　　　　　　　　　　　　29th Jany 1777

Mrs Garrick solicits me much to make her excuses, and to say, how unhappy she is, that she has not paid her respects to you— if nursing and sitting up with a sick Husband for near three Weeks, & now attending him in the Country (that fresh air, & a little horse may finish what the Doctor could not) cannot excuse her, She begs leave to appeal from the forms of Ceremony to your own feelings, which, she is sure, will plead for her.

When she returns to Town, her inclination will lead her to make the first visit to Mrs Thrale: when I had the pleasure of meeting You at the Dean of Derry's, You were pleas'd to take Notice of a particular breed of Fowls we had at Hampton— Should you not have added this Sort to your Collection, Mrs Garrick & I should be greatly flatter'd, if you will permit us to send You two hens, & whatever Number of Eggs You shall please to order.

I am Madam Your most Obedient humble Servant
D: Garrick

I beg to be favour'd with your Commands at the Adelphi. We present our respectful Comp^{ts} to Mr Thrale,[2] Miss,[3] & Mr Johnson.[4]

Source: Hyde Collection; *The R. B. Adam Library,* Buffalo, 1929, I, [11].

1. Hester Lynch (Salusbury) Thrale (1741–1821), wife (1763) of Henry Thrale and friend of Dr. Johnson. She had first known Garrick when she was a child, and late in 1776 sought to renew the acquaintance (Katherine C. Balderston, *Thraliana,* 2d ed., Oxford, 1951, I, 286; James L. Clifford, *Hester Lynch Piozzi,* Oxford, 1952, pp. 8, 152f.).

2. Henry Thrale (1728?–1781), a wealthy Southwark brewer. Garrick was a frequent guest at the sumptuous dinners which Thrale (who died of over-eating) gave at his brewery and at Streatham Park, his country estate (Clifford, *Piozzi,* pp. 35, 84, 96).

3. Hester Maria (1762–1857), the Thrales' eldest daughter.
4. After first being invited to Streatham by the Thrales in 1765, Johnson had become almost a member of the family.

1078   To William Woodfall

Dear Woodfall   Feby 1st [1777]
I am Easy about Your Prol: & Epil:—[1] upon my Word I was not so before I rec'd Yours— thank You for So long & good a Letter in ye Midst of y^r Bustle & fermentation of Spirit— I laugh'd very heartily at Your Character of ye Man in Office— You have hit him point blank much Nearer than Bate did Stoney or Stoney Bate, tho one went thro ye hat, & ye other, thro the Waistcoat—[2] he is a great Character, always in fermentation, & Ever Sore about himself— he is (as you say) very near being a good Man, and a good Writer, but that cursed leaven Vanity spoils ye Whole— It is Emboss'd upon his Sleeve for Daws to peck at—[3]
Every Wish that a true Zeal can Waft to You for the Cause to Night is sent to You from this place— I have no doubts but of the Heroine—[4] prosper You Master Billy—[5] remember a Note to Night; I shall expect but three Lines, & let them Say omne bene, & I shall be Satisfy'd— Your Brother has got a Mouse, I suppose the Captn is gone over to y⟨^{e} other⟩ Side—[6] with all my heart— I trust that Y^r Brother will not let him mention Names & suspect so harmless a Creature, as Your most Sincere

                          Wellwisher & hu Se^t
                          D Garrick

Hull[7] will speak a Serious prologue better than Lewis—[8] he has got reputation in Caractacus[9] & you are well off there— so don't fret pray direct to Me *not at Hampton* but near Kingston Surrey I shall have it 3 hours sooner—

Address: Mr W. Woodfall.   *Seal.*   *Endorsement:* 1 Feby 1777 David Garrick Sir Thomas Overbury.   *Source:* FSL.

1. To Woodfall's revision of *Sir Thomas Overbury*, which was first produced on the night this letter was written. The prologue was by Sheridan, the epilogue by Cumberland.
2. Bate in his *Morning Post* had made some reflections on the Dowager Countess of Strathmore, whose husband had died on March 7, 1776. Andrew Robinson Stoney

(1745–1810), an adventurer and one of the Countess' suitors, challenged Bate to a duel on Jan. 13—Stoney shot off Bate's hat and Bate punctured Stoney's waistcoat—and on Jan. 17 Stoney married the Countess (*LC*, vol. XLI, Jan. 18–21, 1777, pp. 68–70).

3. *Othello*, I, i, 64f.

4. Mrs. Hartley, who played Isabella in *Sir Thomas Overbury*.

5. The name by which Woodfall is addressed in the "Mouse in the Green Room" articles.

6. Presumably a reference to Thompson. From Garrick's remark, it appears that Henry Sampson Woodfall had engaged Thompson to write for the *Public Advertiser* (see the following letter).

7. Thomas Hull (1728–1808), actor at Covent Garden (1759–1807) and author, spoke the prologue to *Sir Thomas Overbury*.

8. William Thomas Lewis (1748?–1811), actor, later (1782–1804) Deputy-Manager of Covent Garden.

9. Hull had created the part of Mador in that play.

1079　To William Woodfall

Sunday Feb^{ry} 2 [1777]

Thank You, Dear Woodfall, a thousand times for your kind attention to me— had You known my anxiety for You & Yours, You would not think this very friendly Care of Me thrown away— I was not merely content to have Your Account, I insisted upon Becket's going & sending me *his* thoughts— which I inclose You— I am glad I did not quite destroy it in lighting my Candle, he seems to speak more confident of prodigious Success than Even Yourself— If the play had not met with the publick approbation, I would never have given my opinion again— if a little Critique in my way, will be of any Service, I will give it You whenEver You please— as to the M[ouse] he must be Dormouse a little, for their Majesties have Employ'd me Every Minute—[1] I have written within these two days 3 Scenes & 2 fables— if you behave well & don't abuse Managers— perhaps You may have a Slice, before they are tasted by Royalty— when Y^r Benefit Matters are to be settled— You cannot, if you have any doubts, have a better Chamber Councillor than the late Manager, who will be always ready to give you ye best advice he can— so much for that— OVERBURY for Ever!— I grieve about *Hull*— & somewhat Surpris'd about Hartley— all a Lottery!— now to my own business— my old Friend Sampson has said in his *Public Ad^r* Yesterday that I was in London to visit M^{rs} B[arry][2] as I am here upon the [King]'s

Business, & got leave to recover myself in yᵉ Country— they may take it ill at Sᵗ James's— could you desire him to say in an unparading paragraph from himself— *that he was Mistaken about Mʳ G— that he was in the Country & had been for some time in order to recover the great weakness which was caus'd by his late illness*— You or He will put it better & Modester for Me than that, which I have written upon yᵉ gallop: pray let it be inserted in yᵉ same paper tomorrow—³ Hᴇ always sees yᵉ *Publick Adʳ*

You must really take care that our Friend is not suspected of the M—— T⟨hompso⟩n if he can, will be rude with C[olman?] or Me— his rudeness I would chuse to have, but letting the Cat (M. I mean) out of yᵉ bag— wᵈ be ye Devil: I promis'd that I would speak to You for him that he may still be conceal'd— I laugh at him— but he is too foolish upon yᵉ Occasion—

Yours Ever most Sincerely under the Signature
I now rejoice in
T: Overbury

Always in a hurry— Pray don't forget yᵉ Contradictory paragraph in yᵉ Publick Adʳ for tomorrow if possible—
I shall be at the Adelphi to Morrow Evening

Endorsement: 2ᵈ Febʸ 1777 David Garrick— Success of Sir T. Overbury &tc.
Source: FSL; Baker, p. 84f.

1. Garrick was engaged in an alteration of *Lethe*, to be read before the King and Queen on Feb. 15, 1777 (*LC*, vol. XLI, Feb. 15–18, 1777, p. 166; see also Frances Burney, *Early Diary*, ed. Annie R. Ellis, 1907, II, 156–158).

2. "Mʳˢ Barry, who had been in the Country on a Visit to her Sister, is returned, and on Thursday Mʳ Garrick paid her a Visit of Condolance on the late Death of her Husband" (*Public Advertiser*, Feb. 1, 1777).

3. "The Paragraph copied into Saturday's Paper, which mentioned Mʳ Garrick having paid a Visit of Condolance to Mʳˢ Barry, cannot be true, as he was in the Country, where he has been for some Time in Order to recover the great Weakness, which was caused by his illness" (*ibid.*, Feb. 3).

1080   To The Countess Spencer

Adelphi, February 4, 1777

Address: Lady Spencer. *In the possession of the Earl Spencer: Not made available for publication.*

1081   To Hester Thrale

Adelphi
Madam.   Feb^ry 12th [1777?]^1
Mrs Garrick & I should have paid our respects to You in the
Country some morning, had not a very particular affair confin'd
me here for near a fortnight—

We shall do ourselves the pleasure of Waiting upon You, When
the Weather is a little Milder, & we shall have the Satisfaction of
hearing that our visit will be proper, & not inconvenient. the
Moment my business is finish'd, which has so much employ'd Me,
& which nothing but the Command I have receiv'd, could have
induc'd me to undertake, We shall return to Hampton, from whence
we propose Ourselves the Pleasure of waiting upon M^r & M^rs
Thrale, Accompany'd with two of the most beautiful ladies the
place can produce. with our best Compliments to Mr Thrale
                    I am Madam Your most Obed^t hum^le Servt
                                                    D: Garrick.

Source: FSL.

1. The conjectural year is derived from the apparent reference to the alteration
of *Lethe* for the King and Queen.

1082   To William Woodfall

Dear Woodfall.   Thursday Night [?February 13, 1777]^1
Thank You for y^r most agreeable present & for the most friendly,
Elegant letter I have receiv'd for some time—

I could not resist my inclination to say thus much, & to repeat
to You that I think myself greatly Oblig'd by your Play, & y^r
Letter—

                                          Yours most truly
                                            D Garrick.

Source: American Academy of Arts and Letters.

1. The date is based upon the conjectural identification of Woodfall's present as
being the published version of *Sir Thomas Overbury*, the advertisement to which is dated
Feb. 13, 1777, a Thursday.

1083   To The Countess Spencer

March 4, 1777

Address: Lady Spencer.   *In the possession of the Earl Spencer: Not made available for publication.*

1084   To The Countess Spencer

March 6, 1777

Address: Countess Spencer.   *In the possession of the Earl Spencer: Not made available for publication.*

1085   To The Earl of Exeter

Hampton
March 24. 1777

Mr Garrick presents his respects to Ld Exeter & his Lordship may be assur'd that no one in this Kingdom should Command his Services & interest before him. M^r G: will never more appear again upon the Stage,[1] if L^d E: is desirous of Seeing him in any Character he begs it may be, when he is most happy & in the highest Spirits which he believes from ye best information (his own feelings) will be ye next time he shall have ye honor of paying his respects to his Lord^p at Burghley. Will Lord Exeter permit Mr Garrick to set his Lordship's Name down, among many very Noble ones male & female to take a Ticket for the Theatrical Fund W^ch will be on Monday the 21st of April.—[2]

Source: Hyde Collection, draft.

1. Garrick's letter is on the back of one from Exeter of the same date asking for a ticket for the following week, if Garrick is to play.
2. It was actually to take place on April 28.

1086   To Peter Fountain?[1]

D[r] S[r]   Good Friday [March 28, 1777][2]
When I come to Town, I will serve y[r] friend to y[e] best of my Power,
always rememb'ring, that I never can oppose the Son of my Old
Friend, Harry Fielding, & the Nephew of S[r] John.[3]
                              Yours in great haste but most truly
                                             D Garrick

Rayner never forgave my speaking in behalf of his Son—

Source: FC.

  1. The conjectural identification of the recipient is made by the familiar references
to Rayner here and in Letter 1038.
  2. The year is supplied by the phrasing of the postscript, which implies Rayner's
recent death (see Letter 1031, n. 2).
  3. Presumably William Fielding (1748?–1820), lawyer, the eldest son of the novelist
(Wilbur L. Cross, *History of Henry Fielding*, New Haven, 1918, II, 61, III, 121f.).

1087   To Jane Burke

                                             Hampton
My dear Madam.   Good Friday [March 28, 1777][1]
The Moment I rec[d] y[r] Note I set pen to paper in order to Obey y[r]
Commands, which I shall always execute with pleasure & to y[e]
best of my power—
    I had given a Letter for y[e] Wife of an Old Serv[t], but My Man
tells me, he never call'd for it; I have order'd Becket to burn that,
& send You this letter— Should the Man unluckily have call'd for
it since I have been here, Becket will give you Notice, that you may
procure a letter from Somebody Else— I have written *preference*
that y[e] poor Woman, may be admitted without a ballot— a Governor
has that right once a Year,[2] & I am happy to be able to Exert it,
for Your recommendation— pray my Love to Your Love, & thank
him for his powerful support of y[e] Birmingham Patriot—[3] he was
better than bargain; & had I known that he would have been so
pleasant, I should most certainly have attended his honour's wit &

humor. pray remember Me most kindly to all— Mrs Garrick with a Sore throat but a slight one, sends Every good wish to You & Yours

I am Dr Madam Most truly Your Obedt & Affecte Sert

D Garrick

Endorsement: Garrick to Mrs Burke Good Friday. *Source:* Sheffield City Libraries.

1. That this letter was written on the Good Friday in 1777 is established by the reference to the "Birmingham Patriot."
2. Garrick had been one of the governors of the General Lying-in Hospital since 1756.
3. Presumably a reference to Yates, who was trying to obtain a license for a theater in Birmingham; a bill for his petition had been read in the House of Commons on March 26, 1777, but action had been postponed until April 22 (*Journals of the House of Commons*, XXXVI, 316). While Burke originally supported the bill, he later, on the insistence of his Bristol constituents, withheld it (see Letter 1096).

1088   To The Countess Spencer

Adelphi, April 3, 1777

Address: Lady Spencer. *In the possession of the Earl Spencer: Not made available for publication.*

1089   To Mrs. Winch[1]

Hampton
April 8th, 1777

Madam,

Last night I received a note from *Kirke*.[2] He remembers very well the taking down three trees, and that old Blanchet brought them over from Mr. Winch with the branches on: at the time, he told me the loppings were mine; but I said that I would have no dispute with a neighbour for such a trifle,— nor will I with you, Madam, for ten times as much, as the widow of one I very much esteemed.

The persons in the parish who understand these matters, all

agree that the loppings are the tenant's, and that there is no instance to the contrary. I likewise believe that your brother thinks so; because, when I saw him, he did not object to my having them, as my gardiner[3] signified to you. Mr. Mansel, whose word I would have taken, could not give it upon this occasion:— in short, be they my property, or be they not, if you think they belong to you, I will certainly have no dispute about the matter, but I will give orders that your will shall be obeyed directly.

I am, Madam, your most sincere well-wisher and humble servant,
D. Garrick.

Source: Boaden, II, 217.

1. So identified in the source.
2. Presumably Joseph Kirke (d. 1791), a nurseryman who lived at Brompton, Middlesex, near Hampton (*GM*, vol. LXI, July 1791, p. 683).
3. Identified by Boaden as one Bowden (II, 253). Hannah More describes him in her *Ode to Dragon* as one who

> is skill'd more roots to find,
> Than ever fill'd a Hebrew's mind,
> And better knows their uses.

1090   To The Countess Spencer

London, April 10, 1777

Address: Lady Spencer. *In the possession of the Earl Spencer: Not made available for publication.*

1091   To Henry Thrale

Sir   April 17 [1777][1]
Mrs Garrick & I are very much distress'd that We are prevented from waiting upon Mrs Thrale & You on Saturday next— a most violent Cold and a very bad Sore throat, attended with a Slight fever obliges me to keep house— to render me still more unfit for

Company, I cannot be heard across a table— Nothing but this mortifying illness should have prevented our doing Ourselves ye honour & pleasure, We have long wish'd for, of seeing Streatham, & bringing our small addition to your family without doors—² We propose ourselves in about a Week, or ten days the great pleasure of calling upon Mrs Thrale some Morning.

> I am Sr Your most Obed^t humble Servt
> D: Garrick

Tho there has been a great Complaint of ye many falsehoods publish'd in ye daily papers, yet we could not help rejoicing lately, that the Complaint was Well founded.³

Source: HTC.

1. The year is determined by the evident reference to the false reports of Thrale's death.
2. Hens from Hampton (see Letter 1077).
3. Boswell wrote Johnson on April 24, 1777, that he had been "in a state of very uneasy uncertainty" by "our worthy friend Thrale's death having appeared in the newspapers, and been afterwards contradicted." In his reply of May 3 Johnson assured Boswell that the original report had been an "April fools" joke (Boswell, III, 107ff.).

1092   To Elizabeth Montagu

My good Madam.   April ye 18 [1777?]¹
I only requested the gentle Stream of Your Bounty, & you have flow'd upon Us with a torrent— I am really asham'd of being ye means of Your abundant kindness to Us— I have a Set of friends, whom I intended to call upon Every year for one pound one— as I cannot return the Overplus, I have set it down in my Book over against Your never to be forgotten Name— par avance 5 Years— 5:5:0 give me leave to let you into a little Secret history of this Charity— a Nobleman in your Street whom I visit & who looks like benevolence itself— had a Ticket from Me at ye same time, that I was impertinent enough to send one to You— Your two Names like A fat & lean rabbit in a poulterer's Shop— stand thus together—

Mrs Montagu   5:5:0— no ticket
Rt. Honble Lord: W. de B——²   0:5:0— one ticket.

Mrs Garrick presents her Respects, wth Mine & I at the feet of
Miss Gregory am

My dear Madam Most devotedly y^rs
D Garrick

before I went out of Town I sent to Hely, but could not find him
then, since my return I have been confin'd wth a Sore throat &
hoarseness, & cannot yet Stir out— if You have any orders of any
kind for your faithful Servant, you may depend upon my Executing
them wth care & fidelity.

Address: Mrs Montagu, Hill Street. *Seal. Source:* Huntington Library;
Blunt, *Mrs. Montagu*, I, 359f.

1. The year is conjectural, depending on the apparent reference to subscriptions for
the Theatrical Fund benefit on April 28, 1777.
2. John Peyto Verney (1738–1816), fourteenth Baron Willoughby de Broke (1752),
at this time Lord of the King's Bed-chamber.

1093　To The Countess Spencer

April 21, 1777

Address: Countess Spencer. *In the possession of the Earl Spencer: Not made
available for publication.*

1094　To Andrew (Stoney) Bowes[1]

Adelphi
April 23 [1777][2]

Mr Garrick presents his best Comp^ts to Mr Bowes— He should have
call'd upon him in Person, but ye Gout, a violent Cold, Sore throat,
& hoarseness confine him at home— M^r G: takes the Liberty of
informing Mr Bowes, that he is made the Father Founder President
&c of the theatrical Fund,[3] & has Engag'd many Gentlemen to

attend the Benefit next Monday, if Mr Bowes will honor him with his Name, & take a Ticket, Mr G: will be oblig'd to him; or if Lady Strathmore[4] chuses a Box, he will procure one for her Ladyship— Mr G: has heard of her Ladyship's Goodness the other Night to Mr & Mrs Johnston,[5] who are persons of great Worth & much regarded by Mr Garrick, if her Ladp will Extend her Bounty to the Old Actors, the Body will think themselves honour'd—

Mr Becket the Bookseller will deliver this to Mr Bowes, & bring his Answer— he is a great Friend to the Charity & an Excellent, as he is a very honest & reasonable Vender of Books—

Address: ———— Bowes Esqr, Grosvenor Square. *Seal. Source:* FSL.

1. On Feb. 11, 1777, the King granted Stoney permission to take his wife's maiden name of Bowes (*London Gazette*, Feb. 11, 1777).

2. The year is established by the recipient's change of name, and is confirmed by the reference to a benefit performance for the Theatrical Fund on Monday: in 1777 that performance took place on Monday, April 28 (see Knapp, No. 435).

3. In the last few years of Garrick's life the Drury Lane Company on several occasions expressed their appreciation for his creation of the Theatrical Fund: on Feb. 25, 1776, the Committee for the Fund voted that thereafter Garrick should "be styled Father founder & Protector— be perty of the Com— with a casting voice & their seal be a Garricks Head Founder round &c" (James Winston, "Theatrical Records," FSL); on March 25, 1777, an elaborately decorated "Testimony of Duty and Affection" to him was drawn up (HTC); and on April 2, 1777, "The Com with Mr I Iohnston Scy assembled in the Gr Room exed the Deed constituting D Gark Esq mast of the Corporation They proceeded in Coaches to his house in the Adelphi Mr G affectionately received them at the Top of the Stairs & inducted them into the Drawg Room— A booke of Laws was then presented to him by I Wrighton A Blue Ribbon from which hung a Medal [by Reynolds, now in FSL] was put round his neck by W. Davis & I Aickin— T King read the Deed— he made a heartfelt oration & invited him to Dinner" (Winston, "Records").

4. Mary Eleanor Bowes (1749–1800), widow of the ninth Earl of Strathmore and wife of the recipient.

5. Presumably to Mr. and Mrs. Roger Johnston, for her benefit performance.

1095   To The Countess Spencer

Adelphi, April 28, 1777

Address: Countess Spencer. *In the possession of the Earl Spencer: Not made available for publication.*

1096   To Edmund Burke

Tuesday [April 22 or 29, 1777][1]
Ten thousand thanks my dear Burke for Your very kind Letter—[2]
God forbid that all yᵉ Patents in the World should injure Your
Interest, where you are so much in Duty & kindness ⟨bound⟩
                                              Ever & Ever Yʳˢ
                                                  D G.

Source: Sheffield City Libraries; Dixon Wecter, "David Garrick and the
Burkes," *Philological Quarterly,* XVIII (Oct. 1939), 376.

    1. This letter must have been written on one of two Tuesdays: April 22, 1777, when
a bill to grant Yates a license for a theater in Birmingham was scheduled to come before
the House of Commons, or April 29, early in the day before the bill was defeated (*Journals
of the House of Commons,* XXXVI, 316, 454). Garrick's letter is in answer to one from
Burke, also written on a Tuesday.
    2. In which he wrote: "The once patentee is worth all the existing patentees in the
world . . . Be assured that your former request had all its weight with me; and what is
strange, outweighed a very powerful recommendation of some of my own constituents.
They have been since so attacked by applications from their connexions in Birmingham,
that I have again had such instructions, as in wisdom, and indeed in common decency,
I cannot wholly resist. You know that I cannot set my face against those to whom I
owe my seat, unless the cause they espouse is indeed a bad one; nor would you in that
case advise me to it . . . But I believe, as far as I can see, that Yates is in no great danger.
The House seems to be with him; & assuredly I do not mean to be a very mischievous
Enemy to him" (FC; Boaden, I, 331).

1097   To Richard Brinsley Sheridan

Monday [May] 12 [1777][1]
Mʳ Garrick's best Wishes & Compᵗˢ to Mʳ Sheridan— how is the
Saint[2] to day? a Gentleman who is as mad as myself about yᵉ
School remark'd that the Characters upon the Stage at yᵉ falling
of yᵉ Screen Stand too long before they speak— I thought so too
yᵉ first Night— he said it was yᵉ Same on yᵉ 2ᵈ & was remark'd by
others— tho they should be astonish'd & a little petrify'd, yet it
may be carry'd to too great a length— all praised at Lord Lucan's[3]
last Night.

Source: HTC; Thomas Moore, *Memoirs of Richard Brinsley Sheridan,* 1825, I,
245.

1. The month and year are derived from the fact that this letter was obviously written on the Monday following the first two nights of Sheridan's *School for Scandal* (DL, May 8, 9, 1777).

2. Mrs. Sheridan (see Charles R. Leslie and Tom Taylor, *Life and Times of Sir Joshua Reynolds*, 1865, II, 103).

3. Charles Bingham (1735–1799), Baron Lucan of Castlebar (1776). He had a house at 20 Charles Street, Berkeley Square, and was a friend of the Spencers (Walpole, ed. Toynbee, XI, 340, XII, 316).

1098   To The Countess Spencer

May 15, 1777

Address: Lady Spencer.   *In the possession of the Earl Spencer: Not made available for publication.*

1099   To The Countess Spencer

May 20, 1777

Address: Countess Spencer.   *In the possession of the Earl Spencer: Not made available for publication.*

1100   To Richard Cumberland

Hampton
[*post* May 23, 1777][1]

Mr Garrick presents his Comp^ts to Mr Cumberland— His late illness in London which confin'd him so long, & was very near oversetting him prevented him from going abroad till very lately— Mr Sheridan hath indeed Shewn a Wonderful Genius in his last play, which Mr Garrick thinks must be of the greatest consequence to the Stage & the present Management— if Mrs Cumberland can make use of the inclos'd this Evening It is much at her Service— M^r & M^rs G: being in ye Country & not receiving Mr Cumberland's letter till Yesterday, is the reason that they could not Send to M^rs C sooner—

Source: FSL, draft.

1. This is the reply to a letter from Cumberland, which, while dated only May 23, was obviously written in 1777 since he asks for a seat in Garrick's box for the following night so that his wife can see *The School for Scandal.*

1101   To Hannah Cowley

Adelphi

dear Madam.   [May 27, 1777]

If my Mind, as You imagined had been chang'd upon y^r account, ye letter I rec'd Yesterday would have dispers'd any little Clouds, that might have been upon it— be assur'd that my Wishes for You were always ye Same— I had indeed been told that Mr Cowley[1] had express'd himself somewhat strangely with regard to me, which surpriz'd me at ye time, & was quickly forgotten— I might indeed have thought (perhaps wth too much Sensibility) that I was rather neglected after the Comedy[2] had been play'd, but I could not have Expected to have seen you in ye Summer because, I was many Miles from London, & my residence at Hampton is always uncertain—[3] as to my Servant behaving impertinently to Mr Cowley, had he sent me word of it, I should immediatly have discharg'd the offender— I never heard of Mr Cowley's calling upon Me, but in an illness & when I was incapable of seeing any body but my own family,—[4] if You should be disEngag'd on Sunday next to breakfast about ten, & ye Morning should be fine, Mrs Garrick & I Shall be happy to see M^r & Mrs Cowley at ye Adelphi—

I am Dr Madam Your most obed^t Servt & hume Wellwisher

                                       D G.

Endorsement by Garrick: My Letter to Mrs Cowley May 27th 1777. *Source:* FC, draft; Boaden, II, 224.

1. Died 1797; at the time of his death he was a captain in the East India Company.
2. Mrs. Cowley's *Runaway* had enjoyed a long run during the preceding season.
3. In her undated letter, to which Garrick is replying, Mrs. Cowley had mourned the loss of Garrick's affection, writing that George Garrick had told her it was the result of the Cowleys not having called upon the Garricks. "Had I conceiv'd that the continuance of our intercourse depended on me, I should have flown to the Adelphi with transport— but I imagined that your engagements in the great world allow'd you no time for little folks ... the last visit, I had the honour to make you ... I really thought from your manner, you would have gladly spared" (FC; Boaden, II, 223).
4. Mrs. Cowley had continued in her letter: "Determin'd, however to preserve *a reason* for calling on you uninvited, I very cunningly kept back a Runaway [published in the preceding year], which was bound in a manner, I remember'd you liked (and in which I had *written* the dedication) reserving it as an apology, for Mr Cowley's intrusion, or mine, whenever we might be admitted. Mr Cowley accordingly put it in his pocket every time he went to the Adelphi, and every time brought it back with concern. Mr Cowley has spirit Sir— he has great spirit, and nothing less than his sentiments for you, could have enabled him to submit, to such repeated denials— deliver'd by your servants in the most insulting manner."

1102   To The Countess Spencer

May 29, 1777

Address: Countess Spencer. *In the possession of the Earl Spencer: Not made available for publication.*

1103   To The Countess Bathurst[1]

Mad^m   [*post* June 12, 1777][2]
Mrs Garrick & I cannot Express how much we think Ourselves honour'd by Your Ladyship's favour— all we can say for ourselves is, that we are grateful & most Sensible of Lady Bathurst's goodness to Us— We have settled in our own Minds to pass a fortnight at Bridehelmstone but since family business cannot be done without Me, prevents my leaving London or Hampton so soon as My Wishes now would prompt me— the Sea & the Situation of ye Town are most agreeable to us; without those allurements which would give the preference in our minds to any place— If it is

possible to make our Short visit, while Your Ladyship continues at Brighthelmstone, we most certainly shall, if not, we shall have no Inducement strong enough to draw Us there this Summer— My humility as a scribbler is in great danger of being Metamorphos'd into a quality the reverse of Modesty if Your Ladyship continues to be pleas'd with my triffles—³ & how can it possibly be otherwise? when Taste & Sincerity are pleas'd to flatter it is not in yᵉ Power of the humblest being not to be somewhat Vain— nay I had almost Said that vanity in a certain proportion & upon such an Occasion is as natural to a feeling heart as Gratitude— as I understand a little of the Drama I cannot act so much against character, as to give your Ladyship yᵉ office you have so kindly solicited,⁴ that you will let Us be *Your* humble Servants any where, will be our greatest pride, & we will assure Your Ladyship Not to return Your favours with impertinence, or ingratit⟨ude.⟩

I am Madam Your Ladyships Most oblig'd

&c

Mʳˢ Garrick begs leave to present her respects—

Source: Fitzwilliam Museum, draft, copy in FC.

1. Tryphena (Scawen) Bathurst (1730–1807), Countess Bathurst, was the second wife of the second Earl Bathurst.
2. This is the reply to Lady Bathurst's letter of June 12, 1777 (FC; Boaden, II, 228).
3. She had written: "I can't be Silent a moment after receiving so agreeable a token of your remembrance as the Serenade, wᶜʰ pleased me extreemly, as every thing does you do or say."
4. Lady Bathurst had asked Garrick to "make Mʳˢ Garrick tell me wᵗ kind of House she wants tell her (wᵗʰ my Compᵗˢ) I'll take care of the *Pots* and *Pans,* and she shall have no other trouble than telling me wᵗ *you* like."

1104   To Hannah More

[*ante* June 16, 1777]¹

Enclosed you have the "Blackbird and Nightingale."² I am afraid it will not please you so much upon paper as from my tongue. I must desire you to mark what is amiss in it, and speak freely to me as to your thinking about its errors. Baretti has printed a volume in octavo against Voltaire,³ and hath, I believe, sent it to me, for I

9*

found a copy upon my table. If it is done well I shall rejoice; if ill, the cause will be much hurt by a weak defender.

I hope you will consider your dramatic matter with all your wit and feeling. Let your fifth act[4] be worthy of you, and tear the heart to pieces, or wo betide you! I shall not pass over any scenes or parts of scenes that are merely written to make up a certain number of lines. Such doings, Madame Nine, will neither do for you nor for me.

Most affectionately yours, Upon the gallop,

D. Garrick.

My wife sends her love.

Source: Roberts, *Hannah More*, I, 73f.

1. The date is from Hannah More's answer of June 16, 1777 (FSL; Boaden, II, 229).
2. Garrick's prologue to his alteration of *Lethe*. It was never printed, but Miss More gives a description of it (Roberts, *Hannah More*, I, 60; Knapp, No. 378).
3. *Discours sur Shakespeare et sur M. de Voltaire.*
4. Of *Percy*.

1105   To John Robinson[1]

Hampton

My dr Sr   Monday [June] 16 [1777][2]

I should have call'd upon You yesterday had I not been prevented by ye bad weather; I have rec'd yr draught[3] in full to ye first of this Month, & shall continue till you say nay— if You think ye business Mr St Paul[4] mentiond to you is worth attention I will Obey yr Summons for a quarter of an hour, whenever you please; if not, just hint as much to Me, & the party shall not be longer in Suspense: a Word from You is oracular & decides the business,[5] if you wd Speak to me to day in ye Country for a few Minutes, for I know yr hurry, I will attend you, or any time in Town, Morning, Noon or Night

I am most truly Yr very Sincere & I hope not

troublesome hule Sert

D G.

I shall be in London to Morrow about one & stay till Thursday—

Endorsement by Garrick: My Letter to R— about my Friend B— June 16th.
Source: FC, copy.

1. John Robinson (1727–1802), politician. As Secretary of the Treasury it was his duty as chief ministerial agent to manage the constituencies so that a favorable majority would be returned at elections.

2. The year is from Robinson's reply of June 16, 1777, a Monday (Boaden, II, 230).

3. Presumably a draft for expenditures to strengthen the position of the ministry in Hampton or Hendon. Robinson "never hesitated to adopt any method of bargain or barter that seemed likely to procure a seat" (John Robinson, *Parliamentary Papers, 1774–1784*, ed. William T. Laprade, 1922, p. xvi).

4. Horace St. Paul (1729–1812), diplomat, formerly (1772–1776) Secretary of the Embassy and Minister Plenipotentiary in Paris (Joseph Foster, *The Peerage, Baronetage, and Knightage*, 1883, p. 563; David B. Horn, *British Diplomatic Representatives, 1689–1783*, Camden Society, 3d ser., vol. XLXI, 1932, p. 24).

5. What this was is not clear, but it seems to be connected with the following: In the *Public Advertiser* for May 29, 1777, there appeared a letter (retracted May 30), signed "One out of the Secret," accusing Robinson of sharing in government contracts and suggesting that Lord North was also guilty. On June 3 St. Paul had written Garrick that he agreed "entirely with Mr Garrick & Mr Bate that a proper answer tomorrow to this troublesome correspondent may silence him for the future & is sure that every thing Mr Bate will say upon this Occasion will be perfectly right" (FC; Boaden, II, 225). After consulting with North, Robinson wrote to Garrick on June 21, "Agreeable to the Assurances I gave you I have talked with Lord North on the proposition suggested to me by Mr St Paul— His Lordship directed me to desire to thank the Gentleman very much for his offer of Services, but at the same time begged that you wd tell him that at present there is not occasion to trouble him" (FC; Boaden, II, 230). In the meantime Robinson had begun a suit to collect £5000 damages from H. S. Woodfall, the printer of the *Public Advertiser*; on July 3 the case was tried at the Guildhall, and Robinson was awarded 40s. and costs (*LC*, vol. XLI, June 12–14, 1777, p. 562; *Annual Register*, p. 191; *Morning Chronicle*, July 4).

1106   To Frances Cadogan

My dear Madam.   [May–June 1777]¹
I write in a great hurry to You on Account of Lady Alg[ernon] Percy,² Mrs Bennet³ & Mrs Hoare— the last was to have ye Box last Night & You toMorrow to the School for Scandal— Now my best Friend, can you for the Sake of accomodating these Ladies, defer your Night till Friday or Saturday next on Which Night ye Same Play will be Acted— if You can you will, if You cannot, say so— for you must not be displac'd but by yr own good will— Lady Al. Percy goes out of Town Thursday which is ye Reason of my troubling You— forgive my hurry & my Errors

Ever & most affecty Yours
D Garrick

My Wife said She would call, but I Write for fear she should forget.

Address: Miss Cadogan, George Street near Hanover Square. *Source:* HTC.

1. Presumably written during the opening run of *The School for Scandal* in the spring of 1777.
2. Isabella Susanna (Burrell) Percy (1750–1812), wife of Lord Algernon Percy (1750–1830) the second son of the Duke of Northumberland (Nathaniel W. Wraxall, *Posthumous Memoirs*, ed. Henry B. Wheatley, 1884, III, 352ff.).
3. Elizabeth Amelia (Burrell) Bennett, Lady Algernon's older sister, wife of Richard Henry Alexander Bennett (*ibid.*, p. 355).

1107 To James Boswell

Hampton

Dear S[r]

July 3[d] 1777

I should have answer'd y[r] letters[1] Sooner, had not I waited to find a curious book for Y[r] friend M[r] Arnott—[2]

You have much oblig'd Me by bringing us Acquainted— Our Club has flourish'd greatly this last Winter, and the addition of Mess[rs] Dunning,[3] Sheridan &c &c &c give us a great Eclat— however we are incompleat till You add Your Skill to the Concert—

tho I am troubled now & then with Short fits of y[e] Stone, &, what I call, long fits of y[e] Gout, No school Boy at a breaking up for y[e] Holidays, had Ever Such rantipole Spirits— I feel such a Weight off my Spirits, that I really feel myself a New Man— however there is no good without some concomitant Evil, I grow fat, & Short-winded— I heard this Morning, that Your Theatre is going to be honour'd with the appearance of Madam Abington— My heart beats to be with You, not to act, or to See y[r] Actors, but to converse & be happy with my friends— You may tell M[r] Robertson[4] that he need not be apprehensive of my arrival in Scotland; I shall not *now* insist upon his Seeing Me play the fool, for I have made a vow never to Set my foot upon any theatre again, & I will keep my vow most religiously— You may assure him with my respectful Compliments to him, that I would not Act again one Winter to double my fortune

Dear Sir most truly Yours

D Garrick

I can scarce write for y[e] Nasty Gout in my fingers.

Address: Boswell Esq[r]. *Seal. Source:* Boswell MSS. Yale.

1. From Auchinlech on March 21 and 22 (Boswell MSS. Yale).
2. Hugo Arnot (1749–1786), Edinburgh advocate and antiquarian, was collecting material for his *History of Edinburgh* (1779). The subject in question, according to Boswell (March 22), "was a Game or Play called Robin Hood of which frequent mention is made in our Acts of Parliament. Your friend & mine Percy in his Reliques of Ancient Poetry tells us of a little dramatich piece entitled Robin Hood & the Friar, in M[r] Garrick's Collection."
3. John Dunning (1731–1783), later (1782) first Baron Ashburton, barrister, was generally recognized as the best lawyer in London and had acted for Garrick in his suit against Kenrick.
4. Presumably William Robertson.

1108   To Thomas King[1]

Hampton
Dear King   Thursday July 17— 1777
Tho You would not *Seek* Me,[2] I have sought You this Morning—
   You are a Male-Coquette M[r] Thomas but have such Winning ways with You, that we readily forget Your little infidelities—
   I must confess that my reception at y[e] Fund dinner[3] was as Surprising as it was disagreeable & unexpected— I Seem'd to be the Person mark'd for displeasure, and was almost litteraly sent to Coventry, tho I ventur'd among You after a very severe illness & had dress'd myself out as fine as possible to do all y[e] honour I could to the day & the Committee— I never was more unhappy for y[e] time— however let it be forgotten & when we meet let not a Word be said of what is past— poor old Drury! It will be, I fear, very soon in y[e] hands of the Philistines—

Yours Ever most truly
D. G.

Endorsement by Garrick: My Note to King in answer to his Letter receiv'd at Mistley. July 13. 1777. *Source:* FSL, draft; Boaden, II, 237.

1. Hearing that Garrick had declared he was "coolly, not to say indelicately treated, on the day [he] honour'd the Theatrical Committee with [his] presence," and that King was "the foremost in tokens of disrespect," King had taken the initiative in a letter of July 11 to preserve their friendship by suggesting that Garrick might have been wrong and by apologizing for the conduct of some of the members (FC; Boaden, II, 235f.).
2. Near the end of his letter King wrote that whether their friendly intercourse should

continue "depends on your own will; for (after having thus open'd myself to you) tho'
I respect you, love you, admire you— yet I cannot, will not *seek* you."

3. Held at the Globe Tavern, Fleet Street, on May 17 (*LC*, vol. XLI, May 17–20,
p. 470).

1109   To Frances Cadogan

July 17 [1777][1]
Why should not I say a Word to my dear Miss Cadogan? When
shall We see & laugh with You at this Sweet place? I long to hear
you idolize Shakespeare & y^r father unimmortalize him: We shall
be here till Wednesday next & return again from London on
Friday Evening after— will You & Y^{rs} come *before Wednesday* or
after Friday take Your Choice?— I hope You have seen how much I
am abus'd in y^r Friend Mrs Brook's new Novel?—[2] she is pleas'd
to insinuate that [I am] an Excellent Actor, a so so author, an
Execrable Manager & a Worse Man—[3] Thank you good Madam
Brookes— If my heart was not better than my head, I would not
give a farthing for the Carcass, but let it dangle, as it would deserve,
with It's brethren at ye End of Oxford Road—[4] She has invented
a Tale about a Tragedy, which is all a Lie, from beginning to y^e
End— she Even says, that I should reject a Play, if it should be a
Woman's— there's brutal Malignity for You— have not ye Ladies—
Mesdames, *Griffith, Cowley* & *Cilesia* spoke of me before their Plays
with an Over-Enthusiastick Encomium?— what says divine
Hannah More?— & more than all what Says the more divine Miss
Cadogan?—[5] Love to y^r Father

Yours Ever most affect^y
D: Garrick.

I never knew Madam Brookes—
    What a Couple of wretches are y^e *Yateses* Brookes's partners—
I work'd with Zeal for their Patent—[6] wrote a 100 Letters, & they
were Stimulating Crumpling all ye while to Mischief, & they deferr'd
ye publication till this time,[7] that I might not cool in their Cause—
there are Devils for You— If you send me a Line, let it go to y^e
Adelphi any day before 12—

Address: Miss Cadogan at Hurlingham near Fulham. *Postmarked. Source:*
FSL; Baker, p. 127f.

1. The year is from Miss Cadogan's answer of July 19, 1777, which Garrick endorsed: "Excell^t Letter from Miss Cadogan July 20, 1777" (FC; Boaden, II, 239f.).
2. *The Excursion*, published on July 10, 1777 (*LC*, vol. XLII, July 8–10, 1777, p. 39).
3. See vol. II, bk. v, chs. 7 and 8.
4. Where stood the Tyburn gallows.
5. Miss Cadogan replied: "'Let it pass by you like the idle wind, that you respect not!' she is not of consequence enough to excite your anger; treat her with the contempt she merits— while you will continue to be good & great, you must expect your share of abuse."
6. See Letter 1087, note 3.
7. Unidentified.

1110   To Doctor Charles Burney

Hampton
My dear Burney   Sunday Night [?July 20, 1777][1]
Ten thousand thanks for your Journals, I will return them in a few days— I rejoice to hear that You like *Linguet's* Journal,[2] It Entertains & instructs me much— his Mistakes, of which there are plenty, afford me pleasure—

I shall be in Town on Wednesday next & will call upon You if possible—

I think Linguet trims our Friend Marmontel finely— sure Marmontel is got into a Scrape with Mynheer Gluck—[3] There is a better Account of New books by being Shorter, than in any other periodical performance— pray my Love to all about You & believe Me most truly

Y^r Ever Affectionate & Obedient
D: Garrick.

My Wife Sends her best to You— Your Friend Madame de Brook has tickled my Toby for Me.

Source: Morgan Library.

1. Conjecturally dated on the interpretation of the postscript as a reference to Mrs. Brooke's *Excursion*; the book had been announced as published on July 10, 1777, and is first mentioned by Garrick on Thursday, July 17 (see preceding letter).
2. Simon Nicholas Henry Linguet (1736–1794), a notorious pamphleteer. Formerly a successful lawyer in Paris, his attacks on the Philosophers in his *Journal politique et littéraire* had lost him his printing license and forced him into exile in England. From March 1777, when the first number was published in London, until 1792 he published *Annales politiques, civiles, et littéraires du dix-huitième siècle.*

3. The first number of the *Annales politiques* (p. 423) contained a review of Marmontel's *Essai sur les révolutions de la musique en France* (Paris, 1777), mentioning Marmontel's attack on Christoph Willibald Gluck (1714–1787) whose operas were to revolutionize the form.

1111   To Doctor Charles Burney

Dearest Burney.   [*?post* July 20, 1777][1]
Thank You for Your Journals—
   I am much Entertain'd with them— is it not very Strange that I cannot find the title again of ye book I wanted, & which I am sure was in La Harpe's Journal;[2] it was an Account of all kinds of Books wth a Critique upon them— it was in some of them for this Year— but I cannot find it— so it is gone, gone gone,
                                   Yours Ever & ay
                                        D Garrick
Love to all about You—

   Address: Dr Burney, St Martin's Street, Leicester Fields. *Seal. Source:* James M. Osborn.

   1. From the reference to Burney's journals, this letter is conjecturally placed as being written shortly after the preceding.
   2. Presumably *Le Mercure de France*, which Laharpe had been editing since 1770.

1112   To Frances Cadogan

My Most Amiable Friend,   *Monday* Night [July 21, 1777][1]
What a Charming Letter have you written to Me! All the Nonsensical Prescriptions of your most learned Father could not have a ten thousandth part of the Effect upon my animal Spirits as Your sweet Words have: There's Magic in Every Line— and Miss Hannah More swears like a Trooper that it is the best letter in the Language. We shall wait for Sunday with impatience.
   My Coach if you please shall meet you half way or rather come for You at your own hour— so if you love me be free. My horses

are young and have Nothing to do— but if your Doctor will not suffer his Cattle out of his Sight, they shall dine with us, lie with us, or what you will with us, provided he will not abuse Shakespeare, and his loving Patient— in short you are to command and we shall obey most punctually. Pray send a Line to the Adelphi with your pleasure at full.

Ever my dear Miss Cadogan's most affectionate
Friend and Servant,
D. Garrick

You will be glad to know that Mrs Barbauld late Miss Aikin[2] wrote ye following distich upon Miss More's shewing her my Buckles my Wife gave me, which I play'd in ye last Night of Acting.

Thy Buckles, O Garrick, thy Friends may now Use,
But no Mortals hereafter shall stand in thy Shoes.

A. L. Barbauld.

Source: Baker, p. 70f.

1. This is the reply to Miss Cadogan's letter of Saturday, July 19, 1777 (Boaden, II, 239f.).

2. Anna Letitia (Aikin) Barbauld (1743–1825), poet and miscellaneous writer, who had been married in 1774 to the Rev. Rochemont Barbauld. According to Fanny Burney, Mrs. Barbauld had a "set smile, which had an air of determined complacence and prepared acquiescence that seemed to result from a sweetness which never risked being off guard" (*Diary & Letters of Madame D'Arblay*, ed. Charlotte Barrett, 1905, V, 419).

1113   To Frances Cadogan

My dear Madam   Friday [July 25, 1777][1]
The Coach shall be ready to Your orders at Richmond Bridge—[2] if the Doctor had rather his horses were under his Eye, I will prepare a Stable with Pleasure, so let him bring them by all means—

Love Me Love my dog— & Every thing from ye Doctor to a Flea from Hurlingham, Shall be Wellcome at Hampton—

The Coach waits for this so I say no more, but Sunday is ye day— the Coach shall be ready— but let ye horses come if y^e

Doctor had rather it should be so— ⟨all in a hurry for yᵉ Coach Waits for this.⟩

Love to All from all here Most Affectionatᵞ

Yours Ever & Ever

D: Garrick

Address: Miss Cadogan, Hurlingham near Fulham. *Postmarked.* *Source:* FSL.

1. Obviously written on the Friday following the preceding letter.
2. Halfway on the road between Fulham and Hampton.

1114 To Martha Hale

Adelphi

Fryday [July 25, 1777][1]

Most unfortunately my dear Haly Paly,[2] The Hamptonians are engag'd to go on Thursday next to Farnborough Place[3] & stay there Five or Six days— But why may not that *Other Party*, take place at our retur⟨n.⟩ We shall expect you and Lady Glyn,[4] *Monday* or *Tuesday*, or what Say you to *Sunday* next? Cadogan, & his very amiable Daughter with the celebrated *Hannah Moore* will be with us, and if you can take any pleasure in a Roasted Doctor, & have no aversion to roasted Venison, we will treat you with both. open your mind to me I beseech you my dearest Haly, in all Naked Simplicity! hearken with Joy & Gladness to Tidings I shall *declare* unto You

On or about the 7ᵗʰ or 8ᵗʰ of the next Month The Royalty of Mistley[5] will honour Hampton with his presence, and as I would chuse to have him in all his Glory, I should wish to have him attended by his Satellites— therefore let the *Halys*, the *Wrotsleys*,[6] the *Mollys*, the *Dimples*, & the *Cupids* be kept for that high Festival!— To which let the *Reynolds* the *Chamier*,[7] and the *Adam*, the first of Men be call'd by the Sound of Trumpet, and let the Loves, and Graces, with the Iniquities attend, like the first of Women Eve, without the Fig leaf— that his Highness may Regale En Turc, not with that unexpected ablution you were pleas'd once to direct him to, but with the most refin'd Spiritual Sensuality in the Temple of Shakespear.— I am writing this half asleep at the hour of Seven, but the Subject has rous'd miraculously (En astronome) *Le pauvre*

Inspecteur de Pavè— And I shall wait for your Answer by the return of my Courier.

Chuse Sunday, Monday, or Tuesday next for the *private* conference— the *Publick* Rejoycings must be Establish'd by Royal Authority—

Yours, My dearest Paly in all truth, Naked truth,
& most affectionate warmth of Mysterious Conjunction

Davy Pavy

Pray if possible an Explicit answer by the bearer

Endorsement by Garrick: A ridiculous Letter to Haly Paly about meeting Mᵣ Rigby at Hampton. *Source:* FC, copy; Boaden, II, 186.

1. Written on the Friday before the Cadogan's visit to Hampton on Sunday, July 27, 1777 (see preceding letter; see also Roberts, *Hannah More*, I, 71).
2. Garrick's nickname for Mrs. Hale (see, for example, a letter from her to Garrick of Dec. 30, 1778, HTC).
3. Hannah More, who accompanied the Garricks to Farnborough Place and met the Wilmots for the first time, gives an account of the visit in a letter to her sister (Roberts, I, 72).
4. Perhaps Elizabeth, Lady Glyn (d. 1814), widow of Sir Richard Glyn, first Bt., and daughter of Robert Carr of Hampton.
5. Rigby.
6. Presumably Mary (Leveson-Gower), Lady Wrottesley (d. 1778), widow of Sir Richard Wrottesley, Bt., and several of her many daughters (see George Wrottesley, *History of the Family of Wrottesley*, Exeter, 1903, p. 346f.).
7. Anthony Chamier (1725–1780), politician, friend of Dr. Johnson, and Under-Secretary of State (1775–1779). One of the original members of the Literary Club, with Cox and Rigby he also belonged to a little coterie of distinguished men known as "The Gang."

1115 To The Countess Spencer

Hampton, July 26, 1777

Address: Lady Spencer. *In the possession of the Earl Spencer: Not made available for publication.*

1116   To Benjamin Van der Gucht[1]

Hampton

Dear Vander Gucht,   July ye 29th, 1777

Many thanks to you for your very kind & most Entertaining letter;
I have read it to many friends & they all agree that You draw &
colour, as well with y^r Pen as with Y^r brush—

I rejoice that Your Expedition has been so pleasant I hope it will
prove *profitable* too— You are luckily arriv'd in France to correct y^e
blunders which Noverre Junr[2] has made in buying half a dozen
books for Me— he has almost mistaken Every one I desir'd him to
buy for Me— I will set down 3 or 4 at ye End of this letter which I
must beg You to bring with You & not to leave them for Your
heavy baggage— whatever Numbers are wanting from the last of
the Collection of Romances was sent me & which You subscrib'd
for Me, they may be brought any how as I cannot read all those I
have for some Months to come— Your Country Parson, when he
expected to be snapt up by a privateer is a most comic picture
indeed, & you must put him upon Canvas— I see him running up
& down, with a face of fear, rage & despair.

Your Accounts of ye Dutch perfectly tally with my own ideas
of them, & I have long laid it down as a Maxim, that minds so
warp'd to traffick, can never bend to the politer Arts, & what is
worse, their hearts are shut up to the finer feelings of friendship &
Affection— I shall wish much to peep among them but to live with
them, I could not be brib'd with the whole produce of their fam'd
City of *Rotterdam*— I think myself highly honour'd to be mention'd
at ye Hague, but how I could get a place in the Conversation there
surprizes me, & raises my Curiosity— all which We'll reserve for
a little chat at Hampton— the books I want are ye following—
Mrs Garrick will not trouble you this Time—

Les trois Teatres de Paris— par Monsr Desessarts—[3] is an Acc^t
of ye Laws &c of the Theatres of Paris— L'Almanach litteraire—
1776. There is likewise a book which I want the title of which I
have forgot— it is I believe in *4 volumes* an Account of all kind of
authors Greek, roman, & french with their Characters and a Small
⟨cr⟩itique of their Works—[4] Noverre brought me *les trois Sciecles de
la litterature Françoise*[5] for it— but this book is an Acc^t of Classick
Authors as well as others— it is a late book, & I would have it more

particularly as it treats of yᵉ Classicks Greek & Roman— pray if
you can search for that book— if You will go & see *Mʳˢ Pye*⁶ who
lives at yᵉ Hotel de Malthe rüe Sᵗ Nicaise— she will be glad to see
You coming from me— she will assist You in yᵉ book way if You
want her— pray tell her I have found yᵉ letter from yᵉ Lady whose
maiden name was Garrick—⁷ she is to be found chez Madame
Garrick sa mere— maison de Monsʳ le Brun, Noʳᵉ [*illegible*] rüe de
la monnoye— her Name now is *Mad* Wity— If you should want
Money— Messʳˢ Panchaud the Bankers will pay you the ballance
of my Accᵗ as it now stands— on seeing my name D Garrick, If
there are any theatrical pamphlets wᶜʰ make a Noise lately published within 5 or 6 weeks pray buy them for me— there is a
Satirical Poem call'd *le dixhuitième Siecle*⁸ by a Monsʳ Clement or
Gilbert— wᶜʰ I should like to have— I give You much trouble but
I am most truly Your friend & hearty well wisher

D: Garrick

Address: A monsieur, Monsieur VanderGucht au Caffe de Conty, vis a vis
le Pont neuf a Paris. *Source:* Garrick Club; T. F. Dillon Croker, "Garrick in
Retirement," *The Era Almanack and Annual,* 1877, p. 58.

1. Benjamin Van der Gucht (d. 1794), painter and picture dealer, the thirty-second
child of the engraver Gerard Van der Gucht. He was well known as a painter of actors
and as a restorer of pictures, and in 1776 had built an art gallery in Upper Brook Street.
2. Augustin Noverre, who appears in the playbills as "Mr. Noverre, Junr" (HTC).
He was living in Norwich at this time.
3. Nicolas-Toussaint Moyne (1755–1810), called Desessarts; his book was published
in Paris in 1777.
4. When Van der Gucht applied to Mrs. Pye for help in identifying this book, she
wrote Garrick: "I fear it will be more difficult, as I have made it my Business to enquire,
the best account I can get is the following . . . 'Il y a en Français un Ouvrage estimé
intitulé Dictionnaire portatif des Gens de Lettres, Artistes, &c qui se sont rendus celebrés
dans tous les Pays du Monde, en 6 Vol: in 8ᵛᵒ. Cet Ouvrage a paru d'abord en 1770 en
4 Vol: L'année derniere on l'a augmenté de 2 Volumes" (FC; Boaden, II, 257). Neither
Garrick's nor Mrs. Pye's reference has been identified (see also *ibid.*, II, 275, 279).
5. By the Abbé Antoine Sabatier de Castres (Amsterdam, 1774).
6. Joel Henrietta (Mendez) Pye (1736–1782?), wife of Robert Hampden Pye, a
soldier, and daughter of Solomon Mendez (d. 1762) of Red Lion Street, Holborn, a rich
merchant. On May 10, 1771, her play, *The Capricious Lady,* had been given its first and
only performance at Drury Lane. In the Forster Collection are over twenty letters from
her to Garrick written from France between 1774 and 1778 (see also Boaden, vol. II).
7. In this letter, dated from Paris, June 12, 1776, and signed "Garrick fᵐᵉ Wity,"
Mme Wity had informed Garrick "Depuis quelque tems, des affaire de Famille m'obligent
a Etablir ma Genealogie" (FC; Boaden, II, 621; see also Mrs. Pye to Garrick, Aug. 26,
1777, FC).
8. By Nicolas Joseph Laurent Gilbert (1751–1780), poet and satirist.

1117 To Mr. and Mrs. Henry Thrale

Hampton
August 1st [1777?]¹

M^r and Mrs Garrick present their best compliments to M^r and Mrs Thrale, and are extremely sorry that their being engaged to dine this day at Mr Wilmot's at Farnborough Place, where they are to spend some days, will deprive them of the honour and pleasure of seeing M^r and Mrs Thrale to morrow morning. As soon as they return they will write to beg the favour of M^r and Mrs Thrale to fix a day for obliging them with their company.

Mrs Garrick is extremely thankful for the chickens, which shall be taken the utmost care of, both on account of their own merit, and that of their late obliging Mistress.

Source: John Rylands Library.

1. The conjectural year is indicated on the assumption that the references here and in Letter 1114 are to the same visit to Farnborough.

1118   To George Colman

Dear Colman.   Tuesday [August] 12th [1777]¹
I would give You an Epilogue wth as much readiness as I would a pinch of Snuff, being both of Equal value— but indeed, my dear Friend, I have Such a listlessness about Me, that I have not Spirit to scribble a distich— I sh^d be most Sorry to refuse You any thing, but I am really Sick of prologue & Epilogue writing— however if I knew for whom the Shift must be prepar'd, I would Endeavour to rouse from my present Poetical Nap, & Squeeze my brains for You, tho upon my Soul, I expect Nothing but foul Water from the Operation: the Weather is so hot, & my No-head (as Abel says) does so Ach,² that I am not alert enough for Action, however if you want it, I must do it & will— so send a Line to ye Adelphi— tell me ye Speaker, & what I must write & I will certainly do it

Ever Yours &c
D Garrick.

What say You to Letexier's thoughts upon Richard?³

My Man got so fuddled at Richmond that he got from behind yᵉ Coach wᵗʰ the Blunderbuss, & has lost his place for his impertinence & Ebriety—

Address: George Colman Esqʳ.   *Seal.*   *Source:* Bodleian Library.

1. This is the reply to a letter from Colman, dated only "Richmond, Monday Night," asking Garrick to write an epilogue for his *Spanish Barber*—an adaptation of Beaumarchais' *Barbier de Seville*—which was to be produced, with an epilogue by Garrick, at the Haymarket on Aug. 30, 1777 (Boaden, II, 265; Knapp, No. 404).
2. *The Alchemist*, III, ii.
3. Presumably a reference to Henderson's acting Richard III at the Haymarket on Aug. 7, 8, and 11 (*LC*, vol. XLII, Aug. 7–9, 1777, p. 144). Walpole wrote in early August that Garrick was "dying of the yellow jaundice" at the success of the "Bath Roscius" (*Horace Walpole's Correspondence with William Mason*, ed. Wilmarth S. Lewis, Grover Cronin, Jr., and Charles Bennett, New Haven, 1955, I, 326).

1119   To Richard Sharp¹

Sir   Augˢᵗ 16ᵗʰ [1777]²
I never answer anonymous letters for very good reasons— If the Writer who has sign'd a letter to Me with yᵉ initials R:S: will be pleas'd to call at yᵉ Adelphi any time in yᵉ Course of yᵉ winter giving me a day's Notice, I will answer his questions as well as I am able—

I am Sʳ yʳ huᵉ Servᵗ
D G.

yʳ letter was mislaid during my illness, & it came not to my Notice till Yesterday.

Address: To Mʳ R: S: at Mʳ Simmons's, corner of Warwick Court near Gray's Inn.   *Source:* The Hon. Mrs. Eustace Hills.

1. So identified by the owner. Richard Sharp (1759–1835) was to amass a fortune as a hatter; throughout his life he was interested in politics and literature and belonged to many clubs and societies.
2. The year has been added by the recipient.

1120   To The Countess Spencer

Hampton, August 22, 1777

Address: Lady Spencer.   *In the possession of the Earl Spencer: Not made available for publication.*

1121   To Sir Thomas Mills

Hampton

My Dear Sir   Augs^t 23^d 1777

Tho' I sho^d Trust your Heart as soon as any be it in what British bosom it may yet in the whirl of Business & the galloping of y^r Ideas wch al'ays ride past you may possibly forgot *the Sons of Dr Jackson*[1] They only wish for leave to attend their Fath. He has got a permiss^n to go there & two finer young Fellows than the Sons I never heard of

Pray remember them & me Your most Sincere F^d

David Garrick

Endorsement with address: To Sir Thomas Mills at Brighthelmstone.   *Source:* FC, copy.

1. Presumably Rowland Jackson, M.D. 1746, who was to go out to Calcutta, where he died about 1787.

1122   To Maurice Jones[1]

Hampton

Sir,   Thursday [August] 28 [1777][2]

Though I am this moment arrived very hot and very dusty, yet I could not rest till I had expressed my surprise at your very strange, unaccountable, and ill founded letter. Indeed, Sir, your sensibility by far exceeds my understanding; and so little conscious am I by word or deed of ever doing or saying anything to Mr. Jones but in a sincere and friendly, and perhaps too in a warm manner, that I cannot conceive the meaning of his letter.

If I spoke to you in the hurry of being too late and losing a post-night on account of your brother, and it is the usual manner, I think that might be excused, as it is a manner in which I treat, without ceremony, all the persons I chuse to be free with. However you may be assured that for the future you shall hear nothing from me that shall give the least offence to your sensibility.

> I am, Sir, Your humble servant,
> D. Garrick.

Give me leave to take notice that I am still more surprised at your letter when I reflect that you asked me to speak to Lord Sandwich after you had received the hurt to your sensibility, and not in the presence of any servant. I hope my declining to speak to him gave no particular offence, for my reasons are very strong why I could not.

Source: FC, copy.

1. Maurice Jones (d. 1820) was presumably the same man who in 1816 was called to give medical testimony at an inquest at Hampton (Henry Ripley, *The History and Topography of Hampton-on-Thames*, 1885, p. 115).

2. The month and year are from Jones's answer of Aug. 28, 1777 (FC; Boaden, II 263).

1123   To Benjamin Van der Gucht

Hampton

Dear Vander Gucht,   Thursday [August?] 28th [1777?][1]

I am this moment return'd to Hampton, and will not lose a moment to tell you that we shall expect you tomorrow, at what time you please, for at any time you will be most agreeable to Madame and, dear Vander,

> Yours ever,
> D. Garrick.

Thank you for ye books. I will pay you for them when I see you. Yours again and again. If you will send me a line directed to me, *near Kingston, Surrey*, and no otherwise, I will send the coach at any hour you please. On this side Richmond Bridge you will find my coach at your time, and you have nothing to do but to walk over ye bridge from Richmond to it.

Direct thus, and only thus:—

To David Garrick, Esq.,
near Kingston
Surrey.

You need not write to-night if you come another way. Come when you will, always welcome.

Source: T. F. Dillon Croker, "Garrick in Retirement," *The Era Almanack and Annual,* 1877, p. 59.

1. Written presumably in Aug. 1777 when the 28th fell on a Thursday, not in June, as given in the source, when the 28th fell on a Saturday.

1124 To James Chouquet[1]

Hampton

Sir   Aug^st 29th 1777

Many Things in my Hurry of Business may have Escap'd my Memory, but I will assure you that I have not at present ye least reccollections of the Circumstances you mention—[2] When I saw a translation of the Comedy Advertized & dedicated to Mr Sheridan, I bought it, but had not the least Suspicion of it's being intended for the Stage, or that I had ever Seen the play in English, or the Translator—[3] If any conversation on this Subject will be of the least service to you, I shall be at ye Adelphi on Tuesday & at your Commands between Eleven & Twelve

I am Sir Your most obed^t humble Servt

D G—

Endorsement by Garrick: My answer to a Mr Chouquet about the Barbier de Seville. Aug^st 31st 1777. *Source:* FC, copy; Boaden, II, 264.

1. James Chouquet was a merchant at No. 17, Sherborne Lane, London.
2. In his letter of Aug. 28, to which this is the reply, Chouquet had written that in the fall of 1775 he had submitted a translation of Beaumarchais' *Barbier de Seville* and that

Garrick had replied that it was too late to include it in the 1775–76 season. On Garrick's retirement, Sheridan had promised to take it under "his protection" (Boaden, II, 264).

3. In Oct. 1776 was published *The Barber of Seville; or, The Useless Precaution; a Comedy by the Author of the School for Rakes* (*LC*, vol. XL), which while ascribed to Elizabeth Griffith was undoubtedly Chouquet's. Hearing of Colman's adaptation of Beaumarchais' play, and realizing Sheridan would probably in consequence abandon the production of his own alteration, Chouquet had requested in the name of "common justice" that Garrick represent to Colman the priority of Chouquet's rights to the comedy. The play was never produced.

1125   To Peter Fountain

Hampton

Dear Sir   Sunday [August?] 31st 1777[1]
The Moment I receive an answer from Sr Thos Mills, I will send it to You— I inclos'd my Letter to Mr Wombwell[2] the Chairman, that Sr Thos if he had forgot my request might immediatly have apply'd— Should the Gentleman & his Sons have business at Brighthelmstone, they would certainly be right to visit Sr Thos & say they were the Gentlemen for whom I made my application, but by no means let them go on purpose, It might distress Sr Thomas & not forward the business.

I am Dear Sr Your most most Obedt Sert
D: Garrick.

I shall take a jaunt for a few days & expect to be at ye Adelphi at ye End of ye Week— when I hope to Shew You an Answer—

Address: Mr Fountain, Maiden Lane.   *Source:* FC.

1. The month is supplied on the assumption that "the Gentleman & his Sons" are the Rowland Jackson family for whom Garrick had earlier in the month applied for Sir Thomas Mills's help.

2. George Wombwell (d. 1780), at this time Chairman of the Court of Directors of the East India Company (Joseph Haydn, *Book of Dignities*, 1890).

1126   To Caleb Whitefoord

Sunday [August] 31st [1777][1]
Thank You, my dear Sir, ten thousand times over for Your charming Letter & Your as charming news—[2] I always knew You to be a

Gentleman endow'd with the best intelligence— I hope that *ding dong* will always be at your Ear, when you write to Me—³ I rejoice our little Friend is come off so triumphantly— by yʳ Account it will be a good addition to his dramatic Treasury.

Dʳ Sir Ever Yours most truly
D: Garrick

I find by yᵉ Publick that yᵉ Husband *sang* yᵉ verses to his Wife— They are certainly very *airy*, & *tuneful*.

Source: BM; *The Whitefoord Papers*, ed. W. A. S. Hewins, Oxford, 1898, p. 165.

1. The month and year are clearly indicated by Whitefoord's letter, to which this is the reply, in which the "charming news" is identified as the success of Colman's production at the Haymarket of *The Spanish Barber* on Saturday night, Aug. 30, 1777 (*The Whitefoord Papers*, ed. W.A.S. Hewins, Oxford, 1898. p. 164f.; see also Letter 1128)
2. Whitefoord had written: "The Barber and myself have both come off with *flying* Colours. *He* has escaped the fury of the Critics, and I have made my escape from *my* party in order to give you some account of the Proceedings of the night. The Prologue was humorously spoken by your Pupil honest Parsons. The Piece was in general well receiv'd. It is tolerably lively and has some good Situations. Only some little hissing in the upper Regions . . . Your excellent Epilogue was very prettily spoken."
3. Whitefoord had concluded his letter: "I have not time to praise it [*The Spanish Barber*] any longer for this plaguy Fellow [the postman] is here again. Ding Dong— rot ye— I wish the Bell was in your Guts."

1127   To Hannah More

Hampton
[August] 31ˢᵗ [1777]¹

He Us'd me very unkindly about yᵉ Epilogue I Sat up half yᵉ Night to cook one for him in his distress, but beg'd my Name might be conceal'd—² but on yᵉ Contrary— Miss Farren³ spoke it so ill, & so unintelligibly, that it of Course had no Effect,⁴ & then he [*trim*] whose it was— My [*incomplete*]

Yours Dear Madam Hannah most affectʸ
D: Garrick.

Source: FSL, fragment, recto and verso.

1. Garrick had dated the letter July, but that is obviously an error since Colman's *Spanish Barber*, for which Garrick wrote the epilogue alluded to here, was first produced on Aug. 30, 1777.

2. In a letter from Colman, written earlier in the month, he had commented: "Not knowing, you were grown so chary of your name, I have mentioned my application to you, so that it is not in my power to answer for that total silence you wish for; but I will certainly observe your directions not to advertise the Epilogue till you give proper authority for it" (FC; Boaden, II, 274).

3. Elizabeth Farren (1759–1829), whose parents were actors, first acted at Bath in 1774 and after several years in provincial theaters made her debut in London at the Haymarket on June 9, 1777. In the fall of that year she was engaged at Drury Lane, and thereafter appeared at both theaters until she retired in 1797 to marry the twelfth Earl of Derby.

4. Contrary to Garrick, Miss Farren "not only acquitted herself creditably in the comedy, but gained applause from the most rigid critics, by her admirable mode of delivering the Epilogue" (Peake, *Colman*, II, 11f.).

1128   To George Colman

Hampton

My dear Colman   Sepr 2^d [1777][1]
In the first place let me sincerely wish You Joy of Your Barber—
I went from this Place Yesterday on purpose to see Your Nonsense,
upon the information of our Friend Whitefoord, who wrote me a
Line of Intelligence on Saturday night, tho Somebody Else would
not— *I like Your Piece, & that other most promising Piece, Miss Farren—
'tis a Shame that she is not fix'd in London— I will venture my Life that I
could teach her a capital part in Comedy, ay & tragedy too, that should drive
half our Actresses mad—* she is much too fine Stuff to be worn &
Soil'd at Manchester & Liverpool— I thank you for the Trans-
position of ye two lines in the Epilogue, they are now much clearer
to ye audience, & better for ye Speaker—
  What can I possibly say to You about Becket?—[2] Ever since I
heard of the transaction, I have been greatly hurt— I would have
given double ye sum for wch he was arrested, that it had never
happen'd— Garton should not have done it without your participa-
tion— I am told too that he got a Note of Becket's from a Printer
to increase the debt— You ask me why I would not speak to you
about it? I had not Seen B: when You came to me, & I was Willing
to know what had pass'd from *himself* before I spoke to *You*— he
came to my door whil'st You was there, & very prudently went
away— besides what could I say, or do in ye Business? it is a very
disagreeable one at best, & why should I mix it, with the Epilogue

business, Which we were to consult about, & not untune our Minds with distresses— I had Set my heart upon reconciling You to him, fail'd in yᵉ attempt, & to Speak of what happen'd afterwards, could be no Entertainment to Us— All I will say in behalf of Becket is this, that upon my word & honour, I never heard him in yᵉ least speak disrespectfully of You, & I fear, that You are hurt with what his Impertinent Acquaintance are pleas'd to say, as if it came from him: I had a long conversation with him this morning, & he disclaims Every offensive word that was utter'd about you at the Globe—³ More, as you say, when we meet— You are really much oblig'd to Me— I left Hampton with yᵉ Gout in my Stomach was in continual pain all the play, & yet was Entertain'd— I really was too bad to see You or write to You last Night—

Yours Ever most faithfully

D: Garrick.

I shall be all yᵉ Week till Sunday at Hampton— On that day I dine with Lady Westmorland⁴ at Hammersmith & shall be at yᵉ Adelphi on Sunday Night— I am preparing for my Welch Journey.

Source: FSL.

1. This is the reply to Colman's letter of Aug. 31, 1777 (Boaden, II, 266).
2. For the right to print Colman's plays in four volumes Becket had given Colman his note for 300 guineas, due in six months. This note Colman made over to Jonathan Garton, Treasurer of Covent Garden during Colman's management. Later, when in some financial difficulties, Becket sought from Colman, by an intermediary, an extension of the time on the note. Through some misunderstanding, Colman misinterpreted the request as a threat, and when Becket, who had earlier lent Colman £1000, sought a loan of £200 from Colman, £60 of which he proposed to use in making the final payment on the note in Garton's hands, Colman refused Becket the loan. Garton then had Becket arrested for debt (Boaden, II, 246–250; James P. Malcolm, *Anecdotes of the Manners and Customs of London,* 1810, II, 257–272; see also Becket's correspondence in FC).
3. The tavern on Fleet Street?
4. Mary (Cavendish) Fane (1698–1778), widow of John Fane, seventh Earl of Westmorland.

1129   To James Chouquet

Sir   Wedʸ Sepʳ 3ᵈ 1777
I have not yet seen Mʳ Colman, nor will I mention the business¹ to him: Indeed I could not well do it, for I am going from home for

some time— but You Sir mistook my proposal— I had no intention to propose Myself for an Umpire, nor do I know of any thing to be determin'd by a 3ᵈ person—² I said I wᵈ speak to Mʳ Colman about yᵉ Liberty of his Theatre but I could not undertake for any thing Else, nor wᵈ it have been delicate to propose Myself as an Umpire between My Friend & a Stranger

I am Sʳ &c
D G.

Endorsement by Garrick: Mʳ Chouquet's 2ᵈ Letter & my answer about Colman. *Source:* FC, draft; Boaden, II, 268.

1. See Letter 1124, note 3.
2. In a letter, dated only "Wednesday Mornᵍ 12 oClo," Chouquet had written Garrick: "Your polite Offer to settle the matter in dispute with Mʳ Colman was too flattering, not to be gratefully acceptᵈ, but as Mʳ Sheridan will be in Town in a few days, I humbly request you will deffer till then taking any notice on this Matter" (FC; Boaden, II, 267).

1130   To The Countess Spencer

Hampton
September 14, 1777

[Epitomized in the Historical Manuscripts Commission Report as follows: "Electrical apparatus at the Pantheon, to show that pointed conductors invite lightning and produce evil; and his Majesty ordered Mr. Wilson, the great electrical performer on the occasion, to take down all the pointed conductors of Dr. Franklin[1] and place blunted ones in their room at the Queen's house . . . no less than 400 drums and many thousand yards of wire in the apparatus; . . . it is to be hoped there is no party spirit in the business . . . Miss Hannah More, whose essays[2] your ladyship did not much fancy, has written a good tragedy lately . . . The subject from Chevy Chase,[3] the quarrels between the Scotch and the English."— Report 2, Appendix (1874), p. 13.]

Address: Lady Spencer. *In the possession of the Earl Spencer: Not made available for publication.*

1. Benjamin Franklin (1706–1790), the American scientist and statesman, was at this time in France. On receipt of the news, he commented in a letter of Oct. 4, 1777,

"The King's changing his pointed Conductors for blunt ones is . . . a Matter of small Importance to me . . . For it is only since he thought himself & Family safe from the Thunder of Heaven that he dared to use his own Thunder in destroying his innocent Subjects" (*Writings of Benjamin Franklin*, ed. Albert H. Smyth, New York, 1905–1907, VII, 64; see also Charles R. Weld, *History of the Royal Society*, 1848, II, 99–102).
   2. *Essays on Various Subjects, Principally Designed for Young Ladies* (1777).
   3. *Percy.*

1131   To Frances Cadogan

My dear Madam   Sepr 15. 1777
We are ye unhappiest of human beings— a Marriage & Other Matters in our family have Occasion'd the forgetfulness & Negligence of my dear Friends at Hurlingham— will You forgive Us? we have been wandering & disconsolate Ever Since You Saw Us— We are Oblig'd to run down to Lichfield with all speed— What We have done, & undone, & what Strange Matters We have Experienc'd, You shall know, when We call upon You at our return to enjoy some calm Society with You at Hampton— we hope to be back in a fortnight, & then I hope, You will hear all, See all, & forgive all—
   Mrs Garrick sends her Love & what not to You & Yours.
                              Ever most cordially & Affectionatly Yours
                                                       D: Garrick.

        Source: FSL.

1132   To The Lord Camden

                                                            Hampton
My good Lord   Sepr the 16. 1777
It is observed by a french writer that many things which seem severe if spoken as a joke will pass as such but that they grow serious by repetition. Your Lordship has long (jokingly as I thought & hoped) been pleased to twit me with a wavering in that faith, in which I have liv'd with pleasure & wish to die— tho this want of virtue in me (for if true it certainly would be so) hath been often

repeated, yet still, being a great laugher myself I always looked upon it as mere pleasantry, & rather as an ironical compliment than any thing else, & yet the message brought me by Mr Palmer of Bath, has made me half consider the matter as a kind of reproach which of course will make me a little serious— whenever I cannot have the honor as usual, & which I flattered my self would be annual at least of seeing Lord & Lady Camden & the Miss Pratts at Hampton I am sincerely disappointed but at the same time am bound to believe for my own credit that other engagements prevent my happiness— your journey into Kent to Mr Pratt,[1] & the expectation of Mrs Stewart[2] were urg'd to soften my disappointment this Summer; to make the fall as easy as possible I beg'd of Lady Camden that Miss Pratt[3] might pass a few days with us— impossible— to give me some small satisfaction for this refusal I was told that I should know when Mrs Stewart came that I might pay my respects at Chiselhurst— I hear that lady has been arrived more than a fortnight in which time I wrote to your lordship upon other matters, but received neither answer nor notice of the lady's being arrived. M^rs G: & I have endeavoured to put off our Welch journey to Sr Watkin[4] & imagined his being at Brighthelm with Miss Grenville[5] would have brought it to bear but all my wishes on that account are frustrated by the inclosed letter, which will oblige us to go immediately to Litchfield, where my family expects me & a marriage to be soon compleated between a niece of mine & a gentleman in the neighbourhood—[6] Let me assure your Lordship from the sincerity of my heart, that our going without paying our respects at Chiselhurst is very mortifying to us, but I cannot agree that this mortification proceeds from my want of gratitude taste or attention nor from any other cause but your lordship's total neglect of me in this business or rather having something better to think of— your lordship calls me a courtier— if I am a Courtier tis without interest or prospect of interest I have friends who are both in & out of place & I hope that my conduct to both is without reproach the greatest[7] man shall not speak ill of my friend without some decent reprehension, & some Opinions I have that my greatest Frend cannot alter— I have many Weaknesses, but I hope among the Number I can never be Seriously accus'd of want of ye most affect^e & Steady fidelity & Attachment to Lord Camden & his family.

I am Ever was & Ever shall be Y^r Lord^p's
most faithful Ser^t
D G.

If I am foolishly Serious in my letter I hope y^r Lordship will Excuse Me—

I beg that my best respects & wishes may be present⟨ed⟩ to all about you.

I spoke yesterday to Mr Wombwell to get Ironmonger[8] some little place in the India-house— If Capt Smith[9] would speak with that gentleman the business would be done.

Source: FC, copy; Boaden, II, 272f.

1. Presumably the Hon. John Jeffreys Pratt (1759–1840), only son of Lord Camden.
2. The Hon. Frances (Pratt) Stewart (1751–1833), Camden's eldest daughter and the "Fanny" of his letters to Garrick. On June 7, 1775, she had become the second wife of Robert Stewart, later (1816) first Marquis of Londonderry. In a letter to Garrick of July 3 Camden mentions the birth of Frances Anne, the first of her seven daughters (FC; Boaden, II, 231).
3. Probably Jenny Pratt.
4. Sir Watkin Williams Wynn (1749–1789), fourth Bt. (1749), M.P. for Denbighshire, Lord-Lieutenant of Merionethshire, and a member of the Dilletanti Society.
5. A sister-in-law of Sir Watkin and one of the daughters of George Grenville (d. 1770).
6. None of Garrick's three nieces, however, married at this time.
7. From here to the words "Excuse Me" in the postscript the copy is in Garrick's hand.
8. On July 3 Camden had written Garrick: "A poor Woman called upon me this morning who pretends she is a great Niece of Mr Beighton for some charitable assistance. Her Husband, accord^g to her account, was lately released from prison by the insolvent debtor's Act & they have 4 Small Children. Her Father was son to Mr. Beighton's own Sister. She signs herself Ironmonger late *Toplis* wch I suppose was her Maiden name . . . I sent her to London with a Guinea in her Pocket, & directed her to apply to you, who fr^m your long friendship with our good friend might probably know more of his family than I c^d & might be abler to detect the imposture, if there was any" (FC; Boaden, II, 230f.).
9. Perhaps Nathaniel Smith (d. 1794), a director of the East India Company at this time (*GM*, vol. XLVII, April 1777, p. 193).

1133   To Peter Garrick

Wynnstay Denbeighshire
Sepr 26 [1777][1]

Dear Peter

We shall certainly be at Birmingham on *Sunday Evening the 5th of October*, & shall stay ye Next day till about 12, so we may have a good deal of Gabble; I hope You will bring Cousin Bailye with You, & let us have a Snug party— I send this by the Chester post,

& you may Send me an answer by yᵉ Same Way— directed to me at *Sʳ Wat[kin] Will[iams] Wynn's Barᵗ at Wynnstay near Wrexham, Denbeighshire* to tell me if you approve yᵉ Party, & it will be convenient— we are very happy here, & cannot stir till Saturday Sen'night the 4ᵗʰ of October— these Welch scenes are quite New to us, & very well worth anybody's Curiosity— at *Shrewsbury* the Town was in an Alarm at my Coming, & the Raven-Inn besieg'd— I little Expected so much honour from Salopian Swains, & Welch Mountaineers— their Observations upon my Person, age &c you shall have at Birmingham on Sunday yᵉ 5ᵗʰ Octʳ if Nothing prevents your making Us happy— a line by yᵉ return of the Post to Chester will oblige

Your most affectᵉ Brother
D: Garrick

The Ladies with Me Send their Love— F⟨osbroke⟩ desires her duty & Love to her Father & Mother— She hopes to see her Brother at Birmingham, who she tells me is gone there to be a Doctor—² prays is it a Horse-Doctor?

Address: Peter Garrick Esqʳ, Litchfield, Staffordshire. *Frank:* Watkin Williams Wynn. *Postmark:* WREXHAM. *Source:* FC.

1. The year is supplied by Walpole in a letter to Jephson of Oct. 1, 1777, in which he reports that Garrick "is gone into Staffordshire to marry a nephew, and thence will pass into Wales to superintend a play to be acted at Sir Watkin William's" (ed. Toynbee, X, 124). The Wynnstay private theater in Denbighshire was a strange edifice that had originally been a kitchen and which consisted "merely, of a commodious Pit" (George Colman the Younger, *Random Records*, 1830, II, 43; [Askew Roberts], *Wynnstay & the Wynns*, Oswestry, 1885, p. 19). The play is identified by the younger Colman, using the cast book of the Wynnstay theater, as "Chrononhotonthologos perform'd October 2d, 1777.— Mr. Garrick was present" (autograph note in HTC copy of *Random Records*, II, 55).

2. Perhaps the "Mr. Fosbrooke, surgeon at Rugby," a town in Warwickshire not far from Birmingham (*GM*, vol. LXIII, Sept. 1793, p. 956).

1134   To Peter Garrick

Wynnstay

My dear Peter   Sepʳ 30ᵗʰ [1777]¹
Would it not be a little too much upon Sᵗ Patrick, to desire You, Honey, to meet me at Birmingham & then return to Lichfield with You, which is much nearer my Dear— In short we beg to see You

at Birmingham next Sunday because we cannot Stay at Lichfield so long as we could Wish— Should You arrive Sooner than We— I beg You'll bespeak beds sufficient for Us all There will be two wanted for You & Cousin Dick—² one for me & my Wife & one for Fosbroke & My Wife's Neice—³ I have Six horses for which I must have a good Stable & four Men Servants— Sʳ Watkin tells me it is a good house— We shall be there before Six in yᵉ Evening—

I wish You would Order a good joint of Meat for yᵉ Servants some fish if any, & some Chickens or fowls boiled or roasted as You like best & whatever Else you & Cousin chuse to be ready about Seven or Sooner—⁴

I am writing in yᵉ Dark & Mʳ Parry⁵ yᵉ famous Harper is playing like an Angel

Source: FC.

1. This letter must have been written shortly after the preceding.
2. Bailye.
3. Elisabeth ("Liserl") Fürst (1766–1840), daughter of Peter Fürst, a retired Viennese municipal inspector, and Therese, Mrs. Garrick's sister, came to London to live with her aunt in June 1777 (*Diary of John Baker*, ed. Philip C. Yorke, 1931, p. 404). After the death of Garrick, who left her £1000 in his will, she returned to Vienna, and on July 2, 1781, married Joseph Peter Adam von Saar (1762–1830), Imperial Royal Councillor of Finance in the Austrian postal service (*Genealogisches Taschenbuch der Adeligen Häuser Oesterreichs*, ed. H. W. Höfflinger, Vienna, 1911, p. 397).
4. Except for the postscript, the rest of the letter has been heavily scored out.
5. Presumably John Parry (d. 1782), the famous blind harper. A Welshman, he was much patronized by Sir Watkin (John T. Smith, *Nollekens and His Times*, 1828, II, 213f.).

1135   To Peter Garrick

[?*post* September 30, 1777]¹

Sʳ Watkin says if you would come to him, You would have suc[h] fishing in yᵉ River Dee, as You never Saw— As this is your high fly Season, I thank You doubly for losing a day with Us at Birmingham

Yours Dear Peter most Affectʸ
D Garrick

Address: Peter Garrick Esqr, Litchfield.   *Frank:* Watkin Williams Wynn. *Postmark:* WREXHAM.   *Source:* Gabriel Wells, fragment.

1. Conjecturally written in reply to a missing letter from Peter and in confirmation of the appointment at Birmingham mentioned in the two preceding letters.

1136   To Marie Jeanne Riccoboni

Hampton
Friday Octr 17th 1777

I am so flatter'd, my dear Madam, by an Extract from a Letter of Yours sent Me by my Worthy friend Mr Johns,[1] that I cannot resist (tho I have ye Gout in my hand) thanking you for it in the most affectionate manner— I return'd last Night from a long journey into Wales, & was very sorry that I could not call upon Mr Johns, but he was too far from the place I was at, & therefore I shall defer that pleasure till next Summer, when, if you please, I will carry You there, which by the bye is ye greatest ⟨favour?⟩ I can confer upon You; it is no less than to ⟨present?⟩ the Object of sincere affection to a younger Rival,[2] which all must allow to be a Service of great Danger— however I will do it for You— *You* Mad^e Riccoboni— before this winter You must, & shall receive some token of my Love—[3] would to Heav'n that I knew what w^d be most agreeable to You: but there is such a Work to manage Your proud Sensibilities, & refin'd delicacies, that Mr Johns & I have puzzled Ourselves often, & cannot yet determine how to make a successful Coup de main upon that impregnable fortress, YOUR GREAT SOUL—!

pray tell Mrs Pye to whom I wrote Yesterday, that I have while I was Writing receiv'd her letter, & will take care of the Business of it most Effectually— ⟨Pray⟩ tell her, that I imagin'd her Understanding ⟨was⟩ superior to such Nonsense—[4] however I will ⟨sac⟩rifice some time to her Weakness, if she will promise to think no more of it— by the bye, let her know that this folly is so strong a feature in ye Picture She sent Me,[5] that I shall put it in, if she will not; and tho I like the Portrait, yet I could add some Strokes to give it a finishing Resemblance:

do You know the great Lawyer *Linguet*? When he came to

England, he sent to me to desire to See Me when I was ill with the
Stone—[6] I sent to let him know that I would call upon him when
I was recover'd— but he took huft, & [in] the Journal politique &c
which he is now printing, he abuses Me with my Old friend Shake-
spear,[7] tho he never Saw Me, & cannot understand a Word of the
Poet— What a true vaut rien he must be!— I am very happy that
I have his Malignity instead of his Company—

My Wife, who sits by me, desires her Love— We were in hopes to
see You long before this, but tho I am at liberty, & quit of my
Theatrical Yoke, it is not yet in my Power to follow my Inclinations.

Ever & most Affectionatly Yours
D. Garrick.

best Wishes & regards to y^r Companion—

Address: A Madame, Madame Riccoboni, rüe poissoniere au Marbrier du
Roy a Paris. *Postmark:* LANGLETERRE. *Source:* FSL.

1. Presumably Thomas Johnes (1748–1816), M.P. for Cardiganshire (1774–1780).
He is mentioned in two of Mme Riccoboni's letters to Garrick (Boaden, II, 631, 633).
2. Mme Riccoboni replied to this remark: "je l'aime tous les jours davantage, mr
johnes, et son exactitude a m'écrire me lie veritablement a lui. ce je dis n'est pas une
finesse pour vous appeller paressex. je vous aime quand vous parlez et quand vous vous
taisez. je vous aimerai toujours parce que vous méritez lestime et lattachement de tous
ceux dont le coeur est sensible et capable de distinguer en vous les qualités au dessus
même des talens qui vous ont rendu lhomme le plus célébre de votre siecle" (FC; Boaden,
II, 633f.).
3. Evidently Garrick asked Mrs. Pye to suggest a suitable gift, for she wrote in her
letter of Nov. 17: "I do believe the only acceptable present you could send would be
Mrs Garrick's Picture & yours for Bracelets, but very plainly set. The Gold Medal she
does not wish" (FC; Boaden, II, 279).
4. In her letter of reply Mme Riccoboni expressed great indignation over the fact
that Mrs. Pye had recently been slandered in the papers (*ibid.*, 632f.).
5. Perhaps her own character sketch (*ibid.*, 215ff.).
6. In her reply Mme Riccoboni remarked: "non, en vérité, je ne *connois* point
linguet, pas même une seul personne qui ait eu la moindre liaison avec lui" (FC; Boaden,
II, 632). Upon his arrival in London, Linguet had written Garrick a flattering but
pompous note, dated Nov. 1, 1776, requesting the honor of his acquaintance (FC).
7. These attacks appeared in the second volume of *Annales politiques, civiles, et littéraires,*
published in August (pp. 18f., 327f.). Among other things, it was asserted that because
of Henderson's great success the general feeling of regret over Garrick's retirement was
rapidly disappearing.

1137   To Frances Cadogan

My Dear Madam   Monday Octr 20th [1777]^1
We are just return'd from North Wales, a most divine Country—
to shorten Matters between Us, will You & Your good Father be
With Us next Saturday to dinner & stay as long as You please, if
as long as *We* please You must spend the Xmas with Us— pray
send a Line by ye Post or to ye Adelphi to let us know if we may
expect You on Saturday to dinner, or if we shall send our Coach
to Richmond Bridge for You— It has Nothing to do but wait y^r
Commands—

                              Y^{rs} most affect^y Ever
                                        D Garrick

Madam Sends her best Love to Both with mine don't tell ye D^r but
I have ye Gout in my Writing Thumb & Middle Finger— Ecce
Signum! Scrawl!

   Address: Miss Cadogan at Hurlingham near Fulham. *Postmarked.* *Source:*
FSL; Baker, p. 67f.

   1. The year is determined by the reference to the return from Wales and by the fact
that Oct. 20, 1777, was a Monday.

1138   To Thomas Becket

                                                  Hampton
Dr B.   Tuesday Night [October 21, 1777]^1
I am glad You have sent ye packet to Sr Watkin, & I hope y^e
Porter will lose no time to send it to Wynnstay:
   To be sure *Garton's* behaviour to You considering ye original debt
was Colman's, is as astonishing, as it was most unjust, cruel, wicked
& unparrallell'd—^{2} It is impossible but he must be very unhappy
in ye End, for ye more it gets Wind, the more will he be condemn'd—
it is really so Strange, that I can yet scarce believe it— do You
think that Garton will dare to go on— it is impossible that they
will Suffer such a Story to be brought into a Court of Justice— I

have been very ill today & so Weaken'd with a purging that I can scarce walk about— It is not Stop'd yet, nor do I chuse it Should, as I believe Nature is throwing off some bad Matter, perhaps not less than a Fever— I am better, & hope to walk Stoutly tomorrow—

Old Carrington has behav'd just as I thought he would— with wicked partiality to Nathan & with cruelty & injustice to yᵉ others—[3] He was a good for Nothing, ignorant old —— You may fill up yᵉ blank as you please— how go yᵉ theatres on?— was Falstaff follow'd this Evening,[4] or did *Mʳˢ Barry* bear yᵉ prize away in *Zenobia*. She has desir'd me to write an Epitaph for *Barry*— I can't refuse her, & yet I don't like yᵉ office—[5] I believe we shall have a Cook come here tomorrow, if so, pray send my things by him—

Yours Ever &c

D G.

Address: Mʳ Becket.   *Source:* FSL; Andrew Becket, *Dramatic and Prose Miscellanies*, 1838, I, xii.

1. The date is established by the reference to the rival popularities of Henderson as Falstaff at Drury Lane and Mrs. Barry as Zenobia at Covent Garden on the evening of Tuesday, Oct. 21, 1777.
2. See Letter 1128, note 2.
3. Nathan Carrington had died on Oct. 20, 1777. In his will, probated on Oct. 29, he made Nathan his residuary legatee and left him £1000 and an estate of £900 a year. George Garrick received 10 guineas "for Mourning," and the other grandchildren the following bequests: Arabella and Catherine, £1500 each; Carrington, £1000 and some property; David, £1000 (Probate Court of Canterbury, Collier 413).
4. As played by Henderson at Drury Lane, Oct. 21, 1777 (*LC*, vol. XLII, Oct. 21-23, p. 396).
5. Garrick, however, did not write an epitaph for Spranger Barry, who had died on Jan. 10, 1777, and his tomb in Westminster Abbey bears none.

1139   To The Countess Spencer

Hampton
October 22, 1777

[Epitomized in the Historical Manuscripts Commission Report as follows: "Mentions Foote's death on his landing at Calais,[1] he had much wit and no feeling; sacrificed friends and foes to a joke, and so has died very little regretted, even by his nearest acquaintance."— Report 2, Appendix (1874), p. 13.]

Address: a la Comtesse Spencer, chez Mesrs. Panchaud, Banquiers, a Paris.
In the possession of the Earl Spencer: Not made available for publication.

1. Foote died on Oct. 21, 1777, at Dover while waiting passage to Calais (*GM*, vol.
XLVII, Oct. 1777, p. 508).

1140   To Richard Bailye

Hampton
Dear Dick—   Octr 22^d 1777
I have no knowledge Myself of Mr Aikin[1] but as a fine writer, My
friend Miss More of Bristol, I believe, is very intimate with his
Sister,[2] & I have wrote to her for a letter immediatly— but if You
take my Young Cousin[3] directly You may shew Mr Aikin that I
have written to Miss More, & it will be the same thing— her
letter may follow You— pray tell my Brother that I rec'd his
letter, & will see Lord Sandwich toMorrow— I offer'd the Young
Man, Bond,[4] a letter of recommendation Sign'd by Me, & he
rather Wav'd it, which surpris'd us all— It might have been of
Some Service to him, but I suppose he thought Otherwise, & we
parted— tell Peter that I have spoken about a Fiddle for him—
and if I send him a *Cremona*, don't let him imagine that I have the
slightest intention of getting *Mona* from him— No— No— *Hams* &
ale are sufficient—
     Old Carrington is gone, & has made a most unjust, partial, &
cruel Will— He has rais'd his Youngest Grandson, as high as he
possibly could to the prejudice of all the rest— He dy'd, as he
liv'd— without principle—
     If You Set out immediat^y for Warrington, I wish You Success
wth Your Nephew, & hope so promising a Youth, will be happily
plac'd at that celebrated Academy.[5]
                              I am Dear Dick Most Sincerely Yours
                                             D: Garrick.

My Wife & I Send Love to all—

Address: Richd Bailye Esqr in the Close, Lichfield. *Postmark:* OC 23. TW.
Source: FSL.

1. John Aikin (1747–1822), physician and author. Having completed his medical
studies, he was now resident in Warrington, Lancashire, lecturing on chemistry and
10*

anatomy at Warrington Academy. Aikin's early writings include *Thoughts on Hospitals*, 1771, *Essays on Song-writing*, 1772, and *An Essay on the Application of Natural History to Poetry*, published at Warrington in 1777 (Lucy Aikin, *Memoir of John Aikin*, Philadelphia, 1824, p. 156f.; Henry A. Bright, *A Historical Sketch of Warrington Academy*, Liverpool, 1859, p. 14f.).

2. Mrs. Barbauld.

3. Hugh Bailye (1761–1833), afterwards Canon-Residentiary and Chancellor of Lichfield, elder son of Richard Bailye's brother William (Reade, II, 76f., IV, 180).

4. Perhaps a son of the Rev. Benjamin Bond (1715?–1782) of Lichfield, Curate of St. Michael's from the 1740's on.

5. After attending the Lichfield Grammar School, Hugh Bailye entered Warrington Academy in 1777 (*Monthly Repository*, 1814, p. 530).

1141   To Peter Fountain

Hampton

Dear Sʳ   Wednesday [October]¹ 22 [1777]
Since my return from North Wales I have been much indispos'd—
I hope to be in Town some time next Week When I shall call upon
You— in yᵉ mean time I must desire You not to publish any of
those things You mention—² they are for private inspection, & it
would be very wrong to make them publick—

I am Dʳ Sʳ Your most Obedᵗ huᵉ Servᵗ

D: Garrick

Address: Mʳ Fountain, Maiden Lane, Southampton Street, Covᵗ Garden. *Postmark:* OC. *Endorsement (by the recipient?):* 22ᵈ Augᵗ 1777. *Source:* FC; Boaden, II, 259.

1. That the August in the endorsement is a mistake for October is confirmed by the postmark and by the reference to the return from Wales. In 1777 Oct. 22 fell on a Wednesday, while Aug. 22 was a Friday.

2. For an example of Fountain's unreliability and indiscretion, see Thomas Evans' letter to Garrick of six months later, April 1: "As that Blockhead Fountaine is handing about a printed account of D'Eon in which there are remarks on your Prologue I hope you will not take the least notice of such a malignant being should chance throw Him in your way I will not say more." The letter is endorsed by Garrick: "1778 Evans's correspᵉ with Fountaine about Me. The last a Rogue yᵉ first a fool" (FC).

1142   To Lady Young

Hampton
My dear Madam   Oct.r 28th 1777
A little rambling to see some of our distant Friends prevented my
receiving Your letter Sooner or I shd have answer'd it immediatly—
We have too exquisite a relish for the pleasures we enjoy'd at
Hampton with Lady Young & Elsewhere not to be selfish enough
to wish for them again & again— We heard that You & Sr Willm
intended to make a little Excursion till ye Winter upon the Conti-
nent, or we Should have intreated the favour of kissing Your hands
upon ye banks of the Thames— but why would not our amiable
Friend let us know by a Line in the Summer that she had leisure &
inclinations to make Us happy?— We did not leave Hampton till
the End of Sepr to go into Wales, where & in other places, we have
loiter'd wth our friends— We are this Moment going to London,
call'd there by a Death,1 & a Marriage— but be We where we
will, We shall always retain the greatest regard & affection for Sr
William & our dear Lady Young.
        I am Dear Madm Most faithfully & Affecty Yours
                                             D Garrick

My Wife Sends her Love & warmest wishes.

Address: Lady Young at Delaford near Uxbridge, Middlesex. *Postmarked.*
Source: FSL.

   1. Nathan Carrington's?

1143   To Nicholas Ramus

Adelphi
Dear Sir   Octor 30th [1777?]1
Notwithstanding all my pains & care to have a correct copy of the
trifle which I was in hopes to lay at her Majesty's feet with the
alterations & additional Characters,2 I find upon examination that
the transcriber has not done his duty—

I have therefore got a person with me who has undertaken to make it less unworthy of her Majesty's acceptance. I shall therefore desire to see you & my other friends to dinner on Friday Se'nnight instead of next Wednesday, when I hope to put it into your hands a better dressed Gentleman than you saw yesterday, tho' like other fine Gentlemen I fear he will be found to have little wit, & not deserving of the honour to be introduced into her Majesty's company.

> I am Dear Sir your most obed^t humble Servt
>> D: Garrick.

Endorsement by Garrick: My Letter to Mr Ramus about the Manuscript Letter I sent to her Majesty.   *Source:* FC, copy; Boaden, II, 354f.

  1. The year is indicated by the conjectural identification of "the trifle" as the alteration of *Lethe.*
  2. Presumably a manuscript copy of *Lethe,* containing the alterations which Garrick had introduced into the piece when he read it before the King and Queen in February. Lady Bathurst wrote Garrick, Sept. 3, 1777, expressing concern lest the copy of *Lethe* which she had returned to the Adelphi in a basket with a haunch of venison would be so contaminated as not to be fit for a Royal apartment" (HTC).

1144   To The Countess Spencer

Sunday [November 30, 1777
[Epitomized in the Historical Manuscripts Commission Report as follows: "A letter written by David Garrick, in Mrs. Garrick's name, in German English."—Report 2, Appendix (1874), p. 13.]

Address: Countess Spencer.   *In the possession of the Earl Spencer: Not made available for publication.*

1145   To James Adam

Hampton
Dear Sir   Friday [December 5, 1777]
I forgot to Speak to You before I came away— I wish You Would Send for Becket's Son & he will Shew You ye Account & I think

very plain & I hope Satisfactory— I beg you will do Nothing in taking yᵉ Books away from him,[1] till you have talk'd with the Son or with

Dear Sʳ Yours most Truly
D Garrick.

I shall be in Town again on Sunday next.

Address: James Adam Esqʳ on the Terrace, Adelphi, Strand. *Seal. Endorsement:* Mʳ Garrick 5 Decʳ 1777—. *Source:* FSL.

1. Adam, knowing of Becket's financial troubles, may have been considering another publisher-bookseller for part five of *The Works of Architecture.* The volume, which appeared in April 1778, bears on its title page the imprint of Becket, J. Robson, and T. Sewell.

1146 To The Countess Spencer

December 11, 1777

[Epitomized in the Historical Manuscripts Commission Report as follows: "Our tragedy[1] succeeded; cordial applause; not a dry eye in the house."—Report 2, Appendix (1874), p. 13.]

Address: Countess Spencer, Althorpe. *In the possession of the Earl Spencer: Not made available for publication.*

1. Probably Hannah More's *Percy*, which had received its first production on the preceding day.

1147 To Luke Gardiner[1]

London
Decʳ 13ᵗʰ 1777

Sir
We are just return'd from a little jaunt into yᵉ Country, or Mʳˢ Garrick would have answer'd yʳ letter sooner & more fully. She inquir'd into yᵉ forms of the habits wᶜʰ were us'd for Macbeth at Covᵗ Garden, & which were much approv'd—[2] We have Sent You

a Sketch of those,[3] made by a person, one Messink,[4] belonging to that house. I wish you may understand it— in Short any becoming dress of that Age or like that Age, will be proper, & you may please Yourselves— as we came late to Town we sent immediately & got the best intelligence we could thinking there was no time to lose—[5] The Ancient dresses are certainly preferable to any Modern ones.

I am Sr Your humble & most Obed^t Ser^t

D: Garrick

Mrs Garrick joins with Me in respects to your Lady.[6]

There is no Occasion for a black dress for Lady Macbeth, & no order was Ever wore by Me.

Address: Luke Gardiner Esqr, Dublin. *Postmarked. Source:* Sir Laurence Olivier.

1. Luke Gardiner (1745–1798), later Baron (1789) and Viscount (1795) Mountjoy. Educated at Eton and Cambridge, he was at this time an officer in the army and a wealthy and prominent citizen of Dublin; he had a taste for the theater which he passed on to his son, the Earl of Blessington. "Mr. Gardiner, to gratify his beautiful lady's taste, fitted up a theatre at his lodge in Phoenix Park [Dublin], of which he and Lord Sackville [were] keepers; and there the people of fashion in Ireland were invited twice or three times a year, to see what was allowed to be the best company of gentlemen and lady performers that ever trod the boards" (*GM*, vol. LIII, Dec. 1783, p. 1064).

2. See M. St. Clare Byrne, "The Stage Costuming of *Macbeth* in the Eighteenth Century," *Studies in English Theatre History in Memory of Gabrielle Enthoven*, 1952, pp. 52–64.

3. *Ibid.*, Plate 6, opposite p. [65], facsimile.

4. James Messink (1702?–1789) had been a scene painter and minor actor at Drury Lane, but after the 1774–75 season he presumably moved to Covent Garden.

5. A criticism of Gardiner's production, with illustrations of the costumes, appeared in January in the *Hibernian Magazine* (p. 53f.).

6. Elizabeth (1751–1783), the daughter of Sir William Montgomery, had married Gardiner in 1773. She and her sisters, Lady Townshend and Mrs. Beresford, "were reckoned the three most beautiful women in Europe, and were called the Irish Graces. Mrs. Gardiner had most remarkable fine theatrical talents, and performed most of Shakespeare's tragic characters . . . Her Lady Macbeth was the finest piece of acting ever exhibited on any stage" (*GM*, LIII, 1064; see also Boaden, I, 528, II, 23).

1148   To George Garrick

Althorp

Dear George   Decr 15th 1777

I have inclos'd Lord Sandwich's Letter & my answer about *Johnstone*,[1] have I spelt his Name right?— if I have not You must rectify it, & send Johnstone with a Note to his Lordship with Your Respects, & direction Where He is to be found— I must desire You at yᵉ Same time to speak to him about Moody, if my Security is not deliver'd up, I will never speak to him again.

If he gets once into a Sloop, we can upon his good behaviour, remove him with my Interest wᵗʰ my Lord— I have another thing to say— Miss More promis'd Me a Copy of the play to read to Lady Spencer if she has it ready & will send it on *Friday Next to the Earl of Jersey*,² *directed to Me*, his Lordship will bring it down here on Saturday— if you have any Letters You may send them inclos'd in yᵉ Same parcel— You need not send me any more papers unless it is the Morning Chronicle, which Becket will take care of, Lord Spencer has all yᵉ Papers Except that, I shᵈ be glad to know what he says of yᵉ *Roman Sacrifice*,³ Mʳ Cumberland has written an excellent Epilogue for it & that B—— Master Y[ates] would not speak it— Mʳ Cumberland will frank any thing for Me, & may be always found at Lord George Germaine's⁴ Office from ten to two— I believe yᵉ office is Somewhere near Mʳ Rigby's— Will you speak to Captⁿ Smith about Ironmonger in Lord Camden's & my Name—⁵ it wᵈ be done directly— I don't think Shirley will appear so Soon as Thursday— I hope not as it will be against *his 6ᵗʰ Night*—

I have sent a Letter for Jolliff⁶ yᵉ Guardian to David's Girl—⁷ will it do?— if it will let it be directed & sent. I have promis'd Wilkes⁸ in Dublin a very Early printed Copy of *Percy* for his friend Ryder— pray take care to speak to Miss More for one as soon as it can be got, & Mʳ Chamier or Mʳ Cumberland will frank it to *Mʳ Wilkes Sycamore Alley Dublin*—

I am Yours Ever &c

D Garrick

remember to seal Lord Sandwich's letter after you have read it to Johnstone— I hope the School for Scandal will [be] done on Friday, for Mʳ Mason— if yᵉ New play perhaps he wᵈ chuse That—

Let yᵉ Play sent to *Lord Jersey* be made into as Slender a *Roll* as possible for [he] comes on horseback— his Lordship desi⟨res⟩ it— don't send anything Else with it— it must be at his house in Grosvenor Square on Friday Night at farthest—

Let yᵉ Play be cut as it is Acted— if it was printed off it wᵈ be better to read & I would stay a day or two for it. then You need not send to Lord Jersey's. Mʳ Chamier would frank it or Mʳ Cumberland—

Address: George Garrick Esqr at the Stage Door of Drury Lane Theatre, Russel Street, Drury Lane (with Care & Speed). *Seal. Source:* FC.

1. John Henry Johnstone (1749–1828), actor and singer, had been at Drury Lane as early as 1774, when he substituted as prompter during Hopkins' illness (Johnstone to Garrick [Dec. 20, 1774], HTC). Apparently Johnstone had persuaded Garrick to assume his debts on the security that he would pay them off by serving in the navy, to which end Garrick was to write a letter to Lord Sandwich. The recommendation seems to have been successful, for Johnstone wrote later from Portsmouth full of gratitude for Garrick's kindness (Dec. 25, 1777, FC).

2. George Bussy Villiers (1735–1805), fourth Earl of Jersey (1769).

3. Shirley's tragedy (DL, Dec. 18) was played for only four nights, and was coldly received (*BD*).

4. George Sackville (1716–1785), known, from 1770 when he assumed the name Germain to 1782 when he became first Viscount Sackville, as Lord George Germain. At this time he held the positions of Commissioner of Trade and Plantations and Secretary of State for the Colonies.

5. See Letter 1132, note 8.

6. William Jolliffe (1744–1802), a Lord of Trade and Plantations at this time.

7. Emma Hart (1758–1813), daughter and co-heir of Percival Hart of Brentford and Ealing, Middlesex (Lysons, II, 567). On July 22, 1778, at Hendon, she was to marry young David Garrick (*LC*, vol. XLIV, July 23–25, 1778, p. 87).

8. Thomas Wilkes (d. 1786), a Dublin friend of Garrick and author of *A General View of the Stage*, 1759 (see Wilkes's letters in Boaden; Wilkinson, II, 151; W. J. Lawrence, "George Farquhar: Thomas Wilkes," London *Times Literary Supplement*, June 26, 1930, p. 534).

1149   To Mrs. Thomas Rackett, Sr.

Althorp

Dear Madam Rackett.   Decr 21st 1777

I have receiv'd a letter from my Neice,[1] full of y^r Goodness to her & her own happiness— Mrs Garrick as well as myself, cannot but be uneasy at the trouble & confinement She must give You, & are conscientiously struck with our unreasonable imposing this hard task upon You— I believe we must give Orders directly that she returns to ye Adelphi, & We shall send Mrs Garrick[2] to take care of her till we come back to London— for Yesterday Morning Lady Spencer in full convocation assembled at Breakfast, declar'd her resolution and vow'd very seriously, that she would not suffer Us to Stir till 8 or 10 days after the Holidays— this tho very flattering to Us distresses M^{rs} G & Me on Your Account— therefore We intend sending our Maid about Friday or Saturday next to free You

from Your Confinement— this must be done— because we are
unhappy till it is done— pray give our Love to Mademoiselle & tell
her she Writes English like an Angel, I will answer it in a day or two
& so will her Aunt that she has written to her— pray let yʳ Husband
& Son know that I shall Send to you all my Warmest Wishes with
my Wife's before the approaching Season: that I hope they will
Enjoy all the Mirth & Happiness of yᵉ Season— however We must
Eat a Minc'd pye together in spite of our present Seperation— We
are very happy here indeed— the Company is Duke & Duchess of
Devonshire— Lord & Lady Jersey—[3] Lord Althorp— Mʳ Stanley—[4]
Mʳ & Mʳˢ Hanbury—[5] Mʳ Egerton—[6] Mʳ Thursby—[7] Lord &
Lady Charles Spencer— Mʳ Stewart—[8] Miss Lloyd— Mʳ Poyntz[9] &
Miss— &c &c &c yᵉ Duke & Duchess of Marlborough are
Expected—I have tir'd You & Myself— pray let me have a Line
from You directly— my Brother will Send it, or rather direct it
to me at Earl Spencer's at Althorp near Northampton Once more
my dear Mʳˢ Rackett adieu

      I am Dear Madam Most truly Yours & most Affectʸ

                       D: Garrick.

Source: FSL.

1. Elisabeth Fürst.
2. Presumably George Garrick's second wife, Elizabeth (Tetley) Garrick (d. 1822).
She was probably the Miss Tetley or Tatley, a dancer, listed in the Drury Lane playbills from 1762 to Jan. 19, 1771, in the Harvard Theatre Collection. It is not known
when they were married, but their only child, George, was born in June 1775 (*Morning
Post*, Feb. 5, 1779; *GM*, vol. LXXXIX, Oct. 1819, p. 380; *GM*, vol. XCII, Feb. 1822,
p. 190; Fitzgerald, pp. xvii, 435n.).
3. The fourth Earl of Jersey had married in 1770 Frances Twysden (1753–1821),
daughter and heiress of the Bishop of Raphoe.
4. Hans Stanley (1720?–1780), politician and diplomat, at this time Governor of the
Isle of Wight, M.P. for Southampton, and Cofferer of the Household. He was later to
commit suicide while staying at Althorp.
5. Charlotte (Packe) Hanbury (d. 1816).
6. Presumably Samuel Egerton (d. 1780), M.P. for Cheshire, great-grandson of the
second Earl of Bridgewater.
7. Presumably John Harvey Thursby (1734?–1798), Hanbury's brother-in-law.
8. Robert Stewart (1739–1821), husband of Lord Camden's eldest daughter. At this
time he was M.P. for county Down, but was later to become Viscount Castlereagh
(1795), Earl (1796) and first Marquis (1816) of Londonderry.
9. William Poyntz (1733–1809), brother of Lady Spencer.

1150   To The Earl of Upper Ossory

Althorp

My good Lord.   Decr 24th [1777?]^1

I should have answer'd Your Lordship's most Obliging Letter immediatly, had not a return of my old Complaint kept me in bed at ye time of the Post going away— Mrs Garrick & I are very unhappy that our Engagements here & in London will prevent Us this time from paying our Respects to Lady Ossory & Your Lordship— had we known that our Company would not have been inconvenient We should certainly have done ourselves that honour & pleasure.

I am My Lord Your Lordship's most Oblig'd &
most Obedient Servt
D: Garrick.

Source: FSL; Adrian H. Joline, *Meditations of an Autograph Collector,* 1902, p. 238.

1. The conjectural year is supplied by the fact that Garrick spent Christmas at Althorp in 1777 (see preceding letter).

1151   To Elisabeth Fürst

Dear Neice   Christmas day [1777]^1

Your Aunt & I have receiv'd Your Letters, & are glad that My Mirth the day We parted, & your Yawning afterwards have not kill'd You— as for my Part, I always follow Nature, & what she is pleas'd to direct me to do, I always obey her Commands, but never mean to offend any body— If a little affectation or Hypo[c]risy was necessary, I could *Act* Melancholly, as well as any body— but Why should I be mellancholly?— I was going to see some of the best as well as the greatest Persons in the Kingdom, & who do Every thing to make me happy— I left You at ye Same time with very good People, who Wish to Oblige y^r Aunt & Me, & have a great regard for You— therefore Your Situation must be comfortable & pleasurable if You please— I hope you were not uneasy that I took this jaunt, I must see my best friends, & can not lose the priviledge of pleasing Myself— however we shall return to You the Moment we can— I thank You for Your letter which is written well & the improvement in y^r English is very Surprizing— I beg You will present my best & Affectionate Wishes to our Friends You are with, & Your Aunt joins with Me in ye Compliments of ye Season to you all— which in plain English is Wishing You from my heart a *Merry* Christmas & a happy New Year.

Your Aunt sends her Love & will Write to you in a few days.
Ever & truly Yours most affectionatly
D: Garrick.

I have very bad pen & can scarce Scribble this letter—

Address: To Miss Fürst at Mr Rackett's in King Street, Cov^t Garden. *Seal.* *Source:* FSL.

1. The year is determined by the fact that Elisabeth Fürst spent Christmas of 1777 with the Racketts.

1152   To The Countess Spencer

January 17, 1778

Address: Lady Spencer. *In the possession of the Earl Spencer: Not made available for publication.*

1153   To The Countess Spencer

January 22, 1778

Address: Lady Spencer. *In the possession of the Earl Spencer: Not made available for publication.*

1154　　　　　To Elizabeth Montagu

My dear Madam　　　　　　　　Sunday [?January 25, 1778][1]
Indeed & indeed You rate the little Matter I did last Night too
highly— if I could give any Idea of Acting to Your Noble Friends,[2]
I have my reward— for I could not see such a desire of hearing Me
in Mrs Montagu's house without running the risk of Exposing
Myself— If I have got off for less, I am well off— I am at this
Moment very well & Escap'd Colds tho it rain'd hard when I went
away— I saw near two Acts—[3] the Audience certainly applauded,
& I believe were sincere; but with all it's Merit, there is something
forc'd in the manner of Writing, a Constant Endeavor at poetical
Images which perhaps by repetition may surfeit the Mind: this
remark only to Your Good Self—

　　　　　　　　I am dear Madam Most truly & affec^{ty} y^r
　　　　　　　　　　　　　　Obed^t humble Ser^t
　　　　　　　　　　　　　　　　D Garrick

M^{rs} G: presents her best & respectful Comp^{ts}

Address: Mrs Montagu.　*Seal.*　*Source:* FSL.

　　1. The conjectural date is indicated by the references to Garrick's acting at Mrs.
Montagu's "last Night" and to the tragedy which he had just seen.
　　2. In a letter to Mrs. Vesey which, while undated, must from its references to the
fifteenth performance of *Percy* (Jan. 26) have been written in the last week of Jan. 1778,
Mrs. Montagu reported: "On Saturday last the French Ambassador and Ambassadress
[the marquis and marquise de Noilles], L^d and Lady Spencer and the Garricks dined
with me, and Mr. Garrick was so good as to act the Dagger scene in Macbeth, and King
Lear on his knees uttering maledictions on his ungratefull daughters" (Blunt, *Mrs.
Montagu,* II, 43).
　　3. Presumably the last two acts of the first performance of Cumberland's *Battle of
Hastings* at Drury Lane, Saturday, Jan. 24, 1778.

1155　　　　　To Frances Abington

Madam,　　　　　　　　　　　　　　Feb. 12th, 1778
I sincerely agree with Montaigne that the smallest token of sorrow
from a Lady ought to melt the hardest heart, and bring it to what

state of feeling she is pleased to give it. If Mrs. Abington has inadvertently mentioned me as the author of the Characters[1] in question, I trust in her justice that she will not suffer any false impression of me to remain among her friends,

I am, Madam, your humble servant,

D. Garrick.

Source: Boaden, II, 287.

1. "Modern Characters from Shakespeare," consisting of quotations from Shakespeare's plays selected to characterize contemporaries, was appearing anonymously in the *Morning Post* (Jan. 2–June 23) and in the *Public Advertiser* (Jan. 27–July 9). It was, in the same year, published as a small book and went through two editions.

1156 To The Honorable Albinia Hobart[1]

Madam   [*post* February 12, 1778][2]
There was too much Company on Sunday Night & you were too Well employ'd for Me to say all I had to say to you upon a Business of very great Consequence to me— A friend of mine assur'd me that You were lately in Company with Mrs Abington, who declar'd that I was the Author of the application of the Words of Shakespear to Modern Characters in ye M^g Post— tho I shall no longer appear before ye Publick yet it is incumbent upon Me to shew, that I am not altogether unworthy of their favour which I certainly sh^d be, were I guilty of what that Mischief Making Lady is pleas'd to accuse Me— I flatter Myself that those who know that Lady & Me, will not give the least Credit to so false & malignant a Suggestion— all I beg of You Madam is, that you will Satisfy Me whether You were in Company & heard Mrs Abington accuse Me of being the Author of the Characters from Shakespear in that paper?

Mrs Hobart may be Assur'd that I will not let her Name be mention'd in any appeal I shall make, & I hope that She will not refuse the request I have Made   I am

Madam Your most Obed^t humble Servt

D: Garrick.

Source: FC, draft; Boaden, II, 287.

1. Albinia (Bertie) Hobart (1739–1816), wife (1757) of George Hobart, later (1793) third Earl of Buckinghamshire. There are two letters from her to Garrick in the Harvard Theatre Collection.

2. From the reference to Mrs. Abington and "Modern Characters," this letter was conjecturally written at the same time as the preceding.

1157   To Messenger Monsey

Dear Dr Feb^y [*post* 13]^1 1778
Let your warmest Friend read our Two Notes, and pronounce which heart has the most Malice in it— Indeed you are grown very peevish, & some of your College Friends Say as much.— I have Sent Two of your Books, and I will get the third,^{2} if there is one to be got in the Three Kingdoms.—

You are in the right to drop your Intelligence about the Duke of Leeds, but you had been more right not to have mention'd at all such a Silly improbable Business.^{3} You are pleas'd to Say that I never gave You any thing for any favour shewn to me— Your favourite Horace, and all the best writers Say that Friendship can interchange no Gifts but those of the heart;— however let us pleasantly reconsider this charge— you as a Physician and I as a Manager of a Theatre, dealt in Tragedy, Comedy and Farce— You had always free Egress & Regress into my Shop, and why should not I have a peep into yours?— our Drugs indeed *work'd* in different ways, but I hope and believe that mine were as wholesome and Salutary as yours— however if you find that any ballance is due to you, for particular *favours*, I am ready to discharge it, notwithstanding Hudibras's Axiom.—

> When Friends begin to take Account
> The Devil with Such Friends may Mount.

Yours my Dear Dr Most Obediently
D G.

Endorsement by Garrick: 1778 Dr Monsey's Two peevish Letters & my answer.
Source: FC, copy; Boaden, II, 289.

1. Written in answer to Monsey's letter of Feb. 13, 1778. Monsey's reply, the second letter referred to in the endorsement, is dated only with the month and year (Boaden, II, 288f.).
2. Monsey had written: "Between fifteen and twenty years ago I lent you Miss Carter's translation of 'Epictetus' and a 'Macrobius's Saturnalia;' I should be glad to

have them again; presuming you have done with them. I also lent you 'Remarks upon the Minute Philosopher,' which are supposed to be Middleton's. This I value full as much as I do either of the others, and should be glad to have it."

3. Monsey had professed that "one thing gave me pain . . . and that was that I had done you *ill offices* with the Duke of Leeds"—Thomas Osborne (1713–1789), fourth Duke (1734), whose friendship Monsey had long enjoyed. "Being fully conscious I had not," he continued, "it gave me so much pain I applied to his Grace, who said in these words, or very like them, 'Done Garrick ill office with me! Lord, Doctor, I dare say I have used you ill, for puffing him to me perpetually, and making me believe there was not his fellow upon the earth.'"

1158 To Captain Frederick Bridges Schaw?[1]

Adelphi
Sir   March 2ᵈ 1778—
I have been very much indispos'd with a bilious disorder & am forc'd out of Town this Morning by my Doctor till the next week,— I will not pretend to be a Stranger to your partiality for Miss Garrick, I heard of it Some Months ago from many of my Neighbors in yᵉ Country & from Some of my friends in Town & was rather Surpris'd that I should be more ignorant of this business than the rest of yᵉ World—

Miss Garrick to this Moment has kept it a Secret from Me & my Wife, nor indeed have We been favour'd with a visit, Message or any civil inquiry after Us, tho both have been ill for Some Months— I am therefore the more oblig'd to You, Sir, for the Information you have given Me in Your letter, & shall be glad of an opportunity to thank you for it, at my return to Town—
I am Sir Your most Obedᵗ humble Servᵗ
D G.

Source: FC, draft.

1. The conjectural recipient is established by the date, for on April 30, 1778, Arabella Garrick was to marry Frederick Bridges Schaw, a widower; from 1763 to 1775 he had been Captain of the 66th Regiment of Foot, retiring from the army in 1776 (*Registers of Marriages of St. Mary le Bone, 1775–83*, ed. R. Bruce Bannerman and Capt. R. B. Bannerman, Publication of the Harleian Society, vol. LI, pt. 3, 1921, p. 38).

1159   To The Countess Spencer

March 2, 1778

Address: Countess Spencer, St James's Place. *In the possession of the Earl
Spencer: Not made available for publication.*

1160   To Mary Hoare

Sweetest of Canaries—   March 9th [1778?][1]
What a Mistake has my poor, foolish, sick head made?— and why
will not You, my dear Madam, gives Your name at full length, that
such confusion may be avoided? Thus stands ye Matter— Mr
Hardinge[2] begs of Me to write him a letter about Nothing upon ye
Circuit— I was so unfit to be Nonsensical, that I desir'd my Brother
to call upon Mrs Hardinge to let her know that I was incapable of
writing, & beg'd that She would signify as much to that genius her
Husband— the next day I rec'd a Note sign'd *M. H*— wch from ye
foregoing Circumstances I took for *Mary Hardinge*[3] instead of *M.
Hoare*— a Letter came this day from ye first, which I have inclos'd
for yr *Secret* perusal, & wch, I am sure, will not a little entertain
You— but what a jolt-headed, hard-hearted Dunce I must be, not
to distinguish the sweet hand, & excellent heart of my next door
Neighbours?, & what a *Brute* must she think me not to have
answer'd sooner her very kind Enquiries?— I am most sorely vex'd
at this Mistake— the Country has had a very great Effect upon
Me, & I begin to recover my Lillies and Roses; indeed so much so,
that I shall bring a face to Town next Wednesday, not unworthy
of the Pencil of a certain Porter-drinking, masquerading, raking
Genius, not many Miles from ye royal Terrace of the Adelphi—
My Wife begs me to ask You, & then Your heart, if You really &
truly think that She *loves* You?— I thought that our affections had
leapt over the bounds of *permission*, & darted through the party
Wall of our houses— in short such things are better *felt* than
describ'd, so I will Say no More— Will You go next Wednesday
with Us to hear Judas Maccabæus—?[4] You shall go when you
please, come back when You please, & sit upon ye Softest chair in

the box?— We shall expect a few Short answers to all these questions to Morrow upon our Arrival at the Adelphi— with our Loves to You & Yours

I am Most devotedly your most Obedient

D Garrick

Source: FSL.

1. Conjecturally written in 1778, after the Hardinges' marriage in Oct. 1777, when Wednesday fell on March 11 and there was a performance of Handel's *Judas Maccabaeus* at Drury Lane.
2. Presumably George Hardinge (1743–1816), writer and barrister, nephew of Lord Camden.
3. Mrs. Hardinge's given name, however, was Lucy (d. 1820). She was the daughter and heiress of Richard Long of Hinxton, Cambridgeshire (George Hardinge, *The Miscellaneous Works, in Prose and Verse*, ed. John Nichols, 1818, I, xvi).
4. "Last night [March 11] Handel's celebrated Oratorio of Judas Maccabaeus was performed at this theatre [Drury Lane], for the first time this season" (*LC*, vol. XLIII, March 10–12, 1778, p. 247).

1161   To Richard Cox

March 12th 1778

What did my Worthy, affectionate & Sincere Richard Cox suspect his old Friend David of bitching last Wednesday? let me assure You upon my word & honour that I deferr'd sending my Excuse to You to the very last Moment, for I am most cordially & particularly attach'd to You & the Company I sh^d have met that day at Your house:

on the *Monday* I was to have attended all my Welsh friends to their festival— I could not go— on the *Tuesday* I was to have din'd with Mr Rigby the Attorney Gen^{ll} &c at Sr George Hay's, & ye day fix'd for my conveniency, and behold I could not go— on the *Wednesday* nothing but a high Fever attended wth lowness of Spirit should have prevented my revelling in Albermarle Street—

The Flesh was guilty, but my heart was free!

and could my dear old Friend the Richard of all Richards, suspect my honour, because a tall, gawky, platter-fac'd papistical dripping-pan, who lives in the Kitchen many fathoms under-ground— who is just arriv'd from Staffordshire, who never sees, or hears of Me, & never sees the light, but when all the rest of the house is in yᵉ Country, & she just wakes from her torpid State to say *Yes* or *No* to silly folks who ask her silly Questions?— if that Period is not long enough for You, I will send You a longer the next time, provided You will take off from my reputation all the Abuse, that high-ton'd abuse, which You cast upon Me before those Men who of all Other's, I love, honour, & Esteem— do this my dearest Dick, & be restor'd to the warm & unalterable Affections

of Your most Sincere friend
D: Garrick

Source: Lloyds Bank, Ltd., Cox and King's Branch.

1. Edward Thurlow (1731–1806), lawyer, had been Attorney-General since 1771; he was to become the first Baron Thurlow on June 3, 1778.

1162   To Lacy, Ford, Sheridan, and Linley

Adelphi
Gentlemen.   March the 16ᵗʰ 1778
Mʳ Bateman¹ of Maiden Lane sent to Mʳ Wallis of Norfolk Street the 14ᵗʰ of Novʳ last to desire an Accᵗ of Mʳ Lacy's Mortgage to Me,² as He, Mʳ Bateman, had authority to pay Mʳ Lacy's debts. Mʳ Wallis comply'd with his desire, but I have not yet had Notice when I was to receive My Money— I must therefore desire You Gentlemen, as You are all parties Concern'd, to take care that Mʳ Bateman's Notice to my Solicitor may be comply'd with on Your Parts, as I am ready to comply with it on Mine—

I am Gentlemen yʳ most humbᵉ Servᵗ
D Garrick.

Endorsement by Garrick: Copy of My Letter of yᵉ 16ᵗʰ of March 1778 to Messʳˢ Lacy Ford Sheridan & Linley. Source: FC, copy; Boaden, II, 291.

1. Gregory Bateman, lawyer, of Maiden Lane (*Browne's General Law-List*, 1777). He was admitted to Lincoln's Inn on Nov. 29, 1765 (*Records of the Honourable Society of Lincoln's Inn: Admissions, 1430–1799*, 1896, p. 457).
2. In the manuscript material in the Harvard Theatre Collection covering the sale of Drury Lane to Sheridan is a memorandum headed "Case of W L," to this effect:

Following the formation of the partnership of James Lacy and Garrick (see Appendix B), Lacy in succeeding years mortgaged his share to Garrick, "proceeding from a very expensive undertaking on his estate in oxfordshire in a Scheme of finding a coal mine" and his share in alterations of the theater. When Willoughby Lacy on his father's death failed to keep up the payments on the mortgage, Garrick, without consulting him, sought to assign the mortgage to the purchasers of his own share; whereupon Lacy "enterd into an eng^t with two Gentlemen to purchase one moity of his share."

Yielding to the opposition of his partners, Lacy, however, agreed to a further loan by Garrick on additional security of his partners and also agreed to have the interest on the loan taken by deputy from the nightly receipts of the theater. (According to the Drury Lane Account Books, 1776–1777, in the FSL, the interest paid Garrick was £6 each acting day.) Lacy's debt, nevertheless, increased, and at the end of the second season, even more "harrass'd" by a balance due, "threathened by Mr Garrick," and "importuned with propositions from Mr Sheridan," Lacy proposed granting "Renters . . . money arising on Mr Lacy moity to be applied in reducing Mr Garricks mortgage, and exonerating M^r L from" the obligations. This proposal did not meet with approval and was dropped.

According to the Winston manuscript in the British Museum (p. 143), James Lacy's indebtedness at his death to Garrick was £4,500; Willoughby Lacy increased the indebtedness to £22,500. (For a fuller account of the negotiations, see Winston MSS, pp. 102–119, 132–159.)

1163   To Joseph Cradock

Dear Sir,   March 18, 1778
A thousand thanks for your luxurious present; but you will make me blush, if your bounty does not stop. We shall regale upon it to-morrow. Alas! I have no money at present: it is all disposed of. I shall keep the secret, though I suppose it will be soon known. You are very obliging, and Mrs. Garrick begs her best compliments and thanks with mine for you[r] very kind invitation. Mrs. Cradock is more particularly included in these acknowledgments. We are all in confusion and hurry at present. A French war![1] rather more bold than welcome! Heaven send us a good delivery! Once more adieu. We shall remember you to-morrow, when we are full of your loving-kindness. I am, dear Sir, your most obliged and obedient servant,

D. Garrick.

The young lady[2] who presents her respects and thanks, will in all probability be in her own county before the time we shall go into Derbyshire.

Source: Cradock, IV, 256.

1. When, on March 13, the French announced their treaty of alliance with the American colonies, England immediately recalled its Ambassador and began to prepare for war.

2. Hannah More, who was then at Hampton (Roberts, *Hannah More*, I, 86).

1164   To The Countess Spencer

March 19, 1778

Address: Countess Spencer. *In the possession of the Earl Spencer: Not made available for publication.*

1165   To Willoughby Lacy[1]

Wimbleton

Sir   Sunday March 22^d 1778

Y^r Answer to my Bro^r to my Message was very unsatisfactory, & has more convinc'd Me that the trouble You have given Me has been very ill return'd— As my Transactions and my Conduct are more particularly known to your Relation Mr Sainsbury,[2] I must desire You will Appoint him to meet Us at Mr Wallis's when I shall make him a Judge of this Matter, and not those persons who have instigated You to write me an unkind, unjustifiable and let me add an ungratefull Letter I shall be ready to meet Mr Sainsbury at Mr Wallis's any time to Morrow or the next day between the hours of Eleven and Two

I am S^r Y^r humb^{le} Servt

D Garrick

I must desire You to appoint Mr Sainsbury as soon as possible that I may appoint Mr Wallis.

Endorsements by George Garrick: To Mr Lacy—; *and:* answer to M^r L's 1st; *and:* Copy of Mr Garricks t[w]o Letters from Wimbleton dat^d 22^d M⟨arch, 1⟩778.
Source: FC, copy; Boaden, I, 293.

1. This letter was sent only as an enclosure (see following letter), and was to have been the answer to Lacy's letter of Thursday, [March 19?] (Boaden, II, 292).

2. Thomas Sainsbury (d. 1795), Alderman of the ward of Billingsgate, who had been one of the witnesses to Lacy's marriage (Alfred B. Beaven, *Aldermen of the City of London*, 1913, II, 136; *Registers of Marriages of St. Mary le Bone, 1754–1775*, ed. W. Bruce Bannerman, and Capt. R. B. Bannerman, Publications of the Harleian Society, vol. XLVIII, pt. 2, 1918, p. 149).

1166   To Willoughby Lacy

Sir   [March 22, 1778][1]
If You had been pleas'd to have written your last Letter without the first, there wou'd have been no Occasion for the inclos'd— which I had written at Lord Spencers before Yours arriv'd; however there are such particular Circumstances in your first Letter that I must again repeat my desire of your appointing a Meeting at Mr Wallis's with your Friend & relation Mr Sainsbury— I will then open my Heart to You, as I hope You will explain somthing very mysteriously *mask'd* in Yours and which indeed You have promis'd by my Brother— If after some particular Proofs of my regard to You, I am to be suspected of partiality against You, it wou'd be much better that our Correspondence shou'd end— I am

Endorsements: Answ^r to his 2^d; *and:* Copy of M^r G——ks let^r to Mr Lacy dat^d London 4 ock[?] Adelphi. *Source:* FC, copy; Boaden, II, 293.

1. This is the answer to Lacy's letter of March 21, 1778 (Boaden, II, 292f.), and is dated from the endorsements to the preceding letter.

1167   To Willoughby Lacy

(A Note after we had met at Mr Wallis's.)
                                       March 24th— 1778
Mr Garrick's Compliments to Mr Lacy; in the hurry and warmth of their Conversation to day at Mr Wallis's— he was pleas'd to Say, that he never had any thoughts of taking the Mortgage out of

Mr Garrick's hands, tho' he had it in his power, as if it were a matter of favour to continue it.— Mr Garrick in Answer to that, begs that if he should have such an Offer again, that he would accept it, as it would greatly oblige Mr Garrick to be paid off.— On the other hand, that Mr Lacy may not be *distress'd*, or *oppress'd*— Mr Garrick will suspend the Notice of calling in the Money, 'till Mr Lacy shall have settled his Matters with his Partners.

Endorsement by Garrick: The last of ye Correspondence. *Source:* FC, copy; Boaden, II, 294.

1168   To Richard Berenger

Dear Berenger   March 29th 1778
I did not hear till last Night—, and I heard it with the greatest pleasure, that Your Friends have generously contributed to your, & their own happiness—[1] No one can more rejoice at this circumstance than I do, and as I hope We shall have a Bonfire upon the Occasion,[2] I beg that You will light it with the inclos'd—

I am My dear Sir most truly Yours
D: Garrick

Endorsements by Garrick: March 29th 1778 Letter sent to Berenger with his Bond for 280–10–; *and:* March 29th, 1778, with the letter on the other side I inclos'd his Bond for two hundred & eighty pounds ten shillings, which bore date the fourth of Feb^r the 2^d Year of the Reign of George the Third 1762.— D.G. *Source:* FC, draft; Boaden, II, 297.

1. Berenger at this time had sunk into debt so deeply that he dared not leave his house. In March 1778 his friends and relations came to his aid, and among themselves they raised the entire amount (£2600) needed to pay off his creditors. According to Thomas Tyers, Garrick not only returned Berenger's bond (see endorsement, and Berenger's letter of thanks in Boaden, II, 297f.) but also donated "a bank note of 300 *l.*" (Blunt, *Mrs. Montagu*, II, 45f.; John Taylor, *Records of My Life*, 1832, I, 325f.; Thomas Tyers, *An Historical Essay upon Mr. Addison*, 1783, p. 75f.).
2. Taylor records that prior to "a grand dinner," given by Garrick in celebration of Berenger's liquidation, the actor "brought forward all the notes and bonds which had been purchased of the creditors and said, 'I'll have the honour of setting it a-light.' He immediately threw them into the grate, and set the pile on fire" (*Records*, I, 325f.).

1169   To The Earl of Rochford

My Lord   April 3ᵈ 1778
In the Gazette of last Saturday Your Lordship is pleas'd to advertise
that there is a want of Officers for the Essex Militia—¹ I have a
Nephew, my own Name, who is a very good Soldier, & a most
Worthy Young Man— He was in Lord Pembroke's Dragoons, &
was so ill at that time that he was oblig'd to sell out— It was very
unlucky for him that he did, as Lord Pembroke & the Officers were
Willing that he should go abroad to recover himself— I will not
say more of his Character, but leave that to his Lordship, Col¹
Philipson,² Major Colman,³ or any of yᵉ Officers belonging to that
Regiment— He is going to be Married, & I have settled upon him
an Estate I have in Essex of 150 pounds a Year;⁴ if Your Lordship
will Accept of his Services He shall be proud to serve under Lord
Rochford, & it would make me very particularly happy.
                    I am My Lord Your Lordship's most humble &
                                        most Obedient Servant
                                                    D. Garrick

He was a Cornet in Lord Pembroke's, & his Lordᵖ would have
given him a Lieutenancy, if he would have remain'd in the Regᵗ

Source: FSL.

1. See the *London Gazette* for March 28. Rochford was Colonel of the West Essex
Militia.
2. Richard Burton Phillipson (d. 1792), at this time Lieutenant-Colonel of the 1st
Regiment of Dragoons.
3. Edward Coleman, who had been Major of the 1st Regiment of Dragoons from
1771 to 1775.
4. This estate, purchased from a Colonel Clarke in 1771, consisted of 192 acres
lying in the parishes of Copford, Great Birch, Little Birch, and Layer Marney, and
yielded a yearly rent of £149.10s. Garrick, however, retained the manor of Copford
(copy of David Garrick II's marriage contract, dated July 21, HTC).

1170   To William Pearce¹

                                                    April 7ᵗʰ 1778
Mʳ Garrick presents his best Compliments and Acknowledgments to
Mʳ Pearce for the great honour he has done him—² Mʳ Garrick is

this Moment return'd from the Country, or he should have return'd his thanks before for Mʳ Pearce's favour.

Address: Mʳ Pearce, The Author of yᵉ Haunts of Shakespere at Mʳ Brown's, Catherine Street, Strand.   *Source:* FC.

1. William Pearce (1751–1842), a brother-in-law of Henry Bate, was a popular writer of comic operas and a frequent contributor to the *Gentleman's Magazine*.
2. Pearce had dedicated to Garrick his newly published poem, *The Haunts of Shakespeare*.

1171   To The Earl of Rochford

My good Lord   April yᵉ 12ᵗʰ [1778][1]
As you are well known to smile upon Me, I am address'd on all quarters to befriend some petition or Other— let me assure yʳ Lordᵖ this is at least as disagreeable to me, as it can be to You— but what can I do?— not to continue the delusion, that I have some interest wᵗʰ Lord Rochford would be such a loss of importance, that I cannot very readily give it up, and as it will only give Your Lordᵖ the trouble of reading now & then my impertinence, I am in hopes from yʳ usual kindness to Me, that you will permit me to indulge my vanity— Mʳ Glover,[2] who is too deserving a Man not to comply with his request, desires Me to apply to yʳ Lordᵖ that he may have the honor of being Surgeon to yᵉ Essex Militia— He is a most Skillful, worthy Man, is a good Writer, & has always been a Steady friend to Government— I have known him long, he is much belov'd; and yᵉ worst thing I Ever heard of him, was, that by his Skill in his profession, he recover'd a Thief after he had hung half an hour, & which Thief before he had quite heal'd yᵉ Circle yᵉ Rope had Made, pick'd his Friend Glover's pocket, by Way of Gratitude, & never so Much as thank'd him for his good Offices— Will Your Lordship favour Me with a Line to convince this Worthy Man that I have not broke My Word with him?
                    I am Yʳ Lordship's Most devoted & Obedᵗ Serᵗ
                                                D G.

as I am made an Essex Gentleman by yᵉ purchase of General Clark's Farm near Colchester, I had some thoughts of applying to y^r Lordship for a Commission as You want Officers, but I believe that I must confine myself to the Command of Bayes's troops.

Source: FC, copy; Boaden, II, 300f.

1. The year is from Rochford's reply of April 19, 1778 (FC; Boaden, II, 301).
2. William Frederick Glover (1736?–1787), surgeon and actor. As a young man he had abandoned medicine for acting, playing first at Edinburgh and later at Dublin, but in 1767 he had resumed the practice of surgery in London. He was later (1779) to serve four years as surgeon in the East Essex Militia (*European Magazine*, vol. XL, March 1787, p. 214f.).

1172   To James Boswell

My dear Sir   April 2[5, 1778][1]
The Ladies commanded Me to breakfast at Hampton— I could not but Obey, tho I should have been particularly happy to have breakfasted with You this Morning

                                        Most truly Yours
                                        D. Garrick

Address: James Boswell Esqr.   *Source:* Boswell MSS. Yale.

1. So dated by the Yale editors of the Boswell Papers, presumably on the basis of the chronology of Boswell's life.

1173   To The Countess Spencer

                                        April 29, 1778

Address: Lady Spencer.   *In the possession of the Earl Spencer: Not made available for publication.*

1174　To Lacy, Ford, Sheridan, and Linley[1]

Gentlemen.　　　　　　　　　　　　　　　　　　May 7 1778

I am rather surpris'd at the Letter I receiv'd from you yesterday, and as it is impossible for me to know when y^r debts and Expences will be discharg'd, & as I imagine that my Mortgage is as just a debt as any upon the Theatre, & that it is as reasonable for Me to Expect my interest should be paid as punctually as any other Expence of the Theatre,[2] I cannot defer a Moment giving You Notice Gentlemen, that I expect the Mortgage to be paid off at the time mention'd in the deeds taking this day for the Notice Which is to be given to you by Gentlemen

Y^r most Obedient Servant
D: Garrick.

Endorsement: To Messrs Lacy, Ford, Sheridan, & Linley—.　*Source:* FC, copy signed by Garrick; Boaden, II, 303.

　1. This is the reply to a letter of May 6, 1778, signed and sent by Benjamin Victor, which runs: "I am directed by the Proprietors to inform you, that it will not be in their power for the future, to pay the Interest of Mr Lacy's Mortgage untill the Debts & Expenses of the Theatre, are discharged" (FC; Boaden, II, 303).
　2. See Letter 1162.

1175　　　To Willoughby Lacy

May 7th 1778

Mr Garrick presents his Comp^{ts} to Mr Lacy & is very sorry to find that the Proprietors have So ill-manag'd their affairs as to make it necessary for them to send him such a letter as he receiv'd Yesterday—[1] He is greatly alarm'd at the Contents of it, & not much pleas'd with the Manner— however he has sent an Answer to the office which he hopes will not be disagreeable to Mr Lacy—

Endorsement with address: To Willoughby Lacy Esqr Great Queen street. *Source:* FC, draft; Boaden, II, 303.

　1. Lacy replied on May 15 that the letter from the proprietors was written without his consent or knowledge, that the interest he owed was completed for the season, and

that as long as he retained any part of the property he would never consent to any defalcation. Garrick endorsed Lacy's letter: "To this I sent as an answer by My Brother from Hampton— that he might depend upon my not distressing him— before George saw him Mr Lacy had bargained to Sell his Share to Mr Sheridan at an Enormous price— D: Garrick" (FC; Boaden, II, 304). The price was £45,000; two years earlier Garrick had sold for £35,000 (Walter Sichel, *Sheridan*, 1909, I, 527).

1176   To Hannah More

My Dearest Nine.   May 9th 1778

Ingratitude is the Devil my dear— said some Gentleman to his Lady upon receiving no thanks for a basket full of dainties— We have receiv'd a Hamper full, & no kind of Acknowledgments to our dear Friend at Bristol— the Pork was Excellent & so was ye Liquor we drunk your health in— no Matter for that— where is ye Letter say You, of ye real Correspondence—?— I should have written a dozen before this, for I like ye business, but I have not had a Moment to Myself— before this Week is out, you shall receive some Nonsense, & which I beg you will put into ye fire, if you find it, as I fear you will, very unfit Company for his female Companion.

Madam sends her love, she has been much troubled with a bleeding at the Nose, & a frequent head-Ach, She Eats & Sleeps & grows as fat as bouncing Bess of Brentford—[1]

We have had great uneasiness at the Death of poor Mrs Thursby[2] My Eldest Niece is married to Captn Shaw, my Nephew David will soon be married to Miss Hart, & I am to pay the Piper— May all of your family that want husbands, get as good ones, as this Country affords, & I'll answer, Whoe'er the happy Men are, that they will get good Wives, & that is a bold word, as times go— Love to all— in great hurry— Ever Yours Most Affectionately Hannah of all Hannahs

                                                    D. Garrick

Source: Baker, p. 49f.

1. See *The Merry Wives of Windsor*, IV, v.
2. On April 22 (*LC*, vol. XLIII, April 23–25, p. 395).

1177   To Richard Tickell[1]

Sir,   [*post* May 11, 1778][2]
I received your letter this moment, which giving me some uneasiness,
I sit down to answer it directly.[3] What your friend said to me about
applying to Lady Bathurst was very much to his honour, and
expressed his great solicitude for your welfare; he thought a release
of your genius from the fetters of obligation a circumstance of more
consequence to you than the place you hold; and I must desire
you not to harbour the least idea of his *indifference* with regard to
you— such a thought would be very unjust to him and painful to
me—[4] we were together last Thursday at Mr. Wilmot's, and there
we met the Lord Chancellor and Lady Bathurst. Sheridan and I
immediately consulted together, and I spoke very warmly to her
Ladyship; she entered as warmly into the business, mentioned some
gentleman, whose name I forget, who had spoken to the Chancellor
in your behalf. I think she said that his Lordship was obliged to
act as he has done, but that your name, if I mistake not, for we
were interrupted by the coming up of Lady Denbigh,[5] might be put
again upon the list. I intend to see her soon again and talk it over—
she desired me to send her the two poems which in great secrecy
I told her were yours.[6] I have been here with company for a few
days, I shall return to town tomorrow, and will take the first
opportunity of speaking to Lady Bathurst.
    I am, Sir, Your sincere well-wisher and most humble servant,
                                                        D. Garrick

The gout has slightly attacked the thumb of my right hand, as you
may see by this scrawl.

Source: FC, copy.

1. Richard Tickell (1751–1793), pamphleteer and dramatist, had originally studied
for the law (entered at the Middle Temple, Nov. 8, 1768).
2. This is the reply to Tickell's letter of May 11, 1778 (FC; Boaden, II, 304).
3. Through some error Tickell's name had been removed from the list of Commissioners of Bankrupts, and at Sheridan's suggestion he had sought Garrick's inter-
cession with Lord Bathurst, the Lord Chancellor. Before his retirement on June 3
Bathurst was to promise Tickell reinstatement, but that promise was not to be honored
by the new Lord Chancellor, Thurlow. On July 25 Lady Bathurst was to write Garrick:
"I am sorry we were both so unsuccessful in our Schemes with the present Chancellor,
I do assure you I did my part for Mr Tickle but I find he has enemies who flung cold
water on my solicitations. I think if you had taken my hint in regard to the place I
mentioned *you* wou'd have succeeded" (Boaden, II, 157, 302, 304, 305; HTC).

4. Tickell had written: "I am sorry Mr Sheridan could . . . treat either my difficulties, or your wish to overcome them with indifference" (FC; Boaden, II, 304).

5. Mary (Cotton) Feilding (d. 1782), wife of the sixth Earl of Denbigh.

6. Presumably *The Project* and *The Wreath of Fashion*, Tickell's two earliest poems; while the first had been published in April the second was not to appear until August, and the supposition is that Garrick had manuscripts of both poems (*LC*, vol. XLIII, April 16–18, p. 369; *Monthly Review*, vol. LIX, August, p. 141).

1178   To The Earl of Sandwich[1]

My good Lord   May 12th 1778

My Surprise at Miles's letter is beyond words to express it— I receiv'd one from him at Sea[2] in which there is not ye least mention of his unaccountable design of writing to y^r Lordship— I have done with him for Ever, & most sincerely sorry I am that I should ever recommend one so wholly unworthy of your Lordship's goodness— the last honest Man y^r Kindness has sav'd from ruin will, I believe, do credit to my recommendation— he is much lik'd by the officers, & having been us'd to ye sea & liking it, will, I am sure, never fail in his duty— I must own that the welfare of this worthy creature has made me happy, and every little promotion hereafter that may proceed from the source of his present felicity will greatly add to mine— and I trust, that the sober discretion of honest Johnston, will attone for the mad unaccountable freaks of Mr William Augustus Miles.

I am Ever most truly your Lordship's devoted

D. Garrick.

I take the liberty to send y^r L^p the inclos'd postscript of Miles's letter,[3] which is dated at sea April ye 26th. Upon reading Miles's letter to y^r Lordship again I find that he mentions ye affair of the Trident[4] & had I not ye Gout in my right hand I should have written this letter over again, but I hope y^r Lordship will excuse me, as I am in a little pain.

Source: Earl of Sandwich, transcript.

1. So identified by the owner.

2. Dated "At sea April 26th 1778, on board his Majesty's Ship the Surprize," it is in the Forster Collection. Among other things, it informed Garrick that "a Subject very

different from Pursery" was occupying Miles's time: the composition of "miserable Sonnets & yet more miserable Dialogues," and an alteration of Dryden's *Don Sebastian* in which Colman was interested. Wishing to dedicate the alteration to Lord Sandwich, to whom he owed his present position, and desiring Garrick's opinion, Miles had enclosed in his letter a prospective dedication.

3. A part of the manuscript has been cut out at the postscripts, presumably that part which Garrick sent to Sandwich.

4. In April the *Trident* sailed for America carrying Lord Cornwallis and three members of the peace commission. Because of the crowded accommodations the commissioners had protested Cornwallis' presence to Lord Sandwich on April 5 (*Private Papers of John, Earl of Sandwich*, ed. George R. Barnes and J. H. Owen, 1932, I, 371n.).

1179   To William Jolliffe

Hampton

Dear Sir   May 21ˢᵗ [17]78
I rece'd yʳ Letʳ and the papers Yesterday, had I been in Town, I shᵈ have waited upon You directly— It gives Me great Uneasiness that I cannot possibly agree to Every proposal that Mʳ Jolliffe makes— but indeed, Sir, my abhorrance of pin-money has been express'd in ev'ry Way my small talents could suggest— I look upon it as a Common destroyer of Marriage happiness, even where a great fortune in a manner makes it necessary from Custom— but I really think a Settlement of a £100 a Year for Pin-Money out of a small fortune, wou'd not only be unreasonable but dangerous— I trust from my Knowledge of You, that my delivering my Sentiments thus freely, will not hurt the good liking which I flatter'd Myself subsisted between Us, & Which I shᵈ for my own honour and pleasure most sincerely wish to cultivate— may I freely acknowledge to You that every delay in the business of this young Couple is as inconvenient to Me as it is I suppose disagreeable to them— I cannot settle any Plan for Myself till They are fix'd, and I shou'd be greatly oblig'd to You, if with your consent, the Lawyers were desir'd to bring this Affair to as speedy a Conclusion as possible[1]
I am Dʳ Sʳ Your most Oblig'd & obedient humble

Servant

D. Garrick

Mrs Garrick begs her best Compᵗˢ may be presented with mine to Mʳˢ Jolliffe.—[2]

Source: FC, copy.

1. It was concluded two months later, the settlement being signed on July 21.
2. Eleanor, daughter and heir of Sir Richard Hylton, Bt., of Hayton Castle, Cumberland.

1180   To The Princess Dashkova[1]

Mistley in Essex

Madam   May 30th 1778

I feel most sensibly the very great honour You have done Me, and I have felt as Sensibly the charming Object of my gratitude:

Yesterday a most Accomplish'd Musician & an Excellent Composer did all the Justice in his power to Your Highness's composition— the Small Audience was in raptures, the Taste, harmony, & pathetic Simplicity of the Airs were felt from the heart— indeed Madam You were judged not as a Princess, but as a great Artist— not the least favour or indulgence was shewn to Your Titles, or Rank, & tho the Musical Jury sat upon You with the most critical rigour, yet your Acquittal was as unanimous as their approbation—[2] in Short I fear what one of our Poets once prophesy'd will most certainly come to pass—

Russia shall teach the Arts to Britain's Isle.

May Your Highness long continue to be an honour to your own Nation and the delight of ours; & may that pure taste for Nature & simplicity get Strength from Your Highness's Example & drive from our Theatres the present vocal, & instrumental Musick, which astonishes the Ears, without ever touching the heart— if with this publick petition I may be allow'd to throw in a private petition for Myself, it is, that I may enjoy a Continuance of that honour, which Your great Kindness has conferr'd upon

Madam Your most Oblig'd and most Obedient

humble Servant

David Garrick.

I should have acknowledg'd yr Highness's favour sooner had I not been from home

Source: FSL; *Memoirs of the Princess Daschkaw,* ed. Mrs. Martha W. Bradford, 1840, II, 138f.

1. Ekaterina (Vorontsov) Romanova (1743–1810), Princess Dashkova, author, had been a favorite of Catherine the Great and was to be (1782) founder and first President of the Academy of Arts and Sciences at St. Petersburg. At this time she was living in Edinburgh, where her son was attending the university (*Memoirs of the Princess Daschkav,* trans. and ed. Kyril Fitzlyon, 1958, p. 146f.).

2. In an undated letter to Garrick, accompanying her music, she had requested his indulgence: "Elle guidira doucement votre *gout* pour decouvrir dans la Musique que je joins ici, les traits que la Sensibilité, avec un peu d'harmonie Naturelle sans le secours de l'art a produits" (FC; Boaden, II, 314).

1181   To Richard Cox

Dear Richard   June 30th [1778][1]

By great good luck I found Mad^m Hale's Note & by that you will see What Misery I have had upon ye Pocket— We din'd with Mr Hoare at Barnes[2] Wed^y ye 17th & I rec'd ye inclos'd ye Friday after ye 19th for the Calvert's[3] & Paly[4] din'd wth us ye Wed^y after (as express'd in ye Note) which was ye 24th— Will that satisfy'd Your perturbed Spirit my dear Friend?— pray let me know by a Line to ye Adelphi if I shall set y^r Name down & have ye Writing made out in y^r Name for a Renter's Share in ye opera house?

                     Y^rs Ever & Ever
                     D Garrick.

Source: HTC.

1. The recipient and the year are determined by the similar references here and in the following letter to buying shares in the Opera House.

2. Richard Hoare of Barn Elms in Barnes, Surrey.

3. Presumably the John Calverts.

4. Mrs. Hale.

1182   To Richard Cox

                                    Lawford[1]

My dear Master Richard.   July ye 4th [1778]

Upon talking with Wallis of Norfolk Street, I find that the Shares are put at 300 pounds, for operas & all kind of Entertainments that shall be exhibited at the Haymarket Theatre— the Managers agree to allow to Each Renter or Sharer a Ticket, which ticket is only personal & not transferable— & they likewise give a certainty of 15 pounds a year to Each Renter—[2] however if you will be one, I may have it in my Power to befriend You, & I certainly will if I can, for We, who have subscrib'd for 4 have an advantage

Y[rs] Ever & most truly
D Garrick

you may sell Y[r] Share & the Ticket with it— but while you keep y[e] Share y[e] Ticket can only admit Y[r] Self into the Theatre.

Address: Rich[d] Cox Esq[r], Albemarle Street, Piccadilly, London. *Postmark:* IY 6. *Endorsement:* M[r] Garrick July 4th 1778. *Source:* HTC.

1. A small town near Mistley where Garrick was visiting at this time.
2. On June 24, 1778, Richard Brinsley Sheridan and Thomas Harris had become proprietors of the Opera House in the Haymarket. On Oct. 1, in return for £300 apiece, they guaranteed to Richard Rigby and others an annual return of £20 and the privilege of the theater for twenty-one years (indentures in Sheridan Collection; Walter Sichel, *Sheridan,* 1909, I, 529).

1183   To Richard Cox

Lawford

My dear Richard   July 9th [1778][1]
If you should call on Monday next at y[e] Adelphi about Eleven or twelve, we will talk more upon the Business of the Opera. I w[d] call upon you if I could—

Yours Ever & most affect[y]
D: Garrick.

Address: Rich[d] Cox Esq[r], Albemarle Street. *Source:* HTC.

1. From the reference to the Opera, this letter was obviously written in the same year as the preceding.

1184   To Hannah More[1]

Essex

My dearest of Hannahs   July 9ᵗʰ [17]78
You must have thought me lost, mad or dead, that I have not sent
You a morsel of affection for some time— I have an Excuse, if
there can be any, for the neglect of such a friend!— Ever since You
left us, I have been hurried & distressed about my Nephew's
Marriage, & which is not for many tedious reasons of Law, yet
settled— the Lass of his heart being under age has given the Lawyers
great trouble, Myself much disturbance, & the Young Couple
(poor souls!) almost a heart-breaking— however the End of all
their Cares, or the beginning of them is at hand— We are now with
Mʳ Rigby & some Ladies our particular friends by yᵉ Sea side, &
While I am Writing this in my dressing Room, I see no less than
fifty Vessels under Sail, & one half an hour ago Saluted us with
13 Guns— I shall return to Town on Sunday to begin the Matri-
monial Cares over again— among all the News foreign & domestic,
that travels thro & about Bristol, have [you] not yet heard that
Mʳˢ Garrick & I were seperated?— tell the Truth, dear Nine & shame—
You know who— to our very great Surprize a great friend of ours
came from London & to his greater Surprize found us drinking
tea & laughing like ten Christ'nings under our Walnut tree— he
took me aside & told Me, it was all over the Town from Hyde
Park Corner to White Chappel dunghill that I had parted with
Mʳˢ Garrick— You may imagine this was great matter of Mirth to
Us, but my friend fell a'Crying & swore that the Devil was abroad,
& the Curse of Heav'n was upon yᵉ Land— we imagin'd Somebody
had a Mind to joke with our friend, but upon inquiry we found
Such a report had been spread— but to comfort yʳ heart, be assur'd
that we are still as much united as Ever & are both so well, that
there is a prospect of dragging on our Clogs for some Years to come—
there was a very particular paragraph in yᵉ *Mornᵍ Chronicle* about
Percy, which I did not understand & sent for an Explanation to
MY FRIEND Colman— it was said— that *Percy continud to have great*
Success in yᵉ Country, which drew the Mind of the Writer of yᵉ Paragraph
upon the distress'd Favourite of the Muses, who had sav'd yᵉ hero of yᵉ Piece
in yᵉ Course of yᵉ Winter from being ill treated by yᵉ Publick— it was
something like yᵉ foregoing Nonsense, but so Mysterious that I had
not yᵉ least Idea of the meaning of it— when I get yᵉ Explanation

A Page from the Drury Lane Account Books, 1750

The River Front of the Adelphi

You shall have it— the Haymarket goes on but heavily— the
Manager applies to Me for Prologues & Epilogues which I have
sent him—² but unless yᵉ Weather changes, all our Wits together
cannot furnish out a full house— his Majesty, God bless him, has
been twice or thrice, but the boxes were not full— Colman is
preparing his Comedy of *4* Acts call'd the *Suicide*, a very dangerous
Subject, but yᵉ Actors say, it must have great Success—³ the Actors
(entre nous) have been mistaken before now— We have at last
got rid of *Bowdens* & his wife— & have got an Excellent Gardener—
an Exchange which promises Comfort to the Hamptonians, & their
friends.

As You mention'd Vinegar with the Lady You most love &
honour, I suppose you may mean my Wife— I shall deliver Yᵉ
Over-flowings of yʳ heart to her in all yᵉ purity of Affection— I
cannot say, whether the *Wreath of Fashion* did as Much as yᵉ Author
& his friends Expected— There are very great promises, if the
res augusta domi⁴ does not nip his blossoms of fancy— I like Farren⁵
in the parts I have seen him Act— I have heard much of Miss
Walpole⁶ in yᵉ Widow Brady, but I have not yet seen her— my
theatrical curiosity diminishes daily & my Vanity as an Author is
quite extinct— tho by yᵉ bye I have written a copy of Verses to
Mʳ Baldwin the Member for Shropshire⁷ upon his attack upon Me
in yᵉ house of Commons— he complain'd that a celebrated Gentleman was admitted into the house when Everybody Else was
Excluded, & *that I gloried in my Situation* upon these last Words My
Muse has taken flight & with Success—⁸ I have describd the
different Speakers & it is said well & strong & true— I read them
to Lord North, Lord Gower, Lord Weymouth Mʳ Rigby &c & they
were all pleas'd, if I had time before I am oblig'd to send away
this long letter, you shall have yᵉ first copy, tho you must take care
Not to suffer them to go from yʳ own hands— I have, upon my word,
given them to nobody— Burke & Mʳ Townshend behav'd nobly
upon yᵉ Occasion yᵉ whole house groan'd at poor Baldwin, who is
reckon'd, par excellence, yᵉ dullest man in it— & a Question was
going to be put to give me an Exclusive priviledge to go in whenever I pleas'd— in short I am a much greater Man than I thought—

Whenever I receive Your Story⁹ I shall con it over most un-
mercifully— my Wife this Moment tells me that I must send You
a double portion of her Love & she has added that if the Vinegar
is but half as sharp as yʳ Pen or as yʳ temper is Sweet she shall be
most thankful for it— there's German wit for You— Sʳ Peter is

asleep in my desk but I shall wake him when you will least expect it— our Loves to all about You— Mes^rs Sheridan & Harris are very great Geniuses indeed they are Engag'd for no less than £100,000 a Crown or a Coffin, that is their Motto Please send them a good deliverance.[10]

I am a little thoughtful at my Situation with them, but not uneasy— my Security is tolerably good— I am sent for in a great hurry & therefore must tear myself away with assuring You that I am

Most affectionatly & faithfully Yrs

D Garrick.

Mad^le Fürst sends her Comp^ts

Source: FSL, draft; Roberts, *Hannah More*, I, 74f.

1. This draft has extensive deletions, and since it is impossible to determine how many of them were finally incorporated in the actual letter the text is given in full.

2. Among others, Garrick wrote the epilogue to Colman's *Suicide* (HM, July 11) and the prologue to Colman's alteration of Beaumont and Fletcher's *Bonduca* (HM, July 30).

3. Between July 11 and Sept. 16 it was played nineteen times at the Haymarket (Genest; see also Boaden, II, 313).

4. See Juvenal, *Satires*, iii, 164; Garrick's words are the end of the lines which, translated, run: "It is no easy matter, anywhere, for a man to rise when poverty stands in the way of his merits."

5. William Farren (1754–1795), a mediocre actor, had made his debut at Drury Lane during the season of 1775–76 and was to continue there until 1784 when he went to Covent Garden (*Thespian Dictionary*, 1805).

6. Charlotte Walpole (1758–1836), actress, had made her debut at Drury Lane on Oct. 2, 1777, where she became a great favorite. In 1779 she was to marry Edward Atkyns (*LC*, vol. XLII, Oct. 2–4, 1777, p. 332; Frédéric Barbey, *Madame Atkyns et la Prison du Temple*, Paris, 1905).

7. Charles Baldwyn, or Baldwin (1729–1801), of Kenlett, Worcester, M.P. for Shropshire 1766–1780.

8. While the occasion for this oft-repeated episode has not been found in the *Journal of the House of Commons* or in the parliamentary reports in the *London Chronicle*, there is no doubt that Davies, the source of all subsequent accounts, gives an erroneous date of spring 1777—the correction to the following spring being established by Garrick's letter. The parliamentary pother presumably took place in May, when on several occasions the debating became so sharp that Mr. Baldwin well may have wished to clear the gallery. "Mr. Burke rose, and appealed to the honourable Assembly, whether it could possibly be consistent with the rules of decency and liberality, to exclude from the hearing of their debates, a man to whom they all were obliged; one who was the great master of eloquence; in whose school they had all imbibed the art of speaking, and been taught the elements of rhetoric. For his part, he owned that he had been greatly indebted to his instruction. Much more he said in commendation of Mr. Garrick, and was warmly seconded by Mr. Fox and Mr. T. Townshend, who very copiously displayed the great merit of their old preceptor, as they termed him; they reprobated the motion of the gentleman with great warmth and indignation.

"The House almost unanimously concurred in exempting Mr. Garrick from the general order of quitting the gallery" (Davies, II, 359f.). Garrick's verses on Baldwin are printed in *Poetical Works* (II, 538f.).

9. Perhaps the plot outline for her tragedy *The Fatal Falsehood* (CG, May 6, 1779).

10. Under their management the Opera was unprofitable, and by Oct. 1780 £300 shares were selling for £250. In 1781 William Taylor bought them out (Walter Sichel, *Sheridan*, 1909, I, 529).

1185 To The Reverend Henry Bate

Lawford

Dear Bate.   Friday July 10th [1778][1]

George is worse to day & I have order'd my Coach to meet Us upon the road at Kelvedon[2] in order to be at home on Sunday Night— his Illness, ye great heat of ye Weather, & the not perfect State of the Camp[3] make me resolve to get thro' ye dusty road as fast and as Well as I can— George was better last Night, but he is much worse this Morning & we must of Course Shorten our Stay here—

I forgot in ye hurry of my last to thank You most kindly for the Wednesday's paper, which I enjoy'd, & put on some importance to have it a day sooner than Ordinary— I shew'd Y^r Letter, Which is a very good one to our Friend— You shall know what he said for we had much talk about it— if you have 5 Minutes to spare to give me Your opinion of the *Suicide*[4] directed to Me at the White Hart at Ingatestone,[5] I will send my Man for it— always supposing that it is Acted on Saturday, & that You write 3 lines after you have seen it— if You are in ye least hurried with Y^r Paper,[6] I must insist upon Your not indulging my foolish curiosity—

The Heat of ye Weather affected me much yesterday, & gave me a disagreeable fix'd pain in my head— all is well today, but George is so shabby that we are not in our wonted Spirits— the eternal Vivacity of our Right Honourable Host[7] disperses almost Every gloom— tho he is grave at George's illness— I write at this Moment upon ye Galop, as all hands are call'd upon to see a famous decoy he has on ye other Side ye Water so I must away.

Most truly & affect^y Yours

D: Garrick

Seal. Source: FSL.

1. Lawford in the dateline and the reference to *The Suicide* determine the year (see two preceding letters).

2. On the way to London.

3. Presumably the great camp at Warley Common, on the road from Mistley and Lawford to London, where troops, numbering about nine thousand men, were quartered in apprehension of a French invasion (*LC*, vol. XLIV, July 9–11, 1778, p. 39).

4. In a letter to Garrick of July 16, 1778, Bate remarked: "The *Suicide* has already *done it's do*, I fancy, for not a word is now spoke of it from one end of the town to the other" (FC; Boaden, II, 309).

5. On the way to London.

6. The *Morning Post*.

7. Rigby.

1186   To John Moody

Dear Moody.   July 16th 1778

Your letter is written with such a Sincerity of Expression, & as I am more willing that an Old friend should appear blameless than culpable, my Mind is again wholly turn'd in Your favour— at the same time let me fairly own that I thought Myself very greatly insulted, but the Evil in great part vanish'd with yr letter; tho I confess that I was surpris'd, after what I desir'd of You, that You would put ye draught into a Banker's hands, & tell other Persons of my folly, when I wish'd the transaction to be known (& You promis'd me very Solemnly it should be so) only to the Parties— I would have paid You at any time— however I have done with *Johnston* for Ever— I have begun to make his fortune, nor shall I tell Lord Sandwich of his Ingratitude to me, but he shall never Enter my doors again— they have deceiv'd me most egregiously & ungratefully— the Wife assur'd me, that you had accepted of an Assignment of his musical property, which was to be paid to You regularly, by the great Shop in Catharine Street— Why was I to be fool'd by such a Senseless Lye?— I am now only Sorry that such a fellow as Johnstone should draw me in to believe his protestations, & that any Person Should *know* of my folly but YrSelf—

As to Yr draught upon Sr C[harles] Asgyle[1] in favor of Lacy, I am at a loss what to say to him— He wants ye money & left me ye draught, wch by ye bye is faulty in many circumstances— I wish you would write to him, for Else He may think himself ill us'd by Us both—[2]

As You gave him a draught upon Sir Charles, why not send an

Order to yᵉ Same Banker to pay yᵉ sum to me upon my giving up
yᵉ other draught, & signing a Receipt for a hundred pounds for
the Use of Lacy— then all may be right, or if you would undertake
to pay Lacy, & let me have no more trouble with it, I should like
it much better.[3]

> I am Dʳ Sʳ Your most Obedᵗ humble Servᵗ
> & sincere Well wisher
> D: Garrick.

I am sorry yᵉ Bristol matters are not so Successful as I could wish
them— I am just return'd from Essex or I should have answer'd
yʳ letter sooner.

Address: To Mʳ Moody at the Theatre Royal at Bristol.   *Postmarked.   Source:*
FSL.

1. Sir Charles Asgill (d. 1788), of the firm of Asgill, Nightingale, and Nightingale at
70 Lombard St. (Frederick G. H. Price, *A Handbook of London Bankers*, 1876).
2. In a postscript to a letter to Garrick of July 24, Lacy wrote from Cork: "I took
the Liberty of requesting your Assistance relative to a Draught I received of Mʳ Moody
in part of the payment of Purchace of my Share in the Bris[tol] Theatre— I Would be
obliged if the Request made in the Letter was not agreeable that you will favor me with
that Draft or be so obliging to send it to Mʳ Moody, as in its present form it is not of any
Use to me" (FC).
3. See Letter 1190.

1187   To Richard Berenger[1]

My dear Sir   [*ante* July 22, 1778][2]
I am about marrying my nephew David & have not a moment
free from Lawyers &c— I am tired to Death, the Moment I am
clear of these incumbrances I will most certainly call upon you, &
tell you in Person what I tell you upon this Paper, that yʳ Imitation[3]
is a good one & many things excellent

> Ever yours in a Calm as a tempest
> DG

Source: George G. Fortescue, Esq., transcript; *The Manuscripts of J. B. Fortescue,*
Esq., Historical Manuscripts Commission, Report 13, Pt. 3, 1892, I, 151f.

1. So identified by the owner.

2. Written before the marriage of young David Garrick on July 22, 1778.

3. In a letter of April 1 Hannah More wrote Berenger thanking him for "one of the finest imitations of one of the finest Epistles of Horace" (see printed source, p. 160).

1188   To Frances Cadogan

My Dearest Second   Thursday [?July 23, 1778][1]
I write to you with my own hand that you may know I am better—

M[rs] Garrick's impudence of sending for D[r] Cadogan was unknown to me, & Nothing but her great fears to see me in such Agonies could have excus'd her—

I have got rid of two or three possessing Devils & the great Devil of 'Em all who has left me I hope Sulphur Brimstone & Sin but has taken the flesh & Spirit along with him too— I shall be well Enough to see you in a day or two or three & Expect Banquo's Ghost to appear in his pale-brown terrors before you— I would not frighten you if I could, but would always wish [to] give you a little flutter— this is Sentiment & y[e] only one, I have in Common with Boulter Roffey Esq[r][2]

Yours Ever & most Affect[y]

D. Garrick

This is y[e] first letter of any length I have written or attempted to write

Omnia vincit amor!

Source: Baker, p. 65f.

1. The conjectural date is derived from the reference to Mrs. Garrick's letter to Dr. Cadogan: on a Tuesday, July 21, she wrote him from Hampton urgently requesting his attendance on her husband, who had been taken ill the day before. Now from 1771, when the Garricks and Cadogans presumably first became acquainted, until Garrick's death, July 21 fell on a Tuesday only in 1772 and 1778; since Garrick was increasingly ill in the last two years of his life, 1778 is the more likely date for the Garricks' letters.

2. Except for the fact that a Boulter Roffey had a London house at No. 8, Upper Walpole Street in 1793, little is known about him (*Directory to the Nobility, Gentry, and Families of Distinction,* 1793; see also Lysons, II, 411; Boaden, II, 239).

1189   To The Countess Spencer

Hampton, July 26, 1778

Address: Lady Spencer.   *In the possession of the Earl Spencer: Not made available for publication.*

1190   To Willoughby Lacy

Dear Sir   Aug^st 5th 1778
I am now writing to You from a Sick room where I have been confin'd for some time, & I can scarce hold a pen to answer Y^r Obliging Letter—[1] I am rejoic'd that Y^r Matters hitherto have turn'd out so well— Mr Murphy bears a good Character, which will insure you good & Gentlemanlike usage from him— that Miss Younge is with You is a very agreeable Circumstance, for without a Woman the real & our Mock World are Nothing— pray when You present my best Wishes & Comp^ts to y^r Lady, don't forget to remember me kindly to Miss Younge— now to y^r Draught— I have got it Safe, & wrote to Moody— I sent it to Wallis, & desir'd him to pay ye Money, but he sent it back again & Said You gone to Ireland— Since that I wrote to Moody & paid him £70 for Johnson— I told him You wanted ye Money & if he would Send me another draught I would get it Accepted by Sr Charles Asgill, & remit You y^r Money directly for you wanted it— He sent me word he *would sell his Shirt,* but you should have it— I have heard to my surprise Nothing more from him, the moment I do, I will let you know— I told him I was ready to give up the other draught to his order— I beg'd he would send You ye Money to Cork but he told me he knew Nobody— ⟨In⟩ Short I am Sorry that I can give you no better an Acc^t— You m⟨ay⟩ be assur'd ye Draught W^ch he gave you without y^r Name in it, I will keep Safe for y^r Orders. I am too weak to say more but that
                I am D^r S^r Y^r most Sincere Well wisher & h^e S^t
                                        D Garrick

Address: To James Willoughby Lacy Esqr at the Theatre— Cork, Ireland. *Postmarks:* AV 6; [*illegible*] 10.   *Source:* HTC.

1. From Cork, July 24, 1778 (FC).

1191 To Lacy, Ford, Sheridan, and Linley[1]

Gentlemen   Saturday August 16th 1778[2]
The rudeness of Your letters Which is always the sign of a bad
Cause, I shall pass over with the Utmost contempt— but as You
have propos'd to my friend Mr Wallis & my Brother, an Arbitration,
I cannot as an honest Man refuse to meet you upon any Ground—
I therefore desire that Your Attorney will without delay in con-
currence wth Mr Wallis Settle & prepare this Matter, & that all
other Correspondence may cease between You &
                                            Y^r humble Servt
                                            D Garrick

Source: FC, draft; Boaden, II, 310.

1. The subject matter provides the identity of the recipients, though the heading
used is a legal fiction derived from Garrick's earlier letters: at this time Linley was dead
and Lacy was in Ireland.
2. Aug. 16, 1778, was actually a Sunday.

1192   To Joshua? Glover[1]

Dear S^r   Friday Aug^st 21st 1778
When in the most kind Manner You permitted me at ye Club to
raise the Wall for my conviency, I was aware that some difficulties
might arise,[2] & therefore would not go to Work (tho I had Every
thing ready) till you had talk'd with Mrs Glover— I am rather
Sorry that she is averse to me, beg oblig'd to You for that small
favour, as at ye worst, I can build the wall I want upon my own
ground, but rather chose that mutual Acts of kindness & good
fellowship should pass between Us—

I have, upon Your Acc^t & your Lady's kept the ground over against your house for some [time?] without yet receiving any thing for it, because I would not have M^r & Mrs Glover in ye least injur'd in their prospects— I have been offer'd `Money to build there, but I valu'd the Obliging my Neigbors at a greater price than Any I could get for ye Land in question.— It has been my greatest desire to live upon the most neigborly terms with a Gentleman & Lady whom I have much esteem'd.

I am Sr Your most hum^l Ser^t
D: G.

I had Company to breakfast or I should have sent this Sooner.

Source: FSL, draft.

1. Presumably the Joshua Glover (d. 1783) who is buried in the church at Hampton (Lysons, V, 82).
2. Glover had written Garrick on the same date: "Mr. Glover presents his comp^ts to Mr. Garrick on mentioning the Circumstance which he hinted at on Tuesday last of raising the Garden Wall to Mrs. Glover, she thinks as well as himself it will be a disagreeable object to the Windows of the Room, where she most frequently sits, as well as making the garden less airy, wch is already too much confin'd" (Sotheby, Catalogue, June 12–18, 1899).

1193 To Mary Hoare[1]

Aug. 25th, 1778

[My heart intended most sincerely that the inclos'd triffle should have been at Stourhead before your arrival there— but][2] Alas, you had not left us 12 hours before I was attacked with a most violent bilious disorder, which has left me so weak that my hand now trembles while I am writing this— so I may very justly cry out with Œdipus in Dryden's play of that name, "My hands are guilty but my heart is free!" I beg that you will present my respects to Mr. Hoare, and tell him that I now rejoice as much as I lamented before that I did not attend you to his paradise, for my illness like the devil of old, would have entered with me and disturbed the joys of it . . . I trust that your husband and my friend will find choice of eatables and drinkables, for in all the records I have searched, I never heard that any of the name of Hoare ever locked up their pantry or cellar. I will say nothing of news, you have it in the papers; and as Doctors differ whether it is good or bad, I will send you nothing equivocal; and, therefore, I shall finish with sending you my wife's and my love and warmest wishes . . .

D. Garrick for himself and wife

Source: J. Pearson & Co., Catalogue No. 11 [*ca.* 1890], Sotheby, Catalogue, June 12–19, 1899, extracts.

1. The recipient is so identified since both of the senior Mrs. Henry Hoares were dead by this time.
2. Matter enclosed in brackets is from the Sotheby Catalogue.

1194   To The Countess Spencer

August 27, 1778

Address: Countess Spencer. *In the possession of the Earl Spencer: Not made available for publication.*

1195   To Frances Cadogan[1]

My Dearest Second.   Sunday 6th of Sep^r [1778][2]
It was only this Morning at breakfast that the light of Conviction broke upon Me, as it did upon St Paul, & I discoverd for the first Moment to whom I was indebted for ye most charming imitation of Horace— O You Wretched Creature! & so you would not tell Me or my Wife?— how could you keep such delightful flattery a Secret, for it has doubled in value, since I know ye hand that administer'd it— the Moment we can return from Hampshire I will give you Notice, & will send the Coach for You— I hope we shall be with you soon enough to take you on Y^r Way to Farnborough & I hope we shall catch you & keep you at your return—

Ever & most affect^y Y^{rs}
D. Garrick

Love to ye D^r. I will write to You from Lord Palmerston's— I am better but n[ot] quite the very th[ing].

Source: Baker, p. 72.

1. So identified in the source.
2. The year is from Mrs. Garrick's note, written on Garrick's letter, saying that they hope to see Miss Cadogan on their return from Hampshire about Sept. 21, 1778.

1196   To Joseph Cradock

Adelphi

Dear Sir

Sepr 14th 1778

You must have heard before this of a violent bilious Attack Which almost renders me incapable of reading, writing or judging— I am, like a State Prisoner, debarr'd the Use of Pen, Ink & paper— I am going into Hampshire for Change of Air, & thence, if I recover but slowly, to Bath— so that my Stay there or Absence from Town will prevent for Some time my Even Seeing a Theatre— indeed, Sir, I am grown unfit for any thing, but sitting in a great chair, or walking, or rather at present, creeping about my Garden— the least business Agitates Me, & My Friends of the Faculty have order'd me Abstinence from all theatrical Matters— I have not seen Sheridan but once since the Death of poor Linley—[1] He call'd Yesterday, & I was out to take the Air— I had promis'd to write him a little Triffle for his opening,[2] but I found myself so unfit for scribbling that, for ye first time, I gave up the business, & was brought in (like ye Tars who are admitted into Greenwich Hospital)[3] *disabled*. As I can only pray for You, be assur'd that You shall have my prayers for Your Success—[4] should I be in Town, & able to attend ye Theatre I will certainly be there—

I am Most truly Y^r Oblig'd hu^le Ser^t

D: Garrick.

Address: J: Cradock Esqr at Gumly-Hall, Market-Harborough, Leicestershire. *Postmarked. Source:* FSL; Joseph Cradock, *The Czar*, 1824, p. viii.

1. Thomas Linley had drowned on Aug. 5.
2. Sept. 17.

3. Established in 1690, with buildings on Crown land by Wren and Vanbrugh, for disabled and old seamen.

4. Of Cradock's *The Czar*, which, however, was never performed.

1197   To The Countess Spencer

Hampton, September 14, 1778

Address: Lady Spencer. *In the possession of the Earl Spencer: Not made available for publication.*

1198   To Frances Cadogan[1]

Broadlands near Romsay— Lord Palmerston's seat
My Dear Madam   Sepr 21st 1778
I must answer Your most friendly affectionate Letter immediatly, tho You would Willingly excuse Me, & indeed, I am always ready to most of my Correspondents to lay hold of any Excuse to be idle— but Were I flannel'd & Muffled with ye Gout, tormented with a Worse disorder & roaring in my bed, I would say something to please Myself be the consequence what it would to my dear Second— I return the Young Man's letter, which is very Sensibly Written, but we have had Accounts as late as ye 6th of August, which gives a more favourable Account of Matters— I am afraid, by what I have learnt here that, while he is in ye American Service, & Lord Howe,[2] Commander of ye Whole, He must remain as he is— for Lord Howe will not let any preferment take place even by ye first Lord of the Ad[miralt]y without his approbation— his Lordship is very jealous of that part of his Office, &, I hear, made it one of his Chief Conditions when he Accepted of the Command— however I will seek farther before I give up Anything, on which You & my dear D^r have set Your hearts— pray let Your Worthy Father know that I feel in *my heart of Heart* all the kind Expressions of his Love & Affection to me, but My health would be of very little Service to me, if I was to purchase it at ye Price of his being

Shot for a deserter;[3] unless indeed before the Cap was pull'd over his Eyes, He would repent of the manifold Sins he has Committed against the God of my Idolatry— Shakespear!— *Him him! He is the Him!*— there is no Other.

My Love I beseech you to all where You are, pray tell 'Em, We will call in our return to take a kiss & away— As there will be no Turkey-pouts & ducklings, and the Weather too hot for pig, I shall make ye best of my Way home— & tell 'Em likewise I have answer'd the precious Cicester Gazette for which I thank them most sincerely— Lady Bathurst will let Em know what a poor figure I make against Such an Army of Wits, Virtues, Youth, & Beauties,—[4] We expect to leave this place in about 8 or 10 days—

My Wife Sends her Warmest Love— We are very happy here— a good host a Sweet place & warm Wellcome—

Most Affectionatly & truly y^{rs}

D: Garrick.

PS. pray when You write to Miss Griffith let her know, if I could have answer'd her flattering Lines as they deserve she should have heard from Me, but I cannot yet Write as I ought, so she must accept my best thanks, till I can have strength to mount my Pegasus—

Source: FSL; Baker, p. 72f.

1. So identified in the printed source.
2. Richard Howe (1726–1799), fourth Viscount Howe (1758), was from Feb. 1776 to Sept. 25, 1778, Commander-in-Chief of the British naval forces in North America. He was to resign his command out of discontent with the conduct of the war.
3. Cadogan was at this time acting as one of the doctors at the army camp on Warley Common (Boaden, II, 313).
4. From Cirencester, Gloucestershire, the Bathursts' country seat, Garrick had received a joint letter from the Bathursts and Wilmots expressing in various ways their "very sincere regard and esteem" for him. His reply, now lost, acknowledged by Lady Bathurst on Sept. 28 (Boaden, II, 314), must have included the following verses: "Upon reading the Cicester Gazette: Extempore"

> Youth, Beauty, & Virtue, can men desire more,
> In the shape of six females, well worth any score,
> Have sent me a letter Each word gives delight,
> That wth. pride & with pleasure my head is turned quite
> To be thus distinguished, no torment I dread:
> For an honour like this, I'd again be half-dead:
> But think ye, kind fate, I'm a gainer by this?
> Excess, is destructive, of pain or of bliss—
> And what is the consequence? sad, very sad—
> Tho cured of my illness, I am now stark mad!

(Sotheby, Catalogue, June 19, 1928, p. 47).

1199 ## To Hannah More

Broadlands

My Dear Nine, [*post* September 24, 1778][1]
I have been half-dead, and thought I should never see you more.
I took care of your property,[2] and have shown my love to you by a
trifling legacy—[3] but that is at present deferred; and if our friendship is like that of some other persons, we may, in a little time, smile
and shake hands, and backbite each other as genteelly as the best
of them. *Sat sapienti.*

I am at the sweet seat of Lord Palmerston, called Broadlands,
near Romsey, in Hampshire, and again growing fat, and over-
flowing with spirits. I was really so ill that I could not write a letter
but with pain. I am not suffered to write or read; therefore I am
now pleasing myself by stealth.

Your friend the Dean of Gloucester has most kindly sent me his
book against Locke and his followers.[4] I have read it with care,
and like it, some few trifling matters excepted; but I cannot be
conceited enough to make my objections in the margin of his book.
What shall I do? You are, I suppose, in the same predicament.[5]

If you will read the last Monthly Review, you will see an article
upon the *Wreath of Fashion*, which has been much approved; and,
what is more surprising, has revived the sale of the poem very
briskly. A word in your ear— but be secret for your life— I wrote it.

Source: Roberts, *Hannah More*, I, 75.

1. While the date given in the source is 1777, a correction to the approximate date
given here is determined by the reference to Garrick's will and by the fact that Miss
More's reply is dated Oct. 10, 1778 (FC; Boaden, II, 314f.).

2. This may refer to a reinvesting of the proceeds from *Percy*, amounting to nearly
£600, which Garrick in March had originally put into securities (Roberts, *Hannah More*,
I, 87).

3. Garrick's last will, dated Sept. 24, 1778, is witnessed by Palmerston, George
Poyntz Ricketts, and Mrs. Ricketts. While it contains no bequests to intimate friends,
they must have been made through an understanding with Mrs. Garrick (see Appendix G).

4. *The Notions of Mr. Locke and His Followers Considered and Examined*, privately printed
and circulated in 1778, by Josiah Tucker (1712–1799), D.D. 1755, Dean of Gloucester
1758 (*Josiah Tucker, A Selection from His Economic and Political Writings*, ed. Robert Schuyler,
New York, 1931, p. 41).

5. In her reply Miss More wrote: "If you, my dear Sir, are at a loss about marginal
notes in the Dean of Gloucester's Book, what must I be? I have told him about your
delicacy and your scruples, and he will be greatly hurt and disappointed, if you do not
criticize" (FC; Boaden, II, 315).

1200   To The Earl of Sandwich

                                                Broadlands Lord Palmerston's
My good Lord   Sept yᵉ 28ᵗʰ 1778
I shall be in London in about a week's time & then I shall be very
explicit indeed with Mʳ William Augustus Miles— there never sure
was so impudent a fellow— he leaves his Purser-ship to be come an
Agent to yᵉ Newfoundland Merchants!—¹ I have had no letter or
Note from him— I believe he would chuse to avoid me, as I speak
my mind very plainly to him, & will, yᵉ moment I get to Town—
Mʳ Bates² has great power over him, I wish he would assist me to
pare the Scribbling claws of this foolish fellow— I will certainly
set about it the first moment I am within reach of him— I cannot
express to your Lordship what I feel upon this occasion, but upon
all occasions, I am
         My Lord Yʳ Lordships Most Oblig'd & Obedient Servᵗ
                                                D. Garrick.

I beg my best Compᵗˢ to Miss Ray.³

Source: Earl of Sandwich, transcript.

   1. Miles, however, did not leave the navy until 1782.
   2. Joah Bates, at this time Commissioner of the Victualling Office, to which post
he had been appointed in 1776 through Sandwich's influence.
   3. Martha Ray (1745–1779), Sandwich's mistress. She was to be murdered by the
Rev. James Hackman, a jealous lover.

1201   To Ralph Griffiths¹

My dear Sʳ   [October 19, 1778]²
I shall think no pains I take for You disagreeable, & I shall be really
happy to shew my regard & attachment to you— I wrote the
Article³ at Hampton, where I could not look into More's fables,⁴
but I had made myself Master of that matter before I had yᵉ
pleasure of yʳ letter—
   I have spoken of Brooke as a good Man,⁵ I wish you would cast
yʳ Eye upon a Note in yᵉ 2ᵈ Vol of yᵉ Batchelor⁶ which our Friend

Becket will send you, & tho I allow much to party resentment yet sure there cannot be so open & dreadful an attack upon a Man's Character without some little foundation— the authors of that Note are respectable men & Wits, how far their last Character have affected the first I cannot tell— if you think any Note necessary pray insert it, & I beg that You will never give Y^{r}Self ye trouble to send proofs of my stuff to me, unless you may have some doubts— I shall Endeavor to do something better for y^r next— this Article has, I fear, got a little of the Weakness, wch troubled me at ye time of writing it.

> I am Dr Sr Most sincerely Yours
> D Garrick.

Source: BM; John P. Collier, *An Old Man's Diary*, 1871, pt. II, p. 46.

1. From the references to Garrick's review of Brooke, the recipient is identified as Ralph Griffiths, the editor of the *Monthly Review* in which the article appeared.

2. The date is from the printed source, and is supported by the reference to Garrick's review.

3. A review of Henry Brooke's *A Collection of Pieces* (1778) which Garrick wrote for the *Monthly Review* (vol. LIX, Oct. 1778, p. 241f., Nov., p. 357f.; Benjamin C. Nangle, *The Monthly Review, First Series, 1749–1789, Indexes*, Oxford, 1934, p. 67).

4. Three of Brooke's pieces had been included in *Fables for the Female Sex*, published in 1744 by Edward Moore.

5. Henry Brooke. Garrick had known him in Ireland in 1741, when he had been much impressed by Brooke's plays.

6. "The Batchelor; or, Speculations of Jeoffrey Wagstaffe," a series of essays appearing in the *Dublin Mercury* from 1767 to 1772, while published anonymously was actually the work of John Courtenay, Robert Jephson, and the Rev. Francis Burroughs. *Select Essays from the Batchelor* (Dublin, 1772) was reprinted, with additions, by Thomas Becket in 1773 in Dublin and London as *Essays from the Batchelor*. The attack which distressed Garrick is contained in the second volume in a long poem, with many annotations, called "An Epistle to Gorges Edmond Howard," part of which runs:

> Next maudlin B——ke, whose novels please,
> Like some old dotard's reveries,
> Without beginning, middle, ending,
> To *utile* or dulce tending.
> With equal art, his genius pliant
> Can drain a bog, or *quell a giant*.
> Whilst one hand wounds each venal brother,
> He for a bribe extends the other.

1202   To Richard Cox

My dear Richard   [*ante October 21, 1778*]
I was near You three Weeks ago,[1] & heard by a friend of yours that
you were at Mr Drummond's—[2] since then, I have been very ill
indeed, and am return'd hither to rest & recruit if possible my
Shatter'd carcass— I had no sooner got rid of the Stone, but I was
attack'd at Mr Stanley's[3] with the Bile, & underwent the torment
of Martyrs. I am now a Yellow beauty & the Stream of Pactolus[4]
which they say is got into my Pocket, has now mounted into my
face, & that Nothing but Bath will restore me to my Lilies & roses:
a Physician from Warley Common, no less than ye great Cadogan,
thinks he can mend my Complexion by that royal beautifying Fluid
the Thames; & here I am Swallowing pills every 4 hours by the
River side— this is my real Situation, & as I am at your Command,
& ready to stay or go, as you please to direct Me, give me but three
Lines with your Sign Manual, & I will most implicitly Obey You—
Non sum qualis eram—[5] nor do I think myself yet worthy of the
Joys of Quarley, & your Company, but I am better, & never so
well as when I can laugh with you— Mrs Garrick says that I shall be
a Madman to trouble You, as I am, & you no better to receive Me—
but as she is a true German, & thinks no Person Well, that can't
Eat like an Emperor, & drink like a Fish, her fears go for Nothing—
You are in this Matter to be my commanding officer & say *March*,
or *halt*—

                 My dear Sir Ever & most truly Yours
                                          D Garrick

our best Comp^ts attend Mrs Cox— I sent to your Son[6] in Craig's
Court[7] but I find he is with You— If you will be pleas'd to send me
Your Commands in a gentle Manner, & suited to ye present con-
dition of my Nerves, I shall receive them at ye Adelphi, I shall be
there on Friday & Saturday to meet my Doctor— I was within an
Inch of Kingdom come at Mr Stanley's.

Address: Richard Cox Esqr at Quarly near Andover, Hants. *Endorsement:*
Mr Garrick with^t date written a few weeks before his death. 1778. *Postmarks:*
OC 21; OC 22. *Source:* HTC.

1. The approximate date is indicated by the postmark and by Garrick's statement
that three weeks earlier he "was near" Cox: Garrick had been at Broadlands and Cox
at Quarley Manor (a country seat inherited from his father in 1757) both being near

Winchester where on Sept. 29, 1778, Garrick had seen the King review the troops (*LC*, vol. XLIV, Sept. 29–Oct. 1, 1778, p. 319; Boaden, II, 315).

2. Henry Drummond (d. 1795), banker, of Grange Park, Hampshire, had formerly been Cox's partner (*GM*, vol. XLV, June 1795, p. 535).

3. Hans Stanley's country seat, Paultons, was close by Broadlands (see Boaden, II, 270f.).

4. Where Midas had washed and the sands turned to gold.

5. Horace, *Odes*, IV, i, 3: "I am not as I was."

6. Richard Bethel Cox (1753–1832) was to become a partner in his father's business in 1779 (*GM*, vol. CII, Sept. 1832, p. 285; Frederick G. H. Price, *A Handbook of London Bankers*, 1876).

7. The office of Cox's firm in Charing Cross (*ibid.*).

1203   To Richard Cox

My dear Friend   Octr the 28th— [1778]
damn all ye Cooks good & bad for I feel them at this Moment—
I eat Nothing but plain boil'd & roast; & bread & Cheese, a clean
Cloth, & good Small beer with Company I like, are preferable to
any dainties in Frigid form & unsocial parade: Ergo Master
Richard— my heart & Soul cry Hey to Quarley; but a little nasty
creeping ungenerous, fever pulls me back & cries— stay at home, &
take y^r Physick quiet[l]y, & don't make an Hospital of Your Friend's
House—

Keep house cries Prudence— tender Love says nay—

In short the Misery I felt at Lord Palmerston's & Mr Stanley's, for
I kept my bed at both places, & at the last, I never thought myself
so near Kingdom come— I am advis'd to be at rest at Hampton for
some time— however if my fever gives way to the prescriptions I
have this day got, & am to Swallow for a fortnight to come, you
may depend upon my going where I know I shall be most wellcome— Madam who wishes most ardently to pay her respects to
Mrs Cox, & Enjoy ye Keen air of ye downs, has put in her Caveat
back'd by my Physician, against my leaving Hampton directly—[1]

Should the Fates be in good humour & y^r humble Servt in Spirits,
I will have a view hollow after the little Harriers, that I will—

I pray for ye best, & live in Hope—

                Ever Yours my dear Richd Most affect^y
                           D. Garrick

Madam sends her Love wth Mine to Madam—

Address: Richd Cox Esqr at Quarley near Andover, Hants. *Postmark:* OC 29.
Endorsement: Mr Garrick Octr 28th 1778. *Source:* HTC.

1. Mrs. Garrick wrote of her husband to Cox on the same day: "I am very much alarmed, for fear he should fall ill again, and as I know that nothing will hinder him from fulfiling his promise but your absolute Coṁand to the contrary, I Beg you will put him off to an other season. I saw him write to you to day but do not know the contents" (HTC).

1204 To Richard Brinsley Sheridan[1]

Dear S^r

Thursday Night almost Eleven
[October 29, 1778][2]

You must oblige Me wth the sight of Fielding's Play or it will be impossible for me to write an Epilogue,[3] which I suppose you intend for Miss Young[4]

pray assure Your Father, that I meant not to interfere in his department; I imagin'd (foolishly indeed) that my attending Bannister's[5] rehearsal of the part I once play'd, & wch y^r Father never saw,[6] might have assisted ye Cause, without giving ye least offence— I love my Ease too well, to be thought an Interloper, & I should not have been impertinent enough to have attended any Rehearsal, had not *You* Sir in a very particular manner desir'd me—

however upon no Consideration will I Ever interfere again in this business, nor be liable to receive such another Message as was brought me this Evening b⟨y⟩ Young Bannister

You must not imagine that I write this in a pet, let me assure You upon my honour that I am in perfect peace with You all, & wish You from my heart, all that Yours can wish.

Ever & very Sincerely Yours
D Garrick

I was well diverted to Night at Cov^t Garden with three hours after Marriage[7] wch I never saw before— it is well acted & very entertaining— I was likewise glad to see a good house—

Source: FC, draft; Boaden, II, 357.

1. Sheridan is identified as the recipient by the reference to the preparations for the production of Fielding's play, which was to appear at Drury Lane under his management, and by the apparent reference to his father's supervision of the rehearsals at Drury Lane.
2. The date is determined by the reference to *Three Hours after Marriage.*

3. Garrick contributed the prologue, spoken by King, as well as the epilogue spoken by Miss Younge to *The Fathers; or, The Good Natur'd Man* (DL, Nov. 30, 1778; Knapp, Nos. 313, 314).

4. *Deletion*: "I was at home till near half after two & then oblig'd to go out upon very particular business for half an hour.

"You are an Idle Gentleman."

5. John Bannister (1760–1836), actor, was to make his debut at Drury Lane on Nov. 11, 1778, as Zaphna in James Miller and John Hoadly's *Mahomet the Imposter*, a part which Garrick had created at Drury Lane on April 25, 1744.

6. A reminder that Thomas Sheridan had been forced out of the management of the Royal Theatre, Dublin, because of the riots there occasioned by the revival of *Mahomet* on March 2, 1754 (Walter Sichel, *Sheridan*, 1909, I, 237f.).

7. Garrick has confused the title of Arthur Murphy's comedy, *Three Weeks after Marriage* (CG, March 30, 1776), which was played at Covent Garden on Thursday, Oct. 29, 1778 (*LC*, vol. XLIV, Oct. 27–29, 1778, p. 416), with that of Gay, Pope, and Addison's *Three Hours after Marriage* (1717).

1205   To William Augustus Miles

Octr 30. 1778

Mr Garrick begs once for all that Mr Miles will not imagine that he wishes him to decline any thing which may produce him any Emolument— he meant in his letter to his Brother to say, that he thought Mr Miles's logic very erroneous— As Mr Garrick has it not in his power to serve Mr Miles more than he has done, he would not in the least dissuade him from doing his best to provide for his family with credit & reputation—[1] At the same time he would have him recollect that it is impossible for any Friend to behave with more generosity & kindness to him than Lord Sandwich has.

Source: FC, copy.

1. The gap in the Garrick–Miles correspondence between Garrick's letter of May 12, 1778, in which he was incensed at Miles, and this letter is partially bridged by two undated letters which Miles seems to have written Garrick within this period (FC). They reveal that Miles was attempting to sell his writing in order to support his family.

1206   To Elizabeth Younge

My dear Young.   Saturday— [?October 31, 1778][1]
If You are to speak the Epilogue to Fielding's play (as I suppose
You are) I will do my best Endeavors to produce Something that
shall neither discredit You or Your

humble Serv[t]
D: Garrick

I will call upon You at y[r] own house when I have done it—

Address: Miss Younge.   *Seal.*   *Source:* FSL.

   1. Conjecturally written on the Saturday following Garrick's letter to Sheridan of
Thursday night [Oct. 29, 1778], in which he discusses his agreement to provide Miss
Younge with an epilogue for Fielding's *The Fathers.*

1207   To The Countess Spencer

Adelphi, November 14, 1778

   Address: Lady Spencer.   *In the possession of the Earl Spencer: Not made available
for publication.*

1208   To The Countess Spencer

Hampton, November 17, 1778
[Epitomized in the Historical Manuscripts Commission Report as
follows: "Have just finished the prologue to Henry Fielding's long
lost comedy;[1] it was given over for gone by the family, but it fell
into my hands after 25 years' absence; it is to be acted on next
Saturday se'nnight."—Report 2, Appendix (1874), p. 13.]

   Address: Lady Spencer.   *In the possession of the Earl Spencer: Not made available
for publication.*

   1. *The Fathers; or, The Good Natur'd Man.*

1209   To Hannah More

                                                    Hampton
My Dear Madam   Novr 23^d 1778
I have read the three Acts[1] & laid them by, & to them again— there
are some Objections, which may be alter'd when we Meet, & can
read them together: the two next Acts must determine of the
former three— there are some Abrupt Endings of ye Acts or rather
Scenes, & I think ye Scene, wch sh^d be capital between *Rivers* &
Orlando in ye 3^d Act not yet warm enough— the last should inquire
whether some Intelligence about his Family, or some female Connection may not lie heavy upon his Mind— Why sh^d he doubt of his
Father's Consent for his union wth *Emiline*? If that had been mark'd
or known before it would have done; & perhaps the Father's
Objecting to marry his Daughter to a stranger &c might be an
addition to the Fable— however do not alter till I have consider'd
ye whole— You have good time before you, & we will turn it
about in our Minds with Advantage— from the Father's Objections
might arise some good Scenes between the Son & him, & y^e
Daughter & him— then indeed *Rivers* might mistake, & *Orlando*
being afraid to tell, might create an animated Scene and more
confusion— but let it alone till I see ye Whole— I have been very
ill with a Cold & Cough wch tear my head & breast to pieces— has
the Sincere, little, very little Gentleman[2] deign'd to visit you— I
have had such proofs of his insincerity to me upon many Occasions
that I am more astonish'd, than displeas'd at his Conduct—
Mrs *Cholomondeley*[3] gave him a fine Dressing at Sr Jos[hua] Reynold's.
He was quite pale & distress'd for ye Whole Company took my
Part— among other friendly Matters— he said, that it was no
Wonder, Wits were severe upon Me, for that I was always Striking
wth ye keen Edge of Satire all that came in my Way— Mrs C. said
*it was ye reverse of my Character & that I was ye gayest Companion without
Malignity— nay, that I was too prudish, & carry'd my dislike of Satire too
far, & that, she was surpris'd to hear a particular Friend of Mine so
Mistake Me so*— this was a dagger— for all were against him— but
let us brush this Cobweb from our thoughts— I have sent some
Nonsense to the Arab—[4] dull truth without Poetry— I forgot her
Christian name, so have given the Mahometan one:
    I wish I could have written better verses for her book, & prov'd

a little better title to my Place than I have done— I have finish'd
my prol: & Epil: for Fielding's play, & have been very lucky— I
have in yᵉ first introduced the Characters in *Tom Jones* & *Joseph
Andrews* pleading at yᵉ Bar of yᵉ Publick for yᵉ Play— it is really
tolerably done— would have sent it, had I written Copy— say
nothing about it—

Yours my dearest Nine at all Times & in all places

D. Garrick

Madam wraps her Love up with Mine to keep it warm, for you, &
your Sisters—

Source: Baker, p. 103f.

1. The first three acts of Miss More's *Fatal Falsehood*, so identified by the references
to the same characters here and in her letter of Oct. 10 (Boaden, II, 315).
2. Hannah More had referred to Colman as "our little friend" and the "little bard"
(Boaden, II, 313, 315).
3. Mary ("Polly") Woffington (1730?–1811), younger sister of Peg, had married
in 1745 Capt. Robert Cholmondeley. According to Farington, before her marriage
Mrs. Cholmondeley "was on the stage for a season, but did not succeed . . . She has
borne the character of a wit, & having sufficient confidence has been much in the world"
(*GM*, vol. LXXXI, April 1811, p. 403; Joseph Farington, *The Farington Diary*, ed. James
Grieg, 1924, I, 141).
4. A nickname for one of Hannah More's sisters (see Boaden, II, 243).

1210   To Curtius[1]

Hampton

Sir   Novʳ 24ᵗʰ 1778

Tho it is not customary to answer letters written in a disguis'd
hand, & with an assum'd Signature,[2] yet I shall pay Curtius a
Compliment, in return for his, to trust Myself with him in Spite of
that *horrid timidity* which, with as little justice, as politeness he has
attributed to Me— there is such a mixture of harsh language with
a Seeming regard for me, that I am at a loss to guess, how I could
deserve the first, & yet be favour'd with the last:

*Curtius says, that He can praise, as well as blame— his resentment has no
rancour— and yet— I am to blacken under his Pen, & my Nature must be
humbled to the dust*: how can these Matters be reconcil'd?— does
Curtius really think of Me as he writes; I hope, I believe not,— for

12+L.D.G. III

If I am not mistaken this terrible, most abominable Culprit has receiv'd some marks of good Will from his present Accuser— Would not Curtius laugh at Me, should I take any Notice of the *Spies* & *Flatterers* which he has made part of my present retinue?— no Flattery has reach'd My retirement, but that, in which Curtius seems to join with Others— viz— the praise of my talents as an Actor— Now, Sir, for the friendly part of Your letter—

You kindly offer *to send me a fair Copy of the three letters*, written purposely against Me, *and if I can obviate some of the heap of Charges against Me, they shall be expung'd from a publication, which, it is conceiv'd, shall travel to futurity, wth the mistaken Character It analyzes.*— Will Curtius take the Word of the Person Accus'd for his Innocence? He cannot surely do it: nor can M^r G: Obviate any charge against him in this Way— But if Curtius is sincere in his exclamation— (*Would to God that it was not necessary to Enrol the downfal of Roscius in the List of his Victories*) He will, he ought to inquire after the Character, not from idle reports, from malicious or disappointed Men, Nor from Roscius himself (as you are pleas'd to call him) but from those who have known him long, & will speak of him, Nothing extenuating, or setting down ought in Malice:[3] do this *Calmly*, *assiduously*, & *impartially*, & then Spar⟨e⟩ or give no Quarter (as Truth will warrant) from the Stage to the State— from the lowest Note to the top of the Compass

All, all but truth drops still-born from ye press![4]

by saying thus much frankly, I hope that Curtius will not think himself treated disrespectfully for *his* Frankness— I will honestly assure You, that I had much rather have Your praise, than Your blame; but I would as much scorn to obtain It meanly, as You would scorn to grant it— I will likewise honestly assure You, that the *horrid timidity*, you Accuse Me of, will not be in ye least alarm'd tho the Pen of Curtius was to drop It's gall to morrow upon the private Character of

Your very humble S^t
D Garrick—

The letters, as You seem to desire, & I would wish, shall never be seen by any Eyes but Curtius's & my own,— as far as that power is in Me—[5]

this answer should have been sent sooner, had not I been from home for some days—

Endorsement by Garrick: Curtius and Answer. *Source:* FC, copy; Boaden, II, 321.

1. The pseudonym used by William Jackson to sign a series of letters appearing at this time in the *Public Ledger* (John Taylor, *Records of My Life*, 1832, II, 327f.). William Jackson (1737?–1795), a clergyman, was a friend and supporter of the Duchess of Kingston, and was an editor of the *Public Ledger*. Foote had satirized him as Dr. Viper in *The Capuchin*, declaring in the second act that as the "doer of the Scandalous Chronicle" he had "mow'd down reputations like muck." In the summer of 1778 Jackson had printed in his paper several articles, the authorship of which he disclaimed, attacking Garrick; when Garrick had complained to their common friend Dr. Isaac Schomberg, Jackson had promised on Aug. 28 that nothing more of the sort would appear (Boaden, II, 310).
2. Boaden, II, 318f.
3. Cf. *Othello*, V, ii, 342f.
4. Alexander Pope, *Epilogue to the Satires* (1738), Dialogue II, line 226.
5. On Dec. 31 "Curtius" was to write Garrick that "Taken up by a duty to the *political Soverign*, he hath been oblig'd to defer that which he owes to the *theatrical Potentate*"; and on Jan. 12, 1779, he again wrote, saying that he had heard of the actor's illness and would withhold his attack until Garrick was "in a State of body to *answer* any public Charges" (FC; Boaden, II, 327, 330).

1211   To The Countess Spencer

Hampton, November 24, 1778
[Epitomized in the Historical Manuscripts Commission Report as follows: "The new comedy[1] will not be ready for next Saturday."—Report 2, Appendix (1874), p. 13.]

Address: Lady Spencer. *In the possession of the Earl Spencer: Not made available for publication.*

1. *The Fathers.*

1212   To The Countess Spencer

Hampton, December 8, 1778

Address: Lady Spencer. *In the possession of the Earl Spencer: Not made available for publication.*

1213 To Jessé Foot[1]

Hampton
Dear Sir,   Dec. 22, 1778
I shall obey your commands with great pleasure, but I am afraid
my journey into Northamptonshire, to Lord Spencer's, which is
only deferred on account of a slight attack of the gout, will prevent
my reading your play till my return from thence.

I must desire you not to say anything of my reading your piece,
as I have refused to peruse many, which have been sent even by
friends.

I am, Sir, Your most obedient Servant
David Garrick

Address: To Jessé Foot, Esq. Salisbury Street.   *Source:* Foot, *Murphy*, p. 330f.

1. Jessé Foot (1744–1826), surgeon and writer, had at about this time begun practice
in Salisbury Street, the Strand, after having served as house surgeon to the Middlesex
Hospital for a number of years.

1214 To The Countess Spencer

Hampton, December 23, 1778

Address: Countess Spencer.   *In the possession of the Earl Spencer: Not made
available for publication.*

1215 To Thomas Becket

Hampton
Dear B.   Xmas Eve [1778]
I believe the Devil has got into my family at yᵉ Adelphi— We left
yᵉ maid Well, & now she is possess'd wᵗʰ a hundred Devils— I hope

to lay them all on Saturday Morning— You surprise me much about *Andrew*, but say Nothing till I come— it must not be— he Mistakes a little my Meaning— if (as he thought) Y^r Staying in y^r present would make things worse, I am most certainly for y^r going away, as you ought to have done— but if without detriment & palaver, You can Stay to Your advantage— He must be ye Devil of a Friend, who w^d advise You to ye Contrary—[1] I am not yet acquainted with ye particulars, & I know, that you warp Matters to your own Inclination, more than y^r Interest:

I hope this is not ye Case now, & then, Who will say nay— Andrew must not leave You—[2] He is a very, very honest Sensible fellow or I am much deceiv'd—

Yours Ever &c
D G

pray will You see my Man Thomas[3] tonight & write a Line for him, or if *you* are Engag'd *Andrew* will, for I want Some intelligence & my Papers by ye Morning Coach tomorrow.

Address: Mr Becket, Adelphi.　*Seal.*　*Endorsement:* 24th Decr 1778. Mr David Garrick to Mr Thos Becket.　*Source:* FSL.

1. Apparently because of his financial difficulties Becket was contemplating leaving the Adelphi, but not until 1782 did he move to Pall Mall (John Taylor, *Records of My Life*, 1832, I, 384).

2. "When reminded of business, to which his father paid unremitting attention . . . [Andrew] consoled himself with the prospect which Garrick's encouragement had held out, of being able, in due time, to take a final leave of the 'weighty affairs of the Strand,' and to fix his abode in the more congenial . . . regions of Parnassus" (Andrew Becket, *Dramatic and Prose Miscellanies*, ed. William Beattie, 1838, I, xiiif.).

3. Presumably the "Thomas Wakeman Servt to Mr Garrick" who was a witness to young David Garrick's marriage settlement.

1216　　To The Countess Spencer

Hampton, December 26, 1778

Address: Lady Spencer.　*In the possession of the Earl Spencer: Not made available for publication.*

1217 To The Reverend Doctor Joseph Warton

Adelphi

My dear Sir,   Dec. 29th, 177[8][1]

It gives me great concern that I am prevented by a slight attack of the gout from waiting upon you; and as I am obliged to post away into Northamptonshire, where I ought to have been on the 22d, I shall lose the sincere pleasure I have always in your company, till your next return to London, when I hope Mrs. Warton[2] will attend you, and make Mrs. Garrick and me happy.— Mr. Gibbon called upon me, and has tantaliz'd me, by saying I might have met you to dinner at his house[3] Friday or Saturday next: I will take care for the future not to meet with these mortifications: could I possibly have sent another excuse to the most amiable of women, Lady Spencer, I should have been tempted by that devil, Gibbon, who greatly allured me from my allegiance by the mention of you—[4] but I have very philosophically withstood his snares, and shall set off for Althorp to-morrow morning at eight o'clock.— The warmest and most affectionate wishes of the season are most devoutly sent to you and dear Mrs. Warton, from the hearts of the Garricks.

Ever and most affectionately yours,

D. Garrick.

I hope your lady got her flower-roots.

Source: John Wooll, *Biographical Memoirs of the Reverend Joseph Warton*, 1806, p. 388f.

1. Obviously misdated 1779 in the source, since Garrick was dead by that time; the correct year is supplied by Lady Spencer's letter.

2. On Dec. 18, 1773, Joseph Warton had married at Winchester, Charlotte (d. 1809), daughter of William Nicholas of Froyle, Hampshire (*LC*, vol. XXXIV, Dec. 18–21, 1773, p. 600). This was Warton's second marriage, both his wives "being most amiable and good women" (John Wooll, *Biographical Memoirs of the Reverend Joseph Warton*, 1806, p. 52).

3. At this time Gibbon lived at No. 7 Bentinck Street, London (Edward Gibbon, *Private Letters*, ed. Rowland E. Prothero, 1897, I, 179, 351).

4. In a letter dated Dec. 28, 1778, Lady Spencer wrote Garrick: "We shall [be] happy to see you on Thursday [Dec. 31] either well or Ill drest but do not put us off any longer" (FC; Boaden, II, 326).

1218   To The Dean of Carlisle

Adelphi
Decr 30th [1778]^1

Mr Garrick presents his best Compliments to the Dean of Carlisle,
& Nothing but a hurry of leaving London to go to Lord Spencer's
should have prevented him from paying his respects & most sincerely wishing him Joy of his late preferment.

Address: Revd Dr Percy, Dean of Carlisle, Northumberland House.   *Source:*
Brander Matthews Dramatic Museum, transcript.

1. The year is determined by the address, for on Nov. 22, 1778, Percy was appointed
Dean of Carlisle (Boswell, III, 365).

1219   To The Countess Spencer

Dunstable, January 14, 1779

Address: Lady Spencer.   *In the possession of the Earl Spencer: Not made available
for publication.*

1220   To The Countess Spencer

Adelphi, January 15, 1779

Address: Lady Spencer.   *In the possession of the Earl Spencer: Not made available
for publication.*

1221   To Anne Louisa Lane^1

[*ante* January 20, 1779]^2

Mr Garrick presents his Comp^ts to Miss Lane— He has sent a little
of Mrs Garrick & his own hair— He has but one lock behind or he

w^d have sent more— Mr Garrick is much Oblig'd to Miss Lane for her politeness about his Picture.

Source: facsimile, beneath the engraving by J. Heath after the miniature by Louisa Lane, published by W. J. White, 1819, FSL.

1. Anne Louisa Lane (d. 1789), was engaged for several years with her sister, Mary, in producing hair pictures. From 1770 until 1777 the two exhibited their work annually in the gallery of the Society of Artists. In 1778 Garrick had ordered from Miss Lane a copy of the Reynolds portrait of John Campbell, later Lord Cawdor, which had been exhibited at the Royal Academy, as well as pictures of himself and Shakespeare done in the hair of Lady Spencer and the Duchess of Devonshire (*GM*, vol. LIX, Dec. 1789, p. 1149; William T. Whitley, *Artists and Their Friends in England, 1700–1799*, 1928, I, 230f.).

2. The approximate date is provided by a note on the reverse of a copy of the engraving of a hair picture of the Garricks: "David Garrick Esq. The Face Mr & Mrs Garrick's Hair mixt with Colours   The Wig Mr Garricks Hair Worked by Miss Lane and purchased of her 20 Jany 1779" (Walter T. Spencer). Beneath the engraving of the picture (by J. Heath and published by W. J. White in 1819), there is the notation: "MR GARRICK sat for the last time and afterwards sent a lock of his hair to MISS LANE, inclosed in a note, for the purpose of her completing the miniature for Mrs Garrick, a few months before his decease."

Epilogue

All of his life Garrick was temperate in his diet. In the first years of his acting at Covent Garden and Drury Lane, from exertion and nervous exhaustion, he suffered disorders that were alleviated by rest and taking the waters at Bath and other watering-places. Otherwise he experienced general good health, except for one severe attack of typhoid in Munich in the autumn of 1764. In the final fifteen years of his life he was, however, afflicted with gout, more often in his hands, though occasionally in the stomach. But his greatest affliction was increasing attacks of kidney stone.

Early in January 1779, while on a visit to the Spencers at Althorp, he suffered a severe seizure, recovering sufficiently to return to the Adelphi by Friday, January 15. During the ensuing five days he bore cheerfully and bravely the increasing complications that resulted in his death.

An autopsy was performed by Dr. Fearon, a full report of which may be found in Murphy's *Life of Garrick* (II, 471f.). From this account, and other information on Garrick's health, the following diagnosis in modern terms has been made (courtesy of J. Butler Tompkins, M.D.): There was a congenital absence of the right kidney; the left kidney was destroyed by infection or it was originally and congenitally cystic. That is, Garrick had only one kidney— a fairly good one as it served him sixty years— and it became infected. In the last few days of his life the kidney failed in its elimination of the products of metabolism and Garrick died of uremia. The distressing symptoms from which he suffered most in his fatal illness and which contributed in some measure to his death were caused by a stone in the bladder but also were consistent with inflammation of the bladder, that is, with cystitis.

The spectacular nature and success of Garrick's life were dramatized in the final ceremonies: "A more magnificent funeral was never seen in London" (Murphy, II, 349). Presumably ordered and arranged by the chief mourner, Richard Brinsley Sheridan, it was magnificent in display, crowds, and in the distinction and sincerity of the mourners. Though envy colors some contemporary accounts of the funeral, no one questioned the fitness of Garrick's interment at the foot of Shakespeare's monument in the Poet's Corner of Westminster Abbey.

Mrs. Garrick survived her husband for forty-three years, preserving at Hampton and the Adelphi the pattern of their lives together— attending new plays, receiving old friends, exchanging letters. She chose the inscription on the monument to Garrick at Lichfield, including Johnson's words on his friend:

> He had not only the qualities of private life,
>   but such astonishing dramatic talents,
> As too well verified the observation of a friend,
>   "His death eclipsed the gaiety of nations
> and impoverished the public stock of harmless pleasure."

The Laſt Time of the Company's performing this Seaſon.

At the Theatre Royal in Drury-Lane,

This preſent MONDAY, June 10, 1776,

The WONDER.

Don Felix by Mr. GARRICK,

Col. Briton by Mr. SMITH,

Don Lopez by Mr BADDELEY,

Don Pedro by Mr. PARSONS,

Liſſardo by Mr. KING,

Frederick by Mr. PACKER,

Gibby by Mr. MOODY,

Iſabella by Miſs HOPKINS,

Flora by Mrs. WRIGHTEN,

Inis by Mrs. BRADSHAW,

Violante by Mrs. YATES.

End of Act I. The Grand GARLAND DANCE,

By Signor GIORGI, Mrs. SUTTON,

And Mr. SLINGSBY.

To which will be added a Muſical Entertainment, call'd

The WATERMAN.

The PRINCIPAL CHARACTERS by

Mr. BANNISTER,

Mr. DAVIES,

And Mr. DODD.

Mrs. WRIGHTEN,

And Mrs. JEWELL.

To conclude with the Grand Scene of The RECATTA:

Ladies are deſired to ſend their Servants a little after 5 to keep Places, to prevent Confuſion.

The Doors will be opened at HALF after FIVE o'Clock.

To begin at HALF after SIX o'Clock. Vivant Rex & Regina.

The Profits of this Night being appropriated to the Benefit of The Theatrical Fund, the Uſual Addreſs upon that Occaſion Will be ſpoken by Mr. GARRICK, before the Play.

A Playbill for Garrick's Final Performance, 1776

Garrick's Death Mask, the Eyes Inserted, 1779

1222   To Frances Abington

Dear Madam.   Saturday Nine o'Clock [1768–1776][1]
I find by Hopkins's Young Man that You sent to Me last Night
about twelve, with all my Family in bed, to let me know You could
not play today— I must desire You to change y^r Mind— I sent
after I knew of the change of ye Play to you, I heard You were in
the house & sent Jefferson[2] after you, for indeed I wanted to speak
with You—

I hope when all ye rest have agreed to do their Parts, that You
will not be wanting this Evening— I beg You, for Your own Sake,
my Sake, & ye Credit of ye house: nay I'll go farther, I will do any
thing I can for You, in my Power— do be in a good humour &
meet me at ye house this Morning— I am my own Bearer of this
                                        I am Dr Mad^m Y^{rs} truly
                                                D Garrick
Excuse a galloping Pen. & great hurry—

Address: To Mrs Abington.   *Seal.*   *Source:* FSL.

1. Written sometime between Jefferson's return to Drury Lane and Garrick's retirement in June 1776.
2. Jefferson (d. 1807) appeared originally at Drury Lane from 1754 to 1758; he
spent the next ten years as an actor and manager in Dublin, Plymouth, and Exeter,
returning to Drury Lane in 1768 and remaining there until his retirement. A friend and
imitator of Garrick, he was "esteemed for his companionable qualities" (*LC*, vol. CI,
Feb. 28–March 2, 1807, p. 206; Thomas Gilliland, *Dramatic Mirror*, 1808, I, 193f., 217;
Robert Hitchcock, *An Historical View of the Irish Stage*, 1788–1794, I, 302ff.; Wilkinson,
III, 249).

1223   To Domenico Angelo

Dear Angelo,   [*ante* March 24, 1773][1]
I never was so mad in all my Life, a Country booby of a Servant
let you go away when I was waiting for you. Lord Chesterfield &
Colman were with me, the first they let in thinking it was you—
his Lordship could not have interupted us, for he was upon the
wing— I send you this to let you know the fools mistake, he said
you would come again but did not say *When*

Yours ever & ever
D. Garrick

My best comp^ts to Madam

Source: P. Astins, transcript.

1. Written before Lord Chesterfield's death on March 24, 1773.

1224   To Doctor Thomas Augustine Arne

D^r D^r   [*post* 1759][1]
I have read y^r play & rode your horse, and I dont approve of
Either— they both want that particular Spirit which alone can give
pleasure to ye Reader & the Rider— When the one wants Wit,
& ye Other ye Spur, they jog on very heavily— I must keep y^e
horse, but I have return'd you ye Play— I pretend to some little
knowledge of the last, but as I am no Jocky, they cannot say that
a Knowing one is taken in.

I am Dr Dr Your most Obed^t Ser^t
D G—

Endorsement by Garrick: designed for Dr Arne who sold me a Horse, a very
dull one, & sent me a Comic Opera ditto. *Source:* FC; Boaden, II, 112.

1. Written after 1759, when Arne received his D.Mus. at Oxford.

1225 To Doctor Samuel? Arnold[1]

Adelphi
Jany 14 [*post* 1774][2]

Mr Garrick presents his Comp^{ts} to Dr Arnold— some particular business obliges him to be at Hampton this Morn^g— He has sent the Draught by his Neighbour Mr Becket if agreeable to ye Doctor— Mr Garrick shall be always glad to see the D^r if he passes this Way.

Address: To Dr Arnold. *Seal. Source:* FSL.

1. Perhaps Samuel Arnold, Mus. Doc. 1773, the composer.
2. Written after Becket's move to the Adelphi in Jan. 1774 (*DP*).

1226 To The Reverend Henry Bate

Adelphi
Monday [*post* September 9, 1773][1]

Dear Bate
Pray thank Your better part in the Name of Me & my rib for her very choice present— they smell so exquisitely, that my mouth waters at 'Em already— Y^r Servant shall always be Welcome because he is so good a one— I wish You had ye fellow of his to recommend to Me, for one of my Good-for-Naughts will be soon sent a packing,

Y^{rs} Ever & most truly
D Garrick

Love to Madam.

Address: Revd Mr Bate. *Seal. Source:* FSL.

1. Written after Bate's marriage on Sept. 9, 1773 (*Bath Chronicle*).

1227   To Grosvenor Bedford

Dear Sir   [*ante* November 4, 1771]¹
I have so little Time upon my Hands, that I have but just enough
to Spare to tell You
                                        I am most Sincerely Yʳˢ
                                             D: Garrick—

Address: To Grosvʳ Bedford Esqʳ at the Excise Office in the Old Jewry—.
Seal. Source: P. J. Dobell.

   1. Written before Bedford's death on Nov. 4, 1771.

1228   To Richard Berenger

My dear Berenger   Easter Sunday [*post* April 1763]¹
Thank you again & again for yʳ very obliging & always agreeable
letters. Your trouble in preventing my fighting yard arm & yard
arm wᵗʰ Capᵗ Hood, (which by yᵉ bye I had rather do, than lick
the whiskers of his cara sposa)² demands my best & warmest
thanks— could not you my dear friend have smuggled my Name
upon a Card, & then, l'affaire est faite.
    But think you, my merry wag, that I will so ill requite yʳ Kind-
ness to me as to bring you down this bliteing weather to Hampton?—
what shall I draw you from those flagrant Dunghills which are
plac'd so near you, & to the breath of which, you open your en-
raptur'd nostrils, to sniff at my Hyacinths, Gillyflowers, Violets,
Snowdrops and Polyanthoses?— Shall the sweet Musick of Hackney
Coaches, Muffins & Teddydoll be exchang'd for the chirping of
Birds, the cackling of Hens, the gobbling of Turkeys, and the
grunting of hogs? Heavens forfend No my dear Richard, I love
you too well to bring you from the Lap of noise & Luxury, to
repose your high-tun'd spirits sub tegmine fagi—³
    let yᵉ sun leave off his playing at Bopeep— put on his flame
colour'd garment, & make the Mews as hot as the Devil's Oven,
and then, my Master, you shall run thro' dust for 14 Miles till you
are almost choak'd, & we will brush you, clean you, & lay you

down softly upon the banks of the Thames, till the Sallads, custards
& Sillibubs are ready to regale you— in short to be plain wth you,
we shall expect that the Echo at Hampton (& there is no finer)
shall repeat your pleasantry very soon, & give you dash for dash,
for she can only match you, & give you as good, as you bring—
so much for that— when did you see the delectable *Rust!*—4 that a
Man with such a head & heart for Society should be laid by y^e
heels for a third of his Life— 'tis a damn'd shame, & we his many
companions should bring an action against the College for false
imprisonment!

but I must stop my nonsensical career, as Sr Sidney's Gallop was
by a Subpone, as the bearer of this will hardly stay, to let me tell
you how much I am

Dear Berenger Yours affect^y till death
D. Garrick

Madam throws her Love at you, for ye messenger won't take it—
what a scrawl— always in a hurry & a damn'd hand at ye best.

Source: George G. Fortescue, transcript; *The Manuscripts of J. B. Fortescue, Esq.*,
Historical Manuscripts Commission, Report 13, Pt. 3, 1892–1927, I, 151f.

1. Written after Hood's marriage in April 1763.
2. Alexander Hood (1727–1814), later (1801) first Viscount Bridport, was at this
time a Captain in the Royal Navy. He married Mary West (d. 1786), a granddaughter
of Sir Richard Temple.
3. Virgil, *Eclogues*, I, i: "Under your spreading beech's covert."
4. Possibly John Rust (1724–1788), son of Edward Rust of London. In 1739 he
was admitted to the Middle Temple, and it is probable that he stayed in London for
that was where he died (*Alumni Cantab.*). For Garrick's friendship with Rust, see the
latter's letters of Jan. 7 and 17, 1777, in the Forster Collection.

1229 To Richard Berenger

Dear Berenger,   Thursday noon
I have corrected the lines I sent you, and have made them much
better. Exempli gratia.

Inscription for Stowe.[1]

Britons, behold the glory of the Isle!
        *Nor tell what ancient art and worth have been;
Greece never saw a fairer, nobler pile,
        Nor *old Rome* boast more virtue than within.

Most truly yours,
D. Garrick.

*Nor tell what ancient Greece and Rome have been.

Source: FC, copy.

1. Garrick's lines (Knapp, No. 77) may have been intended for one of the many classic temples in the gardens of Stowe House, Buckinghamshire, the seat of Earl Temple, to whom Berenger was related.

1230   To James Boswell

My dear Sir   Sunday
I must desire You not to Say a Word Where You are going of my design to play at Drury-Lane next Summer I will give You my reasons When I see You.

Y^rs most truly,
D Garrick

Address: To J. Boswell, Esqr.   *Seal.*   *Source:* Boswell MSS. Yale.

1231   To Doctor Charles Burney

My dear Burney   Tuesday [*post* March 1772][1]
I shall bring the other Volumes wth me to Town to Morrow— I shall be at ye Adelphi about 8 or a little after in ye Evening to

drink tea— can you call?— when yᵉ other Volˢ come to hand, give me a peep of Em!—

> Yʳˢ Ever & Ever
> D Garrick

Source: Berg Collection.

1. Written after Garrick's move to the Adelphi in March 1772.

1232 To Doctor Charles Burney

Adelphi—

Dear Burney   Janʸ 3 [*post* 1773][1]

Another fine Letter from Gossip Joan to Morrow— I am told better than yᵉ former most exquisite Stuff— take care how you Suspect yᵉ Ghost I mention'd to any one but Myself; or He'll vanish— could you bring me his hand Writing this afternoon— We might be satisfy'd— for I may do Something— but for Heav'ns Sake take care

> Yours Ever & Ever
> DG

Shall I see you this afternoon about 5 or Six

Source: Morgan Library.

1. Written after Garrick's move to the Adelphi in March 1772.

1233 To Doctor Charles Burney

Dear Burney.   Monday [1771–1774][1]

I have got 3 places for you in a front Row— if you go to yᵉ Stage door Johnston has orders to admit You the uncrowded way if you go the other, make Use of the inclos'd—

> Ever Yʳˢ
> D: Garrick

Address: To Dr Burney, Queen Square. *Endorsed by the recipient. Source:* Gabriel Wells.

1. Burney lived in Queen Square from Jan. 1771 to Oct. 1774 (Frances Burney, *Early Diary*, ed. Annie R. Ellis, 1907, I, 102, n. 1, 263f., 313, 328).

1234   To Doctor Charles Burney?[1]

My dear Friend   Sunday 9th [*post* June 1777][2]
Et tu Brute!
pray read ye inclose & assist the poor Devil if you can— his Sister brought my Niece over from Germany & I hope Will take her back again— one good turn deserves another You know, & I know you will assist him if you can

> Ever & Ever Y^rs
> D: Garrick.

Source: Batchelder Collection.

1. The conjectural recipient is established by the fact that in July 1930 this letter was one of five in the possession of Gabriel Wells, the other four being to Dr. Burney.
2. Written after the arrival of Elisabeth Fürst in England in June of 1777.

1235   To Frances Cadogan[1]

My dear Madam   [*post* March 1772][2]
I am sorry but My Box is Engag'd to day, the D^r is the Cause that it is, having said to me, that it would not be in either of your Power to come to Drury-Lane before you go out of Town. Will you tell him that I dined out yesterday and was not the better for it. Adieu.[3]

Source: Baker, p. 64.

1. So identified in the source.
2. From Mrs. Garrick's reference to the Adelphi, see below, this letter was written after the Garricks moved there in March 1772.
3. On the back of Garrick's note Mrs. Garrick wrote: "As you could [not?] got to

the Play, why can you not come in *your night gown* and drink your Coffee & Tea at the Adelphi this evening? I am quite by Myself, my Hus^d dines with Ld Mansfield but will come home time Enough to Kiss you. My Coach shall be with you about half after six. I take no Excuse— bring your work" (Baker, p. 64).

1236   To Frances Cadogan

My dear Friend—   Friday Night [*post* May 1774]^1
Your Card will only take You to ye box, the Night it is dated— if You & y^r friends will respite Your Curiosity of seeing Plays, till M^rs G & I have talk'd to You wch will be *Tuesday* or Wed^y Next, We will Settle ye Matter wth You—

Nobody more Wellcome to ye Garricks than the Cadogans— You cannot imagine how I am flatter'd by y^r Letters— & why?— because You write letters like an Angel— My Wife, the Nine, & I have agreed that Matter this Evening—

pray tell ye Doctor of all Doctors that tomorrow, he shall put me to my purgation— I am not so well to day— I have an acid kind of Water that rises often to my Mouth & a little pain in my Stomach— but I'll be at them tomorrow Morning about 6— so bless You both & believe Me most unalterably & affectionatly Yours

Ever & Ever
D: Garrick.

Address: Miss Cadogan, George Street, Hanover Square.   *Source:* HTC.

1. Written sometime after Garrick met Hannah More ("the Nine") in May 1774 (Letter 839).

1237   To Frances Cadogan

My dear Madam.   Easter Sunday [*post* 1776]^1
Mrs Garrick intended to have Written You a *Garming* letter, as she calls it, but ye Person, who is to carry this, Mr Texier being in haste

she desires me to inclose the Card for the Box on Tuesday Next &
to tell You how Much we Love & Esteem You—
                                        Ever & Ever most affect^y Y^{rs}
                                                D: Garrick

Dr Brooke is truly Wellcome.

   Address: Miss Cadogan at Dr Cadogan's in George Street near Hanover
Square. *Source:* HTC.

   1. Written after Le Texier's coming to London in Sept. 1775.

1238   To Doctor William Cadogan

                                                        Hampton
Dear Dr Octr 3 [*post* May 1771][1]
have pity upon ye Bearer, & forgiveness for Me— Mrs Wilmot will
tell You, *Who he* is & for what he follows You to Farnborough—
You will save Your poor Soul by Charitable deeds, & in some
Measure attone for Y^r Infidelity against Shakespear— if I have y^r
Curses for sending business after You in the midst of y^r happiness
forgive me this once & I will do So no more
                My dear Dr Ever & most unalterably Yours
                                                D Garrick
Love to Your Dear Daughter.

   Address: Dr Cadogan.   *Seal.*   *Source:* FSL.

   1. The Garricks and the Cadogans seem not to have known each other before May
1771. This letter was perhaps written in 1776, when allusions to Cadogan's anti-
Shakespearian attitude begin to appear.

1239   To Doctor William Cadogan

                                                        Adelphi
My dear D^r 29 [*post* March 1772][1]
I rec'd at Hampton ye inclos'd— I have promis'd & vow'd many
things in y^r Name to the Mrs Mills, who is a fine Woman & my

Neighbor—² She comes to Town on Purpose to attend You next Saturday I hope You will not disappoint her

Yours Ever & Ever & Yʳ Daughter's too
D Garrick

I shall return as soon as I can to Hampton.

Address: Dʳ Cadogan, George Street, Hanover Square. *Seal.* *Source:* FSL.

1. Written after the move to the Adelphi in March 1772.
2. Presumably the second wife of John Mills (d. 1758); about 1757 the Millses had taken a house at Hampton (*Diary of John Baker*, ed. Philip C. Yorke, 1931, p. 116).

1240   To Doctor William Cadogan

Adelphi

My dear Dʳ   Sunday [*post* March 1772]¹
Your kindness makes me impudent— pray let me ask another favour of You— the famous *Bond*,² who has often, ventur'd his Life, in the publick Service, is now not well, & tho he values life only like a Philosopher, & deserves to be worth Thousands, yet he cannot Well afford to fee an Esculapius. Will You for my Sake let him Add to the number of Your Soul-saving deeds, & to yᵉ obligations, so kindly conferr'd upon Your very Sincere friend, notwithstanding Your Apostacy from the God of my Idolatry Shakespear,

D. Garrick.

Love to yʳ Daughter.

My Brother will bring Bond on tuesday Mornᵍ before ten o'Clock—

Address: Dʳ Cadogan, Great George Street, Hanover Square. *Seal.* *Source:* FSL.

1. Written after the move to the Adelphi in March 1772, perhaps in 1776 when the allusions to Cadogan's anti-Shakespearian attitude begin to appear.
2. Presumably Nicholas Bond (d. 1807), clerk of the Public Office, Bow Street, under Sir John Fielding. Because of his zeal in the pursuit of criminals, he was later made a J.P. for Middlesex and served for many years as a Bow Street magistrate (*GM*, vol. LXXI, Aug. 1801, p. 762, vol. LXXVII, May 1807, p. 494; *LC*, vol. XXXIV, Sept. 21–23, 1773, p. 295).

1241   To Doctor William Cadogan

Nov. 1 [*ante* January 1776][1]

Will you let me see you this afternoon? I have been very sick &c. this morning, I am now much better, but ye sight of you will be a consolation— if you would . . . see Weston on yr way hither, I shall be very much obliged to you— he had kill'd himself with drinking . . . I believe he is almost past yr skill

Address: To Dr. Cadogan at Mr. Wilmot's.   *Source: The Collector*, ed. Mary A. Benjamin, LX (Jan. 1947), 10, extract.

   1. Written before Weston's death in January of 1776.

1242   To Doctor William Cadogan[1]

My Dear D[r]   [*ante* June 1776][2]

Poor Parsons we fear is in a bad way—[3] he has desir'd me to recommend him to any Physical friend of Mine, that will as he terms it *see him at an Easy rate*— will you be so kind to me, & him, as to see him tomorrow Morn[g]? & let me know his Situation: 'tis of great Consequence to us— What shall I say to you for my impertinence—? this I say— when you want any of your friends to be *merry* send them to *Me*, & when I want any of *My* friends to be *well*, I will send them to *You*. done— pray see Parsons to-Morrow Morning—

                                      Y[rs] Ever & most affect[y]
                                                D. Garrick

Parsons lives at N[o] 9 in Queen Street facing the British Museum. I have rec'd some sweet Letters from Y[r] Daughter

   Source: Baker, p. 63f.

   1. So identified in the source.
   2. Written before Garrick's retirement in June 1776.
   3. William Parsons, the comedian, long suffered acutely from attacks of asthma; eventually they were to lead to his death (Thomas Bellamy, *Life of Mr. William Parsons*, 1795, p. 13f.).

1243 To Doctor William Cadogan

My dear D^r   Sunday Even^g [*post* June 1777][1]
Thank You for Your very Comfortable Letter— We will certainly dine wth You on Wednesday, provided You are as good as Y^r Word & give Us friendly food & no prance. pray let ye Bearer know, what time You will dine. Love to Your dear Daughter.

Y^rs Ever & most affect^y
D: Garrick.

I shall deliver y^r Comp^ts to ye Patriot— I see by y^r Letter the time of Dinner a Quarter after 4.
   (N.B. We shall bring our Neice)

    Address: Dr Cadogan & in his Absence to Miss Cadogan.   *Seal.*   *Source:* FSL.

    1. On the assumption that the niece alluded to is Elisabeth Fürst, this letter was written after her arrival in England in June 1777.

1244   To Catherine Clive

Dear Clive   Thursday—
Mrs Garrick, Mr Capell, & Your most Obedient Manager intend themselves ye Pleasure of drinking Tea with You about 5 this afternoon, if so be that You & ye Weather, are willing, & will kindly invite Us—

Ever Thine my dainty Kate
D: Garrick

    Source: FSL.

1245   To George Colman

Sir.   Wednesday [*ante* 1758?][1]
I am Extreamly oblig'd to you for Your particular & Genteel Compliment to Me— and more so as I have not ye Pleasure of Your

Acquaintance: I must assure You that I have more Pleasure than Uneasiness, when I read a true well intended Criticism, tho against myself— for I always flatter Myself that I can attain the Mark which my Friends may point out to me, & I really think myself neither too old or too wise to learn— If you would still add to yᵉ favor confer'd upon Me, I should wish to have yᵉ Pleasure of seeing You in Southampton Street or rather, I will do myself yᵉ Pleasure of waiting upon You, when I return from yᵉ Country, If you will signify to me by a Line that it will not be inconvenient or disagreeable to You

I am Sʳ Your most oblig'd & Obedᵗ Servᵗ

D Garrick.

P.S. I shall return from Hampton the beginning of next week, a Line directed to me there (Hampton in Middlx) will be with me yᵉ next day—

Address: To Geo. Colman Esqʳ at Serle's Coffeehouse, Lincolns-Inn.   *Source:* Berg Collection; Colman, p. 231f.

1. Presumably written shortly before Garrick and Colman met, around 1758 (see Boaden, I, 90).

1246   To George Colman[1]

[*post* 1758?][2]

I am greatly pleased that the few remarks, which I have made upon your play are not wholly useless. They were merely the result of my feelings and zeal for yᵉ subject and its author. I reverence a turn of abilities and integrity, and am never so happy as when my little endeavours can serve such a one

Source: Puttick & Simpson, Catalogue, March 22, 1854, extract.

1. So identified in the source.
2. Written after Garrick and Colman met around 1758 (see Boaden, I, 90).

1247　　　To George Colman

Hampton

Dear Colman　　　　　　　Monday morn^g [*post* January 1770]^1
I beg that you will read these 3 Acts & a half of a Comedy as soon
as You can, & when I see You, I will read a Letter I shall send
with them to ye author— You know ye hand, & I beg that Nobody
may See them but Yourself, & I give You my honour again & again,
that Nobody shall ever know that You have seen them— pray
oblige Me in this particular for a very particular reason, which you
shall know when I see You, which I hope will be tonight, or
tomorrow, for I shall want ye Papers by to Morrow Night— Yesterday an itch of Scribbling seiz'd me, & I have got several things for
ye Packet, wch you shall do what you please with— let me know
by ye Bearer when I may hope to see You

Ever & Ever Yours
D Garrick.

Source: Harold M. Moulton; Puttick & Simpson, Catalogue, July 15, 1853.

1. Written after the founding of the *London Packet* in Jan. 1770, Colman being one
of the organizers of that paper (Eugene R. Page, *George Colman the Elder*, New York,
1935, pp. 226–231).

1248　　　To George Colman

Thursday [*post* September 1775]^1
As Mr. Bate came in I was obliged to speak to hear from some of
Tesseir's friends about the paragraph in his Paper to-day about ye
affair at ye Opera

Address: Geo. Colman, Soho Square.　*Source:* Sotheby, Catalogue, March 17,
1916, extract.

1. Written after Le Texier came to London in Sept. 1775.

1249   To Grey Cooper

[*ante* October 26, 1775][1]

I shall do myself ye honor to call upon You some Morning this Week—

Address: To Grey Cooper Esqʳ. *Seal.* *Source:* FSL.

1. Written before Cooper assumed his title on Oct. 26, 1775.

1250   To Richard Cox

Hampton
May 12th [1758–1765][1]

To my Friend Mr Cox. Extempore.

'Tis said that no Answer, I sent to your letter,
When for Kindness uncommon, I stood much Yr Debtor:
The fault was in *You*, to inform me by Writing,
That You do, & did ever, kind Actions delight in:
Why thank You for that, which is *Selfish* in You;
Small Merit in doing, what's a Pleasure to do:
I own You are Eager, & warm for Your Friend,
But Nature, not You made Yourself, for that End;
And think you that I will with Compliments vapor,
And send You my Gratitude trick'd out on paper?
It is written *Elsewhere*— or I ever should be,
Unworthy of Friendship, unworthy of Thee!
Tho my Fingers don't move, I've my heart & my Pate-full,
And as You to be kind, I am born to be gratefull.

D G.

Address: To Richd Cox Esqʳ, Albemarle Street, London. *Source:* HTC, draft in FSL.

1. From the address, this letter and the two following were written during Cox's tenancy in Albemarle Street from 1758–1765 (Frederick G. H. Price, *A Handbook of London Bankers*, 1876).

1251   To Richard Cox

My dear Cox.   Novr 8th [1758–1765]
do you think that it would not be disagreeable to Mr Churchill[1]
to meet ye loving Company next Fryday at my house?— if it would
not, & he would come without ceremony, it would make us all
happy. Can I say any more, or do any more? If I can tell me how
                    my dearest Richd Y^{rs} Ever & Ever
                             D. Garrick

Address: To Richd Cox Esqr, Albemarle Street. *Source:* HTC.

1. If this is Charles Churchill, this letter was written before his death in Nov. 1764.

1252   To Richard Cox

My dear Riccardetto.   Thursday Night [1758–1765]
I have sent you two dozen of Burgundy, pray let it be kept warm.
You will find it good, if not Send it again to
                      Yours Ever most truly
                           D: Garrick

I wish you well off Saturday— I think to pluck up a Spirit & write
to Mr Bradshaw— we are ruin'd by Suspense.

Address: To Richd Cox Esqr, Albemarle Street. *Source:* HTC.

1253   To Joseph Cradock

                      [*ante* June 1776][1]
Mr Garrick's best Comp^{ts} to Mr Craddock, & he shall with great
Pleasure consider ye Entertainment he mentions, but as it is
impossible to bring it out this Winter, he could Wish that he w^d
let him take it to Bath after Xmas, When he can consider it at his

leisure—— Mr Garrick will be proud to See Mr Craddock any Morning he pleases.

Address: To Josp^h Craddock Esqr.   *Seal.*   *Source:* FSL; Cradock, IV, 255.

1. Written before Garrick's retirement.

1254   To The Countess of Denbigh

Adelphi

Thursday [*post* March 1772][1]

Mr Garrick presents his respects to Lady Denbigh— he had so much Company when her Ladyship's Servant was with him that he c^d not give a full answer to the Note— M^r G did not imagine that her Ladyship would want any Notice of a Play Which was in the Papers the day before; Had M^r G: not settled to play the part of Kitely so soon, he should certainly have given her L^p Notice of it— as it was Mr G. had Secur'd a box for L^y D—— & Expected her Servant all ye Morn^g to know her Commands & must confess, that he was rather Surpris'd to receive a Note of Displeasure when he flatter'd himself he deserv'd Lady D's thanks:

Endorsement by Garrick: Ans^r to Lady Denbigh's Not.   *Source:* FSL, draft; *Notes and Queries,* 3d Series, IV (Dec. 5, 1863), 450.

1. Garrick played Kitely four times on a Thursday between his move to the Adelphi and his retirement: Oct. 29, 1772, Oct. 20 and Dec. 29, 1774, and April 25, 1776. From the apparent urgency of Lady Denbigh's note, it is probable that she wrote on the last date, when tickets were in demand for Garrick's final performance of the role.

1255   To Charles Dibdin

Adelphi

Ap^l 4 [*post* 1772][1]

Mr Garricks Comp^ts to Mr Dibdden, and if convenient to him, will be glad to see him to Morrow at the Adelphi about twelve o'clock.

Address: Mr Dibdden.   *Seal.*   *Source:* FSL.

1. Written after the move to the Adelphi in March 1772.

1256   To Charles Dibdin[1]

July 31

I have a tale to tell, as shall cause each particular hair to shoot
through your hat; if you happen to sit covered when you hear it

Source: Puttick & Simpson, Catalogue, March 8, 1858, extract.

1. So identified in the source.

1257 To The Reverend Doctor John Douglas

Dear D[r]   Thursday [*post* March 1772][1]
half a dozen friends, pack'd togeather in haste, will meet at y[e]
Adelphi at four to day to Eat Sour Krout & a haunch of Venison—
will you make one?

Y[rs] Ever
D: Garrick

I intended to call Yesterday—

Endorsement by Garrick: To D[r] Douglas.   *Source:* BM, facsimile, *Souvenir of
David Garrick*, brochure issued by Criterion Theatre, Jan. 7, 1887.

1. Written after the move to the Adelphi in March 1772.

1258   To Thomas? Evans[1]

D[r] S[r]   [*ante* June 1776][2]
Y[r] letter is very friendly to both & like Y[r]Self— Y[r] Lady is always
wellcome to a renewal of y[e] inclos'd—

Y[rs] most truly
D G

I sh[d] have sent before but forgot— pray let M[rs] Evans go to Night
if she chuses it—

Address: Mr Evans. *Seal.* *Source:* FSL.

1. Presumably Thomas Evans the bookseller.
2. On the assumption that the "renewal of ye inclos'd" refers to a Drury Lane pass, this letter was written before Garrick's retirement in June 1776.

1259 To The Honorable Thomas Fitzmaurice

My dear Sir
It is a fine come off— & you are a fine Gentleman— I hope You'll starve to day for it

Yrs most truly & in great haste
D Garrick

Address: To The H—— Mr Fitzmaurice. *Source:* FSL.

1260   To Mr. Fosbroke[1]

Mr Fosbroke
Pray deliver this directly to Charles Hart— it is of Consequence from Me

D: Garrick.

I am rather better but dread a relapse I have kept my bed 4 days

Source: Enthoven Collection.

1. A Fosbroke was box-bookkeeper and had a benefit at Drury Lane on May 14, 1776.

1261   To Peter Fountain

Hampton
Dear Sir   Thursday [*post* 1754][1]
I have taken James's powder & been bled for a fever, & I am now writing this in my bed—

I am advis'd not to stir from this place, till my fever is abated so I cannot have yᵉ Pleasure of seeing you to Morrow— I am so weak that I can scarce write this.

> I am very truly Yʳˢ
> D: Garrick

Endorsed by the recipient. Source: FC.

1. This letter and the two following were written after Garrick had the Hampton house in 1754.

1262   To Peter Fountain?[1]

> Hampton
Dear Sir   Sunday [*post* 1754]
The Coach was at yᵉ door, when I rec'd Your letter, & As yᵉ Ladies were in yᵉ Coach, I could not stay to read it— As I am here for a little air, I can't be sure of my time, & indeed, I have an affair of great Consequence upon my hands that will Employ all my Mornings this Week with Lawyers &c &c— I must therefore defer yᵉ pleasure of seeing You & Dʳ Bruce till the Week after— if you wᵈ call upon Me any day after Wedʸ, I will tell You more, and then I will give you the book— pray let Mʳ Guiott deliver the inclos'd to Mʳ Corbett.[2] I wish You joy of Success at yᵉ India hous⟨e⟩

> I am Dʳ Sʳ Yʳˢ most truly
> D: Garrick

pray Seal yᵉ Letter to Mʳ Corbett & give it to Guiott.

Seal. Source: FC.

1. The recipient is identified only by the familiar references to Dr. Bruce here and in other letters to Fountain. Lewis Bruce (1708–1779), D.D. 1747, is most probably the Dr. Bruce Fountain mentions. Bruce succeeded in 1741 as Preacher of His Majesty's Chapel, Somerset House, retaining that position until the Chapel was closed at Michaelmas 1775. In 1764 he was appointed Chaplain in Ordinary to the King (*Alumni Cantab.; Alumni Dublinenses*, ed. George D. Burtchaell and Thomas U. Sadleir, Dublin, 1935; Raymond Needham and Alexander Webster, *Somerset House, Past and Present*, New York, 1906, pp. 176ff.).
2. Perhaps Charles Corbett or his son of the same name (1734–1808), who succeeded him as publisher of the *Whitehall Evening Post*.

1263   To Peter Fountain?[1]

Dᴿ Sᴿ   [*post* 1754]
yᵉ above is at yʳ Service— I am sorry that all next Week I shall [be]
particularly Engag'd partly in Town & in yᵉ Country— after that
I shall be Wholly at Yours & yᵉ Dʳˢ Service— I have not been at
Hampton these 5 Weeks

Ever Yʳˢ (with a Wretched pen)
D G—

Source: FC.

    1. The recipient is indicated only on the conjectural identification of the "Dʳ" as
being the Dr. Bruce mentioned in other letters to Fountain.

1264   To Peter Fountain

Novʳ 25 [post 1769][1]

a thousand thanks, dear Sir, for Your present— I don't know what
you hint at of my letting M de M[orande?] into my Secrets— I have
not I assure You— M. de M. was much *better inform'd than I was*,
& more capable of instructing *Me*— be assur'd of this truth, as I
never give my Mind to fibbing— whenever You please to send for
yᵉ Tickets yᵉ Ladies shall have them.

Dʳ Sʳ most truly Yʳˢ
D G.

Address: Mʳ Fountain.   *Seal.*   *Source:* FC.

    1. Conjecturally identified as Morande, who was released from a French prison by
July 14, 1769, and shortly afterwards fled to England; in Aug. 1771 he was publishing
there *Le Gazetier cuirassé* (Paul Robiquet, *Theveneau de Morande*, Paris, 1882, pp. 22ff.).

1265   To Peter Fountain

Dear Sir.   Thursday yᵉ 4 [*post* March 18, 1772][1]
There is a great Mistake indeed between us— all yᵉ afternoon
yesterday I had nothing to do, & wish'd you had Sent me a Note

as you promis'd to let me know that you w^d call upon Me at ye Adelphi— I wish'd much to pay my respects to Mr Lloyd, & will do so tomorrow morning between Eleven & 12 if you don't prevent me— my good Friend your hurry & Business have prevented You from remembring the Compact we made, recollect Y^rSelf & do justice to Me, by excusing me to Mr Lloyd.

Ever Yours
D Garrick

Address: To Mr Fountain at Mr Lloyd, James Street, Bedford Row.   *Source:* FC.

1. Written after Garrick's move to the Adelphi on March 18, 1772.

The addresses given, show that the following fifteen letters must have been written before Fountain moved from Lichfield Street in 1775; the mention of Hampton indicates that the letter must have been written after 1754.

1266   To Peter Fountain

Dear Sir   May 12th [*ante* 1775]
I am this Moment setting off for Hampton— I have seen ye Story of ye M. D'aubade without know^g any thing of ye Matter— the Story of ye other side sh^d be heard before a prudent Man will judge— I am much better, & hope to return to Town quite re-instated— I am in ye mean time

Dr Sr Yours most truly
D Garrick

Address: To Mr. Fountain, Lichfield Street, Soho.   *Source:* FC.

1267   To Peter Fountain

May 21 [*ante* 1775]

Mr Garrick presents his Comp^{ts} to Mr Fountain, & is much Oblig'd to him for setting that much Mistaken affair right, He hopes that want of Manners & incivility, particularly to Strangers, are not among ye Number of his Sins. Mr Fountain knows too Well Mr Garrick's present Labors to be surpriz'd at his not reading over, & giving his opinion of a Matter of such Consequence & of Writings so Voluminous, till he is settled in the Country— in the mean time he begs leave to repeat to Mr Fountain that his obligations to the Duke de Nivernois, & his Knowledge of that most amiable Noble- man are so rooted, that he cannot upon proofs, less than demon- stration, alter his opinion of him— Mr Garrick begs that Mr Fountain would not trouble himself about ye lease, if Such a thing falls in his way, M^r G will be much oblig'd with a Sight of it: Mr G. in return shall be glad at any time to oblige Mr Fountain, & this he says, not merely in ye common language of Ceremony, but with great Sincerity—

Address: To Mr Fountain, Litchfield Street, Soho at Mr Grignions.   *Source:* FC.

1268   To Peter Fountain

Dear Sir   June 24 [*ante* 1775]

As I cannot possibly see You for some time, I have sent my panto- mical General to confer with You about ye Scene You mention'd— if you chuse to trust him wth it— if not, ye Moment I return from an Expedition I have in hand, I will See you myself

I am Dr Sr Sincerely Y^{rs}

D G—

PS. have you heard of a particular letter written to me by *y^r* *Falstaff.*

Address: Mr Fountain, Lichfield Street.   *Endorsement by the recipient:* June 24 about Ross.   *Source:* FC.

1269   To Peter Fountain

Dear Sir.   Oc^r 8 [*ante* 1775]
Don't imagine because I don't answer directly, that I don't think
of you & y^r friend— I will do my best to get a *Labourer's*[?][1] place,
for that I find is ye right name.

Ten thousand thanks for Y^r attention to my disorder, the Remedy
you have Sent me, was given me some time ago, & I take it con-
stantly going to bed— but it is impossible that so pleasant & harmless a thing, sh^d break down *Stone* Walls. I am Well at present &
much

> Y^r hum^le Ser^t
> D Garrick

Address: To Mr Fountain, Lichfield Street.   *Source:* FC.

1. The word is almost illegible.

1270   To Peter Fountain

> Monday [*ante* 1775]
Don't imagine, dear S^r, because I don't write that I am not most
sincerely thankful to You for Your kindness— I will look over
Polly;[1] when I did some Years ago, I thought it a sad piece— but
You have rous'd me again— I am truly sorry for y^r Friend ye D^r[2]
when he is well & not till then, I shall be happy to attend You—
Mr Loyd has my best Wishes & respects.

> Ever Y^rs truly
> D G.

Address: To Mr Fountain, Lichfield Street.   *Source:* FC.

1. Presumably Gay's *Polly*, which, however, Garrick never produced.
2. Presumably Dr. Bruce.

1271   To Peter Fountain

Hampton

Dear Sir   Tuesday [*ante* 1775]

I was oblig'd to retire here with a very bad cold & hoarseness: When I am better & Able to Enjoy yᵉ Entertainment, Which you And yʳ friend have kindly offer'd, I will let you know, by which time, I hope that the Dʳ¹ too will be recover'd: I am sorry for his indisposition

inclos'd is yᵉ order for yᵉ Young Ladies,² had I been in Town, They shᵈ have had it sooner

Dʳ Sʳ most truly Yʳˢ

D Garrick

Address: To Mʳ Fountain, Lichfield Street.   *Endorsed by the recipient.*   *Source:* FC.

1. Presumably Dr. Bruce.
2. Presumably the recipient's daughter, Mary Barton Fountain, and a friend of hers (Fountain's will, Probate Court of Canterbury, Rockingham 320).

1272   To Peter Fountain

Dear Fountain.   Tuesday [*ante* 1775]

Sure Mʳ Lloyd did not Stay at home, when no Day, or rather Evening was fix'd for our Meeting— when will yᵉ Term End, that I may directly propose an Evening for our waiting upon Mʳ Lloyd?

I am quite ignorant of these matters, & you will inform Me, I shall be at yʳ Service wᵗʰ my Coach yᵉ Day we appoint—

To Morrow Evening I intended to propose, but that I suppose will be too Soon— don't imagine that I am mov'd with yᵉ malice in yᵉ daily papers— I take the best Method to avoid vexation for I never read the Nonsense, nor Should Ever hear of it, did not my Friends now & then let me know that I have been Shot at by *the Arrows that fly by Night*—¹ let me be free from yᵉ Stone, & my Wife free from pain, & I defy the *foul Fiend*

Ever Yours

D. Garrick

Address: To Mr Fountain, Lichfield Street.   *Source:* FC.

1. An adaptation of Psalm 91:5.

1273   To Peter Fountain

Dear Sir.   Tuesday [*ante* 1775]
I have waited till this to know if I could be at leisure to Morrow
Morning— I am sorry that my Affairs oblige me to defer ye great
Pleasure you intend me till ye Next Week when I hope that D^r
Bruce will permit to have ye honour of his Company with Yours
some Morning to breakfast. His Majesty will be at our Theatre
tomorrow.

Ever Y^rs
D Garrick

Address: To Mr Fountain, Lichfield Street.   *Source:* FC.

1274   To Peter Fountain

Dear S^r   Tuesday [*ante* 1775]
I am this Moment return'd from ye Country & am much better—
   I shall be ready for You in a day or two— I am much oblig'd to
You, never take any thing ill, & am truly

Y^r hum^le Ser^t
D: Garrick

I hate writing.

Address: To Mr Fountain, Lichfield Street.   *Source:* FC.

1275   To Peter Fountain

Dʳ Sʳ   Fryday 15 [*ante* 1775]¹
How can you tantalize a body so, when I am going into Buckinghamshire for a Week— I shᵈ have been glad to have made one wᵗʰ
you & yᵉ Chevʳ had not other Engagements dispos'd of me— the
Lines you mention are Mine, but sorry I am & surpriz'd, that they
are printed— it is not right to do it without leave— my friend is
wrong. the Boxes shall be at Your Service when Ever You please
& I am in London to deliver them to you—
    farewell I am in such haste to dine wᵗʰ Mʳ Walpole at Twicken-
ham, that I can scarce say,
                              That I am, most Sincerely Yours,
                                               D: Garrick—

    Address: To Mʳ Fountain, Lichfield Street. *Endorsement:* Febry 19ᵗʰ—.
Seal. Source: FC.

    1. The unidentified endorsement appears to be incorrect, for during d'Eon's stay
in England, 1762–1777, Feb. 15 fell on a Friday only in 1765, when Garrick was in Paris,
and in 1771. There is no record that on this latter date Walpole entertained guests at
Twickenham; further, it is doubtful if Garrick would have been absent from the theater
for a week at this season.

1276   To Peter Fountain

                                        Sunday Noon [*ante* 1775]
To Mʳ Fountain from Mʳ Garrick with his Compᵗˢ and thanks for
the perusal of the inclos'd.

    Address: To Mʳ Fountain, Litchfield Street. *Source:* FC.

1277   To Peter Fountain

Dear Sir   [*ante* 1775]
I should be happy to see Mr Loyd & You to day because I can give
my Self up to my friends, to, what Pope calls

         The Feast of Reason & ye flow of Soul—[1]

To morrow I must be in Denmark as you will see by ye Bills—
If I cannot Enjoy y^r Comp^y to Day, I hope next Tuesday will be
agreeable to you both.

                           Ever & truly Yours
                              D: Garrick.

     Address: To Mr Fountain, Lichfield Street.   *Endorsement by the recipient:*
Thursday Morn^g.   *Source:* FC.

     1. "To Mr. Fortescue," l. 127.

1278   To Peter Fountain

D^r S^r   [*ante* 1775]
Don't be impatient if I don't always answer ⟨your Let⟩ters directly,
unless ye Subject requires it— I admire y^r Friend's ⟨spi⟩rits, &
carry mine so far not to kill Spiders— I could make you laugh ⟨at⟩
mine and my Wife's Sensibility— I even go farther than Mr Lloyd,
I ⟨will⟩ not kill ye hare, no more than ye Greyhound. I most sincerely ⟨think⟩ that this Gentleman's cool moderate Virtue directed
by so ⟨good⟩ an understanding is the happiest counterpoise to your
⟨own⟩ honest *combustibility*— It is ye Joy & advantage of y^e [*trimmed*]
& I hope that you will long partake of ye blessing as you ⟨so⟩ well
deserve it by being truly sensible of it— next tuesday ⟨I am⟩
unluckily engag'd, but after Wednesday I am at yours ⟨and h⟩is
Service—

             I am Dr Sr Your very hu^le Servt
                          D Garrick

I kept ye Newspaper to give it you when I see You.

     Address: To Mr Fountain, Litchfield Street.   *Seal.*   *Source:* FC.

1279   To Peter Fountain

[*ante* 1775]

Mr Garrick's Comp^{ts} to Mr Fountain & many thanks for ye perusal of ye inclos'd papers— Mr Garrick is very sorry that it is not in his Power, circumstanc'd as he is, at present, to accept of ye friendly Offer he has made him—

Address: To Mr Fountain, Litchfield Street, Soho.   *Seal.*   *Source:* FC.

1280   To Peter Fountain

D^r S^r   [*ante* 1775]

I read ye Letter in a hurry, having Company, & forgot [to] send ye Enclos'd

Y^{rs} D^r S^r &c
D G

Address: To Mr Fountain, Lichfield Street.   *Seal.*   *Source:* FC.

1281   To Peter Fountain

Adelphi

Dear Sir   May 22 [1772–1775]¹

Thank you for ye Sight of the inclos'd; it is well done I shall attend the Prince & the Chev^r with Pleasure.

Yours most Sincerely
D Garrick

Address: To Mr Fountain, Lichfield Street, Soho.   *Source:* FC.

1. This letter and the following were written after Garrick moved to the Adelphi in 1772 and before Fountain moved to Maiden Lane in 1775.

1282 To Peter Fountain

Adelphi

Dear Sr Tuesday [1772–1775]
I am now with my Leg upon a Chair & not able to Stir— some
business of Consequence hie'd me into ye Country, from whence I
return'd late Yesterday, & sh^d have been wth You, had not this
Thief ye Gout stol'n in upon Me, & lay'd me by the heels— it is
impossible now to *say* when I can attend You— Why won't you
trust me with Y^r friendly designs, & I will send you an answer if
I receive them this Evening to Morrow Morning, & I assure You
not a Single soul shall Ever know ye Contents— it is ye only way
two such lame Creatures ⟨(⟩not Ducks thank Heav'n) can communicate their thoughts to Each Other— I am impatient to know
as We are now about making new Engagements, & y^r Hints may be
a Guide to me in Some Matters— If you write to me again, don't
send it till 7 or 8 o'Clock, as I may perhaps be upon ye Bed

Address: To Mr Fountain, Litchfield Street, Soho. *Endorsement by the recipient:*
Thursday 7th. *Source:* FC.

1283 To Peter Fountain

Dear Sr Monday Evening [*post* 1775][1]
the inclos'd is Nothing but part of a letter from Mr Victor to some
Correspondent I will give it him— Your Pears were exquisite—
M^{rs} G—— is a —— I know it— I am very much Oblig'd to You,
but I have not a Moment to Myself So pray excuse my brevity
                                                      Y^{rs} Ever &c
                                                        D G.

Address: Mr Fountain, Maiden Lane—. *Seal.* *Source:* FC.

1. Written after Fountain moved to Maiden Lane in 1775.

1284 To Peter Fountain

Adelphi
Dear S^r   Monday [*post* 1775]¹
You must excuse Me for not Writing sooner, I have not yet recover'd
my Spirits— as to dining or junketting with You, & the Baronet,
it is not in my power— I cannot leave home or trust myself in
Company the Doctors & my Wife, which is still more powerful
will not Suffer me to Eat from home
I am Dr Sr Most truly Y^{rs}
D Garrick

Address: Mr Fountain, Maiden Lane. *Endorsement by the recipient:* Adelphi
Monday Baronet Sir Thomas. *Source:* FC.

1. While no definite date can be assigned, references to a baronet in both the text
and the endorsement seem to relate this letter to Letter 935 of Aug. 27, 1775. The letter
was certainly written after Fountain moved to Maiden Lane in that year.

1285 To Peter Fountain

Dear Sir.   May 7 [*ante* June 1776]¹
I thank you for your good ⟨opinion⟩² of my first Comedian M^r
Thos King ⟨Your⟩ letter does him honour, & will ma⟨ke other⟩
Men (such as Mr Lloyd, which is a g⟨reat⟩ blessing) think well of
him— ⟨Will⟩ not you tell me what *Moral* [. . .] mean— there is
one has lately ⟨been⟩ wanting to Me— I really wish [. . .] Y^r
affair—

Y^{rs} most ⟨truly⟩
D ⟨Garrick⟩

Address: To Mr Fountain. *Seal. Source:* FC.

1. Written before Garrick's retirement.
2. The manuscript has been badly torn and trimmed.

1286   To Peter Fountain

Dear Sʳ   Tuesday [*ante* June 1776][1]
I have it not in my Power to assist you & Mʳˢ Fountain to get into
yᵉ house before yᵉ doors are open'd— I have been oblig'd from yᵉ
many Clamours private & publick to forbid it, at plays— if you
can make interest at an Oratorio I have no Objection But I have
no Managemᵗ those nights

Dʳ Sʳ Ever Yours.
D: Garrick.

Endorsed by the recipient.   *Source:* FC.

1. Written before Garrick's retirement.

1287   To Peter Fountain

Dear Sir   Fryday [*ante* June 1776][1]
I imagin'd Mʳ Loyd & You would drink Coffee wᵗʰ Me in yᵉ
afternoon— my hurry in a Morning at yᵉ Theatre will make a visit
at 12 uncomfortable— a still quiet Enjoyment of good Conversation
round a Tea table, is great luxury to Me— is it impossible to change
yᵉ hour of 12 in yᵉ morning to Six in yᵉ Evening? I know Nothing
of *Candidus*[2] for I never read yᵉ Papers, nor can I guess at what You
mean by a late Manager— More when I see You—

Ever Yours
D Garrick.

⟨A⟩ll hurry today—

Address: To Mʳ Fountain.   *Seal.*   *Source:* FC.

1. Written before Garrick's retirement.
2. Perhaps an allusion to the two letters written under that name in the *London
Chronicle* (vol. XXVIII, Aug. 30–Sept. 1, 1770, p. 213, vol. XXX, Nov. 5–7, 1771,
p. 445).

1288   To Peter Fountain

Dear Sir   Thursday 30ᵗʰ [1762–1777]¹
I shall [be] proud to pay my Respects & have yᵉ honour to be
introduc'd to the Comte Souverain d'Erbach—² I shall be ready
to obey the Chevʳ D'Eon's or Your Commands on Saturday about
Eleven, if that will [be] Agreeable.

                                                    Yʳˢ Ever
                                                    D. Garrick

Endorsed by the recipient.   Source: FC.

  1. Written during d'Eon's stay in England.
  2. No record has been found of a visit by any of the counts of Erbach in Hesse-
Darmstadt to England during the years of d'Eon's residence (but see Letter 652, n. 3).

1289   To Peter Fountain

Dear Sʳ   Febʳʸ yᵉ 4
Many thanks to you for yᵉ Sight of yᵉ inclos'd— there is great
Merit in yᵉ full length & much more in my opinion than in yᵉ
head— You see I deliver my opinion fairly & Sincerely— I am
Sorry for yᵉ health of yʳ Friend Dʳ Bruce.

                                                    Yʳˢ Ever
                                                    D Garrick

Endorsed by the recipient.   Source: FC.

1290   To Peter Fountain

Dear Sir   March 16
Many thanks to You for your flattering opinion of Me & many
thanks for the sight of yᵉ inclos'd it is very good & like—
  I am always in a hurry but always Yours

                                                Most Sincerely
                                                    D G.

Endorsed by the recipient.   Source: FC.

1291 **To Peter Fountain**

Augst 21st

Mr Garrick's Comp^{ts} to Mr Fountain & thanks him for his Intelligence about the two Elders. He had heard of their Magnanimity Some time ago, & trembled for his Friend Monnet. The last writes, that he is very happy, so his Friends ought to be contented.

Address: To Mr Fountain. *Endorsed by the recipient. Source:* FC.

1292 **To Peter Fountain**

Sat^y 23^d

Mr Garrick presents his Comp^{ts} to Mr Fountain— he is oblig'd to him for a Sight of ye book: He was not made ye Conveyer of it, but it came directly from the Bishop— M^r G: thinks M^r F: Should return a Card of thanks, but he hopes Mr F. will excuse him, for wishing, he would not say, that any body thought him wrong to return ye Papers &c—

He is Surpriz'd that any Gentleman can talk in y^t Manner— M^r G: still as bad, & can scarce write—

Source: FC.

1293 **To Peter Fountain**

D^r S^r   Saturday

I wrote to You from a Sick Bed, upon which I did not close my Eyes last Night— I am so much honour'd & overjoy'd at Mr Lloyd's attention to me, that I cannot find Words to Express my gratitude— When I am able I shall Write, in ye mean time he &

You may be assur'd, that No Eye shall glance upon yᵉ paper which his kindness has put into my hands.

Yʳˢ Ever & truly
D G.

Address: To Mʳ Fountain. *Seal. Source:* FC.

1294 To George Garrick

Mʳ George   Fryday Night [*post* June 22, 1749]¹
I beg Youll send me Word immediatly What you meant by saying that *You allways took my part when Ever You heard me tax'd with any thing*— Mʳˢ Garrick believes you insinuated that I have been thought to coquet with Women— this is a very serious matter & as I must have it clear'd, I beg an answer directly— I must insist upon you declaring what you meant Explicitly— I do not know which to admire most Your kindness in Saying so much, or her's in drawing Conclusions from it.

I am Yours &c
D Garrick

Address: To Mʳ George Garrick. *Source:* FSL.

1. Written after Garrick's marriage on June 22, 1749.

1295 To Peter Garrick

Dear Peter   [*post* April 1747]¹
I desire You will See Mʳ John Levet as soon as possible & let him know the Ticket (We bargain'd about) is ready for him & he may Use it from Xmas as p agreement. however if his Business detains him in yᵉ Country, [*deleted*] for this Season, if it is more convenient for him, he shall have it yᵉ Next. pray tell him this & let me know his Answer immediatly. Our Theatrical Affairs go on Swimmingly, which Mʳ Windham has undertook to acquaint you with more

particularly. You heard (I find) ten thousand Lyes in yᵉ Country about parties, raising yᵉ Prices &c &c &c, but whence they took their Rise I can't guess, for certainly No Play house ever went on So regularly & harmoniously, and 'tis agreed by all that things never appear'd more Satisfactory & Decent Even in yᵉ Augustan Age of yᵉ Theatre Viz. Booth Wilks & Cibber's Time— Fermingnac has got £500 in yᵉ Lottery & I have two blanks & one in yᵉ Wheel— My Lord Huntington² desir'd to be introduc'd to Me by Mʳ Ranby yᵉ Surgeon, & a very fine Youth he is. I shall send you some Oysters next week, & George shall give You Notice.

I am Dear Brothʳ Yʳˢ Affecᵗʸ
D Garrick.

My Love to Sisters—

Source: FSL.

1. Reference to the sale of tickets establishes the date of the letter as after April 1747, when Garrick became co-manager of Drury Lane.
2. Presumably Francis Hastings (1729–1789), tenth Earl (1746) of Huntingdon.

1296   To Richard Glover?¹

Hampton

Dear Sir   Monday [*post* 1754]²
I shall be in London next Fryday, & shᵈ be glad to return the Same Night to Hampton wᵗʰ the Golden Fleece. will You be kind to let me have it, any time before *four* on *Fryday* in the *afternoon*—?

Yʳˢ Dʳ Sʳ most Sincerely
D Garrick

I shall be in Southampton Street on Fryday by Eight o'Clock in yᵉ morning & shall stay at home till ten, then I go out for yᵉ whole Day.

Source: FSL.

1. Conjectural identification of the recipient rests on the assumption that the reference to the golden fleece applies to Glover's tragedy *Medea* (published 1761; DL, March 24, 1767).
2. Written after Garrick had Hampton in 1754.

1297   To Lady Glyn

Hampton
July 8th [1754–1776][1]

The Author of the Extempore lines on the other side presents his respects to Lady Glyn, & as she wish'd to see them, He has run the risk of exposing himself for the great pleasure of Obliging her Lad*ps* Commands— He cannot flatter himself with y*e* least hopes of her applause, for indeed in this instance he little merits it, but as she *once* was pleas'd *unkindly*, so if she would *now kindly* smile upon y*e* author, He shall think himself not only overpaid as a Poet, but will forget the injury done to him as an Actor.

To Lady Glyn upon her laughing at Lear

Why would You cruel Lady Glyn,
At Old Lear's madness smirk, & Grin,
          And harrow up poor David,
He cares not when the house is cramm'd,
Tho He by all the Wits is damn'd,
          So He by You is saved!

By the same means were You but kind,
You might both charm & vex my Mind:
          'Tis what my Wishes drive at;
For if by Fashion I'm decreed,
In publick by your Smiles to bleed,
          They'll *heal my Wounds* in Private.

Source: Sotheby, copy of verses in Garrick's hand in FSL.

1. Written after Lady Glyn's marriage in March 1754 and before Garrick's retirement in June 1776.

1298   To Fulke Greville

Dear Sir.   Saturday— [*ante* 1756][1]

You may depend upon my small Assistance in your very laudable intentions— I approve much of y*r Introductory discourse*, & your Design upon the Criticks— I hope You will paint many of 'Em— they are fine Subjects, & You have Excellent pencils & Colours.

I am Surpriz'd that our Friend has not call'd upon Me, for I wanted to See him—

I am Dr Sr Your most Sincere hum^{le} Ser^t

D Garrick

Address: To F. Greville Esqr. *Source:* HTC.

1. On the assumption that the "*Introductory discourse*" was written for Greville's *Maxims, Characters and Reflections*, this letter was written before 1756 when the book was published.

1299   To Colonel Bernard Hale?[1]

[1762–1767][2]

Difficilis, facilis, Iucundus, Acerbus es idem,
Nec tecum possum vivere, nec Sine te;[3]

My Wife tells Me & I suppose your Wife told her, (for the true Electrical fire is ever emitting from the tips of their tongues & so goes off, snap, crack all ye town over) my Wife I say tells Me, that You take it ill, (not to heart,) that I have not enter'd y^r doors, since my return from Bath, & as a farther aggravation of my offence, that I was gossipping an hour with Lord Ossory & Mr Beauclerk some where or other— I plead guilty to ye first indictment, which is enough of itself to hang a Man,— for a fool— but I can prove an *Alibi* to ye Second— indeed, my dear Col^l I have not once set Eyes upon those Gentlemen since my return from Bath till last thursday when I met 'Em at Col^l St John's[4] at dinner & if You knew what business, I have gone through of all kinds from Morning to Night, You would rather pity than be angry at me— I have not been able to make one Visit, nor Even to take a giddy turn at Ranelagh tho often invited;— I have only din'd out three times, & if You had not been too great an Œconomist these hard times, & kept y^r Legs of Mutton to y^rSelf You might have given me a great Chair & a pint of Port, & I should have forgot my multitudinous Cares for three hours at least. I'll tell you a fact— the Man of all Men I lov'd the best, one *Draper* by name, & now an arch angel in Heav'n, was for many years Every Morning with Me at breakfast time— as we were walking arm in arm together— pray Garrick, says he, when were You at my house?— Why— answ^d I— with a Sort of hesitation— some time last Month. I believe— not these 13 Months reply'd my friend smiling— Zounds!— nay don't be uneasy— nor think that I have been foolish enough to set it down— I know y^o & y^r Cares too well but my Wife told me this, & will prove it to You when You please to call upon her—

—Blush Col'nel blush— let our Wives be foolish, but let us behave like Men. Ever & most Affec^ty

Yours
D G.

This is ye first moment I have had to play ye fool in, so take ye foll^g answ^r to Dr John Hill's letter

To Dr Hill.

1

Never think Doctor Hill,
My Stomach to fill,
With y^r Med'cines so rank & so stale;
The Physician I love,
A Specifick will prove!
Send Me (Dr Hill) Doctor Hale.

2

Tho the Doctor is forward,
And a little untoward,
His Medcines wth me never fail;
Tho at times he is pettish,
Ceremonious, coquettish,
Send Me (Doctor Hill) Doctor Hale[5]

Source: FSL, draft, copy of verses in FC.

1. Hale seems to be the only colonel to whom Garrick wrote in a familiar manner.

2. Hale was a colonel from 1762 to 1772; within this span it seems unlikely that St. John would have entertained Beauclerk after Oct. 1767 when Beauclerk was named correspondent in the divorce proceedings brought by St. John's brother. Within the period 1762–1767 the only mention in the letters of Garrick being in Bath is during March and April of 1766 and from late March to early May of 1767.

3. Martial, *Epigrams,* xii, xlvii, 1: "Difficult and easy-going, pleasant and churlish, you are at the same time: I can neither live with you nor without you."

4. Henry St. John (1738?–1818), son of John, second Viscount St. John. In 1762 he became a lieutenant colonel of the late 91st Foot.

5. Knapp, No. 162.

1300   To The Earl of Hardwicke

Hampton

My Lord   Monday Morn^g [*post* February 1771][1]

I am really very unhappy that I have not had ye honour of seeing Your Lordship; the Moment I had been fix'd for ye Summer at Hampton I intended to pay my respects at Richmond: an Affair of a Farm I have in Essex, has kept me much against my will from Home: Let me assure Your Lordship that it is the greatest pride, honour & pleasure of my Life [to] have the favour of Lord Hardwicke, & my Utmost ambition is to deserve by my behaviour the continuance of the honour his Lordship has been pleas'd to confer upon Me.

I am My Lord Your Lordship's Most obedient &
respectful Ser^t
D Garrick.

Mrs Garrick joins with me in respects to ye Marchioness of Grey & the Young Ladies.

Source: BM.

1. Assuming that the reference to the farm in Essex is to Garrick's holdings at Copford (which he usually calls a farm) rather than to Hendon (which he usually calls a manor), this letter was written after the purchase of the former in Feb. 1771.

1301   To Hall Hartson

[*ante* January 6, 1768][1]

Mr. Garrick would not delay to return yr. Play as soon as he had considered it— the remarks wh. are written in haste are intended for Mr. Hartson's own perusal, and are not so correct as a little more time might have made them

Source: Maggs Brothers, Catalogue, July–Aug. 1913, extract.

1. The date is supplied on the assumption that the play referred to is Hartson's only known dramatic work, *The Countess of Salisbury*: it was produced in Dublin in the 1764–65 season, at the Haymarket in London on Aug. 21, 1767 (*Public Advertiser*, Aug. 22, 1767, p. 2), and for the first time at Drury Lane on Jan. 6, 1768.

1302 To Mr. and Mrs. John Hawkesworth

Tuesday [1749–1756][1]
M^r & Mrs Garrick send their Compliments to M^r & Mrs Hawkesworth, and they beg to know how Mrs Hawkesworth does, having been very Uneasy with Mr Hawkesworth's Account of her Last Night

Source: FSL.

1. Written after Garrick's marriage in 1749 and before Hawkesworth received the Lambeth degree of LL.D. in 1756.

1303 To Doctor John Hawkesworth

London
My dear D^r   Fryday 10 0 Clock [*post* 1756][1]
I am this Moment arriv'd & surrounded with a dozen Artists; I would leave them directly to wait upon You but can't get away: If You don't come this Way in ye Afternoon about Tea time— I will most certainly be with you at 6, or what hour you will in ye Evening— say when

Ever & Affect^y Y^rs
D Garrick

Address: To Dr Hawkesworth.   Source: HTC.

1. This letter and the following were written after Hawkesworth received his LL.D.

1304   To Doctor John Hawkesworth

My dear Friend.   [*post* 1756]
I am much oblig'd to you— You are Wellcome to me & Mine at
all times & Seasons—
    pray command Me without yᵉ least Reserve whenever Mʳˢ
Hawkesworth pleases to honor Us— I have a thought in my head
for You— but of that when I see You

                                        Ever Yours most affectʸ
                                                D Garrick.

Address: To Dʳ Hawkesworth.   *Seal.*   *Source:* FSL.

1305   To William Hawkins

                                                        Adelphi
Sir.   Augˢᵗ 3 [1772–1775]¹
I return You my thanks for the book you have sent Me—
    As to an Engagement as an Actor at our theatre, the Summer
is too far advanc'd to make any Additions— our Company is full
& we cannot now receive any more, except of yᵉ first Merit.
                            I am Sʳ Your most hum Servᵗ
                                                D. Garrick

I have a pain in my hand & can scarce write

Address: Mʳ Willᵐ Hawkins, Anderton's Coffee house, Fleet Street.   *Seal.*
Source: John David Batchelder Collection.

    1. Written after Garrick's move to the Adelphi in March 1772 and before his retire-
ment in June 1776.

1306   To William Hawkins

Decr. 21, 177[?]

Mr Garrick's Compts. to Mr Hawkins, & thanks him for the book. If he pleases to call upon him at any time after ye Holidays, he will talk with him upon the subject of his letter.

Address: To Mr Wm. Hawkins, Anderton's Coffee House, Fleet St.   *Source:* Captain William Jaggard, transcript.

1307   To Doctor George Hay

My Dʳ Dʳ   Friday Mornᵍ [1749–1757]¹

I have settled with Mʳ Ralph to meet you at his house Sunday next to Dinner— Wilson will be with us, & we shall be at Chiswick by two o'Clock— the little Manager of Drury has so much benefited by yʳ last Skillfull dissection of him, that in yᵉ fullness of his Gratitude he has sent a haunch of Venison to regale You on Sunday next— pray do not fail our Feast.

Mʳˢ Garrick & yʳ Selfish humble Serᵗ will be ready at a Day's Warning, to set off for Oxford; so *that* Expedition will wholly depend upon You— once more let me intreat yᵘ to remember Ralpho & Me, who am (notwithstanding your late Pleasantry)

Yʳˢ most Sincerely
D: Garrick

Address: To Dʳ Haye at Dʳ'ˢ Commons.   *Seal.   Source:* HTC.

1. Written after Garrick's marriage in June 1749 and before his falling-out with Ralph in Sept. 1757.

1308   To Doctor George Hay

My dear Sir   [*ante* 1773]¹

My regard for You is greater than my vanity, & that is a bold Word— for damn Me (as Ranger says) if I had not rather have you with that charming Rigby at yᵉ opera than with Garrick at Drury Lane—²

You are too Generous but I shall Obey yʳ Orders

Yʳˢ most truly
D Garrick

Address: To Dʳ Hay. *Seal.* *Source:* FSL.

1. Written before Hay was knighted in 1773.
2. Cf. *The Suspicious Husband*, III, iii.

1309   To The Countess of Hertford

Madam.   [*post* 1766]¹
Your Ladyship's last Note to Mʳˢ Garrick demands our best & warmest Acknowledgments I shall always be proud of shewing the Sense I have of Lady Hertfords great goodness to Me— As I fear, from some late Observations I have made, that I have been un-happy enough to lose his Lordship's Favour, I think My retreat from the Theatre too insignificant to announce to his Lordship, tho I am vain enough to imagine Myself the first & not I hope the least deserving of his Theatrical Servants, If Your Ladyship thinks proper to mention this very triffling Circumstance to my Lord Chamberlain, as I dare not trouble him myself upon the Occasion, It will add to the many favours already conferr'd upon

Madam Yʳ Ladyships Most Obedᵗ &c

Source: FC, draft; Boaden, I, 574.

1. Written after 1766 when Hertford became Lord Chamberlain.

1310   To James Hook¹

Sir   [?1773–1774]²
—I have the greatest opinion of Mʳ Hook's Abilities in his pro-fession, but the Proprietors of the Theatre in Drury Lane have

determin'd at present not to be engag'd to any particular Gentleman as Composer for their house:

If they had not, they know no one would be more Agreeable to them than Mr Hook.

I am Sr yr most hule ⟨Sert⟩
D: Garrick.

PS. a Gentleman who has compos'd for ye house before, has been promis'd the musical departmt if they shd Ever Engage another Composer

The Gout in my thumb makes me scarce able to write.

Address: To Mr Hook, Percy Street, Rathbone Place, London.   *Source:* FSL.

1. James Hook (1746–1827), organist and composer at Marylebone Gardens, 1769–1773, and at Vauxhall Gardens, 1774–1820.
2. Perhaps written about 1773–1774, between Hook's engagements.

1311   To John Hoole[1]

[*ante* June 1776][2]
Mr Garrick's Compts to Mr Hoole he begs to be excusd either tellg When he plays or procuring places for his friends— He has resolv'd that what he has said, shall be minutely done— *first come*, first serv'd, without preference or partiality.

D G.

Source: FSL.

1. This letter is in reply to a note from Hoole dated "Sheer Lane Monday." In September 1770 Hoole had rooms in Clement's Inn (Nichols, II, 406), but the dedication to *Cleonice* is dated from Shire Lane on March 11, 1775. Hoole's note, on the back of which Garrick has written his reply, reads: "Mr Hoole presents his best Complimts to Mr Garrick, begs to know when he appears again or if he may hope, whenever he does that M[r] Garrick could procure him six places for some very particular friends— Mr H: intreats that Mr Garrick would freely give him a short answer concerning the *propriety* of the above request, or if he may send to Mr Johnston for places."
2. Written before Garrick's retirement.

1312   To John Hoole

D^r S^r   [*ante* June 1776][1]
I have sent my Ans⟨wer⟩ to Y^r Card upon ye back of it— which I
desire You will keep, & read to as many as come in Y^r way— 'tis
my confirm'd purpose.

                                          Y^{rs} Ever & truly
                                                  D G.

Address: —— Hoole Esqr.   *Endorsement:* Note & Card from M Garrick.
Source: HTC.

 1. This note accompanied the preceding letter.

1313   To Doctor William? Hunter[1]

                              Saturday Night [*post* 1754][2]
Mr David Garrick presents his Compliments to Doctor Hunter.
begs to know what hour on Monday will be most convenient for
Him to see Mrs Garrick, as she is He's affraid in a very poor Way
and Stands much in need of Doctor Hunters good advice— M^{rs} &
Mr Garrick being at Hampton, if about twelve or one o'clock will
Suit Doctor Hunter they will endeavor to be as punctual as
possible—

Source: Hunter-Baillie Collection.

 1. This letter is more probably written to William Hunter (1718–1783), M.D. 1750,
than to his brother John (1728–1793), since Garrick uses the title of Doctor and the latter
never held a degree. The brothers were generally recognized as the most distinguished
medical practitioners and experimenters in London.
 2. Written after 1754 when the Garricks first lived at Hampton.

1314   To Edward Jerningham[1]

                                                  Adelphi
                              April 23 [*post* 1772][2]
Mr Garrick presents his best Comp^{ts} & thanks to Mr Jerningham
for the great honour he has done him.

Source: Huntington Library.

1. Edward Jerningham (1737–1812), poet and dramatist. His plays were all produced after Garrick's retirement.
2. This letter and the following were written after Garrick moved to the Adelphi.

1315   To Edward Jerningham

Adelphi
May 29 [*post* 1772]

Mr Garrick presents his Comp^ts to Mr Jerningham— He truly reckon'd yesterday without his Host for Upon his Wife's coming home, he found that an Engagement to dine at Lord Hertford's on thursday & at Epsom on Friday will prevent them from being at Hampton till Friday Night— if Saturday Morning or any Morning after Saturday that the Duke & his Friends will please to appoint, They will be ready at any hour to be honour'd with their Company—

Will Mr Jerningham favour Mr Garrick with a few Lines in answer to ye above?

Address: E^d Jerningham Esqr.   Source: Huntington Library.

1316   To Pierre Antoine de Laplace

My good Friend.   [*post* 1764]^1

You have eas'd my heart & I shall ever remember it— I am truly sorry that I should give You so much trouble for such a triffle, but the Baron^2 is as modest as he is Worthy, & he was affraid of making Enemies—

Once again, I am greatly oblig'd to You; and tho Your Qualifications made me wish Your Friendship, yet Your honest & Feeling Heart will ever make me sollicitous to continue it.

My dear Sir most affectionately Yours
D: Garrick

I must insist upon paying all y^r Workmen for this trouble—

Address: A Monsieur, Monsieur de La Place. *Seal. Source:* FSL.

1. Written after 1764 when Garrick met Laplace; perhaps in 1765 when Garrick was visiting in Paris (Hedgcock, p. 319).
2. Presumably Baron d'Holbach.

1317 To The Reverend Evan Lloyd

Hampton

Dear Lloyd   Sunday [April 29, 1773–January 1774]¹

I cannot exactly say what time I can be in London therefore don't delay by a note sent to the Adelphi letting me know in as many words as you please the *two words* you have to say to me— Let it be at the Adelphi on Monday Evening and I will send you an answer on Tuesday or Wednesday at furthest. If the matter be too great or too sacred or too what you will for a letter, I will call upon you as soon as I can; depend upon my secresy if you choose to Commit it to paper. I think the seal a fine one,² the expression bold, but too flattering for y^r humble servant. I hope to find you upon your legs when I shall be in town—

Y^rs Ever & Sincerely
D. Garrick

Did not I hear of you at the Gardens some wet night. O fie I have.

Source: National Library of Wales, transcript.

1. Presumably written shortly after the exhibition of Marchant's seal of Garrick on April 29, 1773, and before Jan. 1774 after which date Lloyd never returned to London (Cecil Price, "David Garrick and Evan Lloyd," *Review of English Studies*, NS vol. II, Jan. 1952, p. 37).
2. By Nathaniel Marchant (1739–1816), gem-engraver, and described as "a sulphur [impression] from an intaglio, the subject Mr. Garrick turning to a bust of Shakespear with this exclamation: Quo me rapis tui plenum" (catalogue of the *Exhibition of the Incorporated Society of Artists*, April 29, 1773). The seal later passed to Lloyd's descendants.

1318 To Charles Macklin

Sir. [*post* 1759][1]

I have this Moment receiv'd y^r Long Letter & the Post goin^g away in half an hour— I would not omit writing to you directly tho I can answer Yours only in part— I mean those passages that regard Myself only; as to ye Matter of Miss Macklin's agreem^t it must be discuss'd & talk'd over by Yourself Mr Lacy & Me, for which purpose I will be in Town next week at a time I hope that will not be inconvenient to You—

Your Paragraph relative to Mrs Macklin is a Mistake through out— I had Ever a great Regard for her both as a woman & as an Actress, this I believe she knew & felt, but when by an ill state of health, she was incapable of appearing upon ye Stage ye Managers were Satisfy'd with what She could do for them, without Ever once making use of such a disagreeable Term as *Encumbrance*— If Miss Macklin was Ever shockt to burst into Tears at what I may have said to her upon this head, I shall most frankly own that I neither know her or Myself, & I am very Sorry that I should so ill-execute my own intentions as to produce a contrary Effect— The other Passage in Y^r Letter concerning a conservation wth Miss Macklin, about Sallary &c &c &c I shall leave to herself to answer & beg to know if the Name of Mrs Cibber was not most particularly & Essentially Mention'd which Name is omitted in y^r Letter & is, I think a full answer to y^t part of ⟨y^r Letter⟩. I shall now come to ye last Charge against Me— it was reported that you had join'd with Mr Foote,[2] sign'd & seal'd wth him— but I did not believe it, to ye truth of wch I can call some Gentlemen of y^r Acquaintance— therefore I now declare that my reporting or sending Word to Mr Foote (with whom I have not had ye least corespondence[)] that I w^d remonstrate to ye L^d Ch[amberlain] upon that Acc^t is a Falsehood, & therefore *Mr Macklin sh^d Surely have had a better Authority for his aspersion* before he had given it under his hand.— My *real intentions* are to sign & seal our Agreem^t wch were settled between Us, I thought fully & amicably, at our last Meeting, & tho my Broth^r may have delay'd ye Execution, yet You cannot imagine that ye Managers would deviate one tittle from w^t was then Settled— I likewise Wish & hope that Miss Macklin will be settled with Us for a term of Years, ye longer the better, & that all agreements between Us may be full & Explicit that mean unmanly disputes, may be prevented for yᵉ future. Whatever part of yʳ Letter I have omitted to answer, You must attribute to my great haste however I shall not let a single Circumstance pass unanswer'd when I see You

I am Sʳ Yʳ humᵉ Serᵗ
D G—

PS. I was told that you ask'd for yᵉ Book of yʳ Farce; it is far better Security in my possession, but you may command it whenever you please.

Source: FC, draft; Boaden, I, 361f.

1. Written sometime after Mrs. Macklin's death in 1758 and Macklin's return from Ireland in 1759. While Miss Macklin and her father appeared at Drury Lane for the end of the 1759–60 season, they were not reëngaged ever again, though negotiations continued during Garrick's management.
2. Foote was not granted a full patent on any theater until 1766, when presumably he would have first come in conflict with other managers over the engagement of actors for the winter season.

1319 To John Moody[1]

[post 1759][2]

You made me very unhappy last night— Mrs. Garrick has sent you some more Gargle— take 4 or 5 spoonfuls at a time warm

Source: Chas. J. Sawyer, Ltd., Catalogue No. 8, 1955, extract, *complete text not made available for publication.*

1. So identified in the source.
2. Written after 1759 when Moody made his debut at Drury Lane.

1320 To Hannah More

My Dear Madam, [post 1774][1]

Write you an epilogue! give you a pinch of snuff! By the greatest good luck in the world, I received your letter when I was surrounded with ladies and gentlemen, setting out upon a party to go up the Thames. Our expedition will take us seven or eight days upon the most limited calculation. They would hardly allow me a moment to write this scrawl: I snatched up the first piece of paper (and a bad one it is) to tell you how unhappy I am that I cannot confer upon you so small a favour directly. If you will let me know immediately, by a line directed to me at the Adelphi, for whom you intend the epilogue, and what are her or his strong marks of character in the play (for my copy is in town, or with Miss Young), I will do my best on my return. I must desire you not to rely upon me this time, on account of my present situation; I could as soon sleep in a whirlwind as write among these ladies, and I shall be so fatigued with talking myself and hearing them talk, or I could sit up all night to obey your commands. Prepare one, I beseech you, for fear I should not have a day for composing an epilogue. Let me know what subject you choose, what character is to speak it, and everything else about it, and when it is to be acted, and if not now, I will most certainly scribble something for the next time. Should I be drowned, I hope you will excuse me, and write my epitaph.

With my best and warmest wishes to you, your sisters, and the whole blood of the Stonehouses,

I am, most sincerely, Your friend and humble servant,

D. Garrick.

P.S.— I write upon a full gallop; the provisions are on board— my wife calls (who begs her compliments), and that is a voice I always obey.

Source: Roberts, *Hannah More*, I, 68f.

1. Written after Garrick and Miss More first met in the spring of 1774.

1321   To The Earl of Northington[1]

[1764–1772][2]

⟨Were I⟩ not bound by Gratitude, Duty & Inclination to Obey Y^r Lordship's Commands, my Pride would induce Me to Execute them to the best of my Power—

I am afraid as their Majesties have commanded tomorrow so favourite a Play, that I shall not be able to get a Side Box, but Lady Northington[3] may depend upon my procuring her Ladyship three or four places & good Ones in a Middle front Box.

> I am My Lord Y[r] Lordship's Most grateful &
> Obed[t] Ser[t]
> D G.

Source: FSL, fragment.

1. The Earl of Northington was Lord Chancellor during the administrations of Bute, Grenville, and Rockingham.
2. The inclusive dates are supplied by Henley's creation as Earl of Northington in 1764 and by his death in 1772.
3. Jane (Huband) Henley (d. 1787).

1322 To The Reverend Doctor Thomas Percy

My dear Sir. [*post* 1770][1]
There will be room for you all if you can come, & most Welcome you will be—

> Ever Yours in all Shapes & Characters
> D G.

Address: Rev D[r] Percy. *Source:* FSL.

1. Written after Percy had received a D.D. from Cambridge in 1770.

1323 To The Performers of Drury Lane

Gentlemen— [1776?][1]
I have long seen and felt the great evil you complain of— It came with double weight upon me this season, but as I resolved to quit the direction of the Theatre, I gave up all thoughts of finding out a remedy for it— As I most Sincerely wish you well, if you can

point out to me any justifiable method of Serving you, I will do
that for *you*, which I have hitherto delayed to do for the Proprietors

I am Gent Your most Servant

D. G.

Endorsement: Endorsed by Garrick, My Answer to the Performers.   *Source:*
FC, copy.

1. It seems probable that Garrick wrote this letter in the spring of the season in which
he retired.

1324   To Jane Pope

Dear Mad^m   [*post* 1756][1]
One of ye Epilogues is too long & ye other too short. if you curtail
ye first & take out all ye dead wood it will do. the other wants a
few points

I am yours most truly

D. Garrick

Address: Miss Pope.   *Source:* A. C. Burney, transcript.

1. Written after Miss Pope's debut at Drury Lane in 1756.

1325   To Thomas Rackett, Sr.

Dear Sir   Thursday Night
My Wife, Mrs Flasby & y^r humble Servant will dine with You on
Saturday next, & hope 4 o'Clock (a late hour for ye Country) will
not be too late for You— I am afraid we shall be troublesome, but
ye trouble is of your own Seeking, so you must bear it.

I am most truly Y^rs

D Garrick

I have been free enough to Ask Mr Becket to meet me at y^r house
on Saturday upon business— I hope it won't be inconvenient.

Address: To Mr Rackett, King's Street.   *Seal.*   *Source:* FSL.

1326   To Richard Rigby

Monday [*post* 1768][1]

Mr Garrick's respects to Mr Rigby— He feels a few twinges at this moment for ye revelry of Yesterday— the Person who lent him the Letter to the Chancellor is gone to Richmond, but Mr Rigby will have it tomorrow.

Could I be sure that Every Stream at ye Pay office would stop, as one did Yesterday, I should defy the Stone, Gout, Devil & all his Works—

Upon the Vin de Grace
being drunk out at Mr Rigby.

No Stream before in this full-flowing place
Did Ever Stop— but always ran apace:
Did e'er before the Master call in vain?
The Sea is Sunk Chaos is come again:

Little Fish

Endorsement by Garrick: Lady Spencer with ye Vin de Grace.   *Source:* FSL.

1. The letter was written after 1768 when Rigby was made Paymaster of the Forces.

1327   To Doctor ? Schomberg[1]

D^r D^r

As You Love & understand the Subject of the follow^g Song better than any body & as the Author loves Nobody more than You, there cannot be found so proper a Patron for it, which is most Sincerely dedicated to You by

Y^r affectionate
D. G.

Song.

1.

Though land-men may boast of their fresh-running streams,
And Cockneys think nothing so fine as the Thames;
Yet what are all waters compared to the Sea,

Whose exquisite food makes a great man of me?
    As are Squibs to Nine-Pounders,
    So hold in proportion,
    Carp, Tench, & Thames Flounders
    To the fish of the Ocean.
To the fish of the Ocean all dainties are toys;
    For when they're before us,
    Our lips smack in Chorus;
What a treasure's the Sea to us British brave boys!

2.

The luscious-finn'd Turbot so firm, & so white;
With rich Lobster sauce is the Glutton's delight:
Though distant in Party, round a Table we close,
Forget all our feuds, & agree with our foes,
    That fine Soles & red Mullets,
    Cod, Pipers, & Dories
    Will charm rival Gullets
    Of Whigs & of Tories.
To the Fish of the Ocean &c—— Chorus.

3.

Each fish of the Sea has its likeness at land;
The Mack'rel are Damsels that ply in the Strand;
In Summer, both swarming, are common & cheap,
Look tempting & fresh, but they never will keep.
    Smelts, so fresh, & sweet flavour'd,
    Are Maidens so fickle;
    Rakes, salt & high-savour'd,
    Anchovies in pickle.
To the Fish of the Ocean &c—— Chorus.

4.

The Sword-fish are Soldiers, shotten-Herrings are Wits;
The flat-Fish are Courtiers, the Cod-fish are Cits:
The Thornback's a Lawyer,— the Scuttle Fish, He
Who seeks for his prey in the 'Change-Alley Sea.
    When he strikes the poor Bubbles,
    And is danger in fear of—
    Then the Water he troubles,
    That he may get clear off—
To the Fish of the Ocean &c—— Chorus.

5.

The Shellfish are Misers, so hard to come at,
Who opens their shells finds 'em fleshy & fat;
The Whale is a Nabob, with stomach so vast,
That much he gulps down, & can swallow it fast.
    Like the Shark, fam'd for biting,
    The Gambler well known is;
    Shrimps, Sprats, & pale Whiting
    Are all Macaronies.
To the Fish of the Ocean &c—— Chorus.

Endorsement by Garrick: New Song about Fish. tolerable. address'd to Dr Schomberg. *Source:* letter only FSL, copy of verses in FSL.

1. It has been impossible to determine which of the Schomberg twins was the recipient.

1328 To The Reverend Joseph Smith

                      From Mr Vaillant's Shop—
Dear Smith.   Monday [?1750–1761]1
Mrs Garrick & yr humble intend to travel yr way tomorrow, *for Reasons & causes look ye;*2 We cannot pass by Stanmore without asking old friends how they do— We shall be with You between Nine & ten, & if yr water boils & Yr Heart is willing why we will adjourn wth thee & thine for half an hour— my best Compts to Mrs Smith & believe me thine

                      Ever & Sincerely
                      D Garrick

Address: To The Revd Mr Smith. *Source:* FC; Boaden, II, 336f.

1. Probably written between 1750 when Vaillant inherited the family bookselling business and 1761 when Garrick began patronizing Becket.
2. *Merry Wives of Windsor*, III, i, 48.

1329 To The Reverend Joseph Smith

Sir.

We have granted all our Charity Plays and Tickets for this Year and our list is full for ye Next— If twenty pounds would make ye family happy, I am surpriz'd a Lady of fashion, Consequence & Humanity should debate a Moment about the Means— I wish it was in my pow'r to Oblige & serve all; I do as much as I can, & I would I could do more— how You come to imagine that you had no Interest with me (as well as ye Coldness of y^r Letter) surprizes Me! But as *I* must imagine that your Notion, is merely ye result of y^r Inclination, you must give me leave to subscribe myself as coldly

S^r Y^r most Obed^t Ser^t
D Garrick

Mrs Garrick joins wth Me in Compliments to Mrs Smith.

Address: To The Revd Mr Smith, Rector of Stanmore, Middx. *Postmark:* DE 21. *Source:* FC; Boaden, II, 336.

1330 To The Reverend Doctor ? Smith

Saturday [*ante* March 1772][1]

Mr Garrick presents his Respects to Dr Smith and Dr Jay & will not give them ye trouble of calling in Southampton Street to Day, as his being at home is quite uncertain on Account of his Business at the Theatre, but Mr Garrick will Take ye first opportunity of paying his Compliments to them at the Mews Gate.

Address: To The Revd Dr Smith at the Mews Gate, Corner of Duke's Court. *Seal.* *Source:* FSL.

1. Written before Garrick moved from Southampton Street in March of 1772.

1331   To The Countess Spencer

Hampton, Sunday Night

Address: Lady Spencer. *In the possession of the Earl Spencer: Not made available for publication.*

1332   To The Countess Spencer

Address: Lady Spencer. *In the possession of the Earl Spencer: Not made available for publication.*

1333   To The Countess Spencer

Address: Countess Spencer. *In the possession of the Earl Spencer: Not made available for publication.*

1334   To Nathaniel? Thomas[1]

Dᵣ Sir.   [*post* 1761][2]
Suppose you were to introduce yᵉ re-printing of yᵉ Prologue by saying— "that You are oblig'd to Your Cornwall Correspondent, & take Shame to Yourself for some Errors in the Performance alluded to, that You think you cannot find out a more ready way to do Justice to yᵉ author, & oblige Yʳ readers, particularly yᵉ aforesaid Correspondent, than by giving a correcter Copy of yᵉ Prologue in question—"
Something of this Kind if You think it worth while to reprint

yᵉ Prologue, will be necessary— but Mʳ Thomas will manage this Business better than I can, & so I will say no more but that

I am Most Sincerely Yʳˢ

D Garrick.

Source: FSL.

1. Presumably Nathaniel Thomas (1731–1795), antiquarian and numismatist, editor of the *St. James's Chronicle* at its inception and later one of the proprietors (Nichols, III, 281).

2. If identification of the recipient is correct, this letter would have been written after Thomas became editor of the *St. James's Chronicle* in 1761.

1335   To Captain Edward Thompson

Dear Thompson.   Novʳ 13 [1772–1775][1]

You will always Squirt out Your foes whenever you please—

I beg You'll take care of Yourself & think not of Me, till you can come to me Safely— that will be yᵉ best way to shew Yʳ friendship to Me. I thought of being at Hampton last Sunday, but was prevented by business— indeed my five weeks absence has provided me a great deal of business at the Theatre. I shall always be glad to see you— my Love to Yours.

Ever & most affectʸ Yours

D Garrick

Address: To Capᵗⁿ Thompson near Kew Green.   *Postmarked.*   *Source:* Maggs Brothers.

1. Written after Thompson moved to Kew in 1772 and before Garrick retired in June 1776.

1336   To ? Thompson

Dʳ Thompson   Tuesday Evenᵍ

I shall be in London tomorrow, & shall be glad to see you about Eleven or Twelve— the Letter shall be ready

Ever most, Sincerely yours

D. Garrick

My best Respects to yʳ Lady—

Source: American Autograph Shop.

1337   To Lady Henrietta Vernon[1]

Hampton

Madam   Sep[r] 25 [*post* 1767][2]

Tho I wrote to y[r] Ladyship Yesterday I must beg leave to trouble You once more— We cannot bear that her H:R:H:[3] wishes to have some place for the pleasure of fishing in this quarter, without doing Every thing in our Power to Accomodate her— We therefore beg leave to make an offer to your Ladyship of our own house which will be more convenient than any which can be had in or about Hampton—[4] With a few hours Notice Y[r] Ladyship may depend upon having y[e] Whole or part without the least molestation from Ourselves or from any Person whatsoever— We have some fear that her R. H.'s delicacy may imagine that y[e] Acceptance of this offer may be inconvenient to us— we beg leave to assure Your Lady[p] that we can so contrive it, that we shall feel Ourselves highly honour'd if this triffling Mark of our great respect & Duty may be Accepted without the smallest inconvenience to ourselves.

I am Madam Your Ladyship's most Obedient hu Ser[t]

D G

PS. The place over against our Terrace is the best for fishing,[5] the temple in y[e] Garden will be very convenient as it is near & we have boats & a very good landing place all within a few Yards

We go to London this Evening.

Endorsement by Garrick: Another Letter to Lady Harriet Vernon W[th] an offer of my house.   *Source:* Garrick Club; Boaden, II, 125.

1. Henrietta (Wentworth) Vernon (d. 1786), daughter of the third Earl of Strafford and wife (1743) of Henry Vernon of Hilton Park, Staffordshire, was a Lady of the Bedchamber to Princess Amelia (*LC*, vol. LIX, April 11–13, 1786, p. 352).

2. Lady Vernon is first listed among the Ladies of the Bedchamber in the *Royal Kalender; or Correct Annual Register* in 1767 (7th ed. corrected to March 25, 1767).

3. Amelia Sophia Eleanora (1711–1786), second daughter of George II.

4. To Garrick's first letter, now missing, Lady Henrietta had replied: "[I] shall not fail to take the first opportunity of informing Her Royal Highness of your obliging offer, tho' in y[e] mean time I cannot help mentioning from my own knowledge of HRH's disposition, (least it should be any restraint to you or M[rs] Garrick), that I do not imagine HRH will give that trouble" (Garrick Club).

5. The portion of the river known as Hampton Deep, extending from the lawn of Garrick's villa to Tumbling Bay (960 yards), seems always to have been popular water for good catches (Henry Ripley, *The History and Topography of Hampton-on-Thames*, 1885, p. 97f.; see also Walpole, ed. Toynbee, II, 21f.).

1338 To William Watson¹

Sir   Sunday [*ante* 1759]²
I am oblig'd to dine with Lord Chesterfield & Dʳ Garnier to
Morrow; but if you'll let me Wait upon you next Wednesday
between four & five, if a fine Day, you'll greatly oblige
                                                        Yʳ most humˡᵉ Servᵗ
                                                        D. Garrick

Address: To Mʳ Watson Apothecary ⟨Aldersgate Street⟩ near Smithfield.
Source: Hyde Collection; *The R. B. Adam Library*, Buffalo, 1929, I, [10].

    1. William Watson (1715–1787), physician. Apprenticed to an apothecary in 1730,
he established himself independently in 1738 (*Catalogue of the Several Members of the Society
of Apothecaries*, London, Sept. 1741).
    2. From the address, this letter seems to have been written before Watson took up
residence in Lincoln's Inn Fields about 1759 (*ibid.*).

1339 To Joseph White¹

                                                Saturday night 27 [1773–1775]²
Mʳ Garrick begs leave to inform Mʳ White that he has the Edition
of Virgil printed in 1529;³ which Mʳ Warner suppos'd he had not.

Address: Mʳ White, Bookseller, Corner of Serle Street, Lincolns Inn Field.
Source: FSL.

    1. Joseph White (d. 1791), bookseller, had a shop in Lincoln's Inn Fields from 1773
until 1778 (*GM*, vol. LXI, Dec. 1791, p. 1161).
    2. The letter must have been written between 1773 (when White is first found in
Serle Street) and April 1775, the date of Warner's death.
    3. This edition (*Opera Virgiliana cum decem commentis, docte et familiariter exposita ab
Iodoco Badio Ascesio*, [Lyons], 1529) does not appear, however, in the auction catalogue
(1823) of Garrick's library.

1340　　　To Sarah Wilmot

Adelphi

My dear Madam. 18 [*post* March 1772][1]

I wish you were not half so good, that I might have an opportunity
of being a little angry with You sometimes for neglecting me—
Your Friendship & affection is all turnpike, & there is not a single
jog upon the whole road— now thanks to the frailty of human
Nature, my other Connections keep me in good exercise, & like
the old pavement don't suffer me to sleep in my coach— When I
am with You, or write to You, my passions are so subdu'd, & made
stagnate, that if I were to see You often, & stay long with you my
blood would grow too thick, & some morning I should be found
dead of an Apoplexy in ye Conservatory among Your Balsams &
Geraniums— I therefore never chuse to stay long with You at a
time, but get home with my dear wife, who takes care by proper
exercise to keep my Springs in motion by wch I throw off those
heavy particles of Ease & happiness which have too much clog'd
them at Farnborough— mais retournons a nos moutons— Why are
you to plague Yourself about 4 Years old Sheep? if ⟨I have a score
of⟩ 3 Years old, or partly one & partly t'other, (if that is possible)
will do very well for me— I want ye Sheep to feed upon my land,
not for me to feed upon— however a piece of Mutton of my own
feeding, tho it be tough & tastless, would certainly give me an
Importance in my Neighborhood— therefore my dear Madam, you
must get me what you can Easily get— pray, should not they be
mark'd with a red G. to ascertain my property should they be given
to wander? If so, pray let y^r *Marksman* do that business, but *pray*
let him be particula⟨rly⟩ careful not to spoil the wool, as I intend
to run it into France at a very great price— & now my dearest
Mrs Wilmot, don't vex y^rSelf from Morning to Night that You
cannot get the oldest, smallest & finest Sheep in the County
for Me— let me have a Score, or what you will, of the first that
come y^r Way, for Without a joke, I want to make my grass finer
than it is, wch I am told Sheep will do, & if I can get a good Chop
into ye Bargain, so much ye better, but I shall hate my flock, & will
never touch Mutton more, if you have the least trouble about this
Matter—

14*

My love to yʳ amiable Sister & Sweet Daughter My Wife sends her best to You all & I am

My dear Mrs. Wilmot Most unalterably yours
D G.

I must desire You wᵗʰ yʳ usual benevolence to cement my friendship wᵗʰ Dʳ Butler more & more— tell him what a prodigious agreeable Creature I am, he will take your word, and not mine, *for that*

Endorsement with address in copy: Mʳˢ Wilmot, Farmborough Place near Bagshot. *Source:* FC, draft, also copy; Boaden, II, 358.

1. Written after the move to the Adelphi in March 1772.

1341 To Henry Sampson Woodfall[1]

Dʳ Woodfall   Saturday [*post* March 1772][2]
I am going to Hampton this Moment— I shall be glad to see You whenEver You pass by The Adelphi— if I should go into yᵉ City, I will most certainly call upon You.

Yours most Truly & in haste
D Garrick

Endorsement with address in copy: To Mʳ Sam. Hʸ Woodfall. Pater Noster Row. *Source:* HTC, traced copy in FSL.

1. The traced copy of this letter in the Folger Shakespeare Library, which provides identification of the recipient, was made before the wrapper was lost.
2. Written after the move to the Adelphi in March 1772.

1342 To Richard Yates[1]

Tuesday[2]
If you have no objection to take my recommendation for a beautiful woman of Quality to have a box at the Opera next year, I will let you have her name and be much obliged to you

Source: John Heise, Catalogue, Jan. 1930, extract.

1. So identified in the source.
2. This letter was perhaps written during the summer of 1774 when Mrs. Yates was managing the Opera House in the Haymarket.

1343   To ? Yorke

Hampton

S^r   Augst 14th [1776?]¹

Tho it is impertinent in Your Situation to give the trouble of opening a mere letter of thanks, yet I cannot answer it to Myself, not to return my most grateful Acknowledgements for the last honour & particular favour I have rec'd from You. When I was upon the Stage, it was my Ambition to merit the approbation of Mr Yorke, & now I am forc'd upon another theatre (as you are pleas'd to call it) it is great consolation to Me that I shall appear there with your approbation, tho I hope, & believe, it will be the last, as it is the first time of my Ever appearing in that Character.

I am Sr Your most Oblig'd and most Obedient
humble Servant
David Garrick

Source: Historical Society of Pennsylvania.

1. Probably written after Garrick's retirement.

1344   To ——

My dear Sir   [*post* 1754]¹

I have never in ye least concern'd Myself about the prize or ye Privateer tho a Sharer— nor can I answer y^r Question— all the Money I venture upon these things I look upon as lost, & never think of it afterwards—

The Enclos'd is from Dr Warburton— when you can steal out I
hope to see You—

Y^{rs} Ever & most Sincerely
D. Garrick

Source: FSL.

1. Written after Warburton received his D.D. in 1754.

1345   To ———

Hampton

Dr Sr Friday Night [*post* 1754][1]
Upon my examination of the Country young fellow, he has own'd
that he remembers y^r giving him a letter, & he confesses that he put
it into his New Livery pocket, wch is now in Town lock'd up— when
I return I shall deliver you ye letter unseal'd to convince You that
I did not neglect to answer it— the poor Lad was so frighten'd
upon my telling him ye Consequences, that I believe he will never
do so again— I am very sorry that it is not in my power to Serve
the Gentleman You have so very Warmly spoken of— my Situation
at present with that Noble Lord does not intitle Me to Solicit your
business— when I see you in Town, I will tell you more

I am Sr Y^r Most Obed^t Ser^t
D: Garrick.

Source: FC.

1. Written after Garrick had the Hampton house in 1754.

1346   To ———

Dear Sir March 14th [1750–1758][1]
I have within this Week had a Second Conference with Lady
Burlington, the Purport of Which Mr Lacy will tell You— he will

call upon You fryday or Saturday— When You come to Town I
should be glad to wait on You in Southampton Street

I am S^r Y^r most Obed^t Ser^t

D Garrick

Source: FSL.

1. Written after Garrick's marriage in June 1749 and before Lady Burlington's
death in Sept. 1758.

1347   To ——

My dear D^r [*ante* 1760][1]
I thank you for y^r very friendly Lett^r the first part of which, I shall
talk with you upon, & answer it face to face; but y^r last paragraph,
which indeed touches my honesty, principles & understanding, I
cannot pass over or delay answering Even one Moment—

There certainly was a report maliciously & industriously spread
by my Enemies ten Years ago, that I had Endeavor'd to Mimic
him,[2] for whom You know, I have ye most cordial reverence from
Principle, & for Whom I would hazard my Life & fortune tomorrow— When I was first told of this, I scarce can say whether I
was most amaz'd or angry— nay this rumour was so industriously
spread, that many hundreds believ'd it, & when I came to y^t
Passage where Bays says— *here are fine troops Mr Johnson!*; there was
a great laugh in ye house; I was so Ignorant of ye Cause (for there
never was any applause at that place before) that I ask'd *Berry*[3]
who play'd Smith, what was ye Matter; all ye Actors were Equally
Surpriz'd, & till ye report spread, Not any behind ye Scenes could
conceive ye Meaning of it.[4] Now S^r if I had been Villain & fool
Enough to have done this, would not ye Actors have known my
Intention, or found it out? but so far from mimicking any body in
that place, I neither alter'd my tone of Voice or Action, but kept
minutely to ye Character of Bayes. these facts I am sure are sufficient
to convince ye unprejudic'd; but I will assure You farther (upon
Oath too if Your friend desires it) that I never heard his M[ajest]y
speak in my life, or was Ever present at a Review, when he was
there— there are some falsehoods that destroy themselves from y^e

over Straining of yᵉ Conceptions of their inventors, & this was of that Species— for could it be imagin'd that yᵉ least grain of Sensé or prudence (let my principles be what they will) would have suffer'd me to do a thing in my public Capacity, by Which I must certainly have most justly offended Nine Tenths of my Spectators? Dear Dʳ let yᵉ Gentleman know, who spoke of this affair to You, that I flatter Myself if he had known me, there had been no occasion for yʳ friendship in my behalf, & likewise say, that with all my failings, I would not belye my Principles, for any profit or applause that could result from yᵉ folly; I love to be merry, & I have no Objection to getting Money, but I am also just Wise enough to know, that both Mirth & Money may be bought too dear.

I am My Dʳ Dʳ Yʳˢ affectʸ

D Garrick

Source: FSL.

1. The performance of *The Rehearsal* "ten Years ago" must have been before the season of 1744–45, after which Bridges and then Burton replaced Berry in the role of Smith. This dating indicates that the reference to the King is to George II and that the letter was therefore written before his death on Oct. 25, 1760 (playbills, HTC; Genest, IV, 175, 292).

2. The King.

3. Edward Berry (1706–1760), a versatile actor, played for nearly forty years at Drury Lane (*ibid.*, IV, 557; Charles B. Hogan, *Shakespeare in the Theatre, 1701–1800,* Oxford, 1952, 1957, vol. II).

4. The rumors may have been occasioned by Macklin's followers in Dec. 1743 when they tried to prevent Garrick's appearing as Bayes (Murphy, ch. vi; Genest, IV, 53ff., 60).

1348 To ——

Dear Sir.   Thursday [1753–1766]¹
as some particular Business will call me into yᵉ Country next Saturday, I beg that I may have yᵉ Pleasure of Yʳ & Dʳ Birch's Company to Morrow night after yᵉ Play.

I am most Sincerely Yʳˢ

D: Garrick

PS. Mʳ Payne will come.

Source: BM; Nichols, *Illustrations,* I, 824.

1 Written between 1753 when Birch received his D.D. and 1766 when he died.

1349   To ——

Dr Sir   [*ante* 1773][1]
You have paragraphs in yr paper which may make a Lady, for
whom I have ye greatest regard, very uneasy— You are too much of
a Man to give pain to the fair Sex, & to one, who I am sure could
never offend You— If Your own Good Sense & Good Nature will
drop this persecution, I shall be very particularly oblig'd to You,
& if You please You shall be as free wth Me at any, & all times.
I am

Dr Sr Yr most Obligd & Obedt Sert
D Garrick

Excuse hurry.
I need not tell you that the Lady I mean is Lady Bridget Lane.[2]

Source: BM.

1. Written before 1773 when Lady Bridget Lane remarried.
2. Bridget (Henley) Lane, daughter of the first Earl of Northington, was the wife (1761)
of Robert Lane (d. 1768) son of George Fox-Lane, Baron Bingley. Known for her wit,
she was a popular figure in society circles.

1350   To ——

Adelphi
March 1st [*post* 1773][1]
Mr Garrick is extremely surpriz'd at receiving any intimation of
an Apology being expected from him— When he is not conscious
of the least improper behaviour on his part, and thinks an apology
more requisite for the Liberties that have been taken with him.

Source: HTC.

1. Written after Garrick moved to the Adelphi in the middle of March 1772.

1351   To ———

Dear Sir   Novr 22^d [*ante* 1775]^1
I knew ye author when I read the paper in ye Morning— You have
put ye Matter well & clearly— the inclos'd order is at y^r Service
& may be us'd any Night when the King is not there— to Night
if you will, but not to Morrow if their Majesties are at ye house

                                    Y^rs Ever but in haste
                                    D Garrick

Source: FC.

1. Written before Garrick retired in June 1776.

1352   To ———

Dear Madam.   Novr 10— [1761–1776]^1
I beg you will not think of appearing upon the Stage, till you can
Send me Word that you are quite able, & I will not think of You,
till I hear from You— pray give me a day or two's Notice— I have
set you down for Mrs Oakly & will for Hypolita, if you have no
Objection— We shall do ye play well, if that part is agreeable to
you— pray let me know by the bearer, how You are.

                                    Your most truly
                                    D: Garrick

Source: Albert C. Meyer.

1. Written between the first performance of *The Jealous Wife* in Feb. 1761 and
Garrick's retirement in June 1776.

1353   To ———

                                                        Hampton
Sir   April 13 [*ante* 1776]^1
I have been in the Country & ill or I should have thank'd you
immediately for your very obliging Letter—
      It is not in my power to take a journey at this time, and indeed

without I knew in what way the Lady you mention performs, that is, what Characters she plays, what her Age, & whether she is not affected (the common misfortune to all Country Actors & Actresses) I cannot guess whether she would be of Service in our Company, could I trouble you (as you have been so obliging) to acquaint me wth more particulars of the Man & Woman, you wrote to me about, I shall be still more indebted to your good Offices

I am Sir Your most obed^t & obliged Ser^t
(signed)   D. Garrick

Pray direct to me in London.

Source: FC, transcript made in 1830.

1. Written before Garrick retired in June 1776.

1354   To ——

My Dear Sir   [*ante* June 1776][1]
first let me thank You most cordially for the Trouble You have taken & ye desire You have Shewn to Serve a Certain Gentleman, & Your friend & humble Servant.

I was sorry last Night that we could not close y^t business at your Chambers & I think Y^r time too precious to trespass more upon it therefore I sh^d be glad to know by Six o'Clock this Evening whether the Gentleman will or will not Accept of our proposals— viz: 10 pounds p Week for two Years with a Benefit after Mr King's— Sh^d he chuse the other proposal for This Winter without ye Benefit we are ready to close with him—

I hope, my dear Sir, that we shall come to an immediate conclusion— I shall leave the decision of my Conduct towards the Gentleman wholly to y^r Arbitration, & hope that We shall say ay or no, without more talking upon ye Subject, for I hate to refuse even when it is not in my power to grant.

Y^rs Ever & most Affe^t
D. G.

I have all my operations at a Stand till this Matter is determin'd

Source: FSL.

1. Written before Garrick retired.

1355   To ———

Sir   Wed^y March 20th
I shall obey Your Commands & the Ladies with the greatest pleasure, and I flatter myself if the thing is to be done that I can do it— I must only desire You to fix what day they will be Set down for a Box, for, I fear, they will expect to be paid for it, tho the Ladies sh^d not be arriv'd— pray consider these Matters & let me have y^r last resolution.

> I am Your most Obed^t Ser^t
> D: Garrick

Source: Society of Antiquaries.

1356   To ———

Decr 17th
M^r G[arrick] would not lose a Moment to return his best thanks to the Person who has honor'd him with the *Argument*, & *Specimens*.

Upon the closest consideration Mr G. humbly conceives that the Story is too romantic, & that the introduction of the Fairies, quarrelling about the Persons they protect, will bear too great a Similitude between the Oberon and Titania, so exquisitely written by Shakespeare. Mr Garrick really thinks that for these reasons, that Camillus & Columne might fail of Success upon the Stage.

Tho this Judgment may be erroneus, as Mr G. has not Seen ye Whole of ye Performance, Yet he thought himself bound from the Author's great politeness to him, to speak his Mind freely upon y^e *Argument* & *Specimens* which were put into his hands.

Source: FSL.

1357   To ——

Dear Mad^m   Monday
I would have seen You on Saturday last, had not a Multiplicity of
Business hinder'd Me—

I have read over ye Papers with great Care & Candor: there are
good things I confess, & apt for ye Times; but there wants a dramatic
Spirit, & the Scenes are too long, but that is Easily remedied.

These might be made to do, provided they were connected with a
little interesting plan, the necessity of Which we talk'd over before—
it is impossible for Me to give an absolute Opinion till I see y^e
Whole— when I do— you may Expect from Me Every thing that
is in ye Power of Goodwill & regard for
                    I am Most Sincerely Y^r Friend & Servant
                                                        D Garrick

PS. My best respects pray to Mr Richardson.

Source: FSL.

1358   To ——

                                                        Tuesday
If tomorrow Morning at ten will be agreeable to You, I shall be
glad to See You at Breakfast
                    I am Sr Your most humble Ser^t
                                                        D: Garrick

Source: FSL.

1359   To ——

My dear D^r.   Friday
Dine with me to day at four, I have Something to say to you
                                        Ever Yours
                                        D. Garrick

Source: Hyde Collection; *The R. B. Adam Library*, Buffalo, 1929, I, [5].

1360   To ———

Dear Sir

I have not only read, but consider'd Your tragedy with a particular attention— You must therefore excuse me for not return^g it before as I did not chuse to give you my opinion of it too lightly, or too hastily— I think there is but one capital Situation in ye whole play & that is the discovery of the Arm'd Men to Lavagna's Guests, which indeed was ye only thing that struck me as a dramatic Circumstance when I read ye Story in De Retz.[1] the rest of ye Play seems to me to be too like all ye other Conspiracies we have had upon ye Stage with fewer Situations— indeed, Sir, I fear there is a languor thro ye whole that will Ever make its Success precarious— I am of opinion too that this Evil is not to be remedied, for it lies in ye Story itself, which has not afforded dramatic Circumstances sufficient to give that particular interest without which no Play in my opinion can be Supported upon ye Stage. The first play you put into my hands with all its blemishes affected Me more than the last— Could I have struck out any additon to ye Plan, as you were pleasd to desire Me, I should have communicated it to You, with ye greatest pleasure

                    I am Sr Your most Obed humble Servt
                                   D G.

I should have waited upon you but I am obliged to go to Town.

Source: FC, draft; Boaden, I, 408.

1. The account of Giovanni Luigi di Fieschi, Conte di Lavagna, in *La Conjuration du Comte Jean-Louis Fiesque* (Paris, 1665) by Jean François Paul de Gondi (1614–1679), Cardinal de Retz.

1361   To ———

A fig for the President and Eke his Secretary— which by ye bye is ye End of an Old Song— I wish you joy from my Soul

Source: Goodspeed's Book Shop, Catalogue, April 1907, extract.

1362   To ——

Dear Sʳ

You have pepper'd my Verses, I wish You had Salted 'Em too—
the following triffle was written Extempore upon a Gentleman's
Showing Me yʳ Several critical paragraphs against my Muse— a
Prologue & Epilogue I have wᶜʰ I send to you to convince You that
in spite of Your Wit I live in Xian Charity with You

Yʳˢ Ever &c

Upon an Old Friend abusing my Poetry
& praising my Loyalty:—

You say my Poetry is bad— agreed—
Clap-traps to speak, & paltry Stuff to read—
I scribbled not for fame, my only End
In spite of Criticks, was to serve my friend—
Friendly I am, & Loyal *You* have said—
Spare but my heart, You're Welcome to my head.

Source: FSL, draft; verse in Sotheby, Catalogue, 1928, p. 49, no. 301.

Appendices

A: Material relating to Mrs. Garrick
  1. Bibliographical sources for the condensed biography given in the Introduction
  2. Two of Mrs. Garrick's letters

B: Contractual and business documents relating to Drury Lane Theatre
  1. Contract of James Lacy and David Garrick as co-patentees, April 9, 1747
  2. Lacy's financial statement, April 11, 1747
  3. Further statement by Lacy and Garrick on the division of responsibilities
  4. Two letters from John Paterson to Garrick, 1766

C: Garrick's memoranda on the Shakespeare Jubilee

D: Dr. Stonhouse's letter to Garrick introducing Hannah More, May 21, 1774

E: Thomas King's letter to Garrick concerning the management of Drury Lane during Garrick's absence, April 26, 1775

F: Two letters from William Hopkins to George Garrick about Drury Lane business, 1774–75

G: Garrick's will

APPENDIX A

Material Relating to Mrs. Garrick

1. Bibliographical sources for the condensed biography given in the Introduction.

Lady Burlington, A.L.s. to Mrs. Garrick, Londesburgh, July 30, 1749, Berg Collection; Therese Fürst, L.s. to Mrs. Garrick, February 4, 1753, FSL; Eva Rosina Veigel, A.L.s, to Mrs. Garrick, Vienna, March 1761, FSL; Ferdinand Veigel, A.L.s. to Mrs. Garrick, Vienna, December 12, 1772, FSL; Elisabeth von Saar, A.L.s. to G. F. Beltz, December 3, 1822, HTC, [February 26, 1822] FSL; Parish Register, St. Stephen, Vienna; Mrs. Garrick's will, Somerset House, London; Marriage Settlement, FSL; "Das Geburtshaus von Garricks Frau in Wien," *Die Presse*, XII (January 21, 1859), No. 16; G. A. Crüwell, "Eine Wiener Tänzerin," *Die Wienerin im Spiegel der Jahrhunderte*, ed. Raoul Auernheimer (Vienna, 1928); Constant von Wurzbach, *Biographisches Lexikon des Kaisertums Oesterreich* (Vienna, 1884), Section 50, p. 71; *ibid.* (Vienna, 1859), Section 5, p. 90; Robert Haas, *Der Wiener Bühnentanz von 1740 bis 1767*, Jahrbuch der Musikbibliothek Peters für 1937 (Leipzig, 1938); Robert Haas, *Die Wiener Ballet-Pantomime im 18. Jahrhundert und Glucks Don Juan*, Studien zur Musikwissenschaft (Vienna, 1923); X; Hoff-Protocoll in Ambts- und Parthey-Sachen, Haus- Hof- und Staatsarchiv, Vienna, vols. for 1733-1746; Hans Niedecken, *J. G. Noverre, sein Leben und seine Beziehungen zur Musik* (Halle, 1919); *The Autobiography of Alexander Carlyle*, ed. John Hill Burton (1910), pp. 192–93; *Prager Zeitung* (1822), No. 198; Frances Burney, *Early Diary*, ed. Annie Raine Ellis (1907), I, 22; Fulke Greville, *Maxims, Characters, and Reflections, 3ᵈ Edition* (1768), pp. 43–47; Guiseppi Baretti, *Epistolario*, ed. Luigi Piccioni (Bari, 1936), I, 212; *The Letters of Laurence Sterne*, ed. Lewis P. Curtis (Oxford, 1935), p. 157; *Autobiography and Correspondence of Mary Granville, Mrs. Delany*, ed. Lady Llanover, 2d Series (1862), I, 284; William Hogarth, A.L.s. to his wife, June 6, 1749, HTC; John Thomas Smith, *A Book for a Rainy Day* (1905), pp. 236–243, 285–290; Walpole, ed. Lewis, IX, 28, 79–82; *GM*, XCII (November 1822), 468–470; Fitzgerald, *passim*; Davies, *passim*.

2. Two letters from Mrs. Garrick to Lady Burlington. Many of Mrs. Garrick's letters are extant, dealing mostly with the routine of family and social life. Only two of her letters are here printed in full. The first, written several months after her marriage, is a commentary on the relationship of the Garricks to each other and to the Burlingtons. The second, written over a year later, is one of the first written without assistance, and illustrates her difficulties, oral and written, with English; she was never completely to master the language.

Merton

th 8 Aug, *1749*

Do you know my Dear madam, that I Shall answer your tow letters another time, (about Scolding me, for being *too trouble Some* for Repeating So often *Lyp.*:) because I have a Sad Cold & Sore throat; I thinke I caught it only out of curiossity, as I Shall inform you this minute; when I went into my Spouse's Roome, I was Really Struk with the Letter he wrote Last post,[1] and had a mind to heare what he possible could invent to fill So many Sides of paper; I Sat by the window without a Stays, only in my night Gown, and so by curiossity was punish'd, but had the Satisfaction (after one hour's patience) to be convinc'd that all what he Say'd was true, but (entre nous) he could have Sav'd yr Ly^p the truble of reading it: we had company Last Sunday to Dinner with us, you imagine how pleas'd I was? The Porter att B[urlington] House is very well againe, Dr Taylor comes to him: we are oblig'd to go to town this after noon, and Stay two Days, to See a Little after ouer Business in the new House; I Shall be So impertinent, as I don't like to be in his Logings under all them Strange people, to lie at B: House in my Little yeallow bed; if we have not room enough, he mus Lie under it; I hope Lord & Lady won't be angry at us? I promise I Shall not be so free another time.

M^r & Miss Stanfart[2] was here yesterday in the afternoon, but did not Stay Long, as we was oblige to returne a vissit which we ought to have pay'd a fortnight a go; She beg'd me to present her complimant to yr Lyp. and I Sent my best Duty to my Dear Lord B: and tell him I am vestly Sorry about his misfortine, and your Doo My Dear Madam, take care another time in Shooting, I receiv'd the gloves, they fit me xactly; I thank you & give you a fat Kiss, for:

your Ta— My Dearest madam you Duty full

E M Gar:

Address: to R^t Honble the Countess of Burlington at Londesburah Near Market: Weighton, Yorkshire. *Postmarked.* *Endorsement by the recipient:* M^r & Mrs G. rec^d Augt 11th. *Source:* FSL.

1. Letter 63.
2. Stainforth?

London

My Dearest Madam. Oct^{br} 6: 1750

I Receiv'd Yor Lady^p's Second Letter with much joy, hearing all ar well, I am a westill better do, for no mor Painting Rooms, withs has allmost kild me, Every own is finish't now, thank god. I was at the Play Les't Saturday at Coven-garden, all what *I* can Say ofit is, that Mr Barry is too jung (in his ha'd) for Romeo, and Mrs. Cibber to old for a garle of 18:[1] the house was praty foul, but hafe Paf[?]s. I wish thie woold finish both, for it is to much for my Little Dear Spouse to Play Every day; I'll bitty Miss Mimpy to be so brety and to have no more Sence, tell Dear Lady Hart, Lady lincoln was at the Play and Schot mor belly then won wisht to See. I would have writ to her Lady^p, but having no news I Shall defere it for another time. I have not Seen jet the little Dear Lady,[2] as he Plays every night, we Dinn at 1: oclock tor fore can I not go to chiswick, but Shall See her Soon, I must finish now, I am all over Dart with Rerching and must wasch my fottles befor he Coms home, & it is all must 9: So God blais my Dear Lady^p and I am

My Dearest madam Dutyful

E: Garrick.

My Duty as jusul to Lord B[urlington] Lord and Lady H[artington], & pray give my Little lord[3] a Kiss but tell him my nem, or els he will forgett me.

I am afred this letter is wars Spelt, then the forst

I forgot to tll that Miss Mustin[4] was four tims at Romeo and juliet, & I belive wer She not gon out of town Shi would go every Day. We have brotiges fine weter that's all.

Address: to The Countess of Burlington. *Source:* FSL.

1. Barry was thirty-one, Mrs. Cibber thirty-six.
2. Lady Dorothy Cavendish.
3. William Cavendish, the Hartington's eldest son.
4. Presumably Betty Mostyn.

APPENDIX B

Contractual and business documents relating to Drury Lane Theatre

1. Contract of James Lacy and David Garrick as co-patentees, April 9, 1747.

This contract was recognized on June 4, 1747, by the grant of a patent "for 21 years, to commence from 2 September, 1753, of full power to gather together & keep a company of comedians for the King's service to act tragedies, play operas on the stage within the House in Drury Lane." The grant was again made Oct. 27, 1761, "for 21 years to commence from 2 September, 1774," by George III (Patent Rolls, 20 George II, Pt. 3, No. 15, and 2 George III, Pt. 1, No. 45).

1747 April 9

Agreement made the ninth of April 1747 Between James Lacy of great Queen Street near Lincolns Inn Fields in the County of Middlesex Gentleman of the one part and David Garrick of James Street Covent Garden Gentleman of the other part.

Whereas it is alledged by the s^d Ja^s Lacy that he is possessed of or entituled unto the present patent under which Plays are exhibited at the Theatre in Drury Lane in the County af'd for the remainder of a Term where of there are now 6 Years to come & of & unto the Scenes & Wardrobe belonging to or used at the s^d Theatre & also to a Lease of the s^d House or Theatre for the remainder of a Term whereof there are now about 5 Years to come, subject nevertheless to certain Trust Incumbrances & Debts Viz—

A Trust as to two equal third parts of the s^d patent Scenes Wardrobe & Lease for Messrs Green & Amber late of the Strand in the County af'd Bankers for their Creditors ⎱

A Mortgage from the s^d Lacy to the s^d Green & Amber for £2250 & Interest with a covenant for Sharing any new patent that should be obtained, the Whole valued at ⎰ £4000

A Mortgage to Hutchenson Meure whereon the principal & Interest that will be due at the End of this acting Season is computed to amount to

The Debts that will then remain due to the Actors & performers of the said Theatre also Computed at about

The Debts that will then remain due to the Tradesmen &c: belonging to the s^d Theatre which are also Computed at about

The Debts that will then remain due from the s^d
Lacy to others & shall have been by him borrow'd
& applied for Discharging any of the Arrears due
to the s^d Actors, Performers & Tradesmen &c:
since the End of the Last Season & which are also
computed at about
An annuity of £300 to Mr Cawthorpe
An annuity of 500 to Charles Fleetwood Esqr

And Whereas it is alledged by the s^d James Lacy that he can & will before the End of the next Month procure a new patent for 21 Years to commence from the expiration of the former without any other gratuity or expence than the common & ordinary fees & to be subject only to a like annuity of £300 to Mr Cawthorpe, or some other person:

And that he can and will within the Time af"^d procure a good & sufficient Assign^t Release or other Conveyance of all the right Title & Interest both equitable and legal of the s^d Messrs Green & Amber & of their Creditors Assigns or Representatives & all other Persons claiming under them in & to both the s^d patents Lease Wardrobe & Scenes for the s^d Sum of £4000.

And that all the above stated incumbrances (Including ye s^d £4000 & the common & ordinary Fees of procuring the s^d new patent but exclusive of the s^d Mr Cawthorpe's & Mr Fleetwoods annuities) will not exceed the sum of £12000 in the whole.

Now it is hereby agreed that incase the said Ja^s Lacy shall & does within ye Time af'd procure such a new patent on the Terms afd in the joint Names of the s^d Ja^s Lacy & Dav^d Garrick & also such assignment Release & Conveyance as afd on the Terms af^d to them the said Ja^s Lacy & Dav^d Garrick.

They the said Ja^s Lacy & Dav^d Garrick their Ex^{ors} Adm^{ors} & & Assigns shall & will from the End of this present acting season become & be jointly & equally possessed of & Interested in the s'd two several patents & the s^d Lease, wardrobe & Scenes subject to the respective incumbrances af^d for the several terms that will remain & be in the s^d Patents respectively but without any benefit of Survivorship & shall & will enter into & execute proper Articles of Copartnership for the carrying on & managing the Business of the s^d Patents for their joint & equal benefit

And that as soon as such new patents & right in the Old patent &c. shall be procured as af'd the same shall be immediately con-

vey'd to two Persons of which each of the s'd parties shall name &
appoint one, upon Trust as a security from each of the s'ᵈ Parties
to the other for the performance of their respective agreements &
Covenants both in these Presents & in the sᵈ Articles of Copartnership to be contained.

That the said Incumbrances on the sᵈ patents shall be paid off
& Discharg'd as soon as may be, by & out of the profits to arise in
the sᵈ Copartnership or equally by & between the sᵈ Parties.

Provided that in case the sᵈ incumbrances (exclusive of the sᵈ
annuites) shall exceed the sᵈ sum of £12000 the Difference or excess
shall be made good, pay'd, & Discharged by the sᵈ Jᵃˢ Lacy or his
assigns or out of his or their moiety of the sᵈ profits & the sᵈ D:
Garrick & his assigns & his or their moiety of the sᵈ Patents &c:
are to be fully endemnified therefrom. Provided also that each of
yᵉ sᵈ Parties shall or may weekly or otherwise take & retain for their
private expences & under the Title of Managers out of the Money
to be in yᵉ Hands of the Treasurer or Cashier of the sᵈ Copartnership
any sum not exceeding the rate of £500 per annum Each

Provided also that in case the Profits shall at any Time fall short
of the sᵈ two sums of £500 per annum to each of the s'd Parties &
either of the s'ᵈ shall not withstanding have occasion for & actually
draw out or receive on account of the sᵈ allowance more than his
share of the net profits then in the Treasury or office shall amount
unto then & in every such case the sᵈ party shall be made debtor
for the sum by him so drawn out or rec'ᵈ to-gether with legal Interest
untill his share of the net profits shall be sufficient to answer the
same & in the mean time his share of the Patent &c: shall stand
charged therewith as a security to the other of the sᵈ parties.

Provided also & it is expressly agreed that the s'ᵈ D: Garrick
shall have & be paid a clear Sallary of 500 guineas per annum as an
actor with a clear Benefit or shall have such better terms as shall at
any Time during the s'ᵈ Copartnership be given to any actor or
actress but the sᵈ D: Garrick shall not During the Time of his being
intrusted in the s'ᵈ patents or either of them act or Perform except
for the joint benefit of the Parties concerning the sᵈ patents.

Provided also that in settling the Incumbrances af'd the sᵈ J:
Lacy is to account for the recepts of this present season it being
the intent of the Parties that the Arrears due to yᵉ Actors, per-
formers, & Tradesmen at the End of the last Season are to be the
Basis of the Respective accounts from or to which the profits o[r]
Loss of this present season are to be respectively subtracted or added.

Provided also that if either Party shall Discharge any of yᵉ sᵈ Debts or Incumbrances or lend or advance any Money to or for the sᵈ Copartnership more than the other of the s'ᵈ parties then & in every such case the Party so lending or advancing shall have & be allowed Legal Interest in the account of the s'ᵈ Copartnership untill the other party shall have Advanced his proportion.

Provided Also that if either party shall be minded to sell or dispose of his shar⟨e⟩ the other party shall have the refusal their of at such price as two Persons one to be named by each party shall value the same at.

Lastly if any dispute or Differences shall happen the same are hereby agree⟨d⟩ to be referred to two arbitrators (each of the parties to name one within 24 Hours after notice from the other) In witness whereof the parties have sign'd these presents the Day & year first abov⟨e⟩ written

Sign'd { James Lacy
{ David Garrick

Source: FC, copy; Boaden, I, 50–53.

2. After Lacy and Garrick had signed their partnership agreement Lacy presented the following financial statement to his former backers, the bankers Green and Amber, as a means of arriving at a settlement with them.

11ᵗʰ April 1747.   Theatre

Due to Mʳ Mure on a Mortgage as settled 30ᵗʰ March last past	4675. – –
Due to him on Sat 11ᵗʰ April	61. – –
Due to Actors &c for Arrears last season	1275. – –
Due to Ditto this Season to Sat. 11ᵗʰ April	676. 19. –
Due to Dancers Ballat Master &c	480. – –
Due to Musick 3 days this Season	15. 15. –
J Lacy Borrow'd and paid into the Office &c for the Use of the Theatre	400. – –
Due to Charles Fletewood Esqʳ on his Annuity from the Theatre at Lady day last	125. – –
Due to Tradesmen for last Season & this £1100 & upwards	1100. – –
	8808. 14. –

Exclusive of the Money now due to J: Lacy out of £500 p Ann.
The Annuitys chargeable on the Theatre are
£500 p Ann. to Mʳ Fletewood

315 Do   to the patent
500 Do   to Mr Lacy.

The Theatre was purchas'd of Mr Fletewood for the Sum
    of £6750 & subject to a Mortgage of £5000   }   11750. — —

If the Sum of £4000 is given for the Theatre &c subject to the
Incumbrances of £8808. 14. it will be sold for £1058. 14 more
than was given to Mr Fletewood when the patent had Two Seasons
& a half more to Come than it has now besides the Money now due
to J. Lacy.

The Money paid by Messrs Green & Amber out of their Shop over
& above the purchase does not amount to more than what was
left in their hands for the Use of the Theatre.

    I told M^r ... the intended purchasor that the whole would not
amount to £12000. He said if it was more it shou'd rest on me, for
that was the Utmost Shilling he wou'd give. But upon a Strict
    Enquiry
I find it will amount to £12808. 14. This difference is not
    Altogether
owing to an Error in Calculation but has been likewise heighthen'd
    by
a falling off of Business, nor is it possible to Ascertain
    the Debt of
a Theatre for a Day it is of so Fluctuating a Nature. Q. whether
this loss ought to light upon me who have endeavour'd to
    get a purchasor
& encreas'd the Value of the Estate to the Utmost of my power—
Errors Excepted

Source: HTC.

3. Further statement by Lacy and Garrick on the division of
responsibilities. Garrick endorsed the statement: "an agreement
between Me & Lacy left in Patersons hands."

Whereas at the time of signing the Original agreement of Copartnership between James Lacy and David Garrick Esquires on the 9th
day of April 1747 It was verbally agreed that the business of the
Stage should be under the management of Mr Garrick there being
sufficient other matters of importance to employ Mr Lacy. And
whereas there have of late some misunderstandings arisen between
them touching the said management of the Stage And whereas It
would be very inconvenient for the Partners to meet to settle the

said Business by joint consent And the Plan of such Business must frequently and sometimes suddenly be broken thro' and altered on account of various accidents *either of a foreign or domestick kind* Therefore to obviate such difficulties & prevent all misunderstandings for the future. It is hereby agreed between the said Partner's as follows: Viz^t

1st That the settling or altering the business of the Stage be left entirely to Mr Garrick who shall immediately communicate the same to the Prompter for the information of Mr Lacy with this proviso that whensoever Mr Lacy shall apprehend that Mr Garrick is pursuing measures injurious to his, Mr Lacy's property he shall state his objection to John Paterson Esqr (who undertakes to act as the common Friend of both) and to him only; and Mr Garrick shall submit to his determination.

2dly That all Actors Actresses Singers Dancers & other Servants shall be hired or discharged and their salaries or allowances settled or encreased by joint consent and not otherwise.

3dly That the Accounts and all other business of the Copartnership shall be jointly carried on at the Office; Mr Garrick by reason of his attendance upon the Business of the Stage being at liberty to employ his Brother George Garrick to attend & act for him in the said Office; But to give his personal Attendance whensoever any Matter of importance shall in the judgement of Mr Lacy appear to require it.

4^{thly} That in case of any future difference the Partner who shall think himself injured shall (without venting any speeches in publick to the disadvantage of the other) state his complaint to Mr Paterson who shall decide thereon & finally settle the dispute between them.

5^{thly} That in case of any future misunderstanding between them being such as cannot be sett right by Mr Paterson either party may give notice to the other of his desire to dissolve the Copartnership and Both parties shall attend Mr Paterson at such time and place as he shall appoint in writing when and where their joint Property shall be put up to auction between them their biddings being in writing and signed by them respectively And when either party Shall refuse or neglect to bid any more the best bidder shall be entitled to the whole joint property upon payment to the other of one half of the Sum last bid by himself And the other party shall upon such payment convey assign and assure his half part of the said property to the said best Bidder free from all incumbrances And in case there shall be any such incumbrances the same shall be discharged out of the money payable to the party whose Incumbrances thes [*part of one line trimmed*]

6^{thly} That in case of the death of either party there shall be the same Auction and proceedings between the Surviving Partner the Executors or Administrators of the partner deceased as are hereinbefore directed between the said Partners themselves in the case of a total Breach.

7^{thly} That this agreement is understood to be honorary and shall not be divulged upon any pretence whatsoever Unless upon a breach of some part thereof and in that case, only so far as relates to the Article supposed to be broken.

Source: FC.

4. Two letters from John Paterson to David Garrick concerning the contractual agreement between Lacy and Garrick.

Dear S^r   [*ante* January 10, 1766]
It was not from any Scruple I so long delayd answering your Letter but a desire of doing it upon ye best recollection I could make at this great Distance of time. If my Memory does not mislead Me It was insisted upon on your part in the course of the Treaty that ye sole Management with regard to Plays & Players should be left to you as a department best suited to you It [in?] which a diversity of opinion might otherwise prove injurious to the common Interest as well as particularly painful to you. To this it was objected on ye part of Mr Lacy that his being expressly excluded from ye management might lessen him in the Eyes of the Performers But that he knew his own Interest and your Abilities too well to interfere in a matter you understood so much better than he and that consequently there was no need of any Stipulation in ye Articles to bind him to what his own Interest would naturally prompt him to And I have always considered this Arrangement so much part of ye agreem^t that I thought it had been punctually complyd with till I have lately heard that it has been ye occasion of some difference between you It gives me concern that Gentlemen so conected should have any disagreement & I sh^d esteem myself happy if I could anyways contribute to restore that harmony which in ye time of my Intimacy with ye Theater so happily subsisted between you.

If therefore I can be useful Command Me as one who is with great Truth

Dear Sr Your most faithful humble Ser^t

John Paterson

Postmark: IA 10. *Endorsment by Garrick:* Mr Paterson's Letter to me about verbal agreem^t with Mr Lacy relative to ye Managem^t. *Source:* FC.

New Burlington Street 4[?]

Dear S^r   March 22 [17]66

Mr Lacy is just gone from me; he bro^t me back the Memorandum I had drawn & absolutely refuses to subscribe to it: he particularly objects to the Mode I had pointed out for the disposal of the property in case of death or separation. He declares ye most sincere desire of continuing with you in Partnership as well as friendship and says that in the 20 years you have been together he does not recollect his having interrupted you in the Management of the Stage more than twice & as to the last time seems to think himself to blame for ye manner of doing it & I really believe is sorry for it He says he desires you may go on upon the old footing & has given me his word of honour that in such case he will never object to your management but in a private & friendly manner and in case you two cannot agree he will Leave it to my determination as the Common friend of both tho originally yours.

Now taking it for granted that Mr Lacy is in earnest I think his proposal fair & reasonable & such as you should agree to. I have heard you express your inclination to continue with him in which I thought you sincere, give me leave to say that I think Mr Lacy equally so & will undertake for his punctually performing what he promises. I have not told him my sentiments of his proposal But on the contrary have appointed to meet Mr Fitzgerald next Saturday But My sincere wish is that you would both agree, disappoint the little arts of those who endeavour to make a total breach between you, & give me the satisfaction of being ye happy instrument of restoring your [*illegible*] harmony & friendship. Pray send me an answer as soon as possible that I may let Mr Lacy know your determination & believe me

Ever Your most faithfull humble Ser^t

John Paterson

Address: To David Garrick Esq, Southampton Street, Covent Garden. *Source:* FC; Boaden, I, 223.

APPENDIX C

Garrick's memoranda on the Shakespeare Jubilee

Memd^s for Stratford

As it has been reported to the great prejudice of Stratford in particular and to others concern'd in the aproaching Jubilee that the Inhabitants of Stratford intend to ask very exhorbitant prizes for their Lodgings, the Steward particularly insists that enquiry be made into the Number of Lodgings that are already taken and of the Number that are vacant, and that they be informed that no more shall be taken than a Guinea a Bed being the same as is usualy taken at the Races,

To take Lodgings for Lord Spencer, 6 Master Bedds, Eight Stall for Horses

To take D^o — for Lord Charles Spencer   Bedds

    D^o — for —

    D^o — for —

To speak to Mr Hunt, and make the Corporation an offer of M^r DG^s runnings the risk of the Expence of Booths &c for the aproaching Jubilee with them by paying half of the Loss (if any) and the Profitts (if any) to be entirely laid out in Honor of Shakespear, If this offer should be thought improper for the Corporation to risk, then to let them know that the whole affair of erecting the Booths, Illuminations, and other things, will be put into the hands of 3 or 4 Persons who have agreed to do everything that shall be necessary, agreeable to the Stewards Plan for accomodating the Numbers of People that may come to Stratford on this Occasion & to stand to all Loss on that Acct. whatever provided.   they shall be entitled to all proffits, from the diversions or Amusements and which are to be regulated by the said Steward, the said undertakers desire it may be understood by the Corporation, that they do not want to receive the proffitts, provided the Corporation shall think proper to take it into their own hands and to pay them for what the Steward shall think necessary to be done; Their determinate and final answer is desired on this matter as soon as possible as there is no time to lose—

Mr Peaton must let the Steward know what he expects ahead at the Ordinary for the several Gentlemen Performers Viz 50/. and likewise for their Bedds, and that In case the Steward can procure a Booth to be Built that will dine 600 or upwards, what he can afford to give either in the lump or yᵉ head for the Number of People that shall dine and Breakfast there

To be particular in regard to the admeasurement of Ground the Fireworks and particularly of the ground opposite—in order, &c,

Mʳ Peaton is desired to purchase a Sign of Shakespeare which cost 150£ and which he may have for 12:12£ as the Steward thinks it will be of the greatest advantage to him, and to be put up the day of the Jubilee—

¹to Enquire if there seems to be any Spirit among the People for Erecting Booths, or if yᵉ Town's-people seem to intend to decorate their houses at yᵉ Jubilee— *They do.*²

To know precisely what boats there are upon yᵉ River Avon, that may be made use of, if thought necessary— & if any Gentlemen there or near Stratford have any pleasure boats— & to take yᵉ Measure of these, large & small, that are made use of there in common— *may have 2 barges & Fishing Boat*

If the Great Booth can't be Erected at yᵉ back of Peaton's house. Whether he will think it too far to have it by River Side— there must surely be a sort of fence or Pallisade at a certain Distance, to keep off yᵉ Mob—

to consider how the bridge may be decorated at yᵉ coming in at yᵉ Town, & which will make a figure at yᵉ fireworks—

that Mʳ G: thinks that Mʳ Hunt in yᵉ name of yᵉ Corporation shᵈ request of Lᵈ Beauchamp to have yᵉ Militia at yᵉ Jubᵉᵉ

that it is adviseable nay necessary, to see what Company has already taken Lodgings, & what Numbers can be lodg'd at Stratford—

To get yᵉ Breadth of yᵉ River, & know why there was a neglect in Sending the Measure to me.

Some consideration about yᵉ Tickets & their Prices. *It is thought that the Price for Tickets is too little, though if the Ball was to be 1/2 a Ga exclusive of yᵉ 1 G—a Genˡ Ticket*

Whether there shᵈ be a land Pageant— whether yᵉ Corporation wᵈ walk in a procession— what Person is to be apply'd to about making yᵉ favors— Mʳ Bird never came to Mʳˢ G—— & that it seems very odd yᵗ he did not come.

If any other things shᵈ strike yᵉ fancy of Mesrs. G. & Latimer to Entertain at yᵉ Jubᵉᵉ to put it directly upon Paper.

to know if Shrewsbury Races are upon ye same Days with ye Jub^ee for It is said Ld Grosvenor[3] intends to desire Mr G. to put it off till ye 8th or 9th that they may not clash.

The Expences of ye 50 beds & ordinary for ye performers sh^d be ascertain'd, it w^d be very hard if ye Town clerk & Corporation will not take care of that & see that Every thing is reasonable

To secure Some good Lodgings for my Friends— a good Bed for Mr Foote— another for Mr Smith (I believe Peyton[. . .] secur'd y^t) If Mr West sh^d speak to my Bro^r about my being wth him, George may tell him that he fear Sr Thos Robinson will attend M^r G & if so, M^r G: can only pay his respects en passant

To take care that Mr Hunt speaks for a Lodging on this side ye Bridge among some of these houses there for ye firework People— it will be right that they should be by themselves— *Mr Hunt has got two, how many more will be necessary—*

Source: FC.

1. From this point on the manuscript is in Garrick's writing.
2. Notations in George Garrick's hand are printed in italics.
3. Richard Grosvenor (1731–1802), first Baron Grosvenor, later (1784) first Earl, a great breeder and racer of horses.

APPENDIX D

Dr. James Stonhouse's letter to Garrick introducing Hannah More

Cheverel near Devizes Wiltshire
Dear Sir   May 21. 1774
Miss Hannah More, my next Door Neighbour, went to London this Month *purposely* to see you act for the Player's Fund, as she was then *sure* of not being disappointed—She had some Time ago Stayed in Town near two Months, & never had an Opportunity of hearing you; you acting but seldom, & she at Times very ill with an ague. What her Sentiments are in an *hasty* Letter to me I have transcrib'd— & had I any Interest with the News-Writers, I would have inserted them in the Papers. I hope you will act once more before she leaves Town, as she will stay about a Fortnight longer, but I fear you will not.

She is a young Woman of an amazing Genius, & remarkable Humility—She is Mistress of the French, Italian, Spanish, & has lately learnt Latin at my Desire. Her Pastoral Drama has pass'd four Editions, & is acted at many boarding Schools by young Ladies. The *inflexible Captive*, (or Regulus) which I put into your Hands last year, & w^ch, as *Havard's* was on that Subject you declind, has passd two Editions, & is much admird.—And it will be the *Interest* of ye Players to *act* it at Bristol—where no Objection can lie against it, as People there are so much prepossessd in it's Favour, Havard's unknown, & where it will be expected from them by the principal People.

She ordered *Cadell* the Bookseller to present you with her Tragedy which I presume He did, & as she is now in Town & lodges at M^rs H[*tear*]'s in Southampton Street just by you, I could wish you w^d call on her to acknowledge the Receipt of it.—You would not be displeasd with the Interview, & I know she would take it very kindly, as she has a great Desire to see you.

I have heard *accidentally* you think the Death of Count Patkule w^d be a fine Subject for a Tragedy. If this be a Fact, & you sh^d think proper of giving any Hints of a plan of that Kind to her, She would probably do Justice to it—if properly encouragd—but She is so very humble in her own Nature, & so indifferent to Applause, that she is easily discouraged. I dont *know*, that she *would* undertake it. She has wrote another Tragedy taken from Metastasio's Olympiad I think the Title is, much more full of Business, than the other, but she does not care to bring it into public View. I have read it, & there are some pathetic & interesting Scenes in it; but I have not Judgement enough to know whether it would be likely to succeed *in Representation*.—She has wrote some little Farces—which I have not seen—but I am told she has a good comic Genius.

If you are so obliging as to call on her, pray send your Servt with a Card to apprize her of it, as she would be extremely vex^d, should she happen to be from Home. Mrs Stonehouse & my Daughter join in Compliments with me to Mrs Garrick—& I am, dear Sir,

Your most obligd & very humble Servt

James Stonehouse

I am now at a Living Ld Radnor gave me in Wiltshire, where I always spend Part of ye Month of April—& the Months of May, & June.

Great Garrick is the Burthen of my Song
Tis *Garrick* treats,* tis *Garrick* gives us Plays,
Pitts, Boxes, Gallery echo with his Name,
While Covent Garden in a Whisper dies.
Do I not see Him where He does not come?
Have I not heard Him where He has not spoke?
For, when *immortal Garrick* left the Stage,
My Eyes were idly bent on those, who talk'd
Thinking there Prattle to be tedious.—

Yes I have seen Him! I have heard Him!—& the Music of his Voice, & the Lightening of his Eyes still act so forcibly on my Imagination, that I see, & hear Him still. He play'd *Lusignan* last Night, & we had the good Fortune to get Places about the Middle of the Pit, which was laid into Boxes. The Part was most barbarously short;—but "the Excess conpensated the Date". His Pronouncing the little Pronoun *you* in a certain doubtfull, apprehensive, tremulous interrogatory Tone gave me a more precise Idea of Perfection, than all the Elocution I ever heard from the *Stage*:—yet divinely, as He speaks, Speech is almost superfluous in Him, & I would undertake to translate his Looks, & Attitudes into Words, tho' perhaps with some Abatement to the Author's Poetry, & *his* Expression.—No Rant, no Pomp, for He never outsteps the Modesty of Nature. What an enchanting Simplicity! What an eternally varying Cadence, yet without one Stop, one Inequality!—I could have murder'd half the audience with great Composure for the ineffable *Non-chalence*, with which some of them behav'd. They took the Liberty to breathe, to look at the other Actors, nay even to blow their Noses, & fan themselves, with many other like Impertinences; nor was *He* clappd more, than that insipid Vegetable, the unpungent *Reddish*, unless indeed on his first Entrance—& then it was "Cato's long Gown, full Wig, & lacquer'd chair," & not *Garrick*. I was so horridly conceited all the Time, that I look'd with Pity on every Body else fancying, that no one enterd into it with so much Energy, as myself. Miss Young playd *Zara* well: The rest of the Performers were below Notice.

But Tuesday was the Day of Days!
How shall I convey to you the remotest, the most glimmering Idea of what were my Feelings at seeing
Garrick in King Lear!

* Demetrius is Dr Young's Brother [Stonhouse's note].

Surely He is above Mortality.—Is it possible He can be Subject to
Pain, Disease, & Death, like *other* Men?—And must those refulgent
Eyes be ever clos'd in Night? Must those exquisite Powers be
suspended, & that Silver Tongue be Stopp'd? His Talents are
capacious beyond human credibility. I felt myself annihilated
before Him, & every Faculty of my Soul was swallowd up in
Attention. The Part of *Lusignan* had only given me a slight *Ebauche*
of his Superlative Abilities: It was but the *Dawning* of the intolerable
Lustre, with which He shone in Lear. I thought I should have been
suffocated with Grief: It was not like the superficial Sorrow one feels
at a well-acted Play, but the deep, substantial Grief of real Trouble.
His Madness was the Madness of Nature, of Shakespear, of Lear, of
Garrick. In the Midst of the Play I whisperd my Sister Patty—
"I could never be angry with Him, if He refusd ten of my Tragedies."—In short I am quite ridiculous about Him.—Whether I
eat, stand still, or walk—Still I can nothing but of *Garrick* talk.

He spoke a charming Epilogue of his own; in which He displayd
an infinite Variety of Powers. *Pope* somewhere says, "that in
Writing there is an *Happiness*, as well as *Care*." This Remark is
agreeably illustrated in this Epilogue—the chief Merit of which
consists in a *lucky Application* of certain well-known Lines, & Circumstances. After having beggd both humourously, & pathetically
for the Fund, he happily (in a Parody of Œdipus) addresses Himself
to the Gallery:

> "To you, good Gods, I make my last Appeal,
> "For you indeed can *judge*, as well as *feel*.

When these lines had producd the Clapping He expected, He
immediately subjoind "Olympus Shakes;" which in Speaking had
an amazing Effect.—Yet *my Heart ach'd* for the Depredations Time
is beginning to make in his Face, which was not visible, till He
appear'd in his own Form in the Epilogue; & of which He affect-
ingly reminded us in these Words "I was *young* Hamlet once."

Address: To David Garrick Esqr, Adelphi Buildings, Wesminster. *Postmark:*
MA 23. *Endorsement by Garrick:* Miss More's Lett^r to Dr Stonehouse upon Lear
1774. See answer. *Source:* HTC.

APPENDIX E

Thomas King's letter to Garrick concerning the management of Drury Lane during Garrick's absence

London

My dear Sir   April 26ʰ 1775

Mʳ Smith is very well satisfied to take the business of next week as it *now* stands.   Mʳˢ Smith has desired to change the play advertised for her night; has given up Cymbeline and takes Love in a Village— Mʳˢ Yates offer'd to play for Davies to oblige Mʳ Palmer who is, as I understand to manage this summer at Birmingham for her husband.   I *think* we shall not have any impediment.   Weston cannot come out, owing (as he says) to the money in the Office not being divided among his Creditors.   Parsons will therefore play Hurry to morrow.   I prevented Hopkins's advertising, as you desired, the Fund play.   I well knew there wou'd be after Saturday next time and time enough and I wish'd the eye of the public might not be turn'd on any other object till the Maid of the Oaks & Matilda were over.   The Latter has been near full for some time but the Maid has not been so much sought after; tho' the book now makes a *goodish* figure.   As to the Garland Dance—Jefferson had it. Slingsby consented to Dance; but just before Hopkins made out the bill he sent word he was not able to undertake the fatigue of the Provencalle but desired the Dance of the Garland might be perform'd.   *I* not knowing it was one out of the Maid of the Oaks gave consent—will take care it shall not be repeated.   I take all possible care; and must say Hopkins does not fuzzle—I am astonish'd how his patience or his paper holds out to answer all the messages &c that these cursed disorderly people send him.   Poor Wrighten had but a so so House.   The Bellman is waiting and I have only time to send the usual complimᵗˢ & professions of

Yʳ most sincere Well wisher & very hble Serᵗ

Thoˢ King

Address: David Garrick Esq., Bath. *Postmark:* AP 26.   *Source:* James M. Osborn, copy in FC.

15*

APPENDIX F

Two letters from William Hopkins to George Garrick about Drury Lane business

London
Sir   14th December. 1774
I hope you have receiv'd as much benefit from the Bath Waters as you could wish; It gave me great pleasure to hear that you are something better— and if you have any regard for your health don't come home till it is perfectly restored; for the fatigue of the Theatre will soon make a Relapse.

The Business of the Theatre viz.
Monday 5th Maid of the Oaks and Register Office.   Good House
Tuesdy 6. Achymist—and Deserter—a good House but the worst
          your Brother has play'd to for a long time.—
Wed— 7 The Chances and Deserter.   by Command.
Thurs. 8 The Country Girl and Genii.   tolerable.
Fridy 9 Venice Preserv'd and The Cobler.   1st time
          The 2nd Act hiss'd all thro'
Sat. 10 Maid of the Oaks and Irish Widow.   pretty good.
Monday. 11. Hamlet and Cobler.   great House
          The Cobler much hiss'd.
Tuesday 12. As you like it and Cobler.   great House
          The Cobler mends upon it and
          hope we shall bring it thro'.
The Cholerick Man is to come out on Monday— I have my fears about its success.   I can't say I am charm'd with it.   We are very busy now about the Pantomime I wish it may be ready for Christmas. Your Brother is very well but has not forgot to Scold I have enough of that, and am not very well in wealth and it hurts me much— so much that my Spirits are not able to bear it, good god what an angel He would be if he would do his business with good temper but that's impossible!—

I believe Mr King is not charm'd with his situation of deputy manager.—The Theatre seems quite Melancholy without you, and I assure you I find a great want of you but necessity has no law.

Mʳˢ Hopkins and the children desire their best respects to you, and if the prayers of our family are heard above You will soon be restor'd to your usual health, strength and spirits.—If at your leisure you will send me a line that you are better it will be receiv'd by our family with the greatest Joy.

I have no particular News to send you the Performers are often enquiring after your health. and I can assure you nobody wishes for it more than

Sir Your most obedient humble servᵗ

Wᵐ Hopkins.

Address: To George Garrick Esqʳ at Mʳˢ Philips, North Parade, Bath.
Source: FC.

London

Sir   14ʰ January 1775

I hope You still continue to get Strength & that you may have no Relapse of your disorder, I assure you we want your Company much in the Theatre; Mʳ K—— is getting the illwill of many of the Company daily; & many prayers & hearty wishes for your health & Safe return are often given in the Green Room; your good Natur'd offices in reconciling the little differences &c that often happen are much wanted— The Play of the Distress'd Mother has been a bone of Contention at both Houses. It has been play'd three times at Drury & four times at Covent Garden there have been great House to it at both Theatres— Mʳ Franklins Tragedy is in great forwardness & will be perform'd for the 1ˢᵗ time on Saturday next. We have a Comic opera of Two Acts now in Rehearsal & will Soon be ready call'd *The Rival Candidates*. I think it is a piece of Merit it is Said that Parson Bates is the Author The Pantomime of Harlequin's Jacket does very well, & brings money

We have had very good Houses for sometime past & hope it will Continue Even the Choloric Man, with Harlequin's Jacket wrapt about him brings very tolerable Houses— & The Maid of the Oaks is Stronger than ever, there was a great overflow to it last Night. Miss Younge has been in her airs for this Week or Ten days past & has given us a good deal of trouble— but 'tis what we must Expect from that Lady— If I am not Mistaken Mʳ K—— is a Constant Attendant at your Brother's Levee— Thank God I am able once more to hobble abroad, hope I shall have no return for the remainder of the Season. Your Brother is in very good health & Spirits &

gives his constant Attendance at the Theatre. Mrs Hopkins & all the Family Join with me in best Respects to You & I can assure You that None can wish more for your health & Safe Return I am

Sir Your most obedient humble Servant
Wm Hopkins

Mr Ralph desires his Duty to you

1775
Jany 2—Gamester & Harlequin's Jacket. great
       3—School for Wives & D°——— good
       4—Distress'd Mother & D°——— great
       5—Maid of the Oaks & Register Office— an over flow
       6—Prov'd Wife & Deserter——— great

{ it was to have been Twelfth Night but it was oblig'd to be deferr'd on acco^t of Mrs Baddeleys Illness

Mr Jefferson could not play & Mr Aick play'd Heartfree.
       7. Distress'd Mother & Harlequins Jacket— great
       9. D° & D°—good
      10. Much Ado——— & Cobler——— great
      11. Twelfth Night & Harl: Jacket——— *a Command*
      12—The Choleric Man & Harlequins Jacket— good
      13. Maid of the Oaks & Guardian——— overflow'd
      14. The Cholerick Man & Harl^s Jacket. good—
           on Monday The Distress'd Mother for the 4^h time—

Address: To George Garrick Esqr at Mrs Philips's, North Parade, Bath. *Postmark:* IA 14. *Endorsement by the recipient:* Hopkins on himself. *Source:* FC.

APPENDIX G

Garrick's will

I David Garrick of the Adelphi and of Hampton in the County of Middlesex Esquire Do make publish and Declare this to be my last Will and Testament as follows I Give and devise unto The Right Honourable Charles Lord Camden The Right Honourable Richard Rigby John Paterson Esqr and Albany Wallis Esqr of Norfolk Street

All that my Dwelling House at Hampton aforesaid and the Out-
houses Stables Yards Gardens Orchards Lands and Grounds there-
unto belonging or therewith now by me used occupied or enjoyed
together with the two Islands or Aytes on the River Thames with
their and every of their Appurtenances and the Statue of Shakespeare And also all that my Dwelling House in the Adelphi with the
Appurtenances And also all and every the Pictures Household Goods
and Furniture of and in both the said Houses at Hampton and
Adelphi at the time of my Decease (of which an Inventory shall be
taken) To hold to the said Charles Lord Camden Richard Rigby
John Paterson and Albany Wallis their Heirs Executors Administrators and Assigns In Trust for and to the use of my Wife Eva
Maria Garrick for and during the Term of her natural life for her
own Residence She keeping the Houses and Premises in Good
repair and paying all the Quit Rent Taxes and other Rents and
outgoings for the same I Give to my said Wife all my Household
Linen Silver Plate and China Ware which I shall die possessed of
or entitled unto both in Town and Country together with my
Carriages and Horses and all the Stock in my Cellars at both Houses
to and for her own use and benefit I also Give to my said Wife One
thousand pounds to be paid her immediately after my Death out of
the first Money that shall be received by my Executors I Give to
my said Wife the further sum of Five Thousand pounds to be paid
to her Twelve Months after my Decease with Interest for the same
at the rate of Four pounds per Centum And I also give to my said
Wife Eva Maria Garrick One clear Annuity or Yearly sum of
Fifteen Hundred pounds of lawful Money of Great Britain for and
during the Term of her natural Life to be paid to her quarterly to
and for her Sole and seperate Use without being subject to the
Debts Controul or intermeddling of any Husband she shall or may
Marry and her Receipt alone to be Sufficient Discharges from time
to time for the same to my Executors and Trustees herein after
named It is my request and desire that my Wife shall continue in
England and make Hampton and the Adelphi her chief places of
Residence, but if she shall leave England and reside beyond Sea
or in Scotland or Ireland, In such Case which I hope will not
happen But in that Case I revoke and make void all the Devises and
Bequests to her or for her use herein before mentioned which shall
on such Event become due and payable to her and instead thereof
I give her only a clear Annuity of One thousand pounds of Lawful
Money of Great Britain for and during the Term of her natural

Life payable Quarterly Provided nevertheless and I hereby declare
that the Provision hereby made for my Wife and the Legacies and
bequests hereby given to her are meant and intended to be in Lieu
of and full Satisfaction for the Dividends Interest and profits of the
Sum of ten thousand pounds which by our marriage settlement is
to be paid and agreed to be invested in Stocks or Securities for the
purposes therein mentioned and also in Bar and full Satisfaction of
her Dower or Thirds at common Law which she may be entitled to
out of my real Estates and I further declare it to be an Express
Condition annexed to the said Legacies and bequests so given to
my Wife that if she shall not within three Calendar Months next
after my Decease testify her Consent in Writing to my Executors
to take under this my Will and to relinquish all claim to the Interest
and Dividends of the said Ten thousand pounds mentioned in our
Marriage Settlement Then and in such Case all the Annuities
Legacies Devises and Bequests to her or for her Benefit hereinbefore
mentioned shall become null and void and the Annuities herein
given to her shall sink into and become part of my Estate And from
and after the Decease of my Wife or from and after the Determination or Forfeiture of her Interest in the Premises as aforesaid
I direct my said Trustees and the Survivors and Survivor or the
Heirs Executors or Administrators of the Survivor to sell dispose of
and Convey my said Houses Gardens and Lands at Hampton and
the Adelphi with their respective appurtenances and the Pictures
Household Goods and Furniture herein before given (except the
Statue of Shakespear) by publick or private Sale as they shall think
proper for the best price that can reasonably be got for the same
and turn the same into Money upon the Trusts and for the Purposes
hereinafter mentioned I Give and devise all that Messuage and
Garden now occupied by and in possession of my Nephew David
Garrick of Hampton and all the Furniture therein and all other my
Messuages Farms and Lands in the Parish of Hampton (except
these given to or for the Use of my Wife) unto & to the use of my
said Nephew David Garrick his Heirs Executors Administrators and
Assigns I Give and devise all that my Manor of Hendon with the
Advowson of the Church of Hendon And all other my Manors
Messuages Lands Tenements and Hereditaments with their and
every of their Rights Royalities Members and Appurtenances unto
the said Charles Lord Camden Richard Rigby John Paterson
Albany Wallis and the Survivors and Survivor of them and the
Heirs of such Survivor In Trust to sell dispose of and Convey the

same together or in parcels by publick or private or one or more Sale or Sales And the clear Money arising from such Sale or Sales as the same shall be received, after defraying the Expenses attending such Sales, to place out upon Government or Real Security at Interest in their Names In Trust and for the purposes hereafter mentioned I Give and bequeath the Statue of Shakespear after my Wife's death and all my Collection of old English Plays to the Trustees of the British Museum for the time being for the Use of the Publick I Give all the rest of my Books of what kind soever (except such as my Wife shall chuse to the value of One Hundred pounds which I give and bequeath to her) unto my Nephew Carrington Garrick for his own use I Give the Houses in Drury Lane which I bought of the fund for decayed Actors of the Theatre there back again to the Fund I Give and bequeath All the rest of my personal Estate whatsoever not specifically given, to the said Charles Lord Camden Richard Rigby John Paterson Albany Wallis their Executors Administrators and Assigns In Trust to be by them with all convenient speed sold and disposed of to the best Advantage and out of the Money to arise therefrom and any other Money or Personal Estate in the first place to pay the said Legacies of One thousand Pounds and five thousand pounds to my Wife and the Residue to be placed in their Names in Government or real security at Interest upon Trust That they the said Trustees and the Survivors and Survivor of them and the Executors Administrators and Assigns of such Survivor shall and do out of the Dividends Interest Profits and Proceed thereof or a Competant part thereof from time to time pay or cause to be paid to my Wife Eva Maria Garrick the said Annuity of Fifteen Hundred pounds herein before given to her during her natural life as aforesaid And for that purpose I Direct that part of my personal Estate and of the Money to arise from the Sale of my real Estates and the Securities on which the same shall be vested shall be set apart, sufficient for the Interest thereof to pay the Annuities of Fifteen Hundred pounds or One thousand pounds as the Case may happen to my Wife during her Life as aforesaid and in Case any such Securities so set apart for the purposes aforesaid shall fail or prove deficient I Direct others to be appropriated to make good the same so as that the said Annuities and provisions may be fully and punctually paid to my Wife in preference to every other Legacy Payment or Bequest whatsoever And I Give to my Brother George Garrick the sum of Ten Thousand pounds To my Brother Peter Garrick the sum of Three Thousand pounds To my Nephew

Carrington Garrick the sum of Six Thousand pounds To my Nephew David Garrick the sum of Five Thousand pounds besides what I agreed to give him on his Marriage I Direct my Executors and Trustees to stand possessed of the sum of Six Thousand pounds part of my personal Estate In Trust for my Neice Arabella Schaw Wife of Captain Schaw and to pay and dispose thereof in such manner as my Niece Arabella Schaw shall notwithstanding her present or future Coverture by Writing signed by her in the presence of two credible Witnesses direct or appoint and in default of such Direction or Appointment to pay One Moiety thereof to her personal Representatives the other Moiety to become apart of my personal Estate I Give to my Niece Catherine Garrick the Sum of Six Thousand pounds to be paid to her at her Age of Twenty one Years or Day of Marriage with Interest at the Rate of four pounds per Centum per Annum I Give to my Sister Meriel Doxey the sum of Three Thousand pounds I Give to my Wifes Niece who is now with us at Hampton the Sum of One Thousand Pounds All which Legacies I direct shall be paid by my Executors out of the Residue of my personal Estate which shall remain after paying the Legacies to my Wife and securing the Annuities as aforesaid And if there shall not be sufficient to answer and pay all the said last mentioned Legacies The Legatees shall abate in proportion to their Legacies and wait until the Death of my Wife when the Money arising by the Sale of Hampton and the Fund for payment of the Annuities will be at Liberty and become part of my personal Estate to answer and pay the said Legacies in full Provided Always That if any one or two of my Trustees shall happen to Die before the several Trusts hereby in them reposed shall be fully and compleatly executed and finished Then and in such Case the Survivors and Survivor of them shall in Convenient time Assign Transfer and Convey such of the Estates Stocks Funds and other Securities as shall then remain undisposed of for the purposes aforesaid so as the same may be vested in the Survivors or Survivor And one or two other Trustees as the Case may happen to be named by the Survivors or Survivor and as often as any of the said Trustees shall die a new one shall be named to be joined with the Survivors so as that the Number may be kept filled up and all such new Trustees shall stand possessed of the Estates Stocks Funds and Securities jointly with the Survivors to the same Uses and upon the same Trusts Intents and purposes hereinbefore declared and appointed Provided also That it shall be lawful for my said Trustees and every of them and all future Trustee and Trustees in the first place to retain to themselves out of the Trust Estates from time to time all such Costs Charges and Expences as they or any of them shall respectively be put unto or sustain in the Trust hereby in them respectively reposed and that none of them or any future Trustee or Trustees shall be answerable for the other or others of them or for more than he himself shall actually receive or wilfully lose or destroy And in Case after payment of all the said Legacies Bequests and Expences there shall remain any surplus money or personal Estate I Direct the same to be divided amongst my next of Kin as if I had died Intestate And I nominate and appoint the said Charles Lord Camden Richard Rigby John Paterson Albany Wallis to be Executors of this my Will which I declare to be my last Will and Testament hereby revoking all former and other Wills by me at any time heretofore made In Witness whereof I the said David Garrick have to two parts of this my Will contained in Seven Sheets of paper set my hand to each of the said Sheets and my Seal to the first and last sheets this the 24th day of September One thousand seven hundred and seventy eight.

David Garrick

Signed Sealed published and declared by the said Testator David Garrick as and for his last Will and Testament in the presence of us who at his Request in his presence and in the presence of each other have subscribed our Names as Witnesses thereto
> Sophia Ricketts
> Palmerston
> George: Poyntz: Ricketts

2d Feb^{ry} 1779

The Right Honble Richard Rigby John Paterson and Albany Wallis Esq^{rs} three of the Executors above named were duly sworn as such
Before me

G: Bogg   Geo. Harris
Surrogate

Testator was late of the Parish of St Martin in the fields in the County of Middlesex Esq. & died last month.
The Right Honble Chas Lord Camden the other Executor renounced.

Proved at London the 5th day of Feby 1779 before the Worshipful George Harris Doctor of Laws and Surrogate by the oaths of the Right Hoñble Richard Rigby, John Paterson and Albany Wallis, Esq^{rs} three of the Exors to whom Admön was granted having been first sworn duly to adm^r the Right Hoñble Charles Lord Camden the other Exör hath renounced the Execution of the Will.

Index

Index

NOTE ON THE INDEX

References are to letter numbers, *not to pages*, and only the letters and their notes have been indexed. There is no entry for David Garrick; subjects such as Garrick's health are indexed under Health. All titled people are indexed under their family names, with cross references from titles held during Garrick's lifetime. Wives follow husbands. The first reference following a name is, where possible, to biographical material; [U] following a name indicates that the person so designated is unknown to the editors. G is used for Garrick but all other abbreviations are the same as those in the notes to the text. Characters in plays are given in quotation marks, with the title of the play following in parentheses. Plays and other works are indexed by title, with the author's name (except for Shakespeare) following in parentheses, and each author at the end of his entry has cross references to his cited works. Because of space limitations, modifications have been omitted wherever possible.

397, 398? 413, 414, 419, 443, 447, 471, 875, 898, 902, 903, 904, 925, 928, 936, 945, 948, 963, 971, 988, 992, 1004, 1019, 1044, 1057, 1058, 1069, 1074, 1118, 1128, 1245, 1246, 1247, 1248. See also *Art of Poetry; Bonduca; Clandestine Marriage; Comedies of Terence; Deuce is in Him; Epicoene;* "Genius"; "Gentleman"; *Jealous Wife; Man and Wife; Musical Lady; New Brooms; Philaster; Polly Honeycomb; Spanish Barber; Spleen; Suicide;* "Terrae Filius"

Colman, Sarah (Ford), Mrs. George, 337, 341, 352, 353, 378? 381, 392, 413, 414, 415, 419, 443, 447

Colman the Younger, George, 341, 381, 413, 414, 419, 443, 447, 936

Columbine, Francis, 3, 4

"Columne" [*U* play], 1356

Comédien, Le (Rémond), 565

Comédie-Française, 317, 347

Comédie-Italienne, 317, 347

Comedies of Plautus (Thornton trans.), 397n

Comedies of Terence (Colman trans.), 321, 329, 341, 346, 352, 362, 380

Comedy, 329, 375, 528, 583, 646, 817, 888, 946

Command performances, 259, 274, 278, 373, 374, 378, 393, 399, 438, 503, 513, 517, 522, 523, 654, 661, 759n, 883, 886, 949, 956n, 1022, 1079, 1081, 1273, 1321

Commissary, The (Foote), 394

Compton, Charles, 7th Earl of Northampton, 356n

Confederacy, The (Vanbrugh), 41

Congreve, Mr. [*U*], 38

Congreve, William, see *Double Dealer; Love for Love; Mourning Bride; Old Batchelor; Way of the World*

"Conjurors, The" (French), 135n

Conscious Lovers, The (Steele), 951n

Considerations on Criminal Law (Dagge), 891?

Conspiracy, The (Jephson; earlier called "Vitellia"), 963? 966

Constable family [*U*], 90, 94, 109

Constant Couple, The (Farquhar), 40n

"Constant, Sir Bashful" (*Way to Keep Him*), 256

"Constant, Lady" (*Way to Keep Him*), 256

Contrast, The (Hoadly), 632n

Conway, Francis Seymour, Earl of Hertford, 346, 347, 350, 353, 540, 925, 1309, 1315

Conway, Isabella (Fitzroy), Countess of Hertford, 1015. LETTER TO: 1309

Conway, Francis Seymour, Viscount Beauchamp, 551, Appendix C

Conway, Henry Seymour, 639

Cooper, Sir Grey, 416? 599. LETTERS TO: 625, 726, 820, 912, 915, 979, 1018, 1249

Cooper, Elizabeth (Kennedy), Lady, 625, 726, 979, 1018

Cooper, John Gilbert, 55, 640. LETTER TO: 55

Cooper (Cowper), Nathaniel, 736, 775

Cope, Sir John, 34

Copford Manor, Essex, 622, 683, 1169, 1171, 1300

Copyright, 829n, 989

Corbett, Charles, 121, 1262?

"Cordelia" (*King Lear*), 574

Coriolanus, 108

Cork, Earls of, *see* Boyle: Hamilton, John, & Richard

Corneille, Pierre, see *Don Sanche d'Arragon*

Cornelys, Theresa, 539n

Cornwallis, Charles, 2d Earl, 1178n

Cornwallis, Edward, 123

Cornwallis, Frederick, 1022

Coronation, The (G), 271, 272n, 560n

Corsica, 479, 493, 544

Corsica, An Account of (Boswell), see *Account*

Costuming, 93, 540n, 726, 733, 950n, 1147

Countess of Salisbury, The (Hartson), 1301?

Country Burial, The (Hoadly), 632

Country Girl, The (Wycherley–G), 414n, 419, 434, 437, 449, 478n, 894, 950, Appendix F

Country Wife, The (Wycherley), 414, 419, 434, 437. See also *Country Girl*

Coure, Mr. [*U*], 665

Courtenay, John, 688, 1201n

"Covent Garden Bellman's . . . Verses" (anon.), 596

Covent Garden Theatre, Proprietors of, LETTER TO: 952

Covent Garden Theatre: & DL, 21, 40, 51, 427, 1138; *Romeo* war, 93, 95, 96; riots, 303nn, 896n; sale of, 391, 414, 419, 455, 456, 457, 458, 459, 486n; & *Jubilee*, 560, 567; & Smith, 770n, 775, 796; & Mrs. Siddons, 932; & *Duenna*, 960, 963, 989; mentioned, 19, 20, 28, 29, 40, 41, 50n, 78, 120n, 140, 144, 323, 434, 437, 531, 653, 657, 659, 713, 714, 806nn, 810, 830nn, 834, 838, 844, 867, 869, 875, 893, 897, 908, 911, 913, 934, 994, 1048n, 1057, 1058, 1147, 1204, Appendix F

Lowe, Sr., Elizabeth, Mrs. Christopher, 5
Lowe, Miss, 5
Lowe, Theophilus, 1, 21
Lowndes, Mrs. [*U*], 1–6
Lowry, Edward, 428, 567
Lowth, Robert, 159, 377, 380
Loxley, Mrs. (servant), 97, 101, 128, 212
Lucan of Castlebar, Baron, *see* Bingham, Charles
"Lucinda" (Griffith character), 422
Lusiad (Mickle trans.), 799
"Lusignan" (*Zara*), 660, 833, 893, Appendix D
Lyddall, G appears as, 14n
Lyddel, Richard, 40
Lydia, ou mémoires de Mylord D (Laplace), 729
Lying Valet, The (G), 15, 20
Lyons, France, 317, 340
"Lysander" (*Agis*), 196, 204
Lyttelton, Charles, Bishop of Carlisle, 526
Lyttelton, George, 1st Baron, 18, 19, 23, 52? 67n, 589, 639, 640, 644, 645, 649, 676, 677, 678, 723, 725, 776. LETTERS TO: 266, 648, 655. See also *Dialogues of the Dead*
Lyttelton, Elizabeth (Rich), Lady, 67, 68
Lyttelton, Thomas, 2d Baron, 655, 678, 723, 940
Lyttelton, Apphia (Peach), Lady, 723n
Lyttelton, Sir Thomas, 6

MacArdell, James, 343
"Macaria" (*Royal Suppliants*), 834
Macbeth: quoted, 70, 355, 357, 366, 694, 821, 856, 976; & Johnson, 32; G parodies, 93; G's interpretation of lines in, 281; & Boswell, 799; & Hardcastle, 851; costuming of, 1147; mentioned, 570, 574, 680n
"Macbeth": G playing, 143, 317, 399, 484, 1154n; G doesn't want to do, 452; & Murphy's critique, 485; & King of Denmark, 517, 522, 523; "most violent part," 726; mentioned, 36, 676, 730, 733, 820
"Macbeth, Lady," 412, 1147
Maccaronique, Histoire [*U*], 717
Macdonaugh, Mr. or Dr. [*U*], 216, 218
Maceuen [*U*], 667n
Mackenzie, George, 3d Earl of Cromarty, 46
Mackenzie, James, 775n
Macklin, Charles, 29, 28n, 34, 40, 43, 131, 806, 808, 896, 902n, 1347n. LETTERS TO: 16**

565, 911, 1318. See also *Henry VII; Love à la Mode*
Macklin, Ann (Purvor, Grace), Mrs. Charles, 144, 1318
Macklin, Maria, 908, 911, 1318
Macpherson, James, 698, 888n, 895. *See also* Ossian poems
"MacSarcasm, Sir Archy" (*Love à la Mode*), 255
Maddockes ("Maddox"), Charles, 12
Maddox, Anthony, 108, 118
Magdalen College, Oxford, 877
Mahomet (the prophet), 1055
Mahomet and Irene (Johnson), 55
Mahomet the Imposter (Miller & Hoadly), 1205n
Maid of Bath, The (Foote), 653
Maid of the Mill, The (Bickerstaffe), 402, 412
Maid of the Oaks, The (Burgoyne), 863n, 865, 869, 890, 894, Appendices E, F
Maid's Tragedy, The (Beaumont & Fletcher), 896
"Malagene" (*Friendship in Fashion*), 85
Malcolm, James?, 1
Male Coquette, The (G), 418?
Mallet, David, 207, 571. See also *Alfred; Elvira; Eurydice*
"Mammon, Sir Epicure" (*Alchemist*), 817
Managers' season, days and nights, 179, 499, 1004
Man and Wife; or, The Stratford Jubilee (Colman), 560, 567, 657
Mancini Mazarini, Louis-Jules-Barbon, duc de Nivernois, 401, 1267. LETTER TO: 401
"Manfred and Matilda" (Hardcastle), 851
Mann, Sir Horace, 321
Man of Family, The (Jenner), 582, 583, 614
Man of Mode; or, Sir Foppling Flutter (Etherege), 147
Man of Taste (Miller), 939, 950
Mansel, Mr. [*U*], 1089
Mansfield, 1st Earl of, *see* Murray, William
Mant, Major [*U*], 449
Marchant, Nathaniel, 1317
"Maria" (*Duel*), 719
"Maria" (Griffith character), 464
Marie Antoinette, 571
"Marius, Young" (*Caius Marius*), 41
Marivaux, Pierre Carlet de Chamberlain de, 571. See also *Fausses confidences*
Market Weighton, Yorkshire, 92, 110

"Pharamond" (*Philaster*), 48
Philaster (Beaumont & Fletcher–Colman), 48, 317
Philip, Duke of Parma, 335, 342
Philip, Mr. [*U*], 91
Philips [*U*], 452
Philips, Ambrose, see *Distress'd Mother*
Philips, Charles Claudius, 799
Phillipson, Richard Burton, 1169
Philosopher, The (Williams), 710
Philosophical Dictionary, 347
Phipps, Constantine John, 2d Baron Mulgrave, 903, 936
"Pid Pad," *see* Garrick, Eva
Pierce, Miss (governess), 413, 414
"Pierre" (*Venice Preserv'd*), 332
Piettero ("Pitro"), 119, 120
Pigott, William, 1041
Piles, 339, 635
Pinchbeck, Christopher, 1060
Piper, William, 1001, 1003
Piracy: of *Grandison*, 133; Walpole, ed., 198, 201; of *Jubilee*, 635; of *Institution*, 654
Pirnon, Mr. [*U*], 328
Pitro, Mr., *see* Piettero
Pitt, George, 1st Baron Rivers, 319, 320
Pitt, William, 1st Earl of Chatham, 18, 279, 280, 326, 414, 418, 419, 423, 678. LETTER TO: 676
"Pivy," *see* Clive, Catherine
Placid Man, The (Jenner), 582, 583
Plain Dealer, The (Wycherly–Bickerstaffe), 425
Plato, 319
Platonic Lovers, The (Davenant), 348n
Platonic Wife, The (Griffith), 348, 351
Plautus, 329, 397, 539n
Playhouse Passage, London, 286
Plays, A Select Collection of Old (ed. Dodsley), 627
Plays and the like, G's, see *Bon Ton; Christmas Tale; Clandestine Marriage;* "Cupid and Damon"; *Cymon; Elopement; Enchanter; Fairies; Guardian; Harlequin's Invasion; Institution of the Garter; Irish Widow; Isabella; Jubilee; Lethe; Linco's Travels; Lying Valet; Male Coquette; May Day; Meeting of the Company; Miss in Her Teens; Neck or Nothing; Ode; Peep Behind;* "Ragand-jaw"; *Theatrical Candidates*
Plays, G's old, 627, 848, 849, Appendix G. *See also* Book collecting; Books, G's

Playwriting, G on, 430, 460, 524, 565, 571, 583, 1360. *See also* Comedy; Criticism; Tragedy
"Pliant," *see* "Plyant"
"Plume, Captain" (*Recruiting Officer*), 25n
Plummer, Richard, 2, 3, 5, 6
Plumptre, John, LETTER TO: 1013?
"Plyant ('Pliant'), Sir Paul" (*Double Dealer*), 59, 67, 72, 88, 449, 653
"Plyant ('Pliant'), Lady" (*Double Dealer*), 59, 67
Plym, Miss, 321, 458
Plymouth, 393
Poems Upon Various Subjects (Browne), 482?
Poetical Amusements at a Villa Near Bath (collection), 976nn
Politeuphuia; Wits Commonwealth (Bodenham), 118
Political Survey of Great Britain, A (Campbell), 824
"Politician Reform'd, The" (Ryder), 774n, 778, 779
Politics: & Walpole, 21, 22; & Granville, 63; & Pelham, 101; Westminster elections, 123, 867; York meeting, 129, 130; Pitt & Barré, 279, 280; Regency Bill, 358; Stamp Act, 399; Pitt &, 414, 418, 419, 423; G &, 426, 1105; election riots, 492; Middlesex, 495; Northampton, 511; Bill of Rights, 567; Vaillant &, 575; & Murphy, 609n, 719, 735; & Denmark, 673; & *Boadicia*, 689; & theater, 784; & America, 820, 823n, 915; at Bath, 903; & Necker, 1061; Burke & Yates, 1087n, 1096n; & *Trident*, 1178. *See also* Jacobite Rebellion; War
Polly (Gay), 1270?
Polly Honeycomb (Colman), 251? 252? 260, 261
"Polonius" (*Hamlet*), 57
Pomfret, 2d Earl of, *see* Fermor, George
Pompignan, Marquis de, *see* Lefranc
Pons coffeehouse, 101
Ponsonby, John, 87
Ponsonby, Lady Elizabeth (Cavendish), 87n
Pop, Miss [*U*], 112
Pope, Alexander, 23, 565. See also *Eloisa to Abelard; Epilogue to the Satires;* "Epistle to Dr. Arbuthnot"; "To Mr. Fortescue"
Pope, Essay Upon the Genius and Writing of (Warton), 163, 174, 283